Organisations and Parties

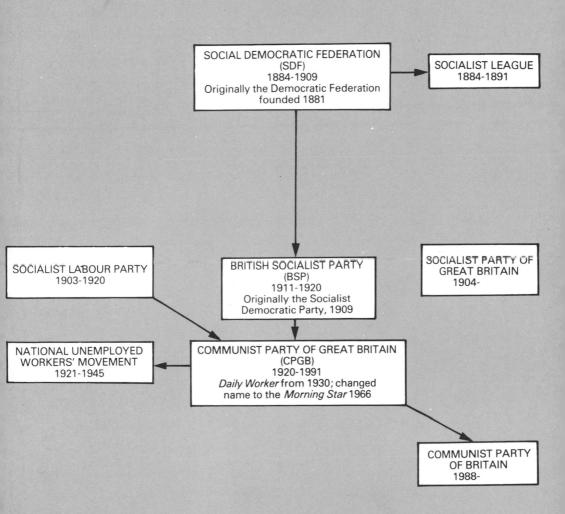

SOCIAL DEMOCRATIC FEDERATION (SDF)
1884-1909
Originally the Democratic Federation
founded 1881

SOCIALIST LEAGUE
1884-1891

SOCIALIST LABOUR PARTY
1903-1920

BRITISH SOCIALIST PARTY (BSP)
1911-1920
Originally the Socialist
Democratic Party, 1909

SOCIALIST PARTY OF GREAT BRITAIN
1904-

NATIONAL UNEMPLOYED WORKERS' MOVEMENT
1921-1945

COMMUNIST PARTY OF GREAT BRITAIN (CPGB)
1920-1991
Daily Worker from 1930; changed
name to the *Morning Star* 1966

COMMUNIST PARTY OF BRITAIN
1988-

SOCIALIST WORKERS' PARTY (SWP)
1977-
Originally International Socialism,
formed 1962

To Build A New Jerusalem

The British Labour Movement from the 1880s to the 1990s

A. J. DAVIES

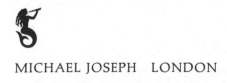

MICHAEL JOSEPH   LONDON

MICHAEL JOSEPH LTD

Published by the Penguin Group, 27 Wrights Lane, London W8 5TZ
Penguin Books USA Inc., 375 Hudson Street, New York, New York 10014, USA
Penguin Books Australia Ltd, Ringwood, Victoria, Australia
Penguin Books Canada Ltd, 10 Alcorn Avenue, Toronto, Ontario, Canada M4V 3B2
Penguin Books (NZ) Ltd, 182–190 Wairau Road, Auckland 10, New Zealand

Penguin Books Ltd, Registered Offices: Harmondsworth, Middlesex, England

First published in Great Britain 1992

Copyright © Andrew Davies 1992

Printed in England by Clays Ltd, St Ives plc
Typeset in 11/13 pt Palatino

A CIP catalogue record for this book is available from the British Library

ISBN 0 7181 3394 3

Contents

Acknowledgements

VARIOUS DRAFT chapters of *To Build A New Jerusalem* have been read and discussed at conferences and seminars such as the 'Brave New World' conference held at the Polytechnic of North London in April 1980; at an economics seminar organised at Cambridge University by Bob Rowthorn; at a talk given at the Imperial War Museum in May 1985; at the Australian Studies Centre at the University of London in June 1984; at a Greater London Council Arts Conference in November 1981; and at the Marx Memorial Library. Thanks for everyone's comments and also to the scores of people who contacted me with ideas and opinions after the publication of my earlier book *Where Did The Forties Go?*

I learnt much from the courses held at the Marx Library, particularly 'The Marxist Tradition in Britain' series I organised in 1983 whose contributors included Asa Briggs, Eric Hobsbawm, John Saville, Royden Harrison, A. L. Morton and Margaret Morris. Other Marx Library speakers included Stuart Hall, Ray Watkinson, Gareth Stedman Jones and David McLellan.

Over the years hundreds of people have talked to me about politics. It would be impossible to list everyone but I would like to thank by name Garron Baines, David Barrs, Simon Blanchard, Andrew Lorenz, Charles Poulsen, Toots Davies, Margaret Jordan, David Coubrough, Dr. Arthur Brown, Max Egelnick, Charlie Hall, Harold Smith, Tony Attienza, Fran Hazelton, Mary Rosser, Margaret Brunel and Peter Sinclair. I owe much to the inspiration of Liz McGuirk. Ahmet Ratip and Munisha Jethwa never minded me disturbing their work as I arrived to do yet more photocopying.

I owe a special debt to the staff of several libraries, particularly those of the British Library, the London Library, the Marx Memorial Library, the Public Records Office, the Bodleian, Cambridge University Library, the Labour Party, the National Museum of Labour History, the British Library of Political and Economic Science, William Morris Gallery in Waltham Forest, the Fawcett Library, Worcester College, Oxford, the *Morning Star* Library, the Communist Party Library, University College, London, Westminster Public Library and Tower Hamlets Local History Library.

For years family meal-times have often been a political forum and I am very grateful to my parents, brother Simon and his wife Julia, sister Emma and her husband Dominic, Grandma and Aunt Mary for their views which ranged from Far Right to Far Left.

In particular I want to thank Simon van der Borgh for his detailed work on several chapters. Andrew Lownie is my friend and adviser first, my agent second, and as always he provided sustained interest and support. Susan Watt and then Louise Haines at Michael Joseph have let me get away with nothing and I am very grateful to them for their hard work and enthusiasm.

Finally, Jean Collingsworth has gone through draft after draft of this book, always asking the awkward questions and making sure that I didn't get lazy or take refuge behind a barrage of jargon. Not only is she an excellent editor, she also taught me to love modern technology in the form of the word processor.

My greatest debt, however, is to adult education in Britain. Not only have the Workers' Educational Association, the Extra-Mural Departments at London and Cambridge Universities, the City University, the Open University and the University of the Third Age supported me financially over the last ten years, their students have been a wonderful source of inspiration and instruction. Any good future society will build upon and revere the fine British tradition of adult education. This book is dedicated to that tradition.

In view of the very different individuals and organisations mentioned above, some of whom will be amazed to find themselves sharing a page with each other, I must stress that all the views and opinions in this book are entirely my responsibility.

Picture Credits

H. M. Hyndman, Will Dyson and Walter Crane's cartoons, the Morris pamphlet, the Marx Library in the 1930s and Harry Pollitt and R. P. Dutt's pamphlet on the Moscow Trial come from the author's collection; Keystone Press Agency were responsible for the image of Gaitskell and Morgan Phillips in 1959, Central Press Agency for Wilson and Healey, Lionel Cherrault of Camera Press for Benn, Scargill and Livingstone and Press Association Photos for the Militant supporter challenging Kinnock. The remainder of the pictures come from the Labour Party Library in Walworth Road, London – thanks to Melanie Cooper for her help.

And did those feet in ancient time
Walk upon England's mountains green?
And was the holy Lamb of God
On England's pleasant pastures seen?

And did the Countenance Divine
Shine forth upon our clouded hills
And was Jerusalem builded here
Among these dark Satanic mills?

Bring me my bow of burning gold;
Bring me my arrows of desire;
Bring me my spear – O clouds, unfold!
Bring me my chariot of fire!

I will not cease from mental fight,
Nor shall my sword sleep in my hand,
Till we have built Jerusalem,
In England's green and pleasant land.

William Blake's Preface to his poem *Milton,*
written c.1800–04

Beginnings

'In writing upon this, as upon every subject, I speak a language full and intelligible. I deal not in hints and intimations. I have several reasons for this: first, that I may be clearly understood. Secondly, that it may be seen I am in earnest; and thirdly, because it is an affront to truth to treat falsehood with complaisance.'

Thomas Paine, *Examination of the Prophecies*, 1806

'Workers of the world forgive me.'

The words printed under a poster of Karl Marx in East Berlin in the summer of 1990

Surveys have shown that one person in three does not know which party their own MP belongs to.

In 1986 one in three company heads could not identify Nigel Lawson as the Chancellor of the Exchequer.

Holiday tour operators report a doubling in bookings when the date of a general election is announced.

Less than one in twenty of the people questioned in a European poll take an active interest in politics.

In view of such findings, why should anyone in their right mind spend a large chunk of their life researching and writing a book of political and social history?

In my case, it is because of a job I once had.

Clerkenwell Green in London can boast many radical associations. In 1381 Wat Tyler's peasants camped nearby on their way to London to complain about the poll tax. In later years the Green was the best-known of all open-air forums until the creation of Speaker's Corner in Hyde Park in the late nineteenth century.

On the north side of the Green stands an elegant and compact house of 1737 which was built on the site of a medieval nunnery whose arches can still be glimpsed in the basement. Number 37 Clerkenwell Green was used as a Welsh Charity School until 1772 when it was taken over by a variety of businesses: a pub, cobblers, dressmakers. In 1872 it became a radical working men's club and was notable for being open to women. In 1893 Britain's first socialist publishing house, the Twentieth Century Press, moved here. The poet, designer and socialist William Morris guaranteed the first year's rent of £50.

It was to this building that Lenin came between April 1902 and May 1903 to edit the Bolshevik paper *Iskra* which was printed on wafer-thin paper and then smuggled into Czarist Russia. The Twentieth Century Press moved out during the 1920s and in 1933 the Marx Memorial Library moved in. Its foundation was both a memorial to Karl Marx on the fiftieth anniversary of his death and an act of opposition to the burning of books then taking place in Nazi Germany. I was Librarian of the Marx Memorial Library from 1982 to 1986.

The Marx Library is a registered charity, open to all regardless of their political views. One of the most regular users when I was there was the *Daily Telegraph* whose journalists were scrupulous in telephoning to check facts and news items. Often television companies came to film, making use in particular of the archives of the International Brigade, those men who fought in the Spanish Civil War in the 1930s. The Library contains a wonderful collection of rare pamphlets, books and periodicals dating back to the English Civil War of the 1640s. There is also a remarkable range of material on American politics assembled by a former Librarian, John Williamson, who was deported from the United States during the McCarthyite era in the 1950s.

As Librarian, one of my most important jobs was to lay a wreath on Karl Marx's grave in Highgate Cemetery at exactly 2.15 p.m. each 14 February, the very moment of his death. I also spent much of my time showing people around the tiny Lenin Room inside the Library where *Iskra* had been edited. 'Around' is perhaps the wrong word since the room with its single desk, chair and filing cabinet barely holds five people at any one time. When dealing with the frequent parties of Soviet visitors, I had to talk to them in batches: 'Next, please'; 'Move along there'; 'Right down inside'. Some of these groups were attentive but others desperately wanted to go shopping in Oxford Street. For them I speeded up my talk.

Sometimes, showing someone the Lenin Room could be a curiously moving experience. One afternoon a black South African socialist arrived and asked to have a look. When I explained to him that this was indeed the very room in which his idol Lenin had worked, he began to weep. It brought home to me that for some people allegiance to their beliefs, whatever they may be, really is a matter of life and death and not just a political game.

The most famous visitor during my time as Librarian was Mikhail Gorbachev who came over with his wife Raisa to meet Mrs Thatcher in December 1984. Once arrived in London, his first call was to the Marx Memorial Library. Everyone could feel his great vitality which seemed to charge the atmosphere around him. Remarkable too was his spontaneity; not generally a feature of Soviet visits. We sat downstairs in the lecture hall and as usual the Soviet party organised itself hierarchically into rows — most Russian groups were very status-conscious. The Gorbachevs sat in front, the interpreter behind, then the Soviet Ambassador in the third row and so on. Raisa was having none of this and insisted that the interpreter should sit in the front row with them.

The contrast between the energy of the Gorbachevs and the weariness of the Mayor of Moscow who had visited the Library a few months earlier was striking. This elderly man looked tired, bored and fed up. He was a Brezhnev appointee and I noticed later that one of Mr Gorbachev's first acts when he became General Secretary was to 'retire' the Mayor.

One of the pleasures of working at the Library was talking to the other people involved there. The Library's President was an old Balliol man who had been introduced to Lenin by his father. The Library Chairman, Chairwoman or possibly Chairperson — no one could ever agree on the ideologically correct terminology — had been educated at a convent school and was now chief executive of the *Morning Star* newspaper. The Library Secretary had begun his working life as an East End tailor during the 1930s and took part in the Battle of Cable Street in October 1936. Members of the Committee included university lecturers, film editors, librarians, trade union officials, a former general secretary of the national Labour Party, the retired and the unemployed.

And me? I went to public school and then read Law at Oxford. I had been a moderately active member of the Saffron Walden Labour Party with a tiny claim to political fame and a footnote in the history books through having organised a 'one member, one vote' ballot of the local membership for the Deputy Leadership contest between Tony Benn and Denis Healey in 1981 — possibly the first time this was ever done and several years before Mr Kinnock took up the idea.

As for users of the Library, I soon learnt to discount popular stereotypes that dismiss political activists as being either dull and boring or loud and abrasive — though it must be said that some were fairly intense. One group of six people used to meet regularly at the Library to plot the overthrow of world capitalism. While waiting for this to happen, they produced a series of pamphlets of impenetrable complexity and occasionally expelled a former comrade for 'bourgeois revisionism' or some other mortal sin. But most people were generous, thoughtful and with an overwhelming interest in the world around them, showing a concern for others which I thought and still think was admirable, however much I might disagree with some of their political opinions.

Working at the Library gave me the opportunity to read my way through shelves of books about the history of the labour movement. How dull many of these publications were; almost as if unreadability was a sign of political virtue. I was sometimes cheered to find that I was not alone in these critical thoughts when Library members returned volumes with despairing marginal annotations or comments such as 'Boring', 'Couldn't get into it' and so on. Most of these dutiful histories were painstakingly stuffed with committee reports and acronyms while being almost completely devoid of that passion and commitment that had led so many people to give up their time and sometimes even their lives for a great political cause.

In his essay *The English People*, published in 1947, George Orwell claims that the English language is peculiarly prone to jargon. How he would have hated the language of exclusivity which has characterised much recent writing produced by the British Left. The irony is that writers supposedly representing or supporting the working class should employ a style comprehensible only to academics. One leading socialist commentator recently remarked on television that those who attack complexity are guilty of 'reverse snobbery'. In which case I have tried to ensure that *To Build A New Jerusalem* contains quite a lot of reverse snobbery.

One mark of how the radical tradition of writing for all in clear and direct language has declined is the increasing use of a 'depersonalised' vocabulary. Indeed, this has become a mark of whether a book is sufficiently 'serious' and 'rigorous' enough to merit critical attention. It is surely no coincidence that many of the best political books published recently have been biographies, diaries or memoirs in which the personal simply cannot be omitted: Ben Pimlott on Hugh Dalton, Anthony Howard on Richard Crossman, John Campbell on Aneurin Bevan, Susan Crosland on her husband Tony, Hugo Young on Mrs Thatcher, Kenneth Morgan's *Labour People*, Timothy Garton Ash's *The Uses of Adversity* and *We the People*, Denis Healey's *The Time of*

My Life, Noel Annan's *Our Age*, sections in the diaries of Beatrice Webb, Barbara Castle, Richard Crossman and Tony Benn, the essays of E. P. Thompson and so on.

I left the Library in 1986 because I wanted more time to write and research my books on the history of London, to give lectures and to lead walks around the capital. Also my political opinions had become so uncertain that I found it impossible to say quite what 'socialism', 'the Left' and so on were all about. I felt I could not give the job of Librarian the commitment it needs. I will always have fond memories of the place, its wonderful volunteer workers, its priceless materials and the wide range of visitors I encountered, especially the kind Soviet groups who gave me painted Russian dolls, LPs of peasant music and, on several occasions, the selected works of Lenin.

It is because of my political uncertainty as well as my determination to produce something about British politics which would be accessible to all that I have spent several years researching and writing this book. I have explored the history and development of the British Left, hoping to answer some of the questions that have bothered me and others for some years.

I am not part of any group or 'magic circle', whether it be around *Marxism Today*, the *Spectator* or *New Left Review*. I do not want to be an MP, a trade union official or obtain an academic post. I have 'called' this book exactly as I see it: a personal interpretation of British history over the last 100 years.

I have tried to integrate the lives of the various people I include into the context of events in Britain and abroad. If it is thought that the book is sometimes too much concerned with individuals, well, Kenneth Morgan has pointed out that although the British labour movement is supposedly against 'excesses of individualism [it] can go to extreme lengths to perpetuate the cult of personality':

> More than the Conservatives have ever done, Labour draws constant inspiration from the ideas and achievements of key individuals, in both the political and industrial spheres. Indeed, it could well be argued that, since Labour necessarily arose to represent the poor and inarticulate, its need for charismatic individuals has been all the greater than that of its better-endowed opponents.

It would be foolish to pretend that a history of the British Left can ever be a swashbuckling romance: a kind of 'Indiana Jones Meets The Transport and General Workers' Union'. Committees, reports and the minutiae of administration have always been important to the way any political organisation operates. But it seemed to me at the Library, and still does today, that any history of the Left, or the Right for that matter, should try to woo and win potential readers rather than make them face some kind of political assault course. If a thing is worth saying, surely it is worth saying clearly.

The justification for the title is not only that the hymn *Jerusalem* is often sung at the memorial services of influential Labour politicians from George Lansbury to Clem Attlee to Tony Crosland, but the British labour movement is and always has been different in important ways from its European counterparts. Although, of course, Blake's poem is not exclusive to British socialism: the verses are printed on the programmes of women's institutes all over the country.

Jerusalem is selective, as any history book must be if it is to avoid becoming an antiquarian exercise. In the preface to *Eminent Victorians*, Lytton Strachey discusses how the 'explorer of the past' should work:

> He will attack his subject in unexpected places; he will fall upon the flank, or the rear; he will shoot a sudden, revealing searchlight into obscure recesses, hitherto undivined. He will row out over that great ocean of material, and lower down into it, here and there, a little bucket, which will bring up to the light of day some characteristic specimen, from those far depths, to be examined with a careful curiosity.

I have not treated the people or events in this book as 'specimens' but it is clear what Strachey means. He was certainly right about 'that great ocean of material', much larger now than when he was writing. Ramsay MacDonald's papers, for instance, amount to no less than 1,600 files which are stored at the Public Records Office. The *Warwick Guide to British Labour Periodicals 1790–1970* lists a grand total of 4,125 separate titles and it is estimated there have been 6,000 different trade unions in Britain since systematic records were first kept from the 1890s.

Hugh Dalton's diaries amount to nearly two million words. Richard Crossman's diaries were published in four weighty volumes which total 1,136, 688, 851 and 1,039 pages respectively. And pity the future biographer of Tony Benn; quite apart from the four hefty volumes of diaries published so far and his thousands of speeches and articles, apparently he receives 2–3,000 letters *each week*. That publishers feel it is worthwhile bringing out so much material illustrates how the labour movement has 'arrived'; in the Victorian period it was generals and churchmen whose works appeared at such length. However, more sometimes means less.

But if the book mountain is daunting, then what about newspapers? I once sat in the Cambridge University Library and blithely ordered up all the copies of the *Daily Worker* newspaper for the 1930s. Half an hour later I saw staff struggling with scores of heavy-bound volumes. To my horror I realised that I had asked them to fetch several hundredweight of material.

With so many thousands of publications in print it is often difficult to distinguish the wood from the trees. In many ways, therefore, this book represents a kind of personal map, trying to provide an overview of what has happened so far and might happen next.

What is 'right' and who is 'left'? The terms derive from which side of the hall groups sat in the French Assembly two hundred years ago, but since then many layers of different meaning have attached themselves to both these words and to others such as 'conservative', 'liberal' and 'socialist'. It is, I think, clear in the following pages who stands for what, but an excellent shorthand definition has been provided by Ben Pimlott:

> Labour is known to be against privilege, social hierarchy, capitalism, personal wealth, inequality, unregulated markets, the powerful, the Establishment, the upper classes, nationalistic fervour, military might; and in favour of equality, civil rights, state intervention, democracy, the working class, internationalism. Little in either list has changed in a hundred years, which is why the attitudes are so readily identifiable with the Left (and why Labour finds it so hard to disassociate itself from them).

One final problem: footnotes. These immediately repel many 'general readers' and one sometimes feels that the notes are designed to show off the author's dedicated research rather than to help the reader. What one historian has called 'the pleasures of the past' can easily become submerged in ostentatious display. On the other hand, if you don't support assertions and claims then critics will correctly reach for the devastating words 'lightweight' and 'insubstantial'.

I have therefore included notes together with a select bibliography at the end of the book, which is the least I can do to acknowledge the excellent work of the scholars and academics on which I have drawn. To find the source of a quotation or statement, just identify the key words or statistic and turn to the back.

Where should *To Build A New Jerusalem* begin? . . .

Short Chronology

1918 February: John Maclean appointed Bolshevik Consul in Glasgow.

1919 January: the Battle of George Square in Glasgow.

1919 March: formation of the Communist International (COMINTERN), the Third International, in Moscow.

1920 July: the Communist Party of Great Britain (CPGB) formed in London.

1921 July: George Lansbury leads the Poplar councillors to the Law Courts.

1922: the Transport and General Workers' Union (TGWU) established with Ernest Bevin as General Secretary.

1924 January: the first Labour Government, with Ramsay MacDonald as Prime Minister; loses office at the October general election.

1926 May: the General Strike lasts nine days.

1928 May: Transport House opened in London, headquarters of the Transport and General Workers' Union and the Labour Party.

1929 May: formation of second Labour Government.

1930 January: first issue of the *Daily Worker* newspaper.

1931 August: collapse of MacDonald's government; the Labour Party is heavily defeated at the October general election.

PART TWO

1932 October: Sir Stafford Cripps helps establish the Socialist League.

1935 November: Clement Attlee elected leader of the Labour Party to replace George Lansbury.

1936 May: the Left Book Club initiated by Victor Gollancz.

1936 July: outbreak of the Spanish Civil War.

1936 August: the first Moscow Trial.

1936 October: the Battle of Cable Street in the East End of London.

1936 October: the Jarrow March led by the town's MP Ellen Wilkinson.

1937 January: first issue of the weekly *Tribune*.

1937 November: the death of Ramsay MacDonald.

1940 May: the Labour Party joins the coalition government.

1942 December: publication of the Beveridge Report.

1945 July: the Labour Party wins the general election with 393 MPs to the Conservatives' 213.

1947 January: a secret Cabinet committee decides that Britain should make its own nuclear weapons.

1948 July: the National Health Service comes into operation.

1949 April: the North Atlantic Treaty Organisation (NATO) is established.

1949 September: the pound is devalued.

1950 February: the general election cuts Labour's majority to six.

1950 June: start of the Korean War.

1951 April: Aneurin Bevan, Harold Wilson and John Freeman resign from the government.

1951 October: the Conservatives win the general election.

1955 December: Hugh Gaitskell succeeds Clement Attlee as the leader of the Labour Party.

1956 October: Anthony Crosland publishes *The Future of Socialism*.

1956 October: the Hungarian uprising is crushed by the Red Army.

1958 January: the Campaign for Nuclear Disarmament (CND) is formed; the first of what becomes annual marches to Aldermaston takes place that Easter.

1959 October: the Labour Party loses its third general election in a row.

1960 July: death of Aneurin Bevan.

1960 October: the Labour Party Conference passes a unilateralist defence motion, prompting Hugh Gaitskell to make his 'fight' speech.

1963 January: death of Hugh Gaitskell; succeeded by Harold Wilson.

1964 October: Labour just win the general election.

1965 July: Harold Wilson makes a secret deal with the American government not to devalue the pound.

1966 March: the Labour government increases its majority.

1967 November: the pound is devalued by Chancellor of the Exchequer James Callaghan.

1969 January: Barbara Castle publishes her *In Place Of Strife* proposals for trade union reform; they are withdrawn in June.

1969 August: Home Secretary James Callaghan sends the troops into Ulster.

1970 June: the Conservatives under Edward Heath unexpectedly win the general election.

1973 January: Britain enters the European Economic Community (EEC).

1974 February: a Labour government under Wilson returns to office and wins a small majority at the October 1974 general election.

1975 June: referendum on the EEC produces a 2–1 result in favour of staying in.

1976 April: James Callaghan succeeds Harold Wilson as leader of the Labour Party and Prime Minister.

1976 December: the Cabinet agrees to the cuts demanded by the International Monetary Fund (IMF).

1977 March: the 'Lib-Lab' Pact signed.

1979 May: the Conservatives under Mrs Thatcher win the general election with a forty-three-seat majority.

PART THREE

1980 November: Michael Foot succeeds James Callaghan as leader of the Labour Party.

1981 February: a special conference held at Wembley to introduce constitutional changes within the Labour Party prompts the breakaway of the Social Democratic Party (SDP).

1981 May: Labour wins the Greater London Council (GLC) elections; Ken Livingstone is elected leader of the GLC.

1983 June: the Conservatives easily win the general election with a 146-seat majority.

1983 October: Neil Kinnock is elected leader of the Labour Party.

1984 March: the miners' strike begins.

1987 June: the Conservatives win the general election with a 102-seat majority.

1990 November: Mrs Thatcher resigns as Prime Minister.

Part One

From Keir Hardie to Clement Attlee

'SOCIALISM IS MUCH MORE AN AFFAIR OF THE HEART THAN
THE INTELLECT.'

Keir Hardie, March 1906

CHAPTER ONE

Who Cares About Keir Hardie?

'I know what I believe to be the right thing, and I go and do it.'

Keir Hardie

'A mere abstraction, be it ever so demonstrable scientifically, will never move masses of people.'

Keir Hardie

'Light is a more important factor than heat.'

Report on Fabian Policy; Tract 70

EARLY ON the morning of 7 August 1892, an unusual procession set out from Canning Town in East London to make its exuberant way to the Houses of Parliament. The noise was provided by an out-of-tune trumpet player, who accompanied the singing of fifty men following a wagonette. Inside this vehicle was a Scotsman called Keir Hardie, the newly elected MP for West Ham South, on his way to take up his seat in Westminster. He was the first ever Labour Member of Parliament.

At the end of the seven-mile journey, the trumpeter launched into the *Marseillaise*, a song associated with French Revolutions and adapted for the present occasion in the absence of any suitable British revolutionary songs. Bystanders and MPs alike were horrified at what was happening; 'The Mother of Parliaments' had never seen anything like this before. Even more shocking was the fact that Keir Hardie, MP, was proposing to enter the House 'unsuitably dressed', wearing not the frock coat and silk top hat hitherto considered obligatory when attending what was effectively the best gentlemen's club in the world but a tweed suit and something which looked very much like a deerstalker. Next morning an outraged Press lambasted the new MP with a vehemence which, over the next twenty-five years, would become customary.

Acutely aware of the symbolic value of clothes, Hardie realised that his arrival in an ordinary working outfit was tantamount to challenging the

Establishment. As his friend and companion in the procession, Frank Smith, observed: 'The man who did not change his garb, simply because of his change in social status, was not likely to change his principles.' Yet, out of the thousands of words written on or about Hardie's arrival in Parliament, only one journalist, the Liberal A. G. Gardiner, seems to have recognised what 7 August 1892 might ultimately lead to:

> I am not sure that when the historian of the future discusses our time he will not find the most significant event on that day in 1892 when James Keir Hardie rode up to Westminster from West Ham, clothed in cloth cap, tweed suit, and flannel shirt, and accompanied by a band. The world scoffed at the vulgarity, or shuddered at the outrage, according to its humour; but the event was, nevertheless, historic. It marked the emergence of a new force in politics.

Within fifteen years of his election, Hardie had broken the stranglehold of the Conservative and the Liberal Parties by creating a new political organisation, the Labour Party, which was based on the trade union movement. By the 1920s this youthful body had replaced the Liberals as the main rival to the Conservatives and had formed its own government. In 1945, less than forty years after Hardie founded the new party, a Labour government came to power with a huge majority. A. G. Gardiner lived to see his prophecy come true. He died in 1946 at the age of eighty.

Keir Hardie is the undisputed father of the modern British labour movement, a pioneer who worked unceasingly for 'The Cause'. He has a secure and honoured place in any socialist pantheon. Yet people seem to know his name and little else. This complex and fascinating man has become submerged beneath layers of ritual hero-worship. Hardie's early biographers, for instance, were in fact hagiographers, glossing over uncomfortable incidents and events in his life in their eagerness to portray a difficult but essentially saint-like individual. What kind of man was this Scot who devoted his life to the early socialist movement? What forces drove him on so that he rarely slept more than three or four hours a night, always looked at least ten years older than his real age, and died almost of a broken heart after the outbreak of the First World War shattered his faith in mankind?

Hardie himself gave posterity little help towards answering this question. Few personal remarks or feelings appear in his letters, and unlike most labour leaders he never found the time or inclination to write his memoirs. But we do have photographs of him and for once perhaps the camera does not lie.

They show an upright, uncompromising, bearded man whose path is not lightly to be crossed. Always unsmiling, he stares out of the photographs like some minor Old Testament prophet about to summon up fire and brimstone to hurl at his enemies. His stubborn and bloody-minded independence is obvious. Hardie's friend Bruce Glasier wrote that he was able to 'stand alone, fight alone, win alone, bear defeat alone.' Hardie himself once remarked that, 'Companionship is good, solitude is best.' But this was also the married man who enjoyed a long, passionate relationship with the suffragette Sylvia Pankhurst.

The sense of determination and grievance often necessary to be a pioneer was derived largely from the circumstances of Hardie's upbringing. Born illegitimate in a one-room cottage in Legbrannock, Lanarkshire, in August 1856, he spent just one day at school before at the age of eight starting work in order to supplement the family income. He was sent down the mines at ten and could barely write until his late teens. In his early twenties he was sacked from his job and blacklisted by the mine-owners because of his trade union activities.

This summary of Hardie's early years sounds as if it comes from a Victorian melodrama. He did later refer to his upbringing with some bitterness and only rarely mentioned his illegitimacy. His mother was a farm worker called Mary Keir but it is unclear who his real father was. The name of a collier appears on the birth certificate of 1856, but there is some suspicion that this was done to hide the identity of the local doctor. It is remarkable that three of the British labour movement's most influential figures – Hardie, Ramsay MacDonald and Ernest Bevin – should all be illegitimate.

Hardie's mother eventually married a ship's carpenter called David Hardie, but his difficulty in finding work meant that the large family – Keir had six half-brothers and sisters – were often on the move all over Scotland as the stepfather sought employment. The latter's frequent drinking, when apparently he used to taunt Keir's mother with the existence of 'The Bastard', led the young boy to a lifelong commitment to the temperance movement.

Of the jobs Hardie had before his teens, it was his dismissal from one that helped fuel his driving determination. He was employed by a baker who was a pillar of the local community, God-fearing and upright, which did not stop him sacking the ten-year-old boy for being marginally late for work and then refusing to pay him his last week's wages. It was an act of spite with terrible consequences for the family with David Hardie out of work.

After the Hardie family left Glasgow, Keir was sent down the mines, working as the trapper responsible for keeping supplies of fresh air on the move. It was a job that meant long hours on his own, but it was now that the young man showed his ambition to get on in life. He taught himself shorthand, using a pin to scratch out the figures on a slab of stone.

While working at another pit in charge of the pony, an accident to the cage which brought the miners to the surface meant that the boy was trapped below ground along with other miners. They were eventually rescued without mishap, but the hazards of this occupation as well as the offhand and penny-pinching attitude the coalowners had towards safety made a lasting impression on Hardie. As late as 1918, 1,300 miners were killed in accidents every year. Hardie was later to write of his time as a boy down the mines:

> For several years as a lad I rarely saw daylight during the winter months. Down the pit by six in the morning, and not leaving it again until half-past five meant not seeing the sun, and even on Sunday I had at that time to spend four hours down below. Such an experience does not develop the sunny side of one's being.

In later life Hardie never forgot these bitter, early experiences. But the crucial thing about Hardie was that he determined to do something about it, to try and improve these primitive working and living conditions. The only possible way was to set up a trade union. This was very much easier said than done.

The first attempts to set up trade unions in Britain were hampered by the passage of the Combination Acts in 1799 and 1800 which outlawed the formation of working men into organised groups in order to press for better working conditions. The Acts were not finally repealed until 1824. The rapid onset of industrialisation and the factory system meant that large numbers of men and women were thrown together as employees, often labouring in appalling conditions for meagre pay. The only way the weak could defend themselves in a so-called 'free labour market' was by banding together into collective bodies, namely trade unions. In the 1820s the Tory statesman Sir Robert Peel justified the existence of trade unions:

> Men who . . . have no property except their manual skill and strength, ought to be allowed to confer together, if they think fit, for the purpose of determining at what rate they will sell their property.

In 1833 the philanthropist and factory owner Robert Owen set up an organisation which he called the Grand National Consolidated Trades

Union. Within a year it could boast a membership of over one million. The union's weaknesses lay in its federal structure, which meant that it was difficult to co-ordinate action, and its lack of money so that strike pay was out of the question. In 1834 the union miscalculated its strength and called a strike that ended in disarray and its own collapse. At the same time the authorities launched a legal counter-attack against union activities, shown at its most virulent in the transportation of the six Tolpuddle Martyrs of Dorset who were sent to Australia simply for joining a trade union.

The disintegration of these early attempts at industrial organisation led to a lull in activity for the next decade and a half. But when attempts were made to establish unions in the 1850s, the industrial climate was very different. Britain was now 'The Workshop of the World' and possessed a 'labour aristocracy' — that is, skilled workers such as engineers, mechanics, carpenters and 'railway servants' who felt that they had a stake in the expanding capitalist system. Whereas the members of Owen's Grand National Consolidated Trades Union had been fighting to overthrow the new system, groups such as the Amalgamated Society of Engineers, formed in 1851, were more interested in trying to improve their status within it.

These 'New Model Unions' rigorously excluded the unskilled by charging high subscriptions and often drawing up rules which specified that they were for craftsmen only. Like the twenty-eight 'Rochdale Pioneers' who had each subscribed £1 in 1844 and helped begin the Co-operative movement, the New Model Unions were thoroughly respectable bodies. Photographs of their leaders such as Robert Applegarth and William Newton and their colleagues on the Trades Union Congress, which first met in 1868, show men who clearly value moderation and sobriety above all else. They were quite content to work patiently and slowly within the parliamentary system for legal reform.

Their strategy seemed to work: trade unions were given legal recognition in 1871 and in 1875 the right to peaceful picketing. As far as possible the leaders of the New Model Unions worked hand in hand with employers. Robert Applegarth claimed that he never 'had a wrong word with an employer in my life, either as a workman or as a representative of working men.' These men were stalwart supporters of William Gladstone's Liberal Party. They looked down on the miners as distinctly inferior workmen as well as being supposedly so anarchic in their habits as to be incapable of being organised into trade unions.

This meant that when Keir Hardie tried to set up a miners' union he could expect no help from the existing unions. A further difficulty was that the only work available in most mining districts meant going down the pits. If sacked by the owner it was almost impossible for a miner to find alternative work. Any organised protest among the miners was countered with lock-outs by the owners who knew that eventually the men would be starved back to work. 'Blacklegs' could always be imported if the strike action looked serious.

Hardie began work in Hamilton, Lanarkshire. His Christian evangelicalism meant that he believed each person was responsible for their own salvation. He did not shrink therefore from criticising the miners themselves, pointing out that it was partly due to their own failure to organise that the owners got away with often callous behaviour. His attitude was quite different from that of some later labour leaders for whom 'the lads' could do no wrong. But Hardie also held that, in the words of a later Scottish socialist James Maxton, 'poverty was a man-made thing' and so open to change.

In 1879 came the blow that Hardie must have been expecting. At the age of twenty-three he was sacked from the pit, along with two of his half-brothers, and blacklisted because of his trade union activities. It could not have happened at a worse time as he had recently married a Miss Lillie Wilson. Hardie managed to support himself over the next few years by accepting a modest salary for his work as the agent for several small miners' unions and by various pieces of journalism. In fact, it was his promise as a journalist that in 1882 brought him the opportunity to edit his local newspaper, the *Cumnock News*. He accepted the offer.

That the *Cumnock News* was a Liberal newspaper suggests Hardie still hoped that the changes he was seeking could be brought about under the aegis of the Liberal Party. Formed in the 1860s, the Liberals were a strange amalgam of elements: wealthy landowners jostled with Nonconformists and Jewish people, trade unionists and Irish Home Rulers with out-and-out radicals. What held them together as the main opposition to the Tory Party was their hostility to all vested interests and unnecessary privilege. Often a radical force, the Liberals had reformed the educational system, the army, the civil service and the drink trade, recognised trade unions and introduced the secret ballot. In 1884 they extended the vote by means of the third Reform Act. The electorate increased from three to five million male voters, constituting about half the adult male population in Britain.

Nevertheless it was clear that on this issue the Liberals were being expedient rather than principled. John Vincent has put it bluntly:

> The Liberals, flatly, were not democrats, their Reform Bill of 1866 was an exclusion Bill, and when they adapted democracy after 1867 for political purposes, they knew neither its feelings nor its justifications.

It was also clear by the 1880s that the Liberal Party's attachment to the idea of *laissez-faire* or of market forces was sacrosanct and beyond challenge. This meant that they were opposed to the government action which, in the view of many observers, seemed the only way to deal with the widespread poverty and squalor that still disfigured parts of the country.

The virtues of private enterprise were of no help to the hundreds of thousands of people whose low wages and lack of any accident or employment insurance condemned them to a knife-edge existence. The workings of the free market economy inevitably meant that the 'have-nots' would experience destitution and perhaps the ultimate degradation of the workhouse. There was no welfare state and only the fortunate few could rely on the 'friendly societies' or workmen's clubs, which had been legally recognised in 1855 and catered for the better-off workman. In the face of overwhelming social problems, charitable gestures, however laudable, were not enough. As the slogans on early socialist banners declared: 'Damn your charity; we want justice.'

Government action was urgently needed. But the Liberal Party was opposed to such intervention.

Keir Hardie spent much of the 1880s trying to set up miners' unions in Scotland, often in the face of opposition from men who were loyal supporters of the Liberal Party. He began to realise that industrial action needed to be backed up by political change and that the Liberal Party was not sufficiently radical for this. The Party hierarchy, for instance, was very grateful for the votes of the newly enfranchised electorate, but it was not prepared to put forward working-class candidates for safe Liberal seats. Hardie's growing dissatisfaction was increased by his contacts with socialists such as Henry George, who advocated sweeping land reforms, and with Friedrich Engels and Eleanor Marx.

In 1888 a by-election helped to crystallise Hardie's views. The sitting Liberal MP for Mid-Lanark resigned his seat on the grounds of ill-health. Hardie argued that in what was largely a miners' constituency a miners' candidate should be nominated to take his place. His own name was put forward. It was rejected by the Lanark Liberals in favour of a 'safe' candidate. With typical obstinacy Hardie decided to stand anyway. It was a decision that was to culminate nearly twenty years later in the establishment of the Labour Party.

The Mid-Lanark Liberals suddenly realised that Hardie's candidature threatened their hopes of retaining a safe seat. Wouldn't he split the anti-Conservative vote? Wasn't he a poor man, with a growing family? Surely he could be bought off. Hardie found himself summoned to a meeting with Sir George Trevelyan, one of the grandees of the Liberal Party. Hardie tells what happened:

Sir George was very polite, and explained the unwisdom of Liberals and Labour [Hardie was calling himself a National Labour Party candidate] fighting each other. They wanted more working men in Parliament, and if only I would stand down in Mid-Lanark he would give me an assurance that at the General Election I would be adopted somewhere, the party paying my expenses, and guaranteeing me a yearly salary − three hundred pounds was the sum hinted at − as they were doing for others (he gave names). I explained as well as I could why his proposal was offensive, and though he was obviously surprised, he was too much of a gentleman to be anything but courteous. And so the fight went on.

Hardie might have found the proposal 'offensive'; many others wouldn't have done. As a miner, he would have earned about £70 or £80 a year, so the offer of £300 was a substantial one. There must have been pressure too from his wife Lillie who was never keen on her husband's political activities. Keir Hardie was in effect fighting on both personal and political fronts − which only made him the more determined to do what he was convinced was right.

At the by-election in April 1888, Hardie polled 617 votes from a total of 7,381, several thousand behind the victorious Liberal. His comparative lack of success underlined what a huge task lay ahead of him. But the decisive break from the Liberal Party had been made. The first steps had been taken towards the creation of a new political party.

The next task was to create some kind of organisation and political machinery. Ever since the Birmingham Liberal Joseph Chamberlain had first introduced the paraphernalia of political organisation in the 1860s, from membership lists to canvassing, it was clear that the days of the independent candidate were coming to an end. In May 1888, a month after the Mid-Lanark contest, twenty-seven people met in Glasgow to found the Scottish Labour Party. Hardie was elected secretary; the President was R. B. Cunninghame Graham, an extraordinary character who had already been a Radical MP, a writer, an international traveller and a gaucho in Latin America. He was the son of a Scottish laird.

Cunninghame Graham's involvement was significant because it showed that any new body would not be an exclusively proletarian grouping. Although Hardie was insistent on the need to create a new party, he was pragmatic enough to realise that he must work alongside sympathetic allies from whatever background. This explains why the Labour Party, for instance, has always welcomed to its ranks recruits from privileged backgrounds. The desire to be inclusive rather than exclusive underlines Hardie's decision to call it the Scottish Labour Party rather than the Scottish Socialist Party − in the 1880s, the word 'socialist' was generally regarded as a foreign and rather frightening label.

Hardie was shrewd enough to understand that creating a new party in Britain would be no overnight job – which is why he cautiously started in Scotland. But he was not starting completely from scratch. By the late nineteenth century Britain had been transformed into a predominantly urban and industrial society, the first in the world. E. J. Hobsbawm has noted that Britain then was:

> . . . first and foremost, a country of workers. R. Dudley Baxter, calculating the size of the various British classes in 1867, reckoned that over three-quarters – seventy-seven per cent – of the 24.1 million inhabitants of Great Britain belonged to the 'manual labour class'; and he included among the 'middle class' all office-workers and shop-assistants, all shopkeepers, however tiny, all foremen and supervisory workers, and the like.

Firmly rooted within this urban working class were the trade unions, trades councils, co-operatives and friendly societies which formed 'a world of labour', a sort of alternative network of loyalties offering members mutual assistance. Though working class, this world was not opposed to the existing system but was, in fact, supplementary to it. This frame of mind reflected the largely consensual and pragmatic character of the British political system.

The historian Henry Pelling has commented that the most important feature of British socialism is the belief that it is possible to achieve a transfer of power without resorting to violence. Hardie decided that Parliament had to be the focus of this transition. He was hostile towards abstract dogma and Marxist theory because 'it does not touch one human sentiment or feeling . . . it entirely leaves the human element out of account.' As proposed by Hardie, British socialists were to work for piecemeal change within the system. It is a tradition often strikingly different from that propounded by other European socialist parties. Marxist historians have dubbed it 'labourism'.

In particular there were two organisations that Hardie wanted to form the bedrock for any new political body. The first were the Nonconformists who opposed the established Church of England and so had been tied to the Liberal Party. To detach as many Nonconformists as possible, Hardie presented socialism as an ethical and moral gospel. This desire 'to build a New Jerusalem' fitted in with his own evangelical beliefs. As he wrote later in his book *From Serfdom to Socialism*:

> Socialism, like every other problem of life, is at bottom a question of ethics or morals. It has mainly to do with the relationships which should exist between a man and his fellows.

Yet fine thoughts and beautiful words would never be enough to create the New Jerusalem. Hardie also required trade union support, even though the leaders of the New Model Unions were happy enough to stay within the fold of the Liberal Party. But without trade union assistance in terms of both finance and membership any new party would simply be a small and insignificant sect without influence.

Within just two months of his stand at Mid-Lanark, a strike took place in London which was to herald the break-up of the old order and gave added force to Hardie's ideas.

On 23 June 1888 an article appeared in a small circulation weekly magazine called *The Link*. Titled 'White Slavery in London', it was written by a journalist, Annie Besant, and highlighted the terrible working conditions of the matchgirls employed at the Bryant and May factory in Bow in the East End of London.

The directors of Bryant and May − prominent supporters of the Liberal Party and instrumental in the erection of the statue of William Gladstone which still stands outside St Mary's Church, Bow − promptly sacked the girls suspected of giving Mrs Besant her information. She had written about their low wages, the regular fines and deductions to which they were subject, and the horrors of 'phossy jaw' caused by the phosphorus used in the matchmaking process which slowly ate away the girls' faces. To the directors' anger, the girls did not just meekly accept the sackings but instead, at the urging of Mrs Besant, walked out en masse. Equally surprised by this unanimity were the New Model Unions.

The campaign waged by these 1,400 girls soon enlisted public sympathy and over £400 was received in donations. Six hundred of the girls were sent fruit-picking in Kent to support the strike fund. Within a few days a report on the dispute by the impartial Toynbee Hall, a settlement established in Whitechapel four years before, confirmed almost all the girls' assertions. Bryant and May were forced to capitulate. Within a fortnight the matchgirls had won their dispute and returned to work.

Their triumph sent shock waves through the labour movement. If one group of unorganised workers − and women at that − could take on their employers, why shouldn't others? The following month the gasworkers in

East London managed to get their working day reduced from twelve hours to eight without having to go on strike. Then, in 1889, came the dispute which marked this 'New Unionism' as a decisive political force which would underpin Hardie's efforts to establish a working-class party.

Conditions on the London docks were unbelievably savage. Too many men chasing too few jobs meant that a foreman could pick out those he wanted with all the arrogance of a rich man at a slave market. Herded together into what was called 'The Cage', grown men fought and struggled with each other to attract the foreman's attention. One of the dock leaders, Ben Tillett, described in his pamphlet *A Dock Labourer's Bitter Cry* how the foreman:

> Walks up and down with the air of a dealer in a cattle-market, picking and choosing from a crowd of men who, in their eagerness to obtain employment, trample each other under foot, and . . . like beasts they fight each other for the chance of a day's work.

As with the miners and the matchgirls, the New Model Unions had always regarded the dockers as being beyond the pale of trade union organisation. Once more they were to be proved wrong. In August 1889 a dispute at the South-West India Dock escalated and the men walked out. Their main demand was for 'the dockers' tanner' — that is, payment of sixpence an hour — but they also wanted employment of not less than four hours at a stretch rather than bits and pieces here and there.

The dockers' leaders conducted a well-organised campaign, making sure that, like the matchgirls the year before, they gained and then held public support. Marches from East London to the dock companies' headquarters in the City were always held in co-operation with the police and passed off peacefully. One socialist who was on the strike committee, H. H. Champion, stressed in his account of the strike just how vital this air of order and calm was:

> . . . though there was little public sympathy shown in the earlier days of the strike, as soon as it became widely known that thousands of the strikers had marched through the City without a pocket being picked or a window being broken, and that at the head of the procession was a man whose public position was a guarantee that 'the mob' had a responsible leader [John Burns], the British citizen felt he might go back to his suburban villa when his day's work was done full of confidence that his warehouses would not be wrecked in the night, and that he could afford to follow his natural inclination

and back the poor devils who were fighting with pluck, good humour, and order against overwhelming odds.

The dockers also received international support, including a donation of £50,000 from the Australian trade unions. Finally, like the matchgirls and gasworkers before them, the dockers were successful.

These industrial disputes gave a surge of confidence to this 'New Unionism' and the number of trade unionists doubled between 1888 and 1892. Not just in Britain but all over Europe new working-class organisations were being created that reflected the new collective spirit of 'all for one and one for all' which had developed out of the massing together of factory workers in towns. For example, working-class parties were formed in France in 1882, in Italy in 1883, in Belgium and in Spain in 1885; they complemented the German Social Democrats founded the previous decade and Keir Hardie's Independent Labour Party which was to be established in 1893. It is no coincidence that socialists now began to use the word 'masses' or that the failure of Sir George Trevelyan's intervention over the Mid-Lanark by-election symbolised the decline of 'the politics of personal influence'.

Nevertheless in Britain many workers remained unrepresented by labour organisations. Few women joined trade unions (even less provision was made for them) and in rural districts the pioneering union organiser Joseph Arch fought long and hard but often in vain to represent agricultural workers. In Scotland, too, trade union representation remained patchy. But it was clear that the underlying trend was in Hardie's favour. The Liberal Party had been conspicuous by its absence from the above disputes — except where, as in the Bryant and May case, it was prominent Liberals who were the unpopular employers.

Yet life remained difficult for Hardie. Year after year he stood up at the annual Trades Union Congress conferences to argue the need for a political party in Parliament which would represent organised labour. There was still much snobbery among the older unions and at the 1890 conference the representatives of skilled labour jeered those representing the unskilled. At the next year's conference, only eleven delegates voted in favour of setting up a Parliamentary Fund to support an independent party. But in the summer of 1892, Keir Hardie's own election as MP for West Ham South helped to give a focus to his arguments.

What was a Scot doing as the MP for an East London constituency? Not even Hardie's bitterest opponents denied the man's extraordinary energy which took him propagandising for 'the Cause' all over the country. Just reading a list of his weekly commitments makes one feel exhausted. His efforts were helped by the skills he had gained through his training as a lay preacher. His oratory was simple and direct and he never used notes, preferring to respond to the mood of the crowd. Hardie's speeches and imagery still have a compelling power today. To give two examples:

> The nation is yours when there is debt to pay, it is yours when there is blood to shed; but if you attempt to rule it, you are told that you are interfering with what does not belong to you.

And, when attacking the idea of monarchy:

> Either the British people are fit to govern themselves or they are not. If they are, an hereditary ruler is an insult; if they are not, they should not be entrusted with votes.

In an age without microphones — one contributory reason why so few women were able at this time to make their mark on the British labour movement — Hardie's powerful voice was able to inspire and control his audiences. Gradually he became a national and not just a local figure. It was a change reflected in the title of the monthly magazine which he also found the time to edit and to write most of its contents. The *Miner* was first published in January 1887; in 1889 it became the *Labour Leader*.

It was his growing national reputation as both organiser and inspirer which prompted Hardie's supporters to put forward his name in West Ham. Fortunately for him the Liberals failed to decide on a candidate and so gave Hardie their tacit support. He stood as an independent Labour candidate against the Conservative, a Major Barnes. Inevitably, the Press called it a battle between 'the Major and the Miner'. Victory came in July 1892 when Hardie was elected by over a thousand votes — and so on 7 August 1892 he went in procession to take up his seat.

Hardie was not the only independent Labour candidate returned to Parliament at the 1892 general election. For Battersea there was John Burns who had been one of the leaders of the dock strike; for Middlesbrough there was the seamen's leader, J. Havelock Wilson. In contrast to Hardie, both men soon began to display all the characteristics of the old trade union MPs, hanging on to the coat-tails of the Liberal Party and sucking up to its leaders in the hope of political preferment.

So why was Hardie different? He never forgot or forgave the early privations he had experienced, and this gave him the courage to do only what he believed to be right. He was impervious to the blandishments of Parliament with its sense of ease and self-importance which often blunted the edge of many once fiery MPs coming after Hardie. He didn't like the House of Commons: 'I feel like a bird with its wings clipped when I am there.' He always remembered the ordinary people outside Westminster and his persistent campaigning on behalf of the jobless earned him the label 'Member for the Unemployed'. His unconventional arrival at Parliament had showed the metal of the man. But the outrage which greeted his actions on that day was as nothing compared with the abuse heaped on his head over 'the Royal Baby' incident.

On 23 June 1894, 260 people died in a terrible mining tragedy at Cilfyndd in South Wales. In that same week President Carnot of France was assassinated and the then Duchess of York had a baby. A telegram was sent by Parliament to the French Assembly deploring the President's death. No telegram was sent to the mourners in South Wales. The House of Commons also decided to send a message of congratulations to the Duchess. Hardie asked the Liberal Leader of the House what message was to be sent to South Wales. Sir William Harcourt replied offhandedly that of course the House sympathised with the Welsh people but there the matter must rest. Hardie was incensed and decided to speak against sending congratulations to the Duke and Duchess. The reaction of his fellow MPs was extreme. Throughout his speech he was interrupted, jeered and hissed. All around him there was commotion. One observer described the scene: 'They howled and yelled and screamed, but he stood his ground.' Hardie never minded being in a minority of one, but he was gratified to receive over a thousand letters of support from the public after this incident.

At the general election of 1895 the Liberals put forward their own candidate at West Ham South and, not unexpectedly, Hardie lost his seat – although the extent of his influence was seen three years later in 1898 when West Ham became the first council in Britain to have a Labour majority. By the time of his defeat, he had set up the Independent Labour Party (ILP) which was founded in Bradford in January 1893. Hardie, Burns and Wilson had stood as individuals without any organised party backing. The ILP was designed to provide this back-up and to draw together British socialists into a national party.

Not everyone, however, accepted the invitation. H. M. Hyndman's Marxist Social Democratic Federation argued that the ILP was not left-wing enough. But nothing would budge Hardie from his strategy of 'labourism', of working carefully and slowly for change. He knew that anything too extreme would frighten off the trade unions which were to be the keystone of the new party or else risk splitting the movement on religious or regional lines as had happened in several European countries.

In 1900 he was instrumental in founding the Labour Representation Committee (LRC), a tentative first step by the unions towards parliamentary representation. That same year he was returned as MP for Merthyr Tydfil, a seat he was to retain until his death in 1915. He still had few colleagues in the House of Commons but again he fought his corner with vigour. In 1901 the House of Lords decision in the 'Taff Vale Case' held that union funds should be at risk from any employer who suffered loss through a strike; a judicial ruling that completely hamstrung the unions. Virtually every union now realised that a political voice in Parliament was vital if their interests were to be properly defended. The major unions began to turn their backs on the Liberal Party and to affiliate to the Labour Representation Committee, supporting it financially. At the 1906 election twenty-nine MPs were elected on the LRC ticket and it was renamed the Labour Party. Keir Hardie was elected its first chairman.

So at last Hardie had achieved what he had been working towards. But at what cost? Journalist A. G. Gardiner described him as 'The Knight of the Rueful Countenance' and Hardie himself once observed, 'I have few friends and cannot, somehow, enter into the healthy and legitimate light side of life.' There was certainly no disjunction between Hardie's political views and his private opinions. His obstinacy and independence were not political camouflage but true aspects of his personality. He was impervious to bribes or corruption. He had turned down Sir George Trevelyan's offer of money and a safe seat years before, and his integrity did not waver when success finally arrived.

'High Society' wooed him in vain. In *From Serfdom to Socialism*, published in 1907, he refers in scathing terms to 'the vicious tastes and luxurious habits of the idle rich . . .' Gardiner claimed that 'You will never find a dress shirt under the red tie of Keir Hardie. He will never be petted by Princes and Peers.'

His emotional life was more complicated. Separated for long periods from his wife Lillie who remained in Scotland with their three children, Hardie took rooms just off Fleet Street. London to him was 'a haunting horror' which no doubt contributed to his melancholy. When Parliament was sitting he allowed himself only a few hours of sleep each night in order to cope with his voluminous correspondence which he managed on his own without a secretary. Everyone noted that he did not eat properly and smoked too much.

Hardie always paid generous tribute to his wife Lillie's support. At the 1914 ILP Conference, for instance, he said 'never has she reproached me for what I have done for the cause I love . . .' But a friend who knew them both well, Katherine Glasier, wrote that Lillie was 'temperamentally unfitted for the storms and vicissitudes of her husband's public life . . .' It is evident too that despite the moral and puritan exterior of Hardie, he was attracted to other women. In the 1890s he fell in love with a young woman called Annie Hines, although it is unclear if they were ever lovers.

There is no uncertainty over his relationship with Sylvia Pankhurst, an affair which lasted for six years between 1906 and 1912. Hardie at forty-seven was more than twice the age of the twenty-two-year-old Sylvia, who was one of the daughters of Emmeline Pankhurst, founder of the Women's Social and Political Union, the main suffragette organisation. It seems clear that the relationship brought much happiness to both sides but eventually petered out. Yet the affair suggests that Hardie was a more complicated man than his early biographers claimed.

Elected chairman of the Labour Party at the age of only fifty, it might have seemed to observers that Hardie was set fair for many more political triumphs. In fact, from this point onwards his career declined. He was above all else a loner who liked to stand defiant against the whole world. Never a good 'Party man', he disliked the slog of committee work and lacked the flexibility to acquire the necessary skills to lead a party in the House of Commons. 'I am an agitator,' he once said. 'My work has consisted of trying to stir up a divine discontent with wrong.' In 1907 he gave up the Labour Party chairmanship with relief and devoted himself to what he was best at: stumping around the country and putting across his political beliefs. The zeal and courage of the pioneer were to be superseded by the more slippery skills of the parliamentarian: Keir Hardie gave way to Ramsay MacDonald.

What kind of men were the first twenty-nine Labour MPs elected at the 1906 general election? Photographs show a widely contrasting group of individuals. There was Keir Hardie, of course, bewhiskered and stern, and the handsome Ramsay MacDonald. There was Will Crooks, the former docker who had held open-air meetings outside the gates of the East India Dock in London each Sunday. Called 'Crooks' College', they functioned as something like a Victorian Open University. Also present are Will Thorne who never went to school, began work at the age of eight and was only taught to read and write by Eleanor Marx; and Philip Snowden, crippled in a bicycle accident and renowned for the invective he directed at political opponents.

One characteristic that unites them is the extraordinary efforts these working-class men had made to educate themselves. Take J. R. Clynes, the Oldham mill-worker who had begun work at just ten years of age. He spent his spare time reading a dictionary:

> I became like a character from an old romance, my body walking and talking by day, but my soul coming to life only at nights under the potency of the magic words I culled from my sixpenny dictionary.

Another common feature is that they were, of course, all men: women did not get the vote until 1918, and even then on unequal terms. Twenty-three of the twenty-nine were trade unionists, which shows how successful Hardie's strategy of obtaining union support had been. Half had links with Nonconformist religion and several were associated with the temperance movement. All were working class, reflecting the solid roots of the new organisation. By 1900 no less than three-quarters of the workforce were manual labourers, and although there were obviously gender and regional differences this relatively unified class was at the heart of Hardie's party. Yet it was clearly a Labour and not a Socialist Party, made up of moderates rather than revolutionaries. The middle-class Marxist H. M. Hyndman claimed that these 1906 MPs displayed 'a dull and deferential respectability'.

What ideas animated these first Labour MPs? In 1906 the magazine *The Review of Reviews* asked the new MPs, and also the thirteen 'Lib-Lab' MPs – mostly miners who eventually joined the Labour Party – what books had led them to become socialists. Their eclectic replies show an extraordinary range of influences. Richard Crossman once claimed that the British labour movement was not 'bookish'; he was wrong. Books have been important, but not those books which are most obviously considered 'socialist'.

For instance, the Bible was mentioned by several MPs as a powerful factor. The books of Charles Dickens came up several times as did writers like Shakespeare, Milton, Shelley, Bunyan and Thomas Carlyle. Karl Marx was named only twice, which would not have been the case if a similar survey had been taken of contemporary French and German socialist MPs. One critic pointed out that none of the writers mentioned, bar Bunyan, was a representative of manual labour. All the works were very general, lacking any economic detail or proposals.

Of course this was not a coincidence. Elsewhere in Europe socialists spent much time drawing up and debating manifestoes, programmes and statements of aim. In Britain, however, Hardie and his colleagues were little interested in theoretical discussion, which didn't mean to say that they had any doubts as to what they were against.

In 1902 the American writer and socialist Jack London visited the capital. Instead of touring the West End like most tourists, London lived in the East End for several months. His book *The People of the Abyss*, published the next year, provided a horrifying picture of what life was like for hundreds of thousands of people in what he called 'The City of Degradation', supposedly the richest city in the world and the centre of a mighty empire. London detailed the widespread drunkenness, the wife beating, the hundreds of prostitutes. Take this description of an horrific 'pass the parcel':

> When a child dies, and some are always bound to die, since fifty-five per cent of the East End children die before they are five years old, the body is laid out in the same room. And if they are very poor, it is kept for some time until they bury it. During the day it lies on the bed; during the night when the living take the bed, the dead occupies the table, from which, in the morning, when the dead is put back into the bed, they eat their breakfast. Sometimes the body is placed on the shelf which serves as a pantry for their food. Only a couple of weeks ago, an East End woman was in trouble, because, in this fashion, being unable to bury it, she had kept her dead child three weeks.

Outrage at such conditions and at both the Conservative and Liberal Parties that had governed the country between them for the previous fifty years helps explain why people such as Hardie were prepared to devote much of their lives to trying to bring about radical change.

Their anger did not necessarily mean that their socialism could readily be defined, as is clear when reading today the speeches and writings of, for instance, the twenty-nine Labour MPs. The word 'socialism' had first been used nearly eighty years before, in the Owenite *Cooperative Magazine* of November 1827, but no one had ever defined exactly what this word meant or implied. Instead there are just vague references to 'the socialist com-monwealth' or 'the New Jerusalem'. Keir Hardie in particular always bathed his New Jerusalem in a warm, heavenly glow: 'I come from a race of seers, and I see clearly in prophetic vision the day, not fifty years ahead, when the cause for which we stand will be triumphant.' He never managed to flesh out his vision.

Hardie's colleagues were rarely more forthcoming but there was one tenet that they would have agreed on, namely the imperative need for collective control rather than private ownership. It was this feeling which inspired the famous Clause Four of the Constitution, drawn up in 1918, calling for 'the Common Ownership of the Means of Production'.

This looseness in spelling out what socialism meant was matched by the Labour Party's lack of organisation. It was, in fact, more a grouping of like-minded individuals than an efficient and relatively disciplined political party as we know them today. There were no local Labour Parties or even individual membership let alone any defined policies. Not until the Labour Party Conference held at Nottingham in January 1918 was a Constitution drawn up which, in historian Margaret Cole's words, finally 'implied that the Party was now set to become an adult political organisation, ready to challenge either or both of the two older parties.'

The man who drew up this Constitution as well as the statement of policy which followed it, *Labour and the New Social Order*, was Sidney Webb. His name is inextricably linked with that of his wife, Beatrice.

People sometimes laugh at the Webbs and they were, in some respects, figures of fun. There was their obsession with facts and yet more facts which, like socialist Gradgrinds, they incorporated into heavy tomes read nowadays only by insomniacs or Ph.D students. They are well-known for their distinctly unromantic marriage. Their honeymoon, for instance, was spent researching trade union records in Dublin. The Webbs' ascetic lifestyle and frugal housekeeping encouraged shrewd dinner guests to eat beforehand. Kingsley Martin, for many years the editor of the *New Statesman*, attended one gathering and tentatively asked the Webbs if he could use their lavatory; he recalled that they seemed surprised that their guests actually possessed such bodily needs.

Yet this summary neglects the Webbs' many virtues, foremost among them being their remarkable disinterestedness as they laboured for many years towards the general good without hope or expectation of financial reward. Both wore rings inscribed with the words 'Pro Bono Publico'. They were never malicious or self-seeking, always generous, dedicated simply to the service of others. And, not least, they enjoyed a happy marriage, which is movingly depicted in Beatrice's *Diaries* and her book *Our Partnership*.

Beatrice Potter was born in January 1858 into a family whose ancestors had done well in business. Her grandfather had been in the cotton industry, her father had prospered in railways and the timber trade. Richard Potter and his wife had nine daughters. Eight of them married men who became pillars of the Establishment. Margaret Cole has listed some of them. There was:

> R. D. Holt, merchant of Liverpool; Leonard Courtney, who became Lord Courtney of Penwith and narrowly missed the Speakership of the House of Commons; Arthur Payne, mill-owner; Alfred Cripps, barrister and subsequently Lord Parmoor; Henry Hobhouse, member of a great Liberal political family, MP for Somerset and Chairman of the Somerset County Council; Arthur Dyson Williams, barrister.

Beatrice, the youngest daughter, was to be different.

Childhood illness meant that she had little in the way of a formal education but she was healthy enough to be launched into the London season, 'coming out' in 1876. This upper-class social institution was supposed to ensure that girls found suitable husbands of their own class. It had the opposite effect on Beatrice, turning her against the conspicuous waste and extravagance of High Society.

She did however meet and fall in love with the rising politician Joseph Chamberlain, whose talents in running his home city of Birmingham in the 1860s and 1870s were now being demonstrated on the national stage. He was several years older than Beatrice, had been widowed twice and was looking for a companion to be his political hostess and to help further his career. Beatrice was astute enough to realise what such a marriage would entail: 'I shall be absorbed into the life of a man, whose aims are not my aims, who will refuse me all freedom of thought in my intercourse with him; to whose career I shall have to subordinate all my life, mental and physical.' Nevertheless Beatrice was deeply drawn towards Chamberlain, both intellectually and physically. After much heartbreak on her side she turned down his proposal of marriage, although at great cost to her own happiness. 'Will the pain never cease?' she asked herself, and at one point even contemplated suicide: 'If Death comes it will be welcome – for life has always been distasteful to me.'

She tried to keep herself occupied, first by rent-collecting for a charitable organisation in the East End and then by helping her cousin Charles Booth on the research for his multi-volume *The Life and Labour of the People of London*; books which did much to stir the late Victorian conscience. Her zeal for detailed research replaced the religious faith which she had lost. It was at this point in her life that she met Sidney Webb, a high-flying civil servant.

Webb was a mine of information on almost every social and political question of the day. He was a leading figure in the Fabian Society, the group established in 1884 which brought together a miscellaneous body of individuals ranging from the aspiring playwright George Bernard Shaw to the philandering journalist Hubert Bland who was married to the writer Edith Nesbit, later to be famous for *The Railway Children*. The Fabians were adept at publicising their ideas; more than 10 per cent of the membership were journalists, so that the trumpeting of their doctrines disguised their small membership. Most radicals at this time were involved with the Fabians, including many people who will bulk large in this book: Keir Hardie, Ramsay MacDonald who sat on the Executive for several years, Annie Besant, H. G. Wells, Dr and Mrs Pankhurst, the Reverend Stewart Headlam, and the playwright and theatre producer Harley Granville Barker.

The Fabians took their name from the Roman general Fabius Cunctator whose policy of caution had gradually worn down and defeated Hannibal. The moderation of the Fabian Society in working for reform within the parliamentary system – what Sidney Webb was later to describe as the inevitability of gradualness – seemed ideally suited to British conditions. The Fabians eschewed revolutionary rhetoric in favour of detailed investigation of the facts, and these facts revealed the inequalities and injustices which flowed from the *laissez-faire* and individualist philosophy that influenced successive governments. The Fabians argued that 'every man for himself' should be replaced by a collectivist emphasis on the public good which would require a much greater role for government. Instead of being a spectator on the sidelines, the state should roll up its sleeves and get into the action as a player. *Fabian Essays* of 1889 was both an indictment of late Victorian society and a constructive call to arms.

It was because she admired Sidney Webb's contribution to *Fabian Essays* that Beatrice arranged a meeting. He seems to have fallen in love almost at first sight with the beautiful and gifted Miss Potter but she was less enchanted, still perhaps bearing the emotional wounds of her relationship with Chamberlain. In her *Diary* Beatrice was brutally frank in her description of Sidney: 'I am not sure as to the future of that man. His tiny tadpole body, unhealthy skin, lack of manner, cockney pronunciation, poverty, are all against him.'

But gradually, over a period of months, she warmed towards him, although making it clear that she was attracted by Sidney's mind and nothing more. After their engagement, Sidney was bold enough to send his fiancée a photograph of himself. Beatrice replied, 'Let me have your head only – it is the head only that I am marrying.' Sidney had to recognise that public-spirited research was the basis for their marriage: 'One and one,' he remarked, 'placed in a sufficiently integrated relationship, make not two, but eleven.' And yet, despite this unpromising beginning – and the fact that some friends like Charles Booth and his wife dropped Beatrice because they felt she was marrying beneath her – the Webbs' marriage, celebrated in the summer of 1892, proved to be enormously happy on both sides.

Over the next fifty-one years they devoted themselves to their work, researching and writing many books together. They agreed not to have children in case it unsettled their work routine. Beatrice once wrote in her *Diary*: 'Are the books we have written together worth (to the community) the babies we might have had?' On the whole, the answer for Beatrice seems to have been yes.

Each Webb book was built from mountainous piles of file-cards, each card recording one 'fact', which was then placed in order. Such an accumulative method squeezed out any human dimension to their books, and it is no coincidence that their most readable works today – Beatrice's letters, diaries and book *Our Partnership* – retain a personal touch absent from the couple's more 'serious' historical researches. But their solid work did provide much of the ammunition used by early labour leaders as they argued the case for the trade unions and the Labour Party.

The Webbs were not just ivory-tower academics. They were instrumental in founding both the London School of Economics and the *New Statesman* magazine. Sidney worked extensively for the London County Council and was a Labour MP during the 1920s. Beatrice was a formidable member of the Poor Law Commission of 1908 and her Minority Report heralded the disintegration of the old Victorian assumptions towards poverty which had held that it was your own fault if you were poor.

There is still argument about the extent both of their influence and that of the Fabians. Like Hardie, the Webbs initially wanted to work through the Liberal Party. Eventually their disillusion with the Liberals convinced them that only the new Labour Party was a suitable vehicle for their policies. That Sidney should draw up the Constitution of the Labour Party in 1918 showed the way in which the Fabians had established their beliefs as the ideology of 'labourism'. It was a reminder, too, that the Labour Party was not an exclusively working-class body. In many ways the Webbs and the Fabians acted as the brains of the Labour Party and their influence grew stronger from the 1930s onwards when the party had to grapple with the problems of administration and government.

But, of course, a heart is also vital to any living body. And here one returns to the lonely, difficult, courageous figure of Keir Hardie as he makes his way to Parliament in August 1892. It was Hardie who recognised that millions of people were not adequately represented by the Conservative or Liberal Parties and that a political organisation was needed which would mitigate the consequences of a capitalism based on market forces. It was Hardie who more than any other person created the Labour Party and so dramatically influenced the course of British society and politics over the next hundred years. That is why one should care about Keir Hardie.

The Mild-Mannered Desperadoes: Revolutionaries in Britain and British Revolutionaries

'Marx himself ... did not wish to be called a "Marxist" and ridiculed the "Marxists" to his heart's content.'

Wilhelm Liebknecht

'We'll ask the man, where do you stand on the question of the revolution? Are you for it or against it? If he's against it, we'll stand him up against a wall.'

V. I. Lenin

FRENCH REVOLUTIONS, American Revolutions, the European Revolutions of 1848, Russian Revolutions – recent world history seems to be one revolution after another. Why hasn't Britain had one? A possible answer is that it did, over 300 years ago. Why then hasn't it had another and more recent revolution? Because, paradoxically, the English Revolution – the Civil War of the 1640s followed by the execution of Charles I – led to the Restoration and then the so called 'Glorious Revolution' of 1688 which ushered in a political system under which change usually takes place gradually and in piecemeal fashion, with a minimum of bloodshed.

There was, however, one occasion in the nineteenth century when it did look as if there might be a modern 'British Revolution'. In the 1830s and 1840s the authorities were almost paralytically scared of the Chartists, the movement which took its name from the six points of the Charter, the programme drawn up in a London pub. The Charter called for the extension of the vote to all men over the age of twenty-one, for constituencies to be the same size, for an end to the property qualification for MPs, for the payment of MPs, and for the secret ballot. Ironically, these five points are now law; the only point missing is the call for annual Parliaments.

Chartist demonstrations were sometimes fond of lurid slogans such as 'Fight to the knife for children and wife' and 'More pigs and fewer priests'.

There had also been an abortive 'Rising' in Newport, Wales, in which fourteen people had died. Yet the Chartist agitation had on the whole been peaceful and law-abiding. However, this did not stop the authorities from fearing the outbreak of revolution when the Chartist leaders announced they would be holding a meeting on Kennington Common in South London on 10 April 1848. The government thought this was to be the English '1789'. They panicked.

Queen Victoria and her family fled London for the safety of the Isle of Wight. The seventy-nine-year-old Duke of Wellington was put in charge of the capital's defences and 150,000 'Special Constables' – more men than the Duke had commanded at the Battle of Waterloo against Napoleon – were sworn in. Troops were stationed in churches, 1,500 Chelsea Pensioners guarded the bridges at Battersea and Vauxhall. Heavy gun batteries were brought up from Woolwich and the ground floor windows of the Foreign Office were blocked by huge bound volumes of *The Times*. Guns were placed on the roof of the Bank of England and gunsmiths were ordered to make their weapons unusable in the event of looting. The government commandeered the national electric telegraph system and also rushed through Parliament a Gagging Act imposing a penalty of seven years' transportation for seditious speeches.

On the morning of 10 April, observers noted that inhabitants of the capital were edgy and nervous – none more so than Feargus O'Connor, the Irishman who was MP for Nottingham and was recognised as the leader of the Chartists. Though he was a fine journalist and orator – one eyewitness said that his voice was so powerful that it '. . . made the vault of Heaven echo with its sound' – O'Connor was already exhibiting that manic streak of vanity which was eventually to see him spend the last few years of his life incarcerated in a mental asylum. He called himself 'the Lion of Freedom' and his delusions of grandeur even extended to signing his letters 'Feargus Rex'.

One reason for O'Connor's nervousness on 10 April was that he and the other Chartist leaders had no idea how to push forward the Chartist cause. Previously they had concentrated on drawing up petitions in favour of the six points and hoping to pressure the House of Commons into debating them. The 1839 Petition had carried the signatures of one million people; the 1842 Petition had been signed by over three million. Six miles in length, this second petition was carried to Parliament in a huge wooden frame that needed thirty men to carry it. Neither petition was debated by the House of Commons, and by 1848 the Chartist leaders were expected to ensure that the third petition met with a better fate than the previous two.

O'Connor arrived at Kennington Common to find a much smaller crowd than expected. Estimates vary but a figure of about 100,000 seems to have been approximately right. He discovered that the Commissioner of Police had banned the proposed mass march to Westminster. Instead, only a small delegation was to be allowed to accompany the petition. O'Connor had to decide whether to challenge this decision, by force if need be. This was the moment when discontent might burst into something more.

It didn't. O'Connor meekly decided to accept the police decision. Several revolutionary speeches were delivered to the crowd, but it was all an anti-climax. The weather was unsympathetic too. It began to rain and most people went home to tea. The Queen returned, the Duke of Wellington retired again to the House of Lords and the Specials were stood down. This third petition was found on examination at the Houses of Parliament to contain thousands of false names, including those of the Queen and the Duke. Although the Chartist movement continued, never again was it to constitute a threat to the British state.

Contrast 10 April 1848 in London – no injuries, no deaths, few arrests – with events elsewhere in Europe: the crumbling of governments, the overthrow of monarchs, troops firing on crowds in the streets.

A few months after the crushing defeat in mainland Europe of the 1848 Revolutions, a penniless German arrived in London where he was to spend the remaining thirty-four years of his life. As a young man Karl Marx had been a typically Romantic and wild student, fighting duels, drinking too much and writing three passionate volumes of poetry dedicated to Jenny von Westphalen, who was later to become his wife. It was while at university in first Berlin and then Jena that Marx became interested in politics. On leaving Jena, he edited a newspaper called *Rheinische Zeitung*, which soon fell foul of the authorities because of its radical views and was shut down by the censor in March 1843.

His ideas were still unclear but he was beginning to stress the economic or materialist basis of human society. He also suggested that with the onset of industrialisation, a proletariat or working class would be created which would in turn wage war on class society. This struggle would lead to the replacement of capitalism by socialism and eventually create a classless society.

In February 1848 Marx and his friend Friedrich Engels published *The Communist Manifesto*. It began with the assertion, 'A spectre is haunting Europe – the spectre of communism' and contained the stirring call to arms, 'Workers of the world, unite. You have nothing to lose but your chains.' Not even Marx, always confident in his own judgements, could have expected such an instant response. Over the next few months uprisings took place all over Europe, appearing to confirm his analysis. But he had failed to realise that the European middle classes, and none more so than in Britain, would at the death prefer social order to social justice. They sided with the forces of law and order and the revolutions were defeated.

Marx was now a marked man. Exiled from France, Germany and Belgium and harassed by the police, he was a fugitive. By August 1849 there was scarcely a country in Europe prepared to accept him, other than Britain, the traditional sanctuary for exiles and refugees. For virtually the rest of his life Marx was dogged by money problems and, in fact, within a few weeks of his arrival he and his family were evicted from their Chelsea lodgings for not paying the rent. Jenny, who over the next thirty years was to be a faithful and loyal partner to her husband, described in a letter to a friend how humiliating it was to have their difficulties witnessed by 'two or three hundred persons loitering around our door — the whole Chelsea mob' who had gathered to watch the eviction.

The Marx household moved to Dean Street in Soho, one of the most overcrowded and unhealthy parts of London. Without the financial support of Engels who was based at his family's textile firm in Manchester, things would have been even more perilous. Even so, the Marx family, together with their devoted maid Hélène Demuth, known as Lenchen, shared two small rooms — which can still be seen today, above a smart and expensive Italian restaurant. Only many years after Marx's death did Engels reveal that a relationship between Karl and Lenchen had resulted in the birth of a son. Mrs Marx bore children too and once, when their child Guido died (Guido because he was born on Guy Fawkes' Night), Marx was reduced to begging in the streets in order to pay for the coffin.

Marx tried to support himself by odd pieces of journalism but his command of English was initially shaky and there was not much of a market either for his ideas or the difficult style in which he expressed them. Once, in desperation, he tried for a job as a clerk on the railway but was turned down because of his appalling handwriting. This scrawl was to cause many problems for Engels and Marx's daughter Eleanor when they came to transcribe his work after his death.

Marx mixed mainly with his fellow German exiles in London, though they seem to have spent most of their time bickering and squabbling. He was particularly jealous of the art historian Kinkel for his heroic part in the 1848 Revolution in Prussia when he bravely led an uprising. Few of these exiles had much contact with the native British labour movement and Marx himself passed much of his time in the British Museum which was conveniently situated nearby. His personal isolation reflected the political isolation of socialists all over Europe as a period of reaction set in after the 1848 Revolutions.

This conservative mood left Marx and his associates like beached whales, waiting desperately for the political tide to turn. He never found it easy to come to terms with the dilemma of being a revolutionary in a decidedly non-revolutionary situation. Only once did Marx get involved in day-to-day practical political activity. In 1864 a group of individuals gathered in London to set up an international body called the International Working Men's Association (later to be known as the First International). Marx was invited at the last moment to the inaugural meeting held in Covent Garden in September 1864 and did not speak. But he was elected to the General Council and drew up the rules, the first of which called for 'the protection, advancement and complete emancipation of the working classes'.

Marx's force of character and his certainty about his own ideas meant that he quickly dominated proceedings. But not even he could overcome the disunity which plagued the International from the start — over one hundred different organisations from many countries were affiliated, and none was prepared to concede a shred of autonomy. The disputes at meetings were so acrimonious that on one occasion an irate Spanish delegate brandished a pistol at his comrades.

In the absence of modern communications it was difficult to know what was going on in labour disputes abroad, although some foreign 'blacklegging' was prevented. Nationalist preferences predominated over internationalist concerns, a portent of what was to happen within the European labour movement on the outbreak of war in 1914. The International did achieve some notoriety during the Paris Commune of 1871 when the authorities blamed them for helping to foment this uprising. But the Commune was crushed and the International forgotten.

Its comparative impotence led to renewed bickering, especially when anarchists, who distrusted any form of organisation or discipline, grew in influence, threatening Marx's control. In the early 1870s Marx moved its nominal headquarters to New York, where he knew it would expire. He preferred to kill off the International rather than let it fall into anarchist hands. It was formally dissolved in 1876. Marx once more retreated to his study.

There is much irony in the attention which Marx devoted to economics in view of his own poverty. As he once ruefully acknowledged, 'Never, I think, was money written about under such a shortage of it.' He was a terrible manager of his own household affairs. Not only was he unable to support himself or his family, but when there were unexpected windfalls he soon squandered them too. A double inheritance received in 1864 was quickly dissipated and later he could not live on an income of £300 per annum, which in Victorian terms was a substantial sum. Without Engels' financial help, the Marxes would have ended up in the workhouse. They were not, however, always very grateful to their benefactor. Engels lived with a factory girl called Mary Burns. Although Mrs Marx was prepared to accept Engels' money, she refused to visit Manchester because she disapproved of Engels' liaison with Mary.

Photographs of Marx show him as a heavily-bearded and stern-looking patriarch, but there was a more appealing side to him. He always carried with him photographs of his mother, wife and eldest daughter. A Prussian police spy, reporting on the Marx household in 1853, left this report:

> Sitting down is quite a dangerous affair: here is a chair with but three legs; there another, which by chance is still intact where the children are playing at being cooks. Courteously this is offered to the guest, but the children's cooking is not removed and you sit down at the risk of ruining your trousers. None of this occasions Marx or his wife the slightest embarrassment. You are received in the most friendly manner, cordially offered pipes, tobacco or whatever else is available. In any case the clever, agreeable talk compensates to some extent for the domestic shortcomings and makes the discomfort endurable . . .

This is a charming portrait by an observer whose job would not have made him especially sympathetic towards the Marxes.

One of their daughters, Eleanor, claims that her parents had a great sense of humour:

> Assuredly two people never enjoyed a joke more than these two. Again and again – especially if the occasion were one demanding decorum and sedateness, have I seen them laugh till tears ran down their cheeks, and even those inclined to be shocked at such awful levity could not choose but laugh with them. And how often have I seen them not daring to look at one another, each knowing that once a glance was exchanged uncontrollable laughter would result.

The Marx family outings to Hampstead Heath each Sunday were highlights of the week as they and their friends ate, played and slept. There is also the famous occasion of Marx's pub crawl down Tottenham Court Road. Having decided to take a drink at each pub along the way, on his departure from the eighteenth Marx and his friends shattered a number of street-lamps with a volley of stones. Whereupon they found themselves chased by four police-men, their long and hard run ending only when Marx's detailed knowledge of London's alleys and passages enabled them to elude their pursuers.

Marx's relative isolation from the world around him, and his lack of English friends, partly explains why he never properly analysed the traditions and institutions of the country in which he now lived. Why, for example, did Britain lack the revolutionary tradition of neighbouring France? One of the specific features which he might have investigated is British rulers' avoidance of violent repression. British socialism remembers the Peterloo 'Massacre' of 1819 as a horrific battle, and indeed six people died. Yet compare this and 'Bloody Sunday' in Trafalgar Square in 1887 after which one person died with the situations elsewhere in Europe where the most violent repression was practised and massacres were common. British riots had a peculiarly national quality – in 1886 the unemployed lustily bellowed out *Rule Britannia* as they smashed shop windows.

It seems as though the British ruling class had a shrewdness not always displayed by its European counterparts. For instance the suffrage was gradually extended throughout the century – in 1832, 1867 and 1884 – before protest could become even pre-revolutionary. In France, revolution became almost commonplace. In Britain, it was difficult to see what form it might take. The murder of Queen Victoria? Stringing up MPs in Parliament Square? Ransacking St Paul's and Westminster Abbey? Even to pose such questions reveals their absurdity.

In his search for the non-existent spirit of British revolution, Marx might also have examined the continuity of national institutions; a continuity which derives from the fact that Britain has not been invaded since 1066 nor suffered the traumatic shock of defeat in a major war. Moreover the traditional moderation of the Church of England prevented any upsurge of the anti-clericalism which provided the basis for several European socialist movements. The Nonconformist influence too, which Hardie recognised and accommodated when he formed the Labour Party, gave the British labour movement a distinctive heritage which was deeply hostile to the materialist Marxist philosophy.

Above all, British moderation, empiricism and the inclination to 'mind one's own business' is thoroughly unconducive to the development of a politically dynamic and informed society. Several commentators have noted the strength of the British non-participatory political tradition in which 'politics is left to the politicians'. It is not that the British are lazy; just that our enthusiasm and voluntary spirit is usually directed towards sport, flower clubs and a myriad of other non-political activities.

So what was Marx writing about? His detailed research into British capitalism, buttressed by the mountain of facts contained in the government 'Blue Books' which he purchased second-hand in Long Acre, Covent Garden, confirmed his bleak assessment that the rich were getting richer and the poor poorer. Sooner rather than later, this growing polarisation would lead to revolution. A passage towards the end of the first volume of *Das Kapital*, published in German in 1867, forecast what would happen:

> Along with the constantly diminishing number of the magnates of capital, who usurp and monopolise all advantages of this process of transformation, grows the mass of misery, oppression, slavery, degradation, exploitation; but with this too grows the revolt of the working class, a class always increasing in numbers, and disciplined, united, organised by the very mechanism of the process of capitalist production itself. The monopoly of capital becomes a fetter upon the mode of production, which has sprung up and flourished along with, and under it. Centralisation of the means of production and socialisation of labour at last reach a point where they become incompatible with their capitalist integument. This integument is burst asunder. The knell of capitalist private property sounds. The expropriators are expropriated.

His materialist philosophy insisted that people were the products of their own society. Although this tenet must presumably apply to Marx himself, later Marxists often claimed that the great man had, in fact, discovered the 'laws' of human society and that his writings were, as the Soviet textbook dealing with *Das Kapital* emphatically put it, *For All Times And All Men*. It is extraordinary how many modern Marxists, in flagrant violation of Marx's own approach, have maintained that his ideas, formed in the very different circumstances of the nineteenth century, still hold true and valid in the twentieth century.

In particular it is noticeable how often Marx formulates his ideas in terms characteristic of the melodramas which dominated the Victorian stage: Capital is implacably opposed to Labour; the rich face the poor; workers battle against owners; class struggle is inevitable. There is a lack of practical detail in his work – 'If I but knew how to start a business . . .' he once wrote despairingly to Engels. In retrospect Marx appears more of a Romantic figure struggling in a garret than the 'scientific socialist' his supporters claim him to be.

One paradox of his writing is that a man claiming to show how and why the working class would eventually triumph should write in a language so difficult for anyone to understand, even though he himself always stressed the value of clarity. In part this reflects Marx's unflattering view of the working class; as his friend Wilhelm Liebknecht commented, 'The masses were to him a brainless crowd whose thoughts and feelings were furnished by the ruling class.'

Certainly this limitation partly explains the lack of English translations of his writings. The first volume of *Kapital* was not issued in English until 1887, four years after his death. The other volumes were not published until 1907. *The Communist Manifesto* itself did not appear in book form in English until 1888. Marx's work was much more widely published in France and Germany – the Continental taste for abstract thought contrasting with English 'feet on the ground' empiricism.

Since little of Marx's work was available in English, few British socialists were familiar with his writings other than those who could speak foreign languages. George Bernard Shaw, for instance, read *Das Kapital* in German while studying in the British Museum. Another initiate was H. M. Hyndman, the powerful and egocentric individual who can claim to be the first British Marxist. He was the first person to try and create a British revolutionary party whose tenets of sweeping and possibly violent change were very different from the approach favoured by Keir Hardie and the Fabians.

Henry Mayers Hyndman was born in 1842 into a comfortably well-off family which had prospered from trade with the West Indies. He was educated privately and then at Trinity College, Cambridge where his chagrin at not winning his cricket blue still rankled when he came to write his memoirs:

> I declare that I feel at this moment, fifty years later, my not playing for Cambridge against Oxford in the University Cricket Match as a far more unpleasant and depressing experience than infinitely more important failures have been to me since.

This failure did not prevent Hyndman from playing county cricket for Sussex for several years. He also qualified at the Bar and began work as a journalist for the *Pall Mall Gazette*. It was while investigating conditions in the East End that his social conscience was first stirred. His socialism was confirmed in 1880 when he read a French version of Marx's *Das Kapital* during a voyage to America. He returned home a convinced Marxist, certain that Britain was about to enter a period of class warfare. He proclaimed his beliefs in an article published in 1881 called 'The Dawn of a Revolutionary Epoch' which predicted the inevitability of upheaval and revolution.

That same year he set up a loose political body called the Democratic Federation, hoping it would build upon the success of London's many radical working men's clubs founded at that time which functioned, in the words of one historian, as 'workers' universities'. Hyndman also published a book titled *England for All* which drew upon Marx's work but did not actually mention 'the German doctor' by name because he felt that this would alienate possible supporters. Naturally such an outrageous act of plagiarism, and what was worse from Marx's point of view, incorrect plagiarism, did not endear him to either Marx or Engels and they quarrelled. It also revealed an anti-German streak in Hyndman which proved so significant in 1914 when he was one of the most rabid 'war mongers' of them all.

By 1884 Hyndman's Marxist convictions had hardened and he changed the name of his organisation to the Social Democratic Federation (SDF), thus linking it with the social democratic organisations on the Continent. If this sounds decidedly moderate and rather like a forerunner of the party founded by Dr David Owen and others in the 1980s, it wasn't. In the nineteenth century the phrase 'social democracy' was equated with being Marxist and militant. The SDF also established its own printing press, the Twentieth Century Press, which produced a weekly paper called *Justice*. Its circulation was always meagre – in his memoirs Hyndman remarked sadly, 'We did not meet a long-felt want, that's certain' – and he later regretted the time and money he spent on it.

What did Hyndman and the SDF stand for? They emphasised the existence of the class struggle rather than any brand of ethical socialism with its 'love thy neighbour' approach. The party was deeply sceptical about the idea of parliamentary change. Hyndman's friend Edward Carpenter wrote in his autobiography that 'We used to chaff him [Hyndman] because at every crisis in the industrial situation he was confident that the Millennium was at hand.' He was reputed to carry around with him a list of the intended members of his first revolutionary cabinet and once remarked that 'I could not carry on unless I expected the revolution at ten o'clock next Monday morning.' He was to spend a great many frustrated Monday mornings.

At first glance, Hyndman certainly does not fit any stereotype of what a Victorian revolutionary should be like. For many years he lived in Hampstead, one of the smartest parts of London, and his house now carries a plaque. He always wore a frock coat and top hat, even when thundering out bitter denunciations of capitalism, and earned his living from speculating in ventures which ranged from gold-rushes in Australia and the United States to Colt guns and pencils. In his private life he seems to have been caring and considerate. Beatrice Webb once referred to British revolutionaries as 'the mild-mannered desperadoes'.

Hyndman's biggest failing was his authoritarian and egotistical personality. He always liked to get his own way, which explains why he was on bad terms with Marx, Engels and also William Morris. But this self-righteousness meant that he never wavered in his decision to turn his back on a traditional career in Establishment politics that might have led him to a position in the Cabinet. Instead he dedicated himself to tramping up and down the country in order to propagate what was a distinctly unfashionable and minority cause. His courage was evident too after the so-called 'West End riots' of 1886 when demonstrators marched along Pall Mall stoning the windows of the smart gentlemen's clubs. Because he had delivered one of the speeches just before the riot began, Hyndman found himself on trial at the Old Bailey for sedition. Helped by his training as a barrister, he defended himself and secured an acquittal.

The SDF's membership remained small, reaching only 3,250 at its height in 1897. Although size is not everything, this figure contrasted unfavourably with, say, the German Social Democrats whose power was seen as so threatening to the authorities that an 'anti-Socialist Law' was in force in Germany between 1878 and 1890. As soon as the ban was lifted, the party gained nearly one and a half million votes and thirty-five seats in the parliamentary elections. The SDF's vote in British elections was numbered in tens and not millions.

Why was the SDF so small? Once more we are back with the inescapable fact that British life and culture is not really happy with the theoretical and political philosophy of Marxism. Hyndman in particular believed in a thoroughly dogmatic and arid Marxism, arguing that Marx's 'scientific laws' were immutable. Such an approach completely devalued the idea of human agency – if something was bound to happen, then there was little incentive to help it on its way.

In particular, the SDF was never able to surmount the obstacle that in Britain the trade unions had preceded Marxism, whereas in mainland Europe it was generally the other way around. But instead of trying to propagate Marxist ideas within the unions, Hyndman dismissed them as 'mere palliatives'. The great Dock Strike of 1889 was written off as 'a waste of energy'. Keir Hardie's attitude, of course, was very different. He argued that the unions, whatever their defects, were the essential roots out of which any significant labour movement in Britain had to grow.

Without these trade union links the SDF was bound to remain small in size and therefore prone to the sectarianism and squabbling that is such a feature of the British Left. William Morris attacked the SDF's 'pedantic tone of arrogance and lack of generosity which is disgusting . . .' Not that Hyndman, with his absolute belief in his own correctness, minded this: 'The reproach of sectarianism carries with it no odium for us. Truth must ever be sectarian: error alone can afford to be catholic.'

The SDF's uncompromising purism meant that it was unwilling to enter into alliances with other groups and in 1901 it made the crucial mistake of withdrawing from the newly-formed Labour Representation Committee, the body which in 1906 became the Labour Party. This decision ensured that Marxism would remain on the fringes of the labour movement. It forms one of the great 'might-have-beens' to ask whether the history of the British labour movement might not have been very different if the SDF had stayed put. But somehow it is difficult to believe that Marxism would ever have ousted cautious and pragmatic labourism. In many ways the SDF's actions prefigured the split between moderates and militants which occurred within the British labour movement after 1917. Hyndman's authoritarian personality often expressed itself in scathing abuse of the working classes. He once referred to them as 'manifest degenerates', echoing Marx's 'brainless crowd', for not doing what he told them to do. The music hall and the rise of mass sport were two popular activities which the SDF blamed for diverting the workers' political energy into trivial pursuits.

The SDF was unable to accept the near unanimous support for existing political institutions and so their propaganda often took on a bleak and gloomy tone. Robert Tressell's novel *The Ragged Trousered Philanthropists*, published posthumously just before the First World War, is a compelling example of this. Tressell was a house-painter who lived in Hastings and was an active member of his local SDF branch. Written in his free time, his novel depicts with unsparing candour the ways in which 'the bosses' manipulate their compliant and stupid employees. For example, he shows an election that takes place between two equally unsavoury candidates, Adam Sweater and Sir Graball D'Encloseland. Sheep-like, the voters do exactly as they are told. Tressell is brutal in his comments:

> In the face of such colossal imbecility it was absurd to hope for any immediate improvement. The little already accomplished was the work of a few self-sacrificing enthusiasts, battling against the opposition of those they sought to benefit, and the results of their labours were, in many instances, as pearls cast before the swine who stood watching for opportunities to fall upon and rend their benefactors.

Tressell's 'swine' reminds one of Hyndman's 'degenerates' and Marx's 'brainless crowd' and his book conveys the frustration and isolation which many early socialists must have felt, struggling in the face of antagonism and indifference. *The Ragged Trousered Philanthropists* does contain humour and passion too, but to Tressell the domination by the authorities seems as total as in George Orwell's later *1984*. It is difficult to see how any kind of dissent or opposition could make itself effective. Tressell died penniless in a Liverpool workhouse in 1912.

It would be wrong to dismiss the SDF as of no importance. Some of their members were extraordinarily innovative in the methods they used to put across their case to the public. They were the first organisation to hold unemployed marches, something later revived in the 1920s and 1930s, as well as introducing 'Church Parades' in which crowds of the jobless attended church services on a Sunday in order to shock the consciences of the well-off. The SDF was prominent too in holding open-air meetings all over the country, often in the face of police obstruction.

The SDF's assertions about the extent of London poverty in the 1880s also prompted the Liverpool shipowner Charles Booth to launch his own investigations into the state of the capital's poor. Booth confidently expected to disprove what he thought were Hyndman's alarmist claims. In fact, as he recognised, he found that if anything Hyndman had underestimated the position. Booth's series *The Life and Labour of the People of London*, which appeared in seventeen volumes between 1891 and 1903, was vital in shifting public opinion towards a more radical frame of mind that accepted the need for government intervention to improve work and living conditions.

It is notable just how many influential people passed through the SDF's ranks. The German socialist Edouard Bernstein estimated that no less than 100,000 individuals had at some stage of their life been members. William Morris, Eleanor Marx and Edward Carpenter will be discussed in the next chapter, but other members of the SDF (and its successors the Social Democratic Party and the British Socialist Party — left-wing groups have always been fond of name changes) include Ernest Bevin, Tom Mann, Ramsay MacDonald, Herbert Morrison, George Lansbury, John Maclean, Harry Pollitt and Willie Gallacher, all of whom will be mentioned frequently in the following pages.

Two other, totally different, SDF members were Jim Connell and Frances, Countess of Warwick. Connell was a huge Irishman who sported an enormous moustache and large red hat. Apart from writing the words to the internationally famous song *The Red Flag*, he also set up a Poachers' Union in which members' subscriptions helped pay the fines. His pamphlet of 1898,

The Truth about the Game Laws, ends: 'The poacher is the incarnation of the spirit of revolt against oppression and injustice. He dares to fling his naked hand against the bayonets that guard the land monopoly.'

The Countess of Warwick on the other hand, reputedly the most beautiful woman in England, had inherited no less than 30,000 acres. A longstanding mistress of the Prince of Wales, later Edward VII, her husband was a Conservative MP. In 1895 he inherited his title of Earl of Warwick and Frances became a Countess. To celebrate this event, she decided to hold a huge ball at Warwick Castle. Hiring an eminent French dress maker to design her costume she went as Marie Antoinette. The dress cost more than 100 guineas, approximately twice what the average worker earned in a year. Two days after the event the Countess' attention was drawn to an article in the socialist weekly *Clarion* which condemned the extravagance of the ball. She was so incensed that she left her guests and caught the first train to London in order to remonstrate with the editor of the paper, Robert Blatchford. Face to face with him, she claimed that the ball had given employment to hundreds of people in Warwick. She describes in her autobiography what happened next:

> And then Robert Blatchford told me, as a Socialist and a Democrat, what he thought of charity bazaars and ladies bountiful. He made plain to me the difference between productive and unproductive labour. One phrase still lingers. He said that labour used to produce finery was as much wasted as if it were used to dig holes in the ground and fill them again.

Blatchford and the Countess talked for several hours. She then paced up and down Paddington Station thinking over what he had said. By the time she returned to Warwick she decided he was right. 'Next day I sent for ten pounds' worth of books on Socialism. I got the name of an old Professor of Economics, and under him I started my period of study without delay.'

From that day the Countess was a staunch supporter of the SDF and of other socialist causes, giving up much of her wealth to fund them. This took courage — most of her friends 'cut' her because of her new allegiance. Occasionally there were incongruous moments. She once hired a private train to take her home after an SDF Conference in 1902, and perhaps she was behind the decision of the SDF to send a loyal address to Edward VII on his coronation that same year — not an action one would have expected from a Marxist party! That Lady Warwick should be so strong a left-winger explains some of the fascination of the history of British socialism, particularly the way in which it repeatedly contradicts stereotypes and confounds expectations.

One SDF member who blazed meteorically in the political firmament but then faded was Victor Grayson who, in July 1907, was elected the socialist MP for Colne Valley. Even his opponents admired Grayson's oratory which drew thousands of people to his meetings. He arrived at Westminster determined, like Hardie fifteen years before, not to be muffled by parliamentary proprieties. Within a few months he interrupted a debate in the House of Commons to demand that something should be done about unemployment. He was rebuked by the Speaker but refused to give way. Finally, he shouted out that this was 'a House of murderers' and passed several withering comments on the timidity of his colleagues, who ironically enough included Keir Hardie.

But Grayson's revolt was very much that of an individualist and soon the unrelenting pressures of being a political rebel got to him. He always scorned the puritan, 'hairshirt' strain within the labour movement embodied by Hardie and some sections of the Independent Labour Party. Edward Carpenter, who was an admirer of Grayson, wrote of him, 'His fund of anecdotes was inexhaustible, and rarely could a supper party of which he was a member get to bed before three in the morning.' Robert Blatchford said that 'I have never met a man so utterly full of the joys of life.'

Sadly these 'joys' led him into an extraordinarily complicated private life – he was bisexual – and his heavy drinking sometimes caused him to miss meetings or else to speak when drunk. Grayson lost his seat at the 1910 general election. He then wrote for Blatchford's paper *Clarion* but his health was continually breaking down. Marriage to an actress brought no relief from debts and drink. In 1916, while in Australasia, he joined the New Zealand Army and was wounded fighting in the trenches in France. His wife died in childbirth. In September 1920 Grayson vanished from the face of the earth. There were various supposed sightings of him over the next thirty years, but nothing definite. There has been speculation that he got caught up in Lloyd George's 'honours for sale' scandal but no one knows for sure. It was a sad and squalid end to a briefly very promising political career – 'Labour's lost leader' as one biographer has called him.

'A fiery Socialist, without any principles and given to mere phrases.' This damning indictment of Grayson was penned by a man who as both a revolutionary and an individual was as different from Grayson as could be: Lenin.

In Tom Stoppard's play *Travesties*, a number of famous individuals are shown meeting in Zürich where they all lived during the First World War. There is Lenin, James Joyce and the Dadaist poet Tristan Tzara. The three men might have met each other, but almost certainly didn't.

Yet in reality an equally disparate group of 'later to be famous' figures did actually meet, in May 1907, at a 'socialist church' in Islington, north London. As well as Lenin, there was Leon Trotsky, Maxim Gorky, Joseph Stalin and the revolutionary Rosa Luxemburg. English observers included two future leaders of the Labour Party, Ramsay MacDonald and George Lansbury.

Why were they meeting and what were the Russians doing in London? The answer lies in Britain's traditional role as a refuge for exiles and outcasts. Twenty years before, the anarchist Prince Kropotkin had been on the run from the Czarist police. He described in his autobiography how he boarded a ship, not knowing which nationality it was and where he might end up:

> Then I saw floating above the stern the union jack – the flag under which so many refugees, Russian, Italian, French, Hungarian and of all nations, have found an asylum. I greeted that flag from the depth of my heart.

British tolerance was not just a cosy myth. Unlike virtually every other country, newcomers could not be prevented from landing. The Special Branch, founded in 1887, did keep an eye on suspects and a statute of 1905 allowed the authorities in theory to restrict the arrival of 'aliens', although in practice they rarely did.

Russian revolutionaries knew of Britain as a haven and in 1907 the Russian Social Democratic and Labour Party, under pressure from the Czarist secret police, decided to hold their 5th Congress in London. Delegates moaned about the inhospitable weather and were scathing about the small size and influence of their British revolutionary counterpart, the SDF, led by Hyndman. They no doubt contrasted the fact that the SDF was a perfectly legal body with their own experiences. Assassination, suicide, terrorism, torture and imprisonment were simply to be expected as part of a Russian revolutionary's life. The Russians scorned people like Grayson as effete and irresponsible.

Take Lenin himself. His older brother had been executed by the Czarist authorities for his part in a suspected terrorist plot. Lenin gave up his legal studies and became a full-time revolutionary. Anything which came in the way of this was discarded. He gave up listening to classical music because, he said, it made him feel too benevolent towards his fellow human beings. He was a good chess player but that had to stop as it was taking up too much time. It is surprising that he found the time to marry Nadia Krupskaya, but her account of their life together, *Memoirs of Lenin*, is largely devoid of personal detail. Instead it catalogues furtive meetings, the relentless exposure of political heresy (that is, anyone whose views did not coincide with

Lenin's) and attempts to get around the Russian censors by means of invisible inks and aliases.

Although Lenin, like Marx and Hyndman, came from a comparatively privileged background, he was bolstered by his confidence that Marxism was scientific and 'true'. Therefore he knew exactly what the working classes wanted, even if they didn't know it themselves. Everything and anything was a means to one single end: revolution. 'We say that our morality is entirely subordinated to the interests of the proletariat's class struggle.'

The difficulty for Lenin was that the working classes showed little sign of trying to bring about the revolution themselves. His solution was to build a political party which, as an elite or vanguard, would guide and lead the masses. Highly centralised and controlled from above, this party would be very different from the British SDF. For Lenin, 'the Party' would not only have a monopoly of the truth it would also, as he made clear in *What is to be Done?*, much of which was written while he was in London, come before everything else: health, honesty, happiness, life even. The revolutionary 'must be ever ready to do anything'. This was the doctrine that was later called 'Marxism–Leninism'.

Lenin knew London well. He lived here for eighteen months between 1902 and 1903, learning English at Speaker's Corner in Hyde Park, researching at the British Museum and editing the Russian Social Democrat paper *Iskra* ('The Spark') at the SDF's printing press on Clerkenwell Green. Other Russian exiles preferred Paris as a refuge because the weather was generally better there. The one place where they could congregate was the Communist Club in Charlotte Street, near Tottenham Court Road. It contained a library, a billiard room and a cheap restaurant.

The Club was always full of tobacco smoke and the babel of foreign tongues as the émigrés argued and disputed, just as Marx and his German colleagues had bickered at the Communist Club fifty years before when it was based in Soho. The Club was closed down by the police in 1914 on the outbreak of war and became a furniture depository. The building was bombed in 1940.

Despite Lenin's prolonged stay in London he participated little in the British labour movement. Again like Marx, his circle of English friends was minute. It was almost as if Lenin feared contamination by the native socialists. Hyndman once said at a meeting that he was '. . . a Socialist unarmed with revolvers or any other dynamite than mental dynamite.' For Lenin, any kind of dynamite was legitimate in the class struggle. The differences between the Russian Social Democrats and the British were exemplified in the 5th Congress of 1907.

The Russians met in the Brotherhood Church, Islington, because the minister in charge, a Reverend Swan who was to be one of Victor Grayson's full-time supporters at the forthcoming Colne Valley by-election, was a Christian Socialist. The interior of the church was plain and simple. Gorky thought it 'unadorned to the point of absurdity'. The 320 delegates, who included Stalin and Trotsky, were greeted by Ramsay MacDonald. Then, courtesies over, they got down to the business of creating a revolutionary party. Lengthy theoretical debate and argument followed as the correct party line was hammered out. One delegate remarked that 'The speeches of the leaders lasted for hours . . .'

Sometimes proceedings were interrupted by the need for the English to hold services but otherwise the delegates kept at it, even taking their meals on the spot due to a makeshift kitchen run by Gorky's wife. A full two days were spent just finalising the agenda for what they were to discuss and then a further week passed in organisational wrangling. The split between those who became Bolsheviks and those who became Mensheviks was developing, and Lenin wanted to clarify the differences between what were essentially militants (Bolsheviks) and moderates (Mensheviks).

Lenin maintained that to the English all foreigners were alike, and they regarded the Russian émigré 'with a native perplexity'. One or two newspapers did try to stir up hostility against what the *Daily Mail* called 'a congress of undesirables'. From time to time a few people gathered outside the Brotherhood Church to hurl abuse but nothing more concrete. As always, Londoners went about their own business.

Quite apart from their un-English preoccupation with theory, the Congress represented a political philosophy completely at odds with that of the new British Labour Party formed only the year before. Hardie's Labour Party was a reformist, constitutional body wedded to parliamentary change. Lenin and the Russian Social Democrats regarded this 'labourist' approach as mistaken and dangerous. Only true believers could be admitted to the revolutionary vanguard, and at the 1907 Congress a resolution calling for a 'broad [Russian] Labour Party' rather than a revolutionary Marxist party was defeated by 169 votes to 94.

But however passionate or learned the debates, the delegates still had to pay for food and lodging. As the weeks passed, a number of them began to leave and return to Russia. Lenin and the other leaders tried to raise money in London, but only Gorky with his international reputation as a writer had access to wealthy Englishmen and he was not prepared to use his contacts because he was disturbed by the political trend of the Congress.

Help finally arrived in the unlikely shape of Joseph Fels, an American based in England who had made a fortune out of laundry soap. Beatrice Webb was very snobbish about him — 'a decidedly vulgar little Jew with much push, little else on the surface' — which did not stop her trying to get Fels to support some of her own political projects.

Fels looked on the Russian delegates as victims of Czarist repression and he was taken to see the Congress in action by his unofficial adviser, George Lansbury. He then agreed to make a loan of about £1,700 to the Russian Social Democrats on condition that the conference ended, because he was worried that the Russian delegates might give British socialists a bad name. Fels insisted too that the remaining delegates should sign the agreement to accept the money — not all of them did — and that the loan should be repaid by or on 1 January 1908. It wasn't. Joseph Fels died in 1914. Eight years later, in 1922, the repayment was made to Fels' widow by the Soviet Trade Delegation in London.

Much had happened during those fifteen years in which the loan was outstanding. In 1907 the Russian Social Democrats had been small and divided, facing the powerful Czarist regime. By 1922 Lenin's Bolsheviks controlled one of the largest countries in the world.

Who could have guessed that this same party and its leaders would in the years after 1917 exert such an immense influence on the development of the British Left?

CHAPTER THREE

Socialism and the New Life:
Standards and Double Standards

'In looking into matters social and political I have but one rule, that in thinking of the condition of any body of men I shall ask myself, "How could you bear it yourself? What would you feel if you were poor against the system under which you live?"'

William Morris, in a letter of 1883

'The aim of socialism is to substitute the word "ours" for the words "mine" and "thine".'

Robert Blatchford

'I do not want the movement to be a depository of old cranks, humanitarians, vegetarians, anti-vivisectionists and anti-vaccinationists, arty-craftys and all the rest of them, we are scientific socialists and have no room for sentimentalists. They confuse the issue.'

H. M. Hyndman

IN JANUARY 1889 a young woman called Marjorie Davidson, a member of the Fabian Society, was planning to set up home with another Fabian. It was a venture fraught with difficulty for a young, self-conscious and wealthy socialist. She asked George Bernard Shaw for his advice: 'We want to know what is the ideal Socialist home – I don't think we ought to have servants but that is an open question.' Another Fabian, Sidney Olivier, suggested that 'the [house]work should be done by unmarried relations.' The Oliviers themselves did, in fact, keep servants, insisting that they ate together with the family – apparently to the acute embarrassment of all.

The problems of everyday life troubled many of Britain's pioneer socialists. How should their high political ideals be translated into their personal lives? How to create a 'Fellowship of the New Life', as the Fabians had originally been called? Some, such as the Webbs, William Morris, H. M. Hyndman and Edward Carpenter, had substantial private incomes and often felt guilty at their prosperity, particularly when so many of the working class whose cause they championed lived in such abysmal physical conditions. No one seems to have emulated St Francis of Assisi and simply given away their money.

A further problem was that the burning desire to bring about social justice often made individuals difficult to live with. John Trevor, the founder of the Labour Church in 1891, noted the paradox in his autobiography:

> What fate is it that makes some of us so uncomfortable to live with and work with; and, by burdening us with ideas [of making the world a better place], makes us such a burden to those who look to us for support and comfort? Is it not possible to reform the world without all this sacrifice of peace and happiness?

He went on to answer his own question: 'No. There is no other way.'

But what did socialists see as being so wrong with 'the Old Life'? In 1916 Edward Carpenter received an address on his seventieth birthday signed by many distinguished friends. In his reply, he looked back and identified all that he deplored in the nineteenth century. He lambasted:

> ... the Victorian Age, which in some respects, one now thinks, marked the lowest ebb of modern civilised society: a period in which not only commercialism in public life, but cant in religion, pure materialism in science, futility in social conventions, the worship of stocks and shares, the starving of the human heart, the denial of the human body and its needs, the huddling concealment of the body in clothes, the 'impure hush' on matters of sex, class-division, contempt of manual labour, and the cruel barring of women from every natural and useful expression of their lives, were carried to an extremity of folly difficult for us now to realise.

This is a pretty comprehensive list of failings! Carpenter's complaints deal both with society and 'the human heart'. But how did socialists propose to change matters?

None of the left-wing traditions discussed so far offered any guidance about moral issues. Neither Keir Hardie's 'labourism', nor the Webbs and the Fabians, nor Hyndman's Marxists, nor Lenin's revolutionary élite showed much interest in the personal or subjective characteristics of political activity. Instead they all tended to demonstrate how political power was the overwhelming necessity, coming well before the need to debate individual morality. 'For the greater good' (of whichever party or group) could easily sanction all kinds of appalling human behaviour. Each of these traditions was associated with 'bigness', with the large and often difficult concepts of 'class', 'mass' and 'state' — none of which gave a meaning to people's existence or offered much practical help. 'Socialism' could often seem an alien and intimidating idea.

Some groups attempted to deal with this aspect of life by advocating 'the religion of socialism', which was the title of several books and pamphlets published in the 1880s and 1890s. In his newspaper *Clarion*, Robert Blatchford tried to explain the impulse behind this phrase: 'If Socialism is to live and conquer, it must be a religion ... If Socialists are to prove themselves equal to the task assigned to them they must have faith, a real faith, a new faith.'

This faith centred on the building of 'a New Jerusalem', a new, fair and just society for all. It is no coincidence that many socialists spoke of their 'conversion' to socialism or, in William Morris' even more striking phrase, crossing 'the river of fire'. John Trevor described the effects of Blatchford's book *Merrie England* in making converts to 'a new life': 'Their eyes shine with the gladness of a new birth.'

This faith has sometimes been called 'Christian Socialism' but it was made up of so many different ideas and beliefs that it defies labels. Some claimed inspiration from Jesus Christ — Keir Hardie thought that Christ's Sermon on the Mount summed up communism. Others looked back to the radical priest John Ball, one of the leaders of the Peasants' Revolt in 1381, who wrote:

> When Adam delved and Eve span
> Who was then the gentleman?

In other words, because there were no servants or classes in the Garden of Eden these must therefore be man-made and, if so, could be 'man unmade'. The clarity of John Ball's language was echoed in the lengthy struggle to have the Bible translated from Latin into English. This campaign gave the radical movement, until recently, a longstanding association with 'plain speech'.

In the late nineteenth century socialist churchmen began to form themselves into groups and organisations. One of the most important was 'The Guild of St Matthew', founded in 1877 by the Old Etonian Stewart Headlam. He had been through a traditional Establishment education at Eton and then Trinity College, Cambridge. It was at university that he came under the influence of F. D. Maurice, an early Christian Socialist, who had lost his professorship at London University because he doubted the doctine of everlasting damnation for sinners. Headlam's early years in the church were spent in the poorer parts of London, and it was while he was at St Matthew's, Bethnal Green, that his ideas began to coalesce. He stressed the practical aspects of Christianity:

I have always deprecated other-worldliness, as it is called, morbid concern about self, hysterical visions of Heaven, as though earth were a place to be despaired of. I have always talked of the Kingdom of Heaven being fulfilled here and now on earth, and deprecated too much dwelling on a future life, fortified by the fact that Christ Himself said very little about the other world, and very much about this.

To Stewart Headlam, the 'New Jerusalem' was a living, realistic possibility.

In 1884 the Guild of St Matthew adopted more explicitly socialist aims. This was some months before Hyndman founded the Social Democratic Federation (SDF), so the Guild can claim to be Britain's first socialist organisation. A resolution passed by the Guild at a meeting in Trafalgar Square in October 1884 indicates the trenchant thrust of its policies:

Whereas the present contrast between the great body of the workers who produce much and consume little, and of those classes which produce little and consume much is contrary to the Christian doctrine of brotherhood and justice, this meeting urges on all Churchmen the duty of supporting such measures as will tend − a) To restore to the people the value which they give to the land; b) to bring about a better distribution of the wealth created by labour; c) to give the whole body of the people a voice in their own government; d) to abolish false standards of worth and dignity.

This was strong meat for Headlam's superior, the Bishop of London. Headlam made himself even more unpopular by establishing the Church and Stage Guild in order to foster closer relationships between the two professions. At a time when the Church still regarded actresses and music-hall performers as little better than prostitutes, this was considered provocative and Headlam found his licence to preach withdrawn. In other words, he was sacked. He devoted the rest of his life to his work as a London County councillor and a member of the London School Board, trying to improve the capital's standard of education. He died in 1924. Although the Guild of St Matthew was never large numerically − at its peak in 1895 it had no more than 364 members − it was important because it attempted to relate socialism to everyday life.

At the same time as the Guild, other churchmen began to question the direction of the Anglican church. Many were 'ritualists' or from the High Church wing and they stressed the importance of the sacraments. More importantly for society as a whole, these priests were determined to share the sufferings of their parishioners and so they moved to the poorer districts of the country. Among them were Father Lowder who built a church in Wapping, London, and Father Dolling in the slums of Portsmouth.

Some socialist groups expressed themselves in religious terms while remaining outside the organised churches. For example, the Labour Church had its own rituals and conduct and was likened by some to 'a kind of Socialist Salvation Army'. The Socialist Sunday School movement was founded in 1892; their activities included much singing and dancing as well as the learning off by heart of 'The Socialist Ten Commandments'. The singing was particularly important in the early days because, as one socialist remembered, it 'made us feel that we were not solitary but in the great accord of the brotherhood of mankind.'

This tradition of Christian Socialism often lived on in the meetings of the first Labour Party branches, some of which started or ended with the hymn 'When Wilt Thou Save the People, Lord?' The labour movement's subsequent immersion in electoral politics, winning parliamentary and council elections and raising the money to run a party machine, did lead to the dissipation of some of this 'religion of socialism'. The practicalities of day-to-day organisation often elbowed out the spiritual dimension.

But not entirely. Certainly when one compares the British labour movement with its European counterparts, one striking difference is the British emphasis on ethical rather than materialist issues. William Blake's poem *Jerusalem* is one of the most quoted of them all. Hugh Gaitskell, leader of the Labour Party in the 1950s and early 1960s, once lamented that he led a religious movement rather than a political party. The controversy over his attempt to drop Clause Four from the Labour Party constitution was, as Gaitskell's biographer has noted, 'studded with biblical terminology'. Participants talked of Tablets of Stone, the Ark of the Covenant, the 39 Articles, the Old and the New Testaments and so on. Tony Benn recently claimed in the House of Commons that socialism emanated from the Book of Genesis when Cain asked: 'Am I my brother's keeper?'

It is impossible to understand the British Left without recognising this important spiritual heritage that has moulded native radicalism. As a result, 'labourism' has a character and set of values different from those which have prevailed in most other European traditions.

Although the religion of socialism offered many telling moral criticisms of Victorian capitalism, it was less convincing when it came to portraying exactly what kind of society might take its place. Generalised benevolence and exhortations to 'love thy neighbour' were often about as far as it went. This lack of precision was evident in books by two influential late Victorian socialists, William Morris and Robert Blatchford.

Both the works, *News from Nowhere* (1890) and *The Sorcery Shop* (1907), are categorised as 'Utopias', following in the tradition established by Thomas More's original book *Utopia*, written in the early sixteenth century. More's book depicts an idealised society some time in the future, implicitly criticising the contemporary reality which surrounded him. The word 'Utopia' itself comes from the fusion of two Greek words meaning 'no place', which suggests that More had a fairly realistic estimation of the likelihood that such a society would ever be achieved.

Karl Marx disliked Utopias because he thought they were unscientific and a waste of time. William Morris was more acute in realising that the majority of people, working on the theory of 'better the devil you know than the devil you don't', are unlikely to welcome widespread social and political change unless it offers them something appreciably better than the present. His *News from Nowhere* was written in the hope of inspiring people to work for radical improvements in society.

It is noticeable how Morris skates over some of the problems that have plagued human life from the beginning. In *Nowhere*, for instance, we are simply told that the instinct for 'manslaughter' and crime has been bred out of him. There are no laws, no buying or selling, no paid work, no government, no prisons and no private property. Morris explains in his story that 'the great change' came about in 1952 (ironically enough, one year after a Labour government was, in fact, turned out of office by Winston Churchill's Conservatives).

A prohibited march sparks off a train of events that leads to a massacre in Trafalgar Square, a General Strike and the eventual assumption of power by the ominously-named Committee of Public Safety. From then on, we are told, people cast off the anti-social attitudes and behaviour characteristic of the previous regime. Morris describes a London in which the Houses of Parliament contain a dung market (he was never a great believer in parliamentary change!), apricot trees grow in Trafalgar Square, and the East End has been cleared of all its slums.

The egalitarian society depicted in *News from Nowhere* is, on the face of it, a surprising fantasy to have been created by a Victorian whose early life seems to have been the pattern of nineteenth-century bourgeois respectability. Morris was born in Walthamstow, London, in 1834. His father was a City stockbroker who sent his son to public school and then Oxford where he originally intended to enter the Church. But it was at Oxford that Morris was influenced by the writings of the critic John Ruskin and began to rebel against what he regarded as the ugly and philistine Victorian machine-made culture. In reaction, he looked back towards the sense of community and wholeness which in his imagination characterised fourteenth-century England

– it is no coincidence that the inhabitants of Nowhere wear medieval costume.

Morris started to write poetry, displaying a fierce Romantic spirit in such works as *The Life and Death of Jason* and *The Defence of Guenevere* whose aspirations and ideals seemed at odds with Victorian gentility and commercialism. His growing hostility towards his own part of society did not rest simply as words on a page. He was, above all, a man of action whose remarkable energy drove him to many different fields of activity, as poet, designer, artist and socialist. In his own words, 'To do nothing but grumble and not to act – that is throwing away one's life.' As Asa Briggs has commented, 'He was an angry young man and an angry old man, but he always knew what he was angry about.'

In part Morris' abundant energies were a displacement from his unhappy marriage. The beautiful Jane Burden, archetypal model for so many Pre-Raphaelite paintings, produced two daughters but she and Morris were clearly out of sympathy with each other, as almost every visitor to their home noticed. The vivacity of Morris, who was always talking, his hands never still, was in no way compatible with the self-absorption of Jane. She subsequently fell in love with the painter and poet Dante Gabriel Rossetti, a liaison which Morris accepted but which brought him much pain. Clearly the idealised figure of Ellen in *News from Nowhere* has a great deal of wish fulfilment about it.

Everyone admired Morris' seeming omniscience but what was admirable was his sincere desire to share his insights. A workman once said of a boat trip down the Clyde with Morris that it was 'as good as a university education'. Neither was he an intellectual snob. George Bernard Shaw has described visiting a police station where Morris was bailing out colleagues arrested during a free speech demonstration. Amid the inevitable delays, Morris, oblivious to the noise about him, sat on the floor reading Dumas' *The Three Musketeers* 'for the hundredth time or so'.

He was by no means a saint and was renowned for occasionally volcanic outbursts of temper. He once threw an employee guilty of bad workmanship into a vat of dye. One sympathetic critic has suggested that the explanation for these rages may lie in some form of epilepsy. It is reassuring that Morris could not do everything brilliantly. He was a poor public speaker and sometimes vented his frustration in scornful comments about his audience. In his diary for January 1881, for example, he describes giving a talk at the Hammersmith Radical Club and calls the audience 'a very discouraging set of men'. He then goes on to castigate 'the frightful ignorance of English workmen'.

Morris' first-hand experience of shoddy Victorian workmanship came in

1856 when he and his friend Edward Burne-Jones shared a flat together in Red Lion Square, London. So dissatisfied was Morris with the quality of furniture available for sale that he designed his own. When he married Jane in 1859, Morris asked another friend, the architect Philip Webb, to build him a house in Bexley Heath, Kent. It is known as 'The Red House' because of Webb's lavish use of red brick. Again he designed his own furniture and two years later, in 1861, founded the firm which was to become Morris and Co.

Morris envisaged this firm as being organised on the lines of the old medieval guilds in order that workers could participate in every aspect of production, rather than experiencing the divison of labour characteristic of capitalism under which labourers repeated the same tasks over and over again. He deliberately did not expand the company beyond about 100 employees and ran the firm with such success that its stained glass, furniture, embroidery and patterns for wallpapers are still much admired in homes today. This practical achievement gives even more force to Morris' economic and political ideas, proving that he was not simply an armchair theorist.

As for his political involvement, during the 1870s he became increasingly disenchanted with the Liberal Party's imperialist foreign policy. In January 1883 he joined Hyndman's Democratic Federation, becoming its treasurer and collaborating with Hyndman on the book *England for All*, published the next year.

Despite his best intentions, however, Morris' restless individualism meant that he was never really a party man, as is shown by his unsuccessful record in terms of practical politics. He soon clashed with Hyndman and in late 1884 he left to form the Socialist League which even at the height of its influence never had more than 700 members. Much of the League's time was spent debating the internal question whether socialists should actually work through the parliamentary process at all. He spent a lot of money — up to £500 a year — on the weekly magazine *Commonweal*. Within a couple of years the Socialist League was taken over by the anarchists and Morris left his own creation. In the opening pages of *Nowhere* he satirises the sectarian rivalries and squabbles which characterised the League (and much of the British Left): 'there were six persons present, and consequently six sections of the party were represented . . .'

Morris carried out this political work entirely selflessly. He had nothing to gain from the undertaking, and much to lose, especially as 'I dread a quarrel above all things . . .' His name was proposed in 1892 as a possible Poet Laureate to succeed Tennyson but his socialist views ruled him out. It took courage to argue for his particular convictions in a society where socialism was derided and often provoked physical attack. His letters are full of reports of his being heckled, jeered and manhandled. He would have liked 'some organised body guard round the speaker when we speak in doubtful places.'

From 1892 Morris confined his political activities to the Hammersmith Socialist Society which met in the converted coach house of his beautiful home, Kelmscott House, overlooking the Thames. This Society was intended to be a debating group, and it attracted G. B. Shaw, H. G. Wells, who flaunted his radicalism by wearing a bright red tie, Oscar Wilde and W. B. Yeats. Morris also showed he was not one to bear grudges by helping out his former rival, Hyndman, putting up the £50 guarantee for the first year of the Twentieth Century Press, the SDF's printing press, when it moved into 37 Clerkenwell Green in 1893.

What was Morris' legacy to future generations? Well, it is certainly diverse and wide ranging — his daughter May remarked that 'My father never takes any recreation, he merely changes his work.' Engels referred to Morris as 'hopelessly muddle-headed' and 'a settled sentimental Socialist' but subsequent Marxists have claimed him as one of their own. So too have ethical socialists. And in 1935 an article appeared in the *Fascist Weekly* asserting that Morris represented a forerunner of fascism because he was supposedly 'imbued with the Viking spirit'!

Leaving aside his political influence, he had a profound effect on British and European design. He was concerned too with the environment. In 1877 he formed the Society for the Preservation of Ancient Buildings (SPAB) which tried to prevent the wholesale vandalism that some Victorian architects wreaked on old buildings. In one lecture he inveighs against 'litter bugs' with heavy irony: 'When we Londoners go to enjoy ourselves at Hampton Court, for instance, we take special good care to let everybody know that we have had something to eat: so that the park just outside the gates (and a beautiful place it is) looks as if it had been snowing paper.' Like Blake, he hated 'dark satanic mills' and invited his readers to 'dream of London, small, and white, and clean . . .'

His insistence that work should be fun rather than some sort of punishment for the privilege of living also strikes a modern chord. Morris and Co emphasised that, wherever possible, workers should experience the whole production process as they had done in the Middle Ages. He was not 'Luddite' in his attitude towards machines; he never rejected them entirely but believed they should be the slaves and not the masters. The drawback to this ideal — and it is one which still remains — is that beautiful, hand-made items are inevitably expensive so that just the wealthy can afford them. Only mass production can supply enough commodities for mass consumption. At least Morris' workforce was better treated than in most Victorian businesses (except perhaps for the workman thrown into the vat).

Morris also stressed the quality of life: what he called 'the art of living', deriving his views from Ruskin's saying that 'There is no wealth but life'. He loved laughter and fellowship and scorned puritanism. This question of just how human beings should treat each other is one in which few socialists before or since have shown much interest. Whereas the legacy of some early British socialists seems today to be of marginal importance only, the ideas of Morris have grown in relevance and interest since his death in 1896. Time and time again, Morris' name will crop up in the following pages.

Robert Blatchford's book *The Sorcery Shop* was subtitled 'An Impossible Romance'. It depicts a world with no money or guns, no government, no meat, no alcohol, no tobacco, no schools, no political parties, no army, no legal system, no religion. In the absence of all these activities, it is difficult to see quite how Blatchford's Utopian inhabitants occupy themselves, other than by playing cricket which was one of Blatchford's passions. Like *Nowhere*, there is a complete absence of conflict and no sense of how either Utopia planned to deal with individual differences, whether it be in terms of intelligence, appearance, strength and so on. But it is not so much this book which made Blatchford one of the British Left's most influential spokesmen but a work with the quaint title *Merrie England*.

Today, Robert Blatchford is largely a forgotten figure. No plaques or statues commemorate the man who was probably the most successful British socialist propagandist of all time. 'For every convert made by *Das Kapital*, there were a hundred made by *Merrie England*' was the *Manchester Guardian*'s verdict on Blatchford's most famous book, which sold a total of over two million copies in Britain and around the world. It has recently been described as perhaps 'the most effective ever [socialist] propaganda'. Remarkably, this success was achieved without any advertising and with few reviews. The book consists of a series of letters addressed by Blatchford to 'John Smith', an imaginary factory worker in Oldham, 'a hard-headed workman, fond of facts', explaining why he should be a socialist. It was an unlikely publication for a man who had had little schooling and spent seven years as a regular soldier in the British Army.

Blatchford was born in 1851, the son of not very successful actors. The early death of his father meant that the family was always on the breadline and so he had little formal education. Apprenticed to a brush-maker in Halifax, he stuck the job for six years but then ran away, ending up in the army. He left after seven years, married his childhood sweetheart and worked in a factory. Writing articles in his spare time and copying out a dictionary in order to expand his vocabulary, he immediately displayed a strong gift for journalism and joined the group of newspapers run by Edward Hulton. It was while he was based in Manchester that Blatchford researched and wrote a series on the slums there – and what he saw made him a socialist.

The increasingly radical tone of Blatchford's articles caused friction with Hulton and in October 1891 he left and set up his own newspaper, the *Clarion*, a weekly which was to become one of the British Left's most influential and best-loved publications. It was a risky project. Blatchford, his artist brother Montagu and two fellow journalists, A. M. Thompson and Edward Fay, only just managed to raise the necessary £400 capital.

From the first the *Clarion* dispensed with heavy theory and abstract language, writing in a style which welcomed rather than alienated readers. The newspaper's slogan was 'instructive without being dry, and amusing without being vulgar'. Its brand of socialism was joyful and happy; in Margaret Cole's phrase, 'it made Socialism seem as simple and universal as a pint of bitter.' The *Clarion* represented the adventurous and 'devil may care' strand within British socialism, very different from the puritan and earnest stance of Keir Hardie and the *Labour Leader*. The *Clarion*'s wide range of interests is shown by its own advertisement which calls the paper 'an illustrated weekly journal of Literature, Politics, Fiction, Philosophy, Theatricals, Pastimes, Criticism, and everything else'. There's not much left out there! As Blatchford once declared:

> If I desired to rouse a people, the figures I should deal in mostly would be figures of speech. Economics are for the very few, God's love is for the many.

The *Clarion* also created its own powerful cultural movement. Like William Morris, Blatchford was keen on the idea of 'fellowship' and there sprang up Clarion Scouts, Clarion Vocal Unions, Clarion Glee Clubs, Clarion Clubhouses, Clarion Handicraft Guilds, Clarion Field Clubs and a National Clarion Cycling Club. 'Clarion Vans' travelled the country – there were six in existence by 1908 – setting up in market squares and on village greens and trying to convey to bystanders the joys of socialism. The movement even had its own language dubbed 'Clarionese'. Crucially, the Clarion Fellowship exhibited a tolerance and humour that has not always characterised the British Left.

Blatchford's writings were all the more powerful because of the clarity and simplicity of his style. He never forgot his readers, imagining them to be the soldiers with whom he had shared the barracks. In 1925 he published a book called *English Prose And How To Write It* in which he advised writers 'never to use a long word if a short one will do. The one-syllable words are the backbone of our language.' He went on, 'clear writing requires clear thinking' and urged 'Study the comfort of your reader.' Unfortunately, Blatchford's suggestions have been disregarded by many later socialist writers.

But style without content is not much good either, and the quality of Blatchford's writing does not disguise the fact that the Clarion movement was always much stronger on emotion and rhetoric than analysis or prescription. Blatchford admits as much in *Merrie England*: 'The establishment and organisation of a Socialistic State are the two branches of the work to which I have given least attention.' Take the vagueness of his reply to the question as to how socialism will come about. Let people desire it, says Blatchford, 'and I am sure we may safely leave them to secure it' – not a very helpful answer. To the question of how this socialist state will operate, Blatchford returns an answer which reminds one of the bureaucratic élitism of some Fabian plans: 'Just get a number of your cleverest organisers and administrators into committee and let them formulate a scheme.' This seems to show a touching faith in committees, but Blatchford actually loathed them.

The *Clarion*'s circulation settled at about 60,000 copies a week. The newspaper was very much a reflection of Blatchford's personality and his patriotic support for the British Army during the Boer War alienated some readers, as did his campaign against orthodox religion. But until 1914 *Clarion* was a distinctive and important mouthpiece for British socialism. Blatchford's hostility towards the German Army led him, like Hyndman, to support the First World War and in effect destroyed his left-wing standing. The *Clarion* limped on until 1934 with dwindling influence and readership. His adored wife Sally died in 1921. Blatchford lived in retirement in Sussex, writing novels and an attractive autobiography titled *My Eighty Years*. He died in 1943, aged ninety-two.

Despite his many admirable qualities, Blatchford's writings remain very much of their period and do not have the universality which would make them of lasting value. It is this, perhaps, which explains his long neglect. Nevertheless, in his life and in his work he exemplified immediacy, humour, toleration and fun, qualities which will win more hearts than the most rigorous theory is ever likely to do.

There has always been friction within the labour movement between those who argue that socialism should foremost be about freedom and happiness, and those who argue that pleasure is a diversion until socialism has been established.

This division can be seen by comparing the remarks of two contemporaries, Victor Grayson and Keir Hardie. It is not surprising that they disliked each other. As seen, Grayson was all for enjoying life and had nothing but 'contempt for the crank socialists who believe that collectivism means living on cabbages and carrots and drinking cold water'. By contrast, Hardie thought that 'Socialism is a serious task, demanding serious work at the hands of its advocates, and anything which introduces levity or frivolity into the movement is hindering, not helping, its progress.'

This tension was even clearer over sexual questions. Many socialists naturally rationalised their own behaviour. H. M. Hyndman and Robert Blatchford both had happy marriages and were strongly in favour of monogamy. H. G. Wells enjoyed making love to different women and so he argued in his novel *The New Machiavelli* (1911) that the élite, like him, should be allowed to enjoy free love.

Double standards were endemic. Most Victorian socialists argued, at least in theory, for equality between the sexes, but somehow this demand often got lost. The early draft for the Charter in the 1830s had called for the vote for both men and women over the age of twenty-one, but more cautious voices maintained that this was impractical and so 'male persons' only appeared in the Six Points – even though the Chartist and historian R. G. Gammage noted that women were even more enthusiastic for the Charter than the men.

Others had no standards at all, reflecting the masculinity of the labour movement. Raphael Samuel notes that 'Socialism, after all, was conceived as a movement of working *men*, and it is evident that male bonding, and the exclusion of women, was one of the very principles of trade unionism.' Women were seen largely as passive beings whose main role was domestic and their grievances were secondary to the concerns of male trade unionists. There was marked inequality in the home too. Not until the Married Women's Property Act of 1870 did a wife retain ownership of her own property on marriage. Or else women and girls were sex objects. Child prostitution was rife – the age of consent was only raised from thirteen to sixteen as late as 1885. What this restricted role for women meant in personal terms is conveyed by Edward Carpenter who in his autobiography provided a chilling picture of the futility of his sisters' lives in Victorian England:

> ... there were six or seven servants in the house, and my six sisters had absolutely nothing to do except dabble in paints and music as aforesaid, and wander aimlessly from room to room to see if by any chance 'anything was

going on'. Dusting, cooking, sewing, darning — all light household duties were already forestalled; there was no private garden, and if there had been it would have been 'unladylike' to do anything in it; *every* girl could not find an absorbing interest in sol-fa or water-colours; athletics were not invented; every aspiration and outlet, except in the direction of dress and dancing, was blocked; and marriage, with the growing scarcity of men, was becoming every day less likely, or easy to compass. More than once girls of whom I least expected it told me that their lives were miserable 'with nothing on earth to do'. Multiply this picture by thousands and hundreds of thousands all over the country, and it is easy to see how, when the causes of the misery were understood, it led to the powerful growth of the modern 'Women's Movement'.

A few women were prepared to challenge this convention of passivity, encouraged by Ibsen's play *A Doll's House*, first performed in this country in June 1889, which showed Nora slamming the door on her past life and going her own independent way. But the path of a pioneering woman in the late nineteenth century was often not helped by the behaviour of many socialist men who acted more like traditional Casanovas or predators than like comrades and help-meets. H. G. Wells, for instance, formed relationships with several women until they had children, whereupon he quickly fled back to the domestic comforts provided by his long-suffering wife Jane. The Fabian Hubert Bland also had several affairs and actually founded an organisation which he called the Anti-Puritan League. Nevertheless when he discovered his daughter's plans to elope with Wells, he went after them like the typical outraged father and punched Wells on the nose at Paddington Station!

SDF member, university lecturer and failed playwright Edward Aveling was another philanderer, in spite of his unprepossessing appearance. Hyndman said that Aveling 'needed but half an hour's start of the handsomest man in London . . .' to make a woman fall in love with him. He lived for several years with Eleanor Marx, youngest daughter of Karl and herself an active participant in the Dock Strike of 1889, systematically fleecing her of her inheritance. When she found out in 1898 that Aveling had secretly married another woman, she killed herself.

One woman who did remain true to herself was Annie Besant, organiser of the matchgirls' strike in 1888. One of the most fascinating characters of the last century, her energy and curiosity led her to try virtually every philosophy of life then available, as Yvonne Kapp marvels: 'she ran the whole gamut from established religion, through High Church Anglicanism, the Oxford Movement, Theism, Atheism, Malthusianism, Radicalism, Science,

Philanthropy, Fabianism, Feminism and Socialism to Theosophy.' In one ten-year period she produced fifty-one books and pamphlets as well as giving hundreds of lectures. That many of the philosophies Besant embraced were seen as heretical by the orthodox was symptomatic of the growing revolt against conventional thought.

She was born Annie Wood in 1847. Her father died when she was a young girl and she developed a fierce determination to try and work things out for herself. Yet in her youth she held romantic Victorian views on the appeal of clergymen as marriage partners: 'To me a priest was a half-angelic creature, whose whole life was consecrated to heaven . . .' Unfortunately, the clergyman she chose to marry after a whirlwind courtship, a Reverend Frank Besant, was in reality a thoroughly unappealing man 'with very high ideas of a husband's authority and a wife's submission.' She was horrified to discover the sexual aspects of marriage, writing in her autobiography that she had had 'no more idea of the marriage relation than if I had been four years old instead of twenty.'

Though she had a son and a daughter, the marriage was unhappy almost from the start. When her baby girl Mabel fell seriously ill, Annie nursed her but the sight of the small child's pain turned her decisively against the idea of a God: 'There had grown up in my mind a feeling of angry resentment against the God who had been for weeks, as I thought, torturing my helpless baby.' She left both the Church and her husband. He kept custody of the son, she of the daughter.

Annie Besant then met the popular free-thought lecturer Charles Bradlaugh, a man who was separated from his alcoholic wife. Bradlaugh and Besant were simply good friends, though inevitably the gossips and scandalmongers soon got to work. As Annie put it, 'the mere fact that a woman is young and alone justifies any coarseness of slander.' She and Bradlaugh spent the next few years touring the country lecturing on secularism, which in the 1870s was another ingredient of the revolt against conventional Victorian thought. Often their lectures were broken up by stick-wielding and stone-throwing mobs.

In 1877 she and Bradlaugh found themselves accused in court of allegedly selling an obscene pamphlet. Called *Fruits of Philosophy*, it had been published forty years before by an American called Dr Knowlton. One section contained some elementary suggestions about birth control, such as withdrawal before ejaculation. Bradlaugh and Besant were in favour of birth control, as they explained in their *Preface* to Knowlton's pamphlet: 'We think it more moral to prevent the conception of children, than, after they are born, to murder them by want of food, air, and clothing.'

After a celebrated trial both were found guilty of publishing a book calculated to deprave public morals, but the verdict, a severe one carrying a fine and imprisonment, was quashed on appeal over a technicality. This did not stop Reverend Frank Besant, Annie's estranged husband, from seizing custody of their daughter Mabel on the grounds of Annie's way of life: 'the little child was carried away by main force, shrieking and struggling, still weak from the fever, and nearly frantic with fear and passionate resistance.' Both son and daughter returned to Annie when they came of age.

In the 1880s Annie helped Bradlaugh in his struggle to take up his seat in the House of Commons as the Radical MP for Northampton. As a free-thinker he claimed the right when taking his seat to affirm rather than swearing the oath. The Speaker refused to allow this and excluded Bradlaugh from sittings. On one occasion, in 1881, ten policemen were required to remove the burly Bradlaugh. Four times he was excluded, but three times the electors of Northampton returned him. Finally, in 1886, a new Speaker allowed Bradlaugh to take up his seat and in 1888 the Oaths Act was passed, allowing affirmation in both the House of Commons and in the law courts.

By the middle of the 1880s Annie had become a socialist, which Bradlaugh was not — he once referred to the socialist movement as being made up of 'poets and fools' — and their friendship cooled, although forty years later Annie still kept many photographs of him on the walls of her home. She sat on the executive of the Fabian Society and agitated on behalf of sections of the workforce such as the matchgirls. Interestingly, her socialism, like that of Hyndman and Blatchford, was precipitated by her shock on visiting England's slums. But to her mind, socialism lacked a vital spiritual dimension. In 1889 she reviewed two books by Madame Blavatsky, the leader of the Theosophy movement, a spiritual creed popular in the late nineteenth century. She visited India and was so affected by its peace and tranquillity that she decided to move there permanently. This was by no means the end of her public career. She dedicated herself to the Indian independence movement and was briefly interned in 1917 by the British authorities for her activities. She died in India in 1933.

Outstanding women in public life such as Annie Besant were fine, but they were, of course, exceptions and there was a need to develop a strong collective voice. One who tried was Emma Paterson, the founder of the Women's Trade Union League in 1874. The TUC was in favour of female suffrage from 1884 and its Congress four years later stated that 'where women do the same work as men they shall receive equal pay.' On the Left, Hyndman's Democratic Federation and the Independent Labour Party at its 1894 Conference also called for votes for women.

However, there was a reluctance to go beyond resolutions on paper and incorporate 'women's issues' into their programmes and day-to-day activities. Some leading socialists were strongly opposed to such ideas. Belfort Bax was an important figure within Hyndman's SDF. Not content with being a member of the Men's Anti-Suffrage League, he argued that women were inferior because they had smaller brains. Even William Morris thought that, 'Of course we must claim absolute equality of condition between women and men, as between other groups, but it would be poor economy setting women to do men's work (as unluckily they often do now) or vice versa.'

One indication of the size of the inequality is shown by comparing the wages of men and women before the First World War. In Sheila Rowbotham's words:

> In 1906 the average wage of the male worker in Britain was around 30s a week. Women's rates were well below this. Textile workers were among the best-paid women, and had a long tradition of unionisation. They earned about 18s 8d in this period. But women in the linen and silk trades, in glass making and in printing earned only half this amount. Below these came the home-workers. A woman carding hooks and eyes at home could earn 5s a week if she worked eighteen hours a day.

Much of the early union activity centred on the struggle to organise women shopworkers, a particularly exploited group of workers. This is how the gifted Mary Macarthur began. In 1903 she became the secretary of the Women's Trade Union League and in just two years raised its membership from 14,000 to 70,000, as well as finding the time to edit the *Woman Worker*. But it was always an uphill struggle, as one study of women made clear when it listed six obstacles to organising women into trade unions: the character of women's work; low wages; the delay in recognising women on the part of men's trade unions; antagonism on the part of employers; the 'broken term' of industrial life; and tradition.

Frustration at the male socialist groups' indifference was one of the reasons why Mrs Emmeline Pankhurst, a member of both the Independent Labour Party and the Fabians, set up the Women's Social and Political Union (WSPU) in 1903, the main suffragette body. The suffragettes were notable for the extraordinary range of their activities, from colourful marches and rallies to bands, theatre groups and art exhibitions as well as their weekly newspaper *Votes for Women*.

Male support for the suffragette movement, especially from the men associated with active suffragettes, seems to have been patchy. Hannah Mitchell notes in her autobiography that her husband was sympathetic towards her suffragette activities, up to a point:

... men are not so single-minded as women are; they are too much given to talking about their ideas, rather than working for them. Even as socialists they seldom translate their faith into words, being still conservatives at heart, especially where women are concerned. Most of us who were married found that 'Votes for Women' were of less interest to our husbands than their own dinners. They simply could not understand why we made such a fuss about it.

Hannah Mitchell's words could be quoted in every chapter of this book and be relevant to each of them.

The work of the WSPU was later overshadowed by their tactics of stone-throwing, arson and hunger strikes – following Mrs Pankhurst's belief that 'The argument of the broken window pane is the most valuable argument in modern politics.' It was not that Labour MPs were averse to votes for women; Keir Hardie and George Lansbury in particular were strong advocates of the cause. But in a two-party system where both major parties were against reform – the Conservatives on principle, the Liberals because they were apprehensive about giving the vote to those they thought would vote Conservative – it was impossible for the suffragettes to succeed. Women (and then not all of them) did not get the vote until after the First World War.

If it was difficult for women, it was no easier for homosexuals. Not only were homosexual acts illegal but the full ferocity of Victorian feeling on the subject was revealed during the trial of Oscar Wilde in 1895. Wilde's plays continued to run in London – but with the playwright's name stripped out. When George Bernard Shaw tried to put together a petition demanding the reprieve of Wilde, only Father Stewart Headlam was brave enough to sign. It was Headlam who stood bail for Wilde and was to meet him on his release from prison in May 1897. Wilde's long article *The Soul of Man under Socialism* was a typically idiosyncratic attack on some worrying tendencies in the labour movement: '... I confess that many of the socialistic views that I have come across seem to me to be tainted with ideas of authority, if not of actual compulsion.'

Some socialists were totally opposed to homosexuality. Engels, for example, wrote of homosexual acts as 'gross, unnatural vices'. Others like George Bernard Shaw, despite his support for Wilde, counselled caution, writing that socialism should not get mixed up with this 'sex-nonsense' and that 'It doesn't help us in the movement to be mixed up with every new fangled idea.'

These remarks of Shaw were expressed in letters to Edward Carpenter, a Victorian socialist who did advocate homosexual love. Like Blatchford,

Carpenter's name today is almost forgotten, but in his own time he was something of a guru, if only because he had the courage to try and live out his ideals in his own life rather than just writing about them. Born in 1844, he spent an unhappy childhood in Brighton before going to Cambridge where he became a Fellow of his college and entered the Church. After several years of this cloistered existence, his growing awareness of his own sexual preferences started to turn him against academic life and 'the everlasting discussions of theories which never came anywhere near actual life . . .'

Carpenter spent the next seven years as a university extension tutor in the north of England, lecturing mainly in astronomy. In 1883 he bought a cottage outside the village of Millthorpe in Derbyshire where he tried to live life as naturally as possible, growing his own food, dressing simply, writing in the mornings and making sandals for his friends. Millthorpe was not a successful commercial venture and without the legacy of £6,000 from his father's will Carpenter would never have survived.

Carpenter lived with a working-class man called George Merrill, who was to be his life-long companion until Merrill's death in 1928. It was brave of Carpenter to set up home with Merrill — several of his friends were horrified by the arrangement. Even more courage was needed to write the books he did, arguing there was no single type of male sexuality. Several publishers ran scared of his work after Oscar Wilde's trial and conviction, and sometimes Carpenter was forced to write in a deliberately oblique way. For instance, his book *Iolaus* (1902) is subtitled 'An Anthology of Friendship' but concentrates solely on male friendship.

One of Carpenter's attractive qualities was his dislike of fixed rules. He was a vegetarian and teetotaller but not fanatically so. His friend Charles Sixsmith noted his feeling that, 'if rigid vegetarians and teetotallers would occasionally have a good fling and devour beef and drink beer it would do them a lot of good.' He also prized tenderness and sincerity, values which contradict the 'macho' image of strength and brute force popular in some circles. He embodied too the tolerance and the questioning of convention that was typical of much of British socialism before 1914. He recognised by the 1920s, however, that the labour movement had taken a more orthodox and rigid path. After his death in 1929, his friend E. M. Forster wrote: '. . . perhaps he never understood that for many people personal relationships are unimportant for the reason that their hearts are small. His own heart was great, and made him a great man.' Carpenter believed that socialism at its core should be about how human beings behave towards other human beings.

There were two problems that the 'New Lifers' were never able to get to grips with. The first was how best to put across their ideas in an often hostile world. Blatchford, Carpenter and many others argued for simple persuasion and argument, for writing, lecturing and debating. But such methods reached only small numbers of people compared with, say, the mass circulation of the *Daily Mail* founded in 1896.

The other difficulty was that it was never very clear how the New Lifers proposed to bring about the changes they wanted, or what, in fact, these changes meant in detail. In part this arose from the almost bewildering variety of the ideas proposed. This chapter alone has looked at individuals ranging from Stewart Headlam, William Morris and Robert Blatchford to Annie Besant, Charles Bradlaugh and Edward Carpenter while the ideas and movements have included Christian Socialism, the Clarion movement, feminism, secularism and so on.

One characteristic that united all these often disparate ideas was the sense of fellowship they gave to often small groups of people. One future Labour Party leader who was an active member of the Independent Labour Party in the East End of London before the war, Clement Attlee, claimed that this 'spirit of exaltation' came because 'We were crusaders in enemy-occupied country.' W. Stephen Sanders, an early socialist, paid a lovely tribute to the unheralded members of these bodies in his autobiography *Early Socialist Days*:

> I desire to pay a personal tribute to the unknown men and women, the rank and file of those early days, who gallantly played their parts in preparing the way for the great movement which now counts its adherents by the million. Recognition is due to those who formed the tiny nuclei at the open-air meetings, held the flag around which the audiences gathered, sold literature, made the modest collections, and cheerfully performed the arduous tasks of electioneering. They never spoke of burdens or self-sacrifice: to them work for the movement was a means of self-expression. In spite of quarrels, bitterness, weakness, personal failings – we were very human – and inadequacy of many kinds, their faces were towards the light, and they produced examples of courage in disheartening surroundings, unselfishness and loyalty to a cause, without expecting or receiving material reward: a firm faith in the abundant capacity of human nature to act from idealistic motives. To them, and the movement they helped to build, I owe a further gain: the discovery of a meaning and a purpose in the tangled medley of events we call life.

Sadly, after 1918 this tradition of pluralism, tolerance and of building a movement from the bottom up was largely, but certainly not completely, squeezed between the pincer movement of labourism, concerned above all with electoral politics and the smooth running of a party machine, and Communism which sacrificed personal considerations to the demands of 'the Party'. Even the idea of 'the New Life' was often scorned by other socialists. George Orwell, hardly the most conventional man himself, was able to write in 1937 in terms which remind one of Hyndman's dismissive remarks quoted at the beginning of this chapter:

> One sometimes gets the impression that the mere words 'Socialism' and 'Communism' draw towards them with magnetic force every fruit-juice drinker, nudist, sandal-wearer, sex-maniac, Quaker, 'Nature-cure' quack, pacifist and feminist in England . . .'

This was a sad and unjust comment.

CHAPTER FOUR

Tho' Cowards Flinch and Traitors Sneer: The Rise and Fall of Ramsay MacDonald

'"I always feel proud, Tommy, that we knew him [Hamer Shawcross, the character based on Ramsay MacDonald] in Ancoats. It's marvellous to think that he sprang from the people."

Sir Thomas patted Polly's stout arm. "Yes, my dear. And while he was about it, he took care to spring a good long way from 'em."'
Howard Spring *Fame is the Spur*

'When the buggers [his own members] are giving you trouble, give 'em a mass meeting. That gets it out of their system.'
Jimmy Thomas, leader of the National Union of Railwaymen

IN 1947 the Boulting brothers produced a film version of Howard Spring's popular novel *Fame is the Spur*. Novel and film depict the growing conservatism of a once fiery radical as personal ambition and vanity make him turn his back on his working-class roots. At the end of the film Lord Shawcross dies alone, but not before he has realised what an empty and unprincipled man he has become. Spring called his protagonist Shawcross, but everyone knew that he modelled him on Ramsay MacDonald, the first Labour Prime Minister who had died in 1937, just three years before the book was published.

In the course of his long political career, MacDonald was once revered by colleagues in the labour movement and detested by the Conservatives for his semi-pacifist stance during the First World War. Horace King, a socialist who eventually became Speaker of the House of Commons, recalled that MacDonald was 'the god, the god of the whole of the Labour Party in Britain.' In 1929, on the eve of a general election, a German observer noted that 'in the slums of the manufacturing town and in the hovels of the countryside he has become a legendary being – the personification of all that thousands of downtrodden men and women hope and dream and desire.'

But after August 1931, when MacDonald as Labour's Prime Minister unexpectedly ditched his Cabinet and formed a National Government which then heavily defeated his old party at a general election, he found himself lauded by Conservatives and reviled as a traitor by socialists. One trade union branch even plucked out the eyes from the portrait of MacDonald embroidered on their banner. MacDonald's career was full of such paradoxes, not least of which was that the man who had struggled to create and unify the Labour Party should then split it from top to bottom. How can the life of the best hated and most loved of politicians be explained? What does it reveal about the British Left?

James Ramsay MacDonald was born in 1866 in a two-room cottage in Lossiemouth, north Scotland, a small fishing village. His parents, Anne Ramsay, a farmworker and dressmaker, and John MacDonald, the head ploughman at a nearby farm, never married. His illegitimacy was something MacDonald never forgot and explains in part his often over-sensitive and prickly character. His father soon vanished from the scene and the boy was brought up by his maternal grandmother. He developed a love of reading and was lucky in being given gifts of books by a neighbouring watchmaker while the local schoolmaster seems to have been an inspirational teacher. MacDonald left school at eleven intending to be a fisherman but instead he worked as a farm labourer before the schoolmaster appointed him a pupil teacher.

After four years as a teacher MacDonald left Lossiemouth in search of wider horizons and he went to Bristol. Although he was there for only a few months, Bristol had a tremendous impact on him. It was virtually the only city in Britain outside of London that had an organised socialist movement in 1886. MacDonald joined the local SDF branch and, helped by a gift of £5 from Edward Carpenter, he set up its library. Like many other pioneering socialists of the 1880s, the zeal of these Bristol socialists compensated for their comparatively small numbers. As MacDonald wrote later: 'We had all the enthusiasm of early Christians in those days. We were few and the Gospel was new.'

Returning briefly to Scotland, he next made his way to London, desperately searching for work. A job addressing envelopes for the Cyclists' Touring Club at ten shillings a week was followed by a post as a warehouse clerk. In his spare time he read voraciously in the Guildhall Library, hoping to win a scholarship to one of the science schools in South Kensington. But he overworked, as he was prone to do throughout his life, and collapsed. He went back to Scotland once more, but again he returned to London after he had recuperated.

This time MacDonald worked as the secretary to an aspiring Liberal politician called Thomas Lough, holding the post for several years. He gave it up to support himself by freelance journalism and by research work for Sir Leslie Stephens, Virginia Woolf's father, who edited the *Dictionary of National Biography*. Apparently, he worked on the entries from the letter 'M' onwards. In his spare time he joined socialist societies, speaking on street corners and, as always, reading everything he could lay his hands on. His character and opinions were largely formed by his mid-twenties and they changed little over the rest of his life.

Hardworking, determined, sensitive, a fine speaker and organiser, the handsome MacDonald often displayed contradictory sides to his personality. On the one hand, there was the dreamy idealist and romantic who became secretary of a group called The Fellowship of the New Life (out of which the Fabian Society had initially grown) and who ran its commune in Doughty Street in London. On the other, there was the cautious, pragmatic and ambitious man eager to play a conspicuous part in building a powerful labour movement. Even in these early days, he once declared his aim was eventually to become Prime Minister.

Already a member of both the Fabians and the Social Democratic Federation, in 1894 he joined the Independent Labour Party (ILP). This showed not only the flexibility of socialist organisations at this period but also MacDonald's realisation that Hardie was right to try and set up an independent working-class party distinct from the Liberal Party. In the 1895 general election he stood unsuccessfully as an ILP candidate for Southampton. A passage in his election address neatly sums up why he and many others were deserting the Liberals:

> . . . I ceased to trust in the Liberal Party when I was convinced that they were not prepared to go on and courageously face the bread-and-butter problems of the time — the problems of poverty, stunted lives, and pauper-and-criminal-making conditions of labour.

In 1895 he met and fell in love with Margaret Gladstone, a young Fabian from a well-off family. They became engaged on the steps of the British Museum in the summer of 1896 and were married soon afterwards. Margaret was crucial to her husband in two ways. First of all, their happy marriage gave him a stability and happiness which he had never known before, removing some of his earlier remoteness. Her sociability meant that their flat at 3 Lincoln's Inn Fields became a kind of socialist salon, introducing

MacDonald to a huge circle of friends which was later to be invaluable.

Secondly, Margaret's private means allowed him to devote himself fully to the labour movement, enjoying as he did an economic security known to few if any of his colleagues. He was thus uniquely placed to build himself a formidable position, and with his capacity for hard work he seized the opportunity. In 1900, for instance, he was appointed secretary of the new Labour Representation Committee (LRC) and concentrated on acquiring trade union affiliations to the new body. This was an arduous task that required all MacDonald's qualities of patient persuasion.

MacDonald also recognised the need to have several LRC representatives in Parliament, providing a focus for the new organisation's efforts. His success in building up the LRC enabled him to negotiate a secret electoral agreement with the Liberal Chief Whip, Herbert Gladstone, who wanted to maximise the anti-Conservative vote. A handful of Liberal and LRC candidates were given clear runs against Conservatives. At the 1906 general election twenty-nine LRC candidates won seats in Parliament, among them MacDonald who was successful in Leicester. At their first meeting the new LRC MPs decided to rename themselves the Labour Party.

Although it was undoubtedly Keir Hardie who was the prime founder and creator of this political party, MacDonald's administrative abilities were crucial in giving it a shape and structure. Hardie disliked the House of Commons and from 1907 MacDonald was effectively the leading personality within the party. In a series of books and speeches he tried to hammer out just what British socialism was all about, seeking to give it a moral and political basis distinct from *laissez-faire* liberalism. The difficulty today is that MacDonald's writings were extraordinarily abstract and unspecific. Reading his books is like trying to wade through an ocean of cotton wool. Churchill once said of MacDonald that no man could pack such a number of words into so small a space of thought. To give just one example of his writing style:

> Though economic creeds are torn to tatters, though the habits and ways of men disappoint the hearts of reformers, though the bright-eyed enthusiasm of youth fades into the yearning disillusionment of age, the guidance of the world will not be left to cynicism and pessimism, for the music of love and beauty will still be heard over faithless sadness, and chivalrous idealism will save us from selfishness and sleep.

This is all one sentence – and you can take your pick as to what he is on about.

Two important points do emerge from MacDonald's work, namely his emphasis on community- rather than class-consciousness, and his belief that communal and collective effort was morally superior to individualism. He insisted too, and this is an issue still relevant to sections of the British Left, that suffering was not likely to lead to socialist political change:

> I know that there is a belief still fairly prevalent amongst one School of Socialist theorists that the more Capitalism fails, the clearer will the way to Socialism be, that from the misery of the people the Socialist future will arise. I have never shared that faith. For with depression has not come more strenuous thinking, but more despairing action. Poverty of mind and body blurs the vision and does not clarify it . . .

Missing from MacDonald's books and speeches is any detail as to what a Labour government might actually do if elected to office. They show clearly what MacDonald is against, in general terms: greed, poverty, suffering and so on. But aren't most people? The question that MacDonald fails to answer is 'what is distinctive and unique about what socialism has to offer?' 'Love thy neighbour as thyself' is an excellent moral imperative but not much of a recipe for political administration. MacDonald's ideas could mean everything, or nothing. Even MacDonald's sympathetic biographer, David Marquand, has remarked that 'In place of the revolutionary utopianism of Marx, he offered, in effect, evolutionary utopianism – a kinder, but not in practice a more useful creed.' His colleague Philip Snowden remarked of MacDonald's speeches at this time: 'He suffered in those years from a failing which has grown upon him with advancing years, of being unable to make a speech which was not open to any interpretation a person chose to place upon it.' It was a characteristic well caught by Howard Spring in *Fame is the Spur*.

When it came to the vital area of economics, the Labour Party's approach was one of 'leave it to Snowden'. His reputed expertise seems to have been based on the two years he spent as a young man working as a tax collector in the Orkneys. But again a study of Snowden's ideas at this time reveals much evangelical zeal and many uplifting visions of a 'New Jerusalem', but correspondingly little financial detail. 'Leave it to Snowden' was a decision which was later to have disastrous consequences.

Despite, or perhaps because of this deliberate policy which did not give many hostages to fortune, the labour movement was growing in strength. Local election results showed that the Labour Party was starting to establish itself as a powerful presence all over the country. In addition, the 600,000 members of the Co-operative movement in 1890 had increased to over three million by 1914 and the *Daily Herald* newspaper, originally a strike sheet produced by the London printers in January 1911, had now become a national newspaper. The growth of factories and of towns and cities encouraged the collective environment and culture in which the labour movement had sunk its roots.

However, there were complaints, and not just from the left wing, that MacDonald's Labour Party was too timid. The Liberal government under Campbell-Bannerman and then from 1908 under Herbert Asquith, succeeded in modifying their Party's historic attachment to *laissez-faire* and passed a series of important social measures which included the introduction of old age pensions, unemployment insurance, unemployment exchanges, trade boards setting a minimum rate of pay in certain industries, and from 1911 the payment of MPs. Stimulated by the energy of Lloyd George and Churchill, the Liberal administration displayed a reforming zeal that the small number of Labour MPs could only applaud from the sidelines. MacDonald, who had been formally elected chairman of the Labour Party in 1911, stuck to his cautious policy of establishing a respectable image for his group.

The Parliamentary Labour Party in particular was criticised for contributing little to the wave of strikes launched between 1911 and 1913, particularly in the mining and transport industries. Influenced by syndicalist ideas that stressed the aim of workers' control at the expense of parliamentary action, these strikes were notable for the violence of the clashes between the strikers on one side, and the police and troops on the other. In November 1910 a miner was killed at Tonypandy in Wales and during the rail strike in the summer of 1911 signal boxes were attacked, track torn up and telegraph systems damaged. At Chesterfield the railway station itself was set on fire and the crowds only dispersed after bayonet charges by the army. Two people were killed at Llanelli when soldiers opened fire.

The 'labour unrest' in the years leading up to the First World War provides one partial exception to the generally non-violent character of the British labour movement. It alarmed MacDonald almost as much as it did the authorities. For him, any activity which hampered the slow, gradual work of building a strong Labour Party in Parliament was counter-productive.

MacDonald's task was made much harder by the unexpected death of his wife Margaret in September 1911. She had herself been active in the labour movement, playing a major part in the National Union of Women Workers which had been founded by Mary Macarthur in 1906. She loved research – her husband noted of Margaret's family that 'A Blue Book was second in rank of sacredness only to the Gospels.' They would work side by side at 3 Lincoln's Inn Fields, their desks awash with reports, books and pamphlets, surrounded by their five children. Domestic life was chaotic – MacDonald seems to have existed on a staple diet of bananas – but rewarding. For recreation the MacDonalds enjoyed walking and also foreign travel.

Her death ended all this and he was inconsolable. He wrote a touching memoir which was later expanded into a full-length book. A fine memorial was erected which still stands in Lincoln's Inn Fields, near to their flat. MacDonald never got over her death. Many years later he was asked why he had never remarried and simply replied 'My heart is in the grave . . .' Without Margaret, his over-sensitive and often difficult personality returned in force. It also meant that he had to face the personal and political traumas of the First World War alone.

The outbreak of the war in August 1914 was a shattering blow to both MacDonald and Hardie – Hardie, in fact, never recovered from the shock to his deeply-held belief in the brotherhood of man and he died in 1915. Although not a pacifist, MacDonald hated war and the suffering it brought. He voted against granting the Liberal government war credits to finance the conflict. It was a stance supported by only four other Labour MPs and so he resigned the chairmanship of the Party that same August.

As usual MacDonald's views were clouded by fine phrases and verbose rhetoric. Take this passage from a letter of September 1914:

> We cannot go back, nor can we turn to the right or to the left. We must go straight through. History will, in due time, apportion the praise and blame, but the young men of the country must, for the moment, settle the immediate issues of victory. Let them do it in the spirit of the brave men who have crowned our country with honour in the times that are gone. Whoever may be in the wrong, men so inspired will be in the right.

On the one hand, MacDonald seems to have felt that now the war was in progress it had to be fought to a finish. Undoubtedly, too, he was worried, as the German Social Democrats were, that if the Labour Party came out totally against the war it might be outlawed, split apart and so undo much of his previous hard work. On the other, he himself opposed the government and what he thought was, at least in its origins, an unnecessary conflagration. In the overheated and jingoist circumstances of the time, MacDonald's criticisms inevitably led many to brand him as a traitor.

The abuse and hostility which MacDonald endured stoically over the next four years contradict the argument that he was essentially an opportunistic and unprincipled man. The Press campaigned against him, smearing him as pro-German. Fellow socialists like H. G. Wells, a bellicose supporter of the war, referred to MacDonald and Hardie's views as 'the spiteful, lying chatter of the shabbiest scum of Socialism.' Horatio Bottomley published the evidence of MacDonald's illegitimacy on the front page of his journal *John Bull*. MacDonald was even thrown out of his local golf club in Scotland. Yet he carried on addressing meetings although he knew that violence was likely; once, at Plumstead Common in South London in August 1918, his opponents issued ex-servicemen with nailed sticks and bottles in order to disrupt a meeting. Finally, when the war was over, the Press made sure that MacDonald lost his seat at Leicester by over 14,000 votes in the 'Khaki' election. All of this MacDonald faced alone, without Margaret's support and advice.

But, and this was perhaps his greatest achievement, he did hold the Labour Party together. Even though only fifty-seven Labour MPs were elected at the 1918 election it was clear that underneath the jingoist fervour whipped up by Lloyd George, the Labour Party was poised to supersede the Liberals as the main opposition to the Conservatives. Their position was helped by the Representation of the People Act of 1918 which gave the vote to all men over the age of twenty-one and most women over the age of thirty (note the chauvinistic difference). The electorate nearly tripled from $7\frac{1}{2}$ million voters in 1910 to over 21 million in 1918. While many working-class people did not necessarily vote Labour the majority did, and in a first past the post system the Liberals faced the perennial difficulty of being squeezed out.

The Labour Party was beginning to transform itself from a loosely federated alliance into a capable, centralised and national organisation. The constitution of December 1918 for the first time allowed both the formation of local branch parties and individual membership. Much of the hard work needed to establish the machinery for this new Party was undertaken by Arthur Henderson, secretary between 1911 and 1934. There were to be reverses in the future, but the Labour Party was now an ineradicable part of the political landscape.

Kenneth Morgan has noted that '. . . it was Henderson who ensured that the unions dominated the machinery of the party at every stage.' This reflected the maxim that he who pays the piper calls the tune. Much of the Party's finance was indeed supplied by the trade unions, embodying Hardie's conviction that they must provide the backbone of any viable working-class party. In return the trade unions controlled the Labour Party machinery; all twenty-three members of the National Executive were elected by the annual Party Conference which meant that because the trade union block vote swamped that of the constituency parties, only individuals favoured by the unions could be successful. In addition, forty-nine of the fifty-seven Labour MPs returned in 1918 were trade union nominees.

The Labour Party's greater efficiency was paralleled by that of the trade union movement. In 1914 there were estimated to be no less than 1,100 unions in Britain – Germany in 1911 had only 51 – but after the war they began to reorganise and amalgamate. The General Council of the TUC was set up in 1921, as was the Amalgamated Society of Engineers. Next year the massive Transport and General Workers' Union was born out of a merger of twenty-three different unions. The General and Municipal Workers' Union was formed in 1924. As the trade unions grew, so too did the Labour Party. It was not a straightforward success story. Trade union membership peaked in 1920 at 8 million and then dropped away to 5 million, but such figures underline how important an institution the trade unions had become.

A symbol of the British labour movement's newly acquired permanence was the eight-storey Transport House specially built for the Transport and General Workers' Union in Smith Square, close to the Houses of Parliament. One of the first steel and concrete frame buildings erected in London, it was opened on 15 May 1928 by Ramsay MacDonald and Ernest Bevin, General Secretary of the Transport and General Workers' Union. The Labour Party moved its headquarters here, demonstrating the umbilical link between itself and the trade union movement. The TUC was also based at Transport House.

In many ways the Labour Party was a thoroughly progressive force far in advance of its political opponents. For instance, the 1918 Constitution allowed for the setting up of Women's Sections, of which there were 2,000 by 1932. Although the inspirational Mary Macarthur had tragically died of cancer in 1921 aged only forty-one, her example lived on in the work of three women in particular. Susan Lawrence and Margaret Bondfield both became MPs in 1923 and then parliamentary secretaries in the 1924 Labour government. Five years later Bondfield became the first ever woman Cabinet minister. Marion Phillips was elected the first women's secretary of the Labour Party in 1925 and also edited Labour Woman.

But the Labour Party's creation of an electoral machine based on the might of the trade union block vote at the annual conference entailed losses too, particularly in the pioneering ardour exhibited by various socialist groups over the previous forty years. The prospect of paid jobs and careers within the movement meant that the committee room began to edge out the unpaid amateur and the street-corner meeting.

A disciplined party machine was bound to place the block vote and the mandate before socialist education or any search for 'the New Life'. The Independent Labour Party, vanguard of the old revivalist spirit, went into irreversible decline. Some of the old-style revivalism survived in the love and affection which Labour Party members displayed towards inspirational figures such as the miners' leader A. J. Cook, the Clydeside MP James Maxton and the East End MP George Lansbury. It is also true that the reverence with which many in the labour movement looked upon Ramsay MacDonald owed much to the way in which he embodied popular hopes and aspirations. Take this description of a MacDonald visit to the mining valleys of South Wales in 1924:

> When the time arrived for the meeting to begin, the hall was packed to suffocation and the street outside was crowded with people, many with tickets, who had failed to get in. When Ramsay arrived the vast audience inside – and outside – joined in the singing of one of their favourite hymns – the bard Watcyn Wyn's vision of the day when every continent 'neath the firmament would hail the Nazarene. The address was in tune with the hymn – with peace on the horizon if only we had the courage to reach out. The crowd was thrilled and after the Prime Minister had gone on his triumphant way to Aberavon the streets rang with shouts and songs till the early hours of Sunday.

Yet MacDonald and a handful of other 'old-style' revivalists were a dwindling exception. The quest for 'the New Jerusalem' undoubtedly remained but now it was a far-off and probably unattainable hope, secondary to the administrative detail of running a practical, down-to-earth organisation worried about the payment of subscriptions.

Organisational efficiency was not matched by any precision in policy. Both the Constitution of 1918 and the statement *Labour and the New Social Order* which accompanied it were largely the work of Sidney Webb. However, his main concern was with what David Howell has called the 'maximisation of support' and Webb gave few if any hostages to political fortune. Take the famous Clause Four of the Constitution that proposes:

> To secure for the producers by hand or by brain the full fruits of their industry and the most equitable distribution thereof that may be possible, upon the basis of the Common Ownership of the Means of Production and the best obtainable system of popular administration and control of each industry and service.

Every phrase and almost every word in this clause is open to widely differing interpretations.

It was clear, however, that the British labour movement was committed to change within the system. A few individuals might still talk of 'revolution' and of emulating the Bolsheviks but their rhetoric was a million miles from the centre of power. Instead leaders like Ramsay MacDonald stressed the need for caution and compromise: 'Change must proceed from the bottom upwards, otherwise it has no foundation. That means patience, work, trouble.'

One event demonstrated the fundamentally constitutional and non-revolutionary nature of this mainstream British Left. In 1919 a rash of strikes was launched by the 'Triple Alliance' of miners, railwaymen and transport workers which hoped to turn the political agitation of that year into wage increases and better working conditions. Sections of the Establishment feared that Britain might be going the way of Czarist Russia. Prime Minister Lloyd George was more shrewd. He called together the union leaders. As the miner Robert Smillie recalled, they were determined not to be talked over by this 'seductive and eloquent Welshman':

> 'He was quite frank with us from the outset,' Bob went on. 'He said to us: "Gentlemen, you have fashioned, in the Triple Alliance of the unions represented by you, a most powerful instrument. I feel bound to tell you that in our opinion we are at your mercy. The Army is disaffected and cannot be relied upon. Trouble has occurred already in a number of camps. We have just emerged from a great war and the people are eager for the reward of their sacrifices, and we are in no position to satisfy them. In the circumstances, if you carry out your threat and strike, then you will defeat us.
>
> '"But if you do so," went on Mr Lloyd George, "have you weighed the consequences? The strike will be in defiance of the government of the country and by its very success will precipitate a constitutional crisis of the first importance. For, if a force arises in the state which is stronger than the state itself, then it must be ready to take on the functions of the state, or withdraw and accept the authority of the state. Gentlemen," asked the Prime Minister quietly, "have you considered, and if you have, are you ready?" From that moment on,' said Robert Smillie, 'we were beaten and we knew we were.'

It is doubtful if Lenin would have reacted in quite the same way.

The parliamentary road to socialism did seem attainable, particularly when Ramsay MacDonald and the first Labour government took office in January 1924. MacDonald had been returned to Parliament in 1922 as MP for Aberavon and in the first ever party leadership contest he just defeated J. R. Clynes by sixty-one votes to fifty-six. He won mainly because of the support of the left-wing Clydeside MPs – one of them wore a label which read 'High explosive, handle carefully' – who were swayed by MacDonald's brave stand during the war and by the fact that he was a fellow Scot. At the 1923 election, despite Press smears that the Labour Party if elected would introduce 'compulsory free love' (surely a contradiction in terms!), the Party increased its representation to 191 seats. The Conservatives were still the largest party with 255 seats while the Liberals held 158 seats. The Conservatives decided to give the Labour Party the taste of office without the power, knowing full well that as a minority government they would be unable to introduce radical measures.

As MacDonald went about forming his minority administration, some members of the Establishment absurdly over-dramatised what this socialist party might do. They would have been less anxious had they known the reverential thoughts of J. R. Clynes, one of the Party's leading figures, as he and his colleagues went to Buckingham Palace to receive their seals of office:

> As we stood waiting for His Majesty, amid the gold and crimson magnificence of the Palace, I could not help marvelling at the strange turn of Fortune's wheel, which had brought MacDonald the starveling clerk, Thomas the engine-driver, Henderson the foundry labourer and Clynes the mill-hand, to this pinnacle beside the man whose forebears had been kings for so many splendid generations. We were making history! We were, perhaps, somewhat embarrassed, but the little, quiet man whom we addressed as 'Your Majesty' swiftly put us at our ease.

Some Labour MPs in the House of Commons were excited enough to sing *The Red Flag*. MacDonald solemnly promised George V that he would try to break this unfortunate habit. And when it came to the question of the correct ceremonial garb for their meeting with George – would they or wouldn't they dress up? – of course they did. It is interesting to speculate what Keir Hardie would have done. Beatrice Webb describes in her diary 'laughing over Wheatley [one of the Clydeside militants] – the revolutionary – going down on both knees and actually kissing the King's hand.' Not that Mrs Webb advocated anything different. She founded a club for the new Cabinet members' wives so that they could be schooled in the proper etiquette. Left-wing commentators always flay MacDonald and his colleagues for this 'flunkeyism' but Philip Snowden pointed out that 'the constituents of the Labour members who appeared in the full uniform were rather pleased to see the photographs in the newspapers of their representatives in all this glory.'

The first Labour government was an extraordinary mix of individuals.

There was MacDonald himself, handsome, dignified and applauded by sections of the Press that only a few years before had labelled him a traitor. He also took the post of Foreign Secretary, necessitating horrendous sixteen-hour days. Snowden was at the Exchequer, directing his venomous speeches not so much at the Opposition but at his own left-wingers. Arthur Henderson was at the Home Office, Sidney Webb at the Board of Trade. Jimmy Thomas was in charge of the Colonial Office, determined to prove that the Empire was safe in his hands. George Bernard Shaw turned down the offer of a peerage and the post of government spokesman in the House of Lords, arguing that he liked his own name as it was and it was all a waste of time anyway. The one left-winger in the administration, John Wheatley, Minister of Housing, turned out to be the most constructive, passing legislation which led to the building of half a million new homes.

Apart from Wheatley's Act, the ten months that the Labour Party was in office from January to November 1924 did little other than to demonstrate its caution. Admittedly, it was very much a minority government – less than one in three MPs were Labour – but the experience revealed several major weaknesses. This first generation of Labour MPs, most of whom were veterans of the early pioneering days, were essentially propagandists, full of evangelical enthusiasm and passion but often short of practical ideas. Without a programme or sense of direction they were content to drift, waiting for the Conservatives sooner or later to remove them from office. They did this by first of all fomenting a row over a supposedly seditious article published in a Communist journal, causing the Liberals to withdraw their support, and then in the subsequent election by the forged 'Zinoviev letter', which whipped up fears of the Bolshevik menace to Britain. The Conservatives duly returned to power in November 1924.

One area in which MacDonald's Labour Party lost out to the Conservatives was in the sphere of political propaganda, surprisingly so in view of the early socialists' success in building support by means of rallies, marches and open-air meetings. But in many ways the Left had become fixated – and still is, to some extent – on these methods, failing to get to grips with modern communications. As early as 1910 Conservative Central Office was overhauled, the role of its party agents was upgraded and 'Literature' and 'Speakers' departments were created. The Conservatives also produced huge quantities of material: in 1927 alone over 18 million anti-union leaflets were issued. By the 1920s they were financing fleets of mobile film vans which crisscrossed the country as well as residential colleges where speakers were trained to put over suitable anti-socialist arguments.

One telling episode from the October 1924 general election demonstrates how, in this respect at least, it was the socialist MacDonald who was the hidebound reactionary and the Conservative leader Stanley Baldwin who was the innovator. For the first time ever the British Broadcasting Company (later Corporation) allowed the leaders of the three main political parties to broadcast on the radio, reaching an estimated audience of some 3/4 million listeners – a figure much larger than any reached in a lifetime of street-corner oratory. Despite the warnings of the Company's head John Reith, Ramsay MacDonald spoke live from the City Hall in Glasgow and made no attempt to adapt his platform style to the intimacy of radio listening. At times he even turned his face away from the microphone. One observer commented tactfully:

> He raised his voice to its highest pitch and he dropped it to a whisper. He turned to the right and to the left, and even behind him, and spoke to all parts of the hall. He strode up and down the platform and was at varying distances from the microphone all the time. This is extremely effective for those who are present in the hall, but very detrimental for broadcasting.

Asquith, the Liberal leader, also relayed his speech from a live meeting. Baldwin, in contrast, broadcast from the BBC's headquarters in London, making sure that he arrived early and was thoroughly briefed on how to alter his delivery in order to communicate effectively.

MacDonald's 1924 government was bedevilled by the fact that few if any of its ministers had carried out homework as to how radical policies might be drawn up and then implemented. In one way, of course, this can be excused by the fact that only a handful of the Cabinet, usually ex-Liberals, had ever experienced office before. But it might be thought that after the failures of 1924 the Labour Party would have seriously and methodically hammered out effective measures for the future. They didn't. The German journalist Egon Wertheimer commented on this omission on the eve of the 1929 general election; he thought that the Party was placing its hopes in 'the right improvisation at the right moment.'

Very different from this rather lackadaisical attitude was the work of four young Conservative MPs, among them Harold Macmillan, who in 1927 published a book called *Industry and the State* that argued for 'economic democracy', National Wages Boards and a great expansion in welfare work. And it was the Liberal Party which in March 1929 issued a manifesto called *We Can Conquer Unemployment* demanding much greater government intervention in the economy. Both these plans contained ambiguities and evasions but at least they were attempts to grapple with the problems of a new era, notably the prolonged period during the 1920s when the unemployment rate remained constant at 10 per cent of the workforce.

The lack of preparation in the Labour Party was tragically echoed too by the events leading up to the General Strike of May 1926 in which the unions showed themselves to be poor strategists when faced by an antagonistic government. British mineowners were trying to enforce cuts in the already meagre wages of their men. On 31 July 1925 the Conservative government agreed to step in and avert a possible strike by means of a nine-month subsidy – a temporary union victory which somewhat prematurely was termed 'Red Friday'. It was clear that when the subsidy ran out a conflict was inevitable. The government used the breathing space to organise and make detailed plans, beefing up its Organisation for the Maintenance of Supplies (OMS) while the trade unions did nothing. When the strike began on 3 May 1926, the trade union leaders were amazed at the spontaneous upsurge of grassroots support shown by workers all over the country for the miners. For example, more railwaymen came out on strike in 1926 than in support of their own dispute in 1919.

But it was obvious that the trade union leaders were appalled at the tiger which they had unleashed. In the words of critic and historian Julian Symons, they 'feared the consequences of complete victory more than those of a negotiated defeat'– just as they had in 1919. They made little attempt to give a lead to their side, turning down the offer of the Independent Labour Party to help put across to the public their case. As one commentator notes, 'This machine, easily the most efficient and widespread socialist organisation in Great Britain, could organise more than 700 public meetings a week, yet the offer was never taken up.' It was with acute relief that the General Council of the TUC found a way of calling off the General Strike after nine days, leaving the miners to fight on alone and be defeated.

One notable feature of the strike has been stressed by Symons, whose account of the conflict was first published in 1957. The 1987 edition has a new preface by the author in which he contrasts the lack of bitterness and sabotage shown in 1926 with the much more acrimonious atmosphere surrounding the miners' strike of 1984–85: 'The strikers of 1926 were a war-weary generation, almost all of whom remembered the horrors of trench warfare and poison gas. They shrank from violence because they had suffered it.'

Throughout the 1920s the Liberal Party, already split between the followers of Asquith and of Lloyd George, found themselves squeezed out by the

British 'first past the post' electoral system as the Labour Party established itself as the major rival to the Conservatives. This was confirmed by the results of the general election held in May 1929 when the Labour Party won 287 seats, the Conservatives 260 and the Liberals just 59. This meant that MacDonald's second administration was a minority government like his first, but this time the minority was much less than in 1924. Moreover it was clear that sections of the Liberal Party were prepared to accept a radical strategy – just as Labour had supported the Liberals between 1906 and 1914.

The story of the next two and a half years in which the Labour Party was in government is quickly and sadly told. The New York stock exchange crash of October 1929 led to economic depression in Britain and world-wide. Business confidence collapsed, men and women were laid off. Unemployment began to rise inexorably above the 10 per cent figure. In 1930 alone it doubled to over two and a half million people out of work. Philip Snowden at the Exchequer, wedded to traditional ideas of free trade, the gold standard and *laissez-faire*, pinned his hopes on world economic recovery. When this didn't happen, he was lost. The Prime Minister relied on a cheery but totally false optimism; when the newly-elected Labour MP Aneurin Bevan went to see MacDonald in 1930 about the economic crisis he was breezily told that 'Recovery is just around the corner'.

There was, however, one alternative to hand. Sir Oswald Mosley, a junior minister in the government, presented a memorandum in January 1930 calling for the public control of imports and banking and an increase in pensions in order to boost purchasing power. When the memorandum was rather perfunctorily turned down, Mosley resigned.

By the summer of 1931 the crisis had worsened. Snowden's only policy was to cut back on government spending and he demanded a 10 per cent reduction in unemployment pay. The Cabinet split. Outside the government the General Council of the TUC refused to accept this cut. This meant that the trade union or industrial wing of the labour movement was now at odds with the Labour Party or political leadership, thus contradicting the alliance on which the entire movement was based.

For the first but not the last time, this dispute showed how difficult it was to locate exactly where ultimate power within the labour movement was to be found: did it lie with the Labour Prime Minister, the Cabinet, the Parliamentary Labour Party, the Party Conference, the trade unions or the constituency Labour parties? In the years to come this uncertainty was to dog future Labour leaders and governments.

At the end of August 1931 MacDonald suddenly ditched his Cabinet when the majority of them refused to accept his policies. Instead he formed a National Government made up of himself, Snowden and Jimmy Thomas together with Conservatives and Liberals. MacDonald justified his actions by arguing that only a National Government could solve the country's economic problems.

At the October 1931 election the National Government, in reality the Conservatives, scored an extraordinary victory by returning 554 MPs to the Labour Party's meagre 46. Virtually overnight it seemed that the gains and achievements that MacDonald and the Labour Party had won over the course of twenty-five years had been wiped out and that it had shrunk to little more than its 1906 level of parliamentary representation.

The economic crisis had overshadowed the entire period in office of MacDonald's second Labour government. MacDonald himself preferred to concentrate on foreign affairs but eventually he realised that the growing difficulties meant he had to devote himself to the domestic front. In the end this made little difference. MacDonald was not able to deal with the crisis; later Labour administrations, whether led by Clement Attlee, Harold Wilson or James Callaghan were all to experience similar problems when handling a recalcitrant economy. One explanation for MacDonald's failure was his incapacity to ask for, let alone accept, colleagues' advice.

In February 1885 William Morris' Socialist League had published a manifesto which claimed that 'we shall look to it that there shall be no distinctions of rank or dignity amongst us to give opportunities for the selfish ambition of leadership which has so often injured the cause of the workers.' Such an approach had long since been discarded by MacDonald. By the late 1920s even his supporters remarked on his aloofness. Egon Wertheimer observed that 'One can perhaps more readily picture him sitting and dreaming by his fireside or wandering with a knapsack on the moors alone with Nature . . .' than cajoling his administration into wide-ranging socialist change. When backbenchers went to see their party leader he used to read his correspondence as they talked to him. His social circle contained rather more Duchesses than trade unionists.

Philip Snowden as Chancellor had lived off his reputation as the Labour Party's economics expert for years and his views were rarely challenged within the Party. He had always been noted as a fine emotional speaker, typical of the first generation of pioneers. One famous speech ended:

> But the only way to regain the earthly paradise is by the old, hard road to Calvary — through persecution, through poverty, through temptation, by

the agony and bloody sweat, by the crown of thorns, by the agonising death. And then the resurrection to the New Humanity – purified by suffering, triumphant through Sacrifice.

After such a peroration it must have been difficult for Snowden to come back down to earth and work out the nuts and bolts of the Labour Party's economic approach – and he didn't. Instead he relied on the orthodoxies of Victorian Liberalism, as his biographer has noted: 'He was raised in an atmosphere which regarded borrowing as an evil and free trade as an essential ingredient of prosperity.' The Treasury thought likewise and, as Churchill put it in one of his telling phrases, 'The Treasury mind and the Snowden mind embraced each other with the fervour of two long-separated kindred lizards.'

Throughout the economic crisis of 1929–31 Snowden maintained that the only answer to a recession lay in wage cuts. In his autobiography he claimed that he never prepared his speeches, preferring instead to draw from 'the stock of accumulated material.' As Chancellor he likewise depended on accumulated economic wisdom suitable for the past but inadequate for the present crisis. Professor Robert Skidelsky, who has analysed the events of 1929–31 in detail, concludes scathingly that 'With him at the Exchequer, no Government stood much chance in the circumstances of 1929.'

Nothing could be expected of Jimmy Thomas who was specifically in charge of finding a solution to mass unemployment. Not even his most fervent supporters ever claimed that fresh thinking was Thomas' forte. He also had a drink problem. Others who might have helped the administration were unavailable. John Wheatley had blotted his copybook with a botched libel case and Ernest Bevin was not in Parliament, preferring to wield much greater power outside.

But the disaster which destroyed the government was due to much more than personal failings. The Labour Party had completely failed to prepare for the economic situation, unlike some other social democratic parties such as the one in Sweden which by judicious use of government intervention managed to cope with the same sort of difficulties. The whole nature of MacDonald's Labour Party was to shy away from hard and detailed thinking about policy: Snowden and MacDonald's cloudy rhetoric was symptomatic of the Party's approach. To quote Skidelsky again, 'Socialism explained the past and promised the future; it had nothing constructive to offer the present.' A party dominated by trade unions which were concerned above all with 'bread and butter issues' was not, in the 1920s at least, best placed to be innovative. Few of the Labour ministers had ever run anything in their lives; their economic and financial experience was usually meagre and ensured that they were no match for Treasury and business interests.

It is unfair to place all the blame on MacDonald himself. His biographer David Marquand has shown that throughout the crisis he often received contradictory and ambiguous advice from the Treasury, the rest of the civil service, his Cabinet and Labour MPs. There was no clearcut radical course of action open to him. But MacDonald would almost certainly not have tried it even if there had been.

His last few years were tragic. Pledged to defend the Gold Standard and the old economic order, instead he took Britain off it — with no discernible result. He was genuinely upset to see the Labour Party so badly defeated at the October 1931 election; Snowden on the other hand rounded on his former colleagues with a vengeance, accusing their programme of being 'Bolshevism run mad'. The young Harold Wilson witnessed the bewilderment that Snowden's behaviour caused in his own constituency of Colne Valley: '. . . I saw the Valley almost flooded with the tears of those who a month earlier would almost have died for Snowden, and I saw those tears gain a new bitterness as Snowden attacked his colleagues in those acid election speeches and broadcasts.'

MacDonald always hoped to return to the Labour Party, regarding the formation of the National Government as a temporary measure. But it was not to happen. He underestimated the loathing which his former Party now felt for him; in their view he had brought down an elected government and then nearly destroyed it as a parliamentary force. He was therefore surprised and deeply upset to receive a letter from the Party's national organiser expelling him: 'It began "Dear Sir", and it ended not with a signature, but with a rubber stamp and initials underneath. They wanted to insult me.' He lost his seat at the 1935 election, beaten by a former supporter of his, Manny Shinwell, but regained a place in Parliament at a by-election. He died in November 1937. His ashes lie beside those of Margaret in Spynie churchyard, near Lossiemouth.

The sad fate of Ramsay MacDonald, the man who had done so much to build up the Labour Party but then brought it crashing down, is often dismissed as the inevitable outcome of his essentially vain and opportunist character. This 'betrayal complex' has always appealed to sections of the British Left who have applied it to several other figures in decline or disgrace. Conveniently it means that they don't have to examine their own ideas or ways of trying to bring about political change and can simply blame individuals for the failures of the movement.

The 'betrayal' interpretation ignores the fact that for many years MacDonald was the undisputed and enormously popular leader of the Labour Party and that his basic strategy of gradually ousting the Liberals by Labour as the opposition to the Conservatives in a two-party system barely altered over three decades. This could not be accomplished by wild revolutionary antics because it was imperative to win over 'the middle ground' of voters who had for years voted Liberal.

Few within the labour movement quarrelled with this approach at the time and it seems unfair to accuse him of inconsistency. His career vividly revealed both the merits and flaws of 'labourism' in that he was prepared to work within the system as he understood it and to cling to that same system when it was threatened, as in 1931. He was the pioneer who had to govern, but didn't know how. And yet the permanence of his achievement was, paradoxically enough, shown even in the October 1931 election. Despite all the forces ranged against it, the Labour Party still managed to attract 6 million votes.

But 'labourism' is not a single and coherent set of ideas. The challenge facing the Labour Party was how to try and create a different form of labourism which, unlike that associated with MacDonald, could win power in a parliamentary democracy and then use it. How best, in other words, to progress from the first pioneering phase towards the next administrative phase?

MacDonald's labourism was not unchallenged in the 1920s. Lenin had attacked MacDonald for his 'inability and lack of desire to really prepare the party and the class in a revolutionary manner for the dictatorship of the proletariat.' That MacDonald would probably have had no idea what Lenin was talking about shows how deep was the schism between the reformist and revolutionary strands within the British Left. How successful, then, were Britain's revolutionaries, banded together in the new Communist Party, in their attempt to introduce 'the dictatorship of the proletariat'?

CHAPTER FIVE

British Revolutionaries in the 1920s

'A Red football team was recently formed in South Shields.'
News item in the *Workers' Weekly*, 10 February 1923

'Lenin's name rang like magic in my ears ... That day on which I met Comrade Lenin was the greatest of my life.'
Harry Pollitt, General Secretary of the Communist Party of Great Britain

'The one outstanding and – by contemporary standards – highly original quality of the English is their habit of *not killing one another*.'
George Orwell

WHICH BRITISH revolutionary was sometimes called 'Britain's Lenin', was imprisoned five times for his political beliefs, has a Moscow street named after him, and whose centenary in 1979 was marked in the Soviet Union by the issue of a special commemorative stamp? The answer is John Maclean. Until recently, most people hearing this name would justifiably have responded 'Who?', so completely has his name been omitted from the history books.

In the last few years, however, there has been renewed interest in Maclean and, just as happened with William Morris, various factions are busy fighting over his legacy. He has been claimed as an anarchist, a Scottish nationalist and a Communist as well as being dismissed as mentally unbalanced. It doesn't seem to matter that for all his personal bravery he never came anywhere near leading a revolution. In fact, when the British authorities did with some reason fear that a rising was about to take place – in Glasgow on 31 January 1919 when thousands of people demonstrated in favour of a forty-hour week – Maclean was a hundred miles away lecturing in Manchester. It is difficult to imagine Lenin missing the October Revolution in Russia. That Maclean managed to be in the wrong place at the right time somehow sums up the lack of success experienced by British would-be revolutionaries.

Leon Trotsky once tried to identify, in characteristically leaden prose, an important British political phenomenon:

> ... the most radical elements of the contemporary British Labour Movement are mostly of Scotch or Irish race. The union in Ireland of social with national oppression, in face of the sharp conflict of an agrarian with a capitalist country, gives the conditions for sharp changes in consciousness. Scotland set out upon the road of capitalism later than England; a sharper break in the life of the masses of the people causes a sharper break in political reaction.

In more comprehensible English, why is 'the Celtic fringe' so important to the history of the British Left? Invariably, the Welsh, Irish or Scots have played significant roles out of proportion to their numbers. In part this reflects a political interest and consciousness often more aware and informed than in England. These national groups have had much to complain about. The Irish famine in the 1840s, for instance, led to mass migration to Scotland, where the nineteenth-century 'clearances' of the Highlands later forced thousands of people out of their homes and generated a lasting sense of outrage. Irish famine victim and Scottish clearance refugee alike were often sucked into Glasgow which by 1914 had a population of one million and several of the worst slums in Europe with over 1,000 people to an acre in some particularly squalid areas.

John Maclean was born in Pollokshaws near Glasgow in 1879. Both his parents had witnessed the clearances at first hand as children and Maclean's grandmother never let the small boy forget what anguish had been caused. He was brought up under a strict Calvinist regime and although he became a Marxist early on in his life and used to join left-wing friends in playing cricket on Sundays in order to scandalise the elders of the kirk, some of this Calvinism clung to him until his death. A non-smoker, teetotal and heartily opposed to gambling as 'counter-revolutionary', even his best friend James MacDougall could not claim much for Maclean's levity: 'He had little sense of humour, and when ... he introduced a joke ... it was clumsily done.'

Maclean trained as a teacher and, by studying at nights, obtained a part-time MA at Glasgow University in 1904. By this time, however, his complete and absorbing passion was left-wing politics. Influenced by Robert

Blatchford's writings and then by Marx – he once declared '*Merrie England* is the primary school of socialism, but *Das Kapital* is the University' – he joined Hyndman's Social Democratic Federation (SDF) in late 1902 in spite of the fact that the SDF, weak in England, was even weaker in Scotland.

Maclean threw himself into political agitation, holding hundreds of open-air meetings and expounding Marx's ideas tirelessly. Maclean called himself 'a dispeller of ignorance' and even his summer holidays were devoted to propaganda tours in Scotland and the north of England. He attracted extraordinarily large numbers of students for classes which, as his lecture notes show, called for hard, abstract thinking. At one point his regular weekly attendance in Glasgow was 493, a figure inconceivable today. There is no doubt that Maclean was helped by his considerable powers of oratory, which have been hinted at by MacDougall. He was writing about an occasion in 1914 when Maclean was fiercely opposed to the war:

> Who that ever saw can forget the tense, drawn face of the orator, his broad features, high prominent cheekbones, his heavy, bushy eyebrows, firm, cleanshaven mouth, his glowing eyes, and the stream of natural eloquence that fell from his lips? As he drove on, his prematurely grey hair shone in the reflected light of the street-lamps, and his forehead became covered with sweat. The soul of the man leapt out of his eyes and took possession of that vast audience. Not a man, woman or child but knew that they saw a David before them casting defiance against the capitalist Goliath. They knew that all the organised power of the British state was against him, ready to crush him whenever the ruling parties in London might say that it would further their cause. His hearers knew that for these precious words of exhortation and of hope the man would have to pay, and pay dearly.

It is surprising that Maclean found the time to get married, but his wife Agnes must soon have realised that she and their two daughters Jean and Nan would come second to his political work. Eventually, Agnes made her husband choose between her and politics: he chose politics. Maclean regretted their separation, imploring Agnes to return, but not if it meant giving up his propaganda.

It was the outbreak of war in August 1914 that brought Maclean to prominence. As already seen, some left-wing leaders such as Hyndman and Blatchford welcomed the chance to fight Germany as they had always inveighed against 'the German menace'. They were patriots first, socialists second. Maclean opposed the war. Still based in Glasgow, which was an important munitions and shipbuilding centre, he led the campaign against the raising of rents, against conscription and against 'dilution' under which trade unions agreed to accept the temporary suspension of certain labour customs and practices for the duration of the war.

In 1915, after a dispute with his headmaster, Maclean lost his teaching job and became a full-time revolutionary. He supported himself from the fees received for his classes and by the sale of political pamphlets. In 1916 he was sentenced to three years' imprisonment after a typically inflammatory speech and had to endure the harsh Scottish prison conditions. His spirits were lifted by the October 1917 Revolution in Russia, which seemed to confirm his diagnosis of impending capitalist collapse and also gave revolutionaries a sense that history was indeed on their side. As one of Maclean's colleagues, Harry McShane, later wrote of this revolution's impact: 'We had only known working-class revolt; now we could talk about working-class power.' Maclean's growing international reputation was shown by his appointment in February 1918 as the Bolshevik Consul in Glasgow, a post in which he tried to advocate Soviet interests.

Released from gaol, Maclean was soon back there again in 1918 after further 'seditious' speeches brought a harsh sentence of five years' imprisonment. Maclean suspected the prison authorities of poisoning his food. According to the evidence available, this seems unlikely. More probable is that Maclean's unending labours had brought about a nervous breakdown. To mark the end of the war in late 1918 he was released early.

Most men would have convalesced and taken it easy for a few months. But not Maclean. Like Keir Hardie before him, he never for a moment doubted the righteousness of his beliefs or that he must devote himself body and soul to communicating them, whatever the cost.

When the war ended the authorities were worried about possible threats to political stability from a number of sources. The suffragettes planned to continue their often violent campaign for the vote and the troops soon realised they were not returning to 'homes fit for heroes'. Many of them were fed up at the slowness of demobilisation or at the prospect of being sent to Russia to fight in the war launched by fourteen Western European countries in an attempt to crush the new Bolshevik regime. Various mutinies broke out in Britain, details of which are still being uncovered by historians, but Winston Churchill wrote that 'in several cases considerable bodies of men were for some days entirely out of control.' Police forces in parts of the country went on strike, as too did the workforce in many industries. In Glasgow, or 'Red Clydeside' as it was dubbed by journalists, the strike was led by the engineers who called for a forty-hour week. By the end of January 1919 things were coming to a head, although, as already mentioned, Maclean himself was away lecturing in the north of England.

On 31 January 1919 the strikers planned to march to the Council Chambers in George Square, Glasgow. The authorities feared that the strikers might be prepared for an uprising and were worried that many of the marchers had only recently been well-trained soldiers. Scotland Yard's Director of Intelligence noted, 'It must be remembered that in the event of rioting, for the first time in history, the rioters will be better trained than the troops.'

Between 30,000 and 40,000 marchers gathered and then set off in an orderly fashion. On reaching the Square, however, they were attacked by the police who seem to have completely lost their heads and lashed out indiscriminately with their batons. One newspaper described the scene: 'The square soon assumed the appearance of a miniature battlefield. Figures prone and sitting strewed the ground.' Scores of arrests were made and the wounded were taken inside the Chambers where the ground floor began to resemble, in the words of another journalist, 'a field hospital during the war. Dozens of the victims were laid out on the floor . . .'

The strikers dispersed. Next day the government ostentatiously sent six tanks to Glasgow which were displayed in the streets. Armed troops were given explicit instructions that their fire should be 'effectual': 'it is undesirable that firing should take place over the heads of rioters or that blank cartridges should be used.' Such an exhibition was indeed effective. There was no further talk of revolution – not that there had been much among the strikers – and within a few days the strike was over. Why had this potential revolution come to nothing?

There were several reasons. For one thing, only sections of the Glasgow workforce, mainly the skilled craftsmen, were out on strike. The national leaderships of other unions had wanted no part in the forty-hour week agitation and therefore the strikes failed to spread outside Glasgow. Nor was there any strike pay, so it was always doubtful how long the strikers could stay out. The strikers were also unarmed and no one really contemplated using force.

Finally, the leaders of the strike had no idea what they were doing, as one of their leaders, Willie Gallacher, later admitted; we had 'no plan, no unity of purpose, watching one another and waiting for and wondering what was going to happen. We were simply playing with the masses who were behind us, although we didn't stop long enough or think deeply enough to understand it.' When the strikers were attacked by the police, the first reaction of Gallacher and the other leaders was, laudably, to get them away to safety. It is doubtful if Lenin would have responded so humanely. Unlike the British, he was prepared to accept the bloodshed that accompanied revolution.

Would Maclean's presence have made any difference? Almost certainly not. No single individual, not even Maclean, could have overcome the formidable obstacles in the way of a rising in Glasgow in January 1919. Journalists and participants later wrote lovingly of 'Red Clydeside' and Britain's 'near' revolution (in Britain revolution always seems to be 'near'), but in hindsight the discontent barely seems 'pinkish'. At the general election in December 1918, just the month before, ten out of Glasgow's fifteen constituencies had been won by Conservative candidates.

Maclean himself realised that although the Glasgow working class was upset and angry, there was a long way to go before that mood could be considered even pre-revolutionary. The authorities moved quickly to ensure that such events would not happen again and they adopted a carrot and stick approach. The carrot was the Insurance Act of 1920 which entitled some unemployed men to financial benefit; the stick was the Emergency Powers Act of 1920 that strengthened the hands of the authorities in times of crisis, as was later demonstrated during the General Strike in 1926.

One other weakness of the non-Labour Party Left was its fragmentation. A list of some of the associations brings this out. There was the SLP, SPGB, NSP, SLF, BSP, WSF, the South Wales Socialist Society (SWSS), the National Shop Stewards' Committee and the National Guilds League. All had very small memberships, which didn't stop any of them from being convinced of their own rectitude. More energy was expended in attacking the errors of their comrades than was spent assailing the Conservatives. They differed widely in their beliefs; some, as seen, had opposed the recent war, while others had revelled in it – H. M. Hyndman, for instance, had actually written to Whitehall offering to investigate the activities of 'German spy waiters' in London.

Lenin and his Bolshevik party, disgusted at the way in which the Second International, formed in 1889, had collapsed into its national divisions on the outbreak of war in 1914, were determined to found a new International. This, the Third or Comintern (Communist International), was formed in Moscow in March 1919 to direct the activities of the various national Communist Parties. Bolstered by the unique prestige of having successfully carried through a revolution, it was inevitable that the Soviet Communist Party would call the Comintern tune.

Lenin wanted to fuse the various left-wing factions in Britain into a single Communist Party and he was prepared to finance such an amalgamation. The man responsible for carrying out this process was Theodore Rothstein, a distinguished journalist and historian of Russian birth who had lived in

England for over twenty years. His role as the dispenser of 'Moscow gold' has been the subject of considerable speculation. It is difficult to know exactly how much money Rothstein had available. His son Andrew has estimated the figure at £15,000 over two years. Jim Braddock, who was on the committee which handled the Communist Party's finances, put it at £85,000 over an eighteen-month period, a massive sum when compared with the income from contributions which totalled just £7,500 over that same time.

Much ink has been spilt on the question whether, without this money, a Communist Party would have been formed in this country. It seems likely that there would have been, as most British revolutionaries could see that the sectarianism of the many factions was only helping their opponents. The biggest stumbling block was the bickering among the groups about the 'correct' attitude to be taken towards the Labour Party. But the financial assistance did finally bring most of the sects together and then ensure that the new organisation would be on the lines laid down by the Bolsheviks.

In the 'Circular of Invitation' sent out to interested groups by the committee setting up the new body, three 'fundamental bases' were laid down as imperative for unity. They were acceptance of 'the dictatorship of the proletariat', that is of working-class power and the need for forcible suppression of opponents if required; acceptance of the Soviet system as the best available; and recognition of the authority of the Comintern itself, situated in Moscow. This last condition was immediately attacked by several British revolutionaries who argued that the Russians, at a distance of several thousand miles, were not best placed to pronounce on the tactics and strategy to be adopted in Britain. As John Maclean put it, 'The less the Russians interfere in the internal affairs of other countries at this juncture, the better for the cause of revolution in those countries.'

The counter-argument was put by Theodore Rothstein who claimed that although 'every country is "peculiar"', the same social factors — modern industry, capitalism, the proletariat and now the world war — influenced them all and 'are bound to produce the same effects.' In other words, communism, or at least the Bolshevik version of it, had universal validity which outweighed the specific circumstances, whether it be its history or culture, of individual countries.

This conflict between nationalist and internationalist views might seem an academic irrelevancy. In fact, it was a battle of ideas crucial to the development of British socialism and hence of British politics. Was the non-Labour Party Left to go its own way, adapting to British circumstances and events? Or was it to cede authority to an outside organisation which, as was the case with the Comintern, was devoted to the short-term interests of the

Soviet Union and knew little about Britain. Lenin, for instance, always referred to 'John Maclean of England', which in the light of Maclean's pronounced Scottishness was a stupid mistake.

In effect, Lenin and the Comintern were calling for the European Left to be divided into two rigid and opposing camps. In one corner was to be labourism or the social democrats whom Lenin despised as weak and vacillating. In the other were to be the various Communist Parties, disciplined and determined in their pursuit of 'the class struggle'. In mainland Europe, splits within the labour movement resulted in the formation of the German Communist Party in December 1918, the French Communist Party in December 1920 and the Italian Communist Party in January 1921.

Britain, however, was different. Here the labour movement had not split apart over the war, mainly due to Ramsay MacDonald's efforts. Neither was Marxism an influential tradition. These factors meant that the British Communist Party was almost certain to be a small minority grouping. Yet the British were subject to the same rules as everyone else. The 16th thesis of the Comintern read: 'All the decisions of the Congresses of the Communist International, as well as the decisions of its Executive Committee, are binding on all parties belonging to the Communist International.' No room for doubt or equivocation there.

The Communist Party of Great Britain was formally set up in July 1920 after a meeting in London. It was founded at a time when the radical political tide of 1919 was ebbing fast. The Party claimed a membership of only 3,000 – much less than the combined total of the various groupings such as the BSP and the SLP which were absorbed into the new body. John Maclean was one person who did not join, another was Sylvia Pankhurst.

For eight years she had run, in the face of much difficulty, a newspaper called *Workers' Dreadnought*. The new Communist Party wanted to take it over, dictating policy and appointing a different editor without even consulting Pankhurst. She argued that this was typical of the authoritarian behaviour of the Party: '. . . in the weak, young, little-evolved Communist movement of this country discussion is a paramount need, and to stifle it is disastrous.' She was expelled from the Party and the newspaper closed down.

From the outset the new Communist Party showed that Moscow's wishes were imperative, no matter what was happening in Britain. One of its founder members, J. T. Murphy, attended a Comintern session at which the Soviet leaders tried to hammer the 'correct' ideas into their obstinate British comrades: 'We had *got* to learn that a Communist Party was the general staff of a class marching to civil war, that it had to be disciplined, a party organised on military lines, ready for every emergency, an election, a strike, an insurrection.'

The British Communists were prepared to jettison hard-won gains acquired over decades, such as the right to vote. The 1920 Circular of Invitation, for example, laid down that an essential principle of the new party would be 'the Soviet idea as against Parliamentary democracy ie a structure making provision for the participation in social administration only of those who render useful service to the community.' Chilling words. Who was to decide what was or was not 'useful service'? The British Communist Party also applauded the Bolshevik suppression of minority groups whose views were conveniently labelled 'counter-revolutionary'. They made no protest when Trotsky put down the rising of the Kronstadt sailors in 1922 and two years later the leadership actually wrote to *Pravda* stating that a British revolutionary government would ban groups whose policies were deemed to be against the revolution.

There was, however, little likelihood of a British revolutionary government. Britain simply was not, much though Moscow might have wanted it otherwise, in any kind of radical mood. Instead of trying to adapt itself to the difficult situation, the British Communist Party found itself lumbered with a set of policies and ideas repugnant to the majority of the population. Pleas from the Party's own supporters that this was a suicidal approach made no difference. Apart from the warnings of Maclean and Sylvia Pankhurst, even Communists such as John S. Clarke, one of the delegates at the 1920 meeting of the Comintern, argued that 'Ideas imported from Russia must be modified to suit the changing conditions'; 'To copy their [Soviet] tactics under our conditions, and without their backbone, will be the acme of folly.' A Soviet Bolshevik party, fighting desperately for its life in a civil war, understandably adopted a highly disciplined and centralised system. In Britain it was, or should have been, different.

Many early members of the Communist Party had enjoyed varied careers. John S. Clarke, for example, had been first a sailor and then at seventeen a lion tamer. He even started his own zoo in Newcastle as well as working as a journalist. There was the fiery trade union organiser Ellen Wilkinson; the historian and journalist Raymond Postgate who had been gaoled for his anti-war activities and was later to found *The Good Food Guide*; the distinguished typographer Francis Meynell; and the oddball J. Walton Newbold who dressed as scruffily as possible because he thought this made him more proletarian. When elected MP for Motherwell in 1922, he sent Lenin a telegram which claimed 'Have won Motherwell in Scotland for Communism'.

The growing centralisation of the British Communist Party meant that individuals such as Clarke and Wilkinson soon left because they disagreed with the inordinate amount of Comintern influence. Their departure exacerbated the feeling that intellectuals were 'objectively' allies of the ruling class and also helped to give the Party an exclusive class-based approach typical of no other British left-wing organisation.

John Maclean gave his reason for not joining as 'The Communist Party has sold itself to Moscow, with disastrous results both to Russia and to the British revolutionary movement.' The tragedy for Maclean and others like him was that no space remained on the British Left for any organisations other than the Labour and Communist Parties. Individuals who refused to submit to either were doomed to impotence. This isolation increased the physical and mental ill-health which now plagued Maclean. He was left very much alone; even his former colleague, Harry McShane, felt there was no alternative to joining the Communist Party.

Maclean instead set up the small Scottish Workers' Republican Party but it lacked both members and influence. He continued his exhausting round of propaganda, even though friends such as Dora Montefiore noticed that two further gaol sentences left him 'a mental wreck'. In November 1923, aged just forty-four, he caught pneumonia after he had given away his overcoat to a destitute West Indian, and he died. The Jamaican wrote to Maclean's widow Agnes: 'He was the greatest Man in Scotland one great lump of kindness and sincerity.' It was a moving epitaph to a life which had promised much but in fact achieved little.

By 1922 the fledgeling British Communist Party was in trouble. Lenin had predicted that when Britain lost much of its overseas empire its living standards would drop and the working-class would become more receptive to Marxist ideas – but there was no evidence that this prediction was coming true. The stiff and formal Marxism – or Marxism-Leninism as it was increasingly called – propagated by the Party duplicated many of the flaws of Hyndman's ideas.

The Party was stuck in a ghetto largely of its own making. Its dull and linguistically-impoverished Marxism rejected the pluralism and tolerance that had characterised much of the British Left up to 1914. Members were expected to read and then learn off by heart passages from the works of Lenin, Marx and Stalin. Talking of this era, the historian A. L. Morton remarked that 'there had to be a Marxist view of everything from biology to postage stamps':

> . . . we still had, in the Marxist education of those very early days, a form of catechism – you asked: what is a class? – and you had an answer; what is a commodity, and you had the answer. What is value? What is surplus value? And when you had grasped the answers to all the questions you were Marxists!

One critic has noted that Lenin's writings are full of aggressive words and metaphors such as camps, offensives, guerilla warfare, firing squads, shooting, attack, seize, exterminate. The Communist Party followed him in its 'militarisation' of language, turning its back on the old radical traditions of accessibility and tolerance. Party publications abound with talk of 'rank and file', 'cadres', 'vanguards', 'comrades' and so on – all terms which, like a masonic handshake, identified the faithful but excluded everyone else. And any party which called for a 'dictatorship', as in the dictatorship of the proletariat, completely misread British public opinion.

The Comintern had bought the Party its headquarters at 16 King Street, Covent Garden in 1921, but not even its subsidies could disguise the British Communists' desperate plight. Instead of examining the situation on its merits, Moscow held to a 'line' which was supposed to apply in each and every country. In Germany, France and Italy the respective Communist Parties did not have a large Labour Party to contend with; in Britain it did. No matter: Moscow's solution to the crisis was to insist that the British party was not 'Bolshevik' enough and that immediate steps should be taken to rectify this.

A Commission of Inquiry was set up headed by two young men who were very different from each other and yet who between them ran the Communist Party for the next thirty-five years. One was Harry Pollitt, an exuberant, outgoing Lancashire boilermaker who was a fine public speaker. The other was Rajani Palme Dutt, a forbidding and very serious intellectual. Sent down from Balliol College, Oxford, in 1917 for his anti-war views and then imprisoned, Dutt had returned to Oxford the next year and still obtained a First. His father was an Indian doctor, his mother was Swedish. When Harry Pollitt was in Wandsworth Prison during the General Strike of 1926 he learnt to fart the *Internationale*. It is difficult to imagine Palme Dutt having bodily functions.

Pollitt's autobiography *Serving My Time* is, at least in the first half, a lively picture of the life of a political agitator in the early years of this century. He begins with a moving portrait of his mother, a millworker who had to bring up her family on little money. The young Pollitt knew Blatchford's writings by heart and enjoyed the friendly atmosphere of the local Clarion Fellowship Cycling Club. He showed much courage in 1914 by holding open-air meetings attacking the war and was frequently manhandled and assaulted. Once he returned to his lodgings to find that he had to run a gauntlet through maimed and jeering soldiers. He was involved in virtually every left-wing campaign between 1914 and 1920 and then joined the Communist Party. Harry Pollitt was most certainly not the foreigner or opportunist that Fleet Street loved to believe made up the Party's membership.

Subsequently, however, *Serving My Time* becomes very dull as Pollitt dutifully parrots the Party line, even printing huge chunks of his speeches and articles. This mind-numbing exercise is a feature of most Communist autobiographies and starkly reflects the deadening effect of Comintern Marxism. Pollitt did once, in 1939, go against Moscow's directives and was briefly sacked from the post of General Secretary which he had held for ten years. Palme Dutt never, despite all the vagaries and inconsistencies, expressed any doubts. He edited *Labour Monthly* magazine for over fifty years, writing its 'Notes of the Month'. It is a remarkable exercise to read them and see how Dutt could argue something one month and completely contradict himself the next. For this 'British Pope', God was indeed in Moscow.

The Commission of Inquiry recommended a new conception of what the Communist Party was and should be – in effect a thorough 'Bolshevisation' which meant instituting 'democratic centralism'. This powerful doctrine, enshrined in a horrible, 'masonic' phrase, laid down that orders should flow from above down to party members – centralism yes, democratic no. Once a 'line' had been announced from on high, each Party member had to act on it unreservedly, no matter what he or she really thought. It was a concept that left no room for individual conscience let alone discussion or debate. Left-wingers like George Lansbury hated it: 'I told Lenin that the Bolshevik doctrine of discipline was abhorrent to me, that I could never put my mind into someone else's keeping.'

The Bolshevik approach – which Lenin had largely formulated during his stays in London in the early years of the century – meant the application of an authoritarianism all the more damaging because the Comintern was concerned with what Joseph Stalin in 1925 called 'Socialism in one country', that is, the Soviet Union. If Moscow knew it all, disagreement was heresy and heretics had to be reviled and then expelled. The British Communist Party operated a 'panel' system under which only people nominated by the old Executive could be elected to the new Executive. This ensured a stable and quiescent leadership: only twenty-seven men and one woman served on the Politburo (another unattractive term) between 1922 and 1952. This loyalty to Moscow was evident in the other European Communist Parties: Palmiro Togliatti effectively ran the Italian Communists between 1926 and 1964 and Maurice Thorez the French Communists between 1930 and 1964.

Such practices and beliefs explain why the national Labour Party turned down the Communist Party's requests for affiliation and in 1924 decreed that individual Communists could no longer be members of the Labour Party as well. Two years later, nearly a quarter of the Communist Party were still individual members of the Labour Party but they were then systematically expelled. The British Left was now irrevocably split between the Labour Party and the Communist Party, as Lenin had wanted, but without the sort of results he had expected.

The British Communist Party was in a catch-22 situation. Being so small it was dependent on the Soviet Union, but being dependent on the Soviet Union meant that it could not grow. The ideological hold of Moscow was confirmed when, from the middle of the 1920s, Party branches set up 'Lenin Corners'. These were shrines before which members were expected to stand reverentially for a few moments in silence. It was a deification of Lenin totally contrary to anything taught by Marx and so similar to rites within the Catholic Church as to be perverse. Moscow's hold was strengthened from 1926 when promising young Party recruits were sent to the Lenin School in Moscow where they were trained as revolutionaries in the Bolshevik mould. One indication of the closeness of the links was that Harry Pollitt claimed to have visited Moscow twenty seven times between 1921 and 1930.

In such circumstances few British Communists showed much dissent — Trotsky's expulsion from the Soviet Union in 1928 caused barely a ripple. One who did was Shapurji Saklatvala. An Indian born in Bombay to a wealthy family, he had come to Britain in 1905. 'Sak' had many political friends of all persuasions but it was his hatred of imperialism that made him join the Communist Party. In the early years of the Party some parliamentary candidates were able to stand simultaneously as both Labour and Communist Party candidates because, as we have seen, it was possible until 1924 to belong to both.

In 1922 Saklatvala was elected MP for North Battersea in London. He lost his seat in 1923 but won again in 1924. In 1926 he was gaoled for two months for sedition after a speech he delivered in Hyde Park. On the face of it, therefore, he was a model revolutionary. But, in fact, Sak had not completely discarded his background and upbringing. In 1927 he initiated his five children into the Parsee religion at a huge meeting at Caxton Hall and was promptly censured by the Party. He lost his seat in 1929 and died in London in 1936.

Saklatvala's defiance was virtually unique. On a whole range of issues the 'line' as laid down from above was absolute. The multitude of ideas put forward by William Morris, Edward Carpenter, Robert Blatchford and others was sacrificed at the altar of 'scientific socialism'. Moral questions were unimportant as too was any discussion of, say, women's issues; as David Marquand has noted, '. . . scruples are presumably as out of place in the class war as in any other war.' There was more debate whether the new newspaper, the *Daily Worker*, should carry racing tips than there was on more substantial political issues.

Nationalism was another issue which was never tackled – as John Maclean found out – and largely forgotten too was the artistic and cultural side of the movement on the grounds that this could be dealt with only 'after the Revolution'. Socialism was no longer about human beings but about power. In some places there did grow up an alternative 'red' culture, such as in Lumphinnans in Scotland, Mardy in Wales and Chopwell in Durham. Here, in or near to the 'Celtic fringe', activities included 'Red funerals' and the provision of reading rooms and bookshops. Hywel Francis and David Smith have described a few of the activities in Mardy:

> . . . there were the Young Pioneers and the 'Redlets' for the children removed from the Scouts and Wolf Clubs, competitions for boxers for Russia, and to raise a soccer team to visit the Soviet Union, 'Lenin weeks' in the coalfield and secular funerals that replaced one form of pomp with another – red ribbons in place of black ties, with wreaths in the shape of the hammer and sickle not the cross, and rendition of the 'Red Flag' or the 'Internationale' instead of Welsh hymnology . . .

But these Red Moscows were exceptional. Elsewhere the overwhelmingly working-class members of the Communist Party, many of whom were unemployed or had been victimised because of their political opinions, were isolated.

The opportunity had been there for the creation of a left-wing party which was outside of and alternative to Ramsay MacDonald's Labour Party. The remarkably high proportion of votes received by Communist Party candidates in the general elections of 1922 and 1923 – their (admittedly few) candidates averaged 25 per cent of the poll – confirmed this. But the chance was thrown away by the leadership's subordination to Moscow. Instead of trying to come to terms with all the problems of being revolutionaries in a non-revolutionary situation, they abdicated independence of both thought and action. No 'good' socialism can be built on the foundations of servility.

The nadir of this attitude came in 1928 when the Comintern decided that, owing to internal Soviet demands, Communist Parties all over the world should switch to a 'Class versus Class' stance. Again, note the jargon. What this meant was that Communists now drew no distinctions between the vast majority of people who did not think as they did. Labour Party voters and members alike were considered as 'bad' as Conservatives. It was argued that because the mainstream of the labour movement deceived the workers into the illusion of gains, they should be condemned as 'social fascists'. Social democracy was, in fact, the same as fascism.

This approach could only increase the Party's isolation and unpopularity. In 1929 Party members were advised to spoil their ballot papers at the general election, a thoroughly negative action which summed up the depths to which the Party had sunk. Over the next four years, as membership dropped to below 3,000, the Party virtually ceased to exist.

What makes this so tragic is the often admirable qualities of individual Communists. Many went to prison for their views, and during the General Strike of May 1926 most of the leadership were in Wandsworth gaol where they conducted heated political discussion on bits of toilet paper which were passed around from cell to cell. One of the prisoners, Tommy Jackson, a voracious reader, discovered the novels of Jane Austen and read them pressed against the bars in order to make as much use of the daylight as he could. Another remarkable founder member of the Party was Tom Mann, a veteran socialist who had been heavily involved in the dock strike of 1889 and whose sincerity was never doubted even by political opponents such as Philip Snowden.

Quite apart from the leaders, over 1,000 other British Communists were arrested during the General Strike, which is a remarkable tribute to their energy and courage. To join the Communist Party offered no prospect (except for the party functionaries) of material gain, but instead victimisation and the disruption of one's personal life.

The tragedy was that these sacrifices were made in the name of a cause and a Party which was unworthy of them. Because the 'New Jerusalem' had become identified with the Soviet Union, important sections of the British Left set off down a road which was certain to prove a dead end.

Part Two

From Clement Attlee to James Callaghan

'THE GOAL I ASK US TO AIM AT IS NO NEW JERUSALEM,
SIMPLY A COUNTRY WITH STABLE PRICES, JOBS FOR THOSE
WHO WANT THEM AND HELP FOR THOSE WHO NEED IT.'
Denis Healey interviewed in the *Guardian*, 17 March 1980

CHAPTER SIX

The Thirties: A New Beginning

'Marxism, in the hands of Marx and Engels, is the most fruitful conception both for the study of society and for action in it which we have yet achieved.'

A. L. Rowse, 1933

'. . . most English people [in the 1930s] were enjoying a richer life than any previously known in the history of the world: longer holidays, shorter hours, higher real wages.'

A. J. P. Taylor

'. . . if our concern is with practical politics, we do better to decide the direction of advance than to debate the detail of Utopia. We must see clearly the next stretch of the journey. But we need not spend time now in arguing whether, beyond the horizon, the road swerves left or right.'

Hugh Dalton, 1935

AFTER FAILING to cope with an economic crisis, the Labour government was soundly defeated at the subsequent general election. Several leading figures split off to form a new political party while the Labour Party swung to the Left. The militant wing within the Party was led by the MP for Bristol South East who was the son of a peer. After a bitter internecine struggle the Left was defeated and a more moderate political programme was produced. Despite further election defeats it was these policies which eventually brought the Labour Party, after more than a decade out of office, to a stunning victory at a general election.

What period does this synopsis refer to? It may sound like a summary of the 1980s, but in fact it describes the 1930s, a decade which in uncanny ways foreshadows recent events. For the election defeat of 1979, read 1931; for the Social Democrats, read MacDonald's National Labour Party; for Tony Benn, MP for Bristol South East and the son of Lord Stansgate, read

Sir Stafford Cripps, MP for Bristol South East and the son of Lord Parmoor; for the 1983 and 1987 defeats, read 1935. Of course the next question is: will there be a contemporary parallel to Labour's triumph at the 1945 election?

'The Thirties' have been much fought over by politicians and historians. Was it a 'Red Decade' in which a generation of gullible young men threw in their lot with Stalin's Russia? Or a decade of Hunger Marches, dole queues and the means test? A period dominated by a so-called 'National Government' which appeased fascism on the continent – W. H. Auden's 'low, dishonest decade'? Or a time of rising living standards for the majority; not of dole queues but of cinema queues – 20 million British people went to the cinema each week. Some 2,000 Britons may have fought for the International Brigade in Spain, 45 million didn't. There were indeed Hunger Marches, but just as significant was George V's Jubilee celebrations of 1935 which proved so popular that they were extended. Was the success of Victor Gollancz's Left Book Club a more accurate barometer of the new period than the political apathy noted by such observers as George Orwell and J. B. Priestley?

The year 1931 marked the end of the first phase in the history of the British labour movement. The Labour Party had established itself as the main opposition to the Conservative Party by squeezing out the Liberals. Keir Hardie and his successors had created a modern political party rooted in the trade union movement which was pragmatic, moderate and constitutional. The Far Left in the shape of the Communist Party was weak and unpopular.

But the problem with this first phase was that Hardie and the other pioneers had never been clear what the Labour Party should actually do now that it was here to stay. It was a formidable electoral machine certainly, but to what end? James Jupp has commented that left-wing propaganda was always better at stressing wrongs than proposing remedies, but to bring about lasting social and political change the labour movement, particularly the Labour Party, had to come up with viable programmes and policies. How best should the 'New Jerusalem' be achieved? Was it to be 'talk, talk' or – 'plan, plan'?

After Ramsay MacDonald's departure in 1931, the initial problem was to find a new leader from the handful of forty-six Labour MPs, one-half of whom had been miners, who survived the October 1931 general election. The only Cabinet minister to retain his seat, and the last of the pioneering generation of Keir Hardie socialists, was George Lansbury, and he was elected to the post by his fellow MPs.

Lansbury was only three years younger than Keir Hardie and more than seven years older than Ramsay MacDonald. Although born in Suffolk in

1859 where his father was a navvy on the new East Anglian railways, Lansbury was always identified with the East End of London. Here he was brought up and lived for the rest of his life, apart from a brief spell in Australia. Several of the individuals mentioned so far in this book have been Scots, embodying Scotland's fertile contribution to British socialism. Lansbury represented the East End's significant role.

He was certainly one of the most attractive and appealing personalities that the British Left has ever produced. Photographs of him invariably show a happy smiling man whose obvious sense of humour contrasts with the severity of, say, Keir Hardie or John Maclean. The novelist Naomi Mitchison has described what used to happen at the end of a meeting where Lansbury had spoken: 'Afterwards men and women in the audience crowded round just to touch his coat sleeve and to feel comfort and refreshment.'

Lansbury was a devoted family man and a convivial friend whose home at 39 Bow Road was open to all-comers at almost any hour. He once explained that he would rather live among his constituents and receive complaints from them in person, even if this meant a brick through the window, than just get a letter. Many MPs before and since Lansbury's day would not agree. His son-in-law, Raymond Postgate, has described Lansbury's day-to-day work in Bow:

> He was, in Bow itself, a sort of universal consultant – doing by himself the work which 'Citizens' Advice Bureaux' try to do to-day. Almost daily the house in Bow was called at by men and women who were in legal, personal or financial difficulties and wanted 'G.L.' (the initials were by now commonly used) to advise and help.

His unostentatious style of living was very different, for example, from the splendour of Ramsay MacDonald's later career. Lansbury was unusual in combining his ethical socialism – he always regarded the Bible as a revolutionary document – with a wealth of practical and administrative experience. Not only did he run his own sawmill and timber business, he was for many years the leader of Poplar Council, probably the poorest council in Britain. His efforts on behalf of his local constituents earned him the nickname 'the John Bull of Poplar'.

Lansbury was always prepared to make a stand for his beliefs. In 1912 he had resigned his seat as an MP in order to publicise his support for the suffragettes, not regaining it until 1922. In 1921 he led the movement known as 'Poplarism'. No matter how poor Poplar was, it still had to pay the same sums to central government as did much wealthier boroughs like

Westminster and Kensington. In 1921, for example, West London with a rateable value of £15 million had just 4,800 people out of work. Poplar with a rateable value of £4 million had to support 86,500 people who were unemployed. In Lansbury's words, 'the poor had to keep the poor.' Lansbury and his fellow councillors decided to do something about this injustice.

Poplar Council illegally stopped collecting the rates for outside bodies such as the police. On 29 July 1921 the councillors led by Lansbury marched five miles to the Law Courts in the Strand to put their case. Lansbury explained succinctly: 'If we have to choose between contempt of the poor and contempt of Court, it will be contempt of Court.'

In September 1921 the Poplar councillors were found guilty and were imprisoned; the men in Brixton, the women in Holloway. Over the following weeks daily processions were held outside both gaols and Lansbury often addressed the crowds through the bars of his cell. He carried on handling council business in the governor's office. After six weeks the councillors were released and a measure of 'rates equalisation' enacted.

Lansbury was also a renowned journalist, editing the *Daily Herald* and then his own weekly. Like almost all the first generation of British socialists, he was a fine speaker. A firm patriot, his programme for reform was revealingly titled *My England*. He steadfastly fought against MacDonald and Snowden's demands for economic cuts during the second Labour government.

In view of all these qualities, why wasn't this seeming paragon of a socialist a brilliant success as Labour Party leader? Lansbury was not a failure, for he certainly helped restore party morale, especially when it is remembered that the National Government had more than ten times their number of MPs. Yet essentially the Party under his leadership marked time. The main reason is that Lansbury became leader too late. By 1931 he was a man of seventy-two who had behind him years of unceasing activity. For the rest of his life he was dogged by ill-health, spending six months in hospital in 1934 after he had fallen and broken his thigh. His adored wife Bessie had died the year before. One of the big 'ifs' is what might have happened if Lansbury had led the Labour Party in the 1920s and not MacDonald. But he didn't.

There was one other reason for Lansbury's comparative ineffectiveness. He was a convinced pacifist, reflecting, along with Keir Hardie, one important and honourable strand within the British Left; in his own words, '. . . are we not taught that because Christ Himself became flesh, therefore all life is sacred?' The difficulty with this belief was that in the context of the 1930s the rise of Hitler made pacifism an almost suicidal position. To turn the other cheek to the Nazis ensured the infliction of further physical damage.

Pacifism might be claimed as a moral victory, but in human terms it entailed much suffering.

Lansbury resigned as leader at the 1935 Labour Party conference over this issue, his exit hastened by a brutally realistic and hard-hitting speech from Ernest Bevin, who argued that might had to be met by might. Lansbury spent much of the late 1930s visiting Hitler and Mussolini, trying to persuade them to change their views and actions. Like Neville Chamberlain, he had little success.

The failure of Lansbury's missions abroad should not obliterate his many achievements. His death in 1940 marked the passing of the last of 'the old guard', those individuals who had been socialists in the late nineteenth century when the labour movement was often weak and ineffective. He left only a small sum in his will, having been generous with his resources to the end. It is very moving to sit in the Tower Hamlets Local History Library and read the scores of letters sent to his family by people of every class, background and opinion who all admired and revered Lansbury. His political ideas and beliefs sprang from a deep-rooted love and affection for his own country and its people. A. J. P. Taylor has called him 'the most lovable figure in modern politics' and George Lansbury has left behind an example of personal and moral integrity which offers a benchmark for future generations.

Before 1931 there had been little interest in Marxism, but after the collapse of the MacDonald administration it became fashionable to espouse Marxist views. The writer and poet Kathleen Raine recalls: 'Not to be a Marxist then was held to be a mark either of incorrigible selfishness or lack of seriousness.' Historian Robert Blake has echoed this: 'In the 1930s it was intellectually disreputable to be a Tory – anyway if you were a young man.'

At the universities of Oxford and Cambridge two parallel actions revealed the shift in attitudes. Students were no longer such automatic members of the Establishment as they had been in May 1926 when the majority cheerfully blacklegged during the General Strike. In February 1933 the Oxford Union passed a resolution stating that 'in no circumstances' would they fight for King and country. And in Cambridge on Armistice Day, 11 November 1933, some students laid an anti-war wreath on the war memorial and were attacked by their conservative colleagues. The outrage was predictable: the Daily Express claimed that the Oxford resolution had been supported by 'woozy-minded Communists and sexual indeterminates'.

In Cambridge the October Club was founded as was a town branch of the Communist Party. Much of the intellectual excitement which surrounded the new-found interest in left-wing ideas was stimulated by a group of remarkable individuals. The careers of three successive student Communist Party organisers show how talented some of these people were. David Haden Guest was a star pupil of the philosopher Wittgenstein before teaching in Moscow, starting a 'People's Bookshop' in Battersea, London and then lecturing at University College, Southampton. His successor was Charles Madge who had to leave the university because of a relationship with Kathleen Raine. He subsequently founded the influential organisation Mass Observation which from the late 1930s pioneered the study of popular beliefs and opinions. Madge was in turn succeeded by John Cornford, a poet and political activist whose charismatic personality galvanised everyone he met. None of these students was just an armchair theorist; both Guest and Cornford were later killed fighting for the Republicans in the Spanish Civil War.

At Oxford, student radicalism was less spectacular – although even here the future Barbara Pym, surely an unlikely revolutionary, was prompted to march behind the October Club banner. The movement was guided by the economics don G. D. H. Cole, a prolific writer and lecturer who formed a one-man think tank. In addition he found the time to write a detective novel each year with his wife Margaret, herself an influential historian.

At the London School of Economics an important figure was Professor Harold Laski, a journalist and academic much loved for his inspiring lectures and his personal generosity towards his students – there were always queues outside his door as individuals waited for advice. Also a councillor in Fulham, Laski's writings explored the relationships between liberty, democracy and socialism.

Some of the students, especially in Cambridge – namely the much studied circle of Philby, Blunt, Burgess, Maclean and now John Cairncross – gave their allegiance to the Soviet Union. But the question for the majority of individuals not prepared to be spies was how could their radical mood find a suitable political expression? Which parties or groups could they join on leaving university? The Socialist League, led by Stafford Cripps, was one important outlet.

Today Cripps is best remembered for his 'austerity' measures taken to promote economic growth when he was Chancellor of the Exchequer in Attlee's post-war government. His hairshirt asceticism was a prominent feature of his own life. A lifelong teetotaller, service in the Red Cross during the First World War had destroyed his digestive system so that for the rest of his life he was a vegetarian. His two meals a day consisted of raw fruit or vegetables, soured milk, brown bread and butter with the occasional baked potato thrown in as a luxury. As if this wasn't punishing enough, he used to get up at four each morning and plunge straight into a cold bath.

Thirteen of the original twenty-eight 'Rochdale Pioneers' who each subscribed £1 in 1844 to begin the co-operative movement.

One of the imaginative tableaux used by the dockers during the strike of 1889 in order to publicise their campaign.

A FACTORY AS IT MIGHT BE.
By WILLIAM MORRIS.
With PREFACE by JAMES LEATHAM.

PRICE ONE PENNY.

INTERNATIONAL·SOCIALIST·&
TRADE·UNION·CONGRESS·1896.

·INTERNATIONAL·SOLIDARITY·OF·LABOUR·
·THE·TRUE·ANSWER·TO·JINGOISM·
·DEDICATED·TO·THE·WORKERS·OF·THE·WORLD·
·BY·WALTER·CRANE·MAY·1ST·1896·

(*above left*) Keir Hardie (1856–1915). 'He will stand out for ever as the Moses who led the children of labour in this country out of bondage' – J. Ramsay MacDonald.

(*above centre*) Robert Blatchford (1851–1943), ex-Army man who created the Clarion movement and wrote the bestseller *Merrie England*.

(*above right*) H. M. Hyndman (1842–1921), lawyer, journalist, county cricketer and the founder in 1884 of Britain's first Marxist Party.

(*left*) Walter Crane's cartoon for an International Congress of 1896 shows the influence of William Morris and the Arts and Crafts movement.

(*opposite*) A banner for the Iron and Steel Workers celebrates not just the workforce but also the means of production themselves such as the steam hammer and the Bessemer converter.

NATIONAL AMALGAMATED ASSOCIATION of IRON and STEEL WORKERS.

PUDDLING

STEAM HAMMER

BESSEMER PIT

This is to Certify that Sidney Garvey was admitted a Member of the No 1 Newport Branch of this Society in the 15th day of March 1877

GENERAL SECRETARY.   BRANCH SECRETARY.

Sidney Garvey

BOARD OF ARBITRATION

George Bernard Shaw's photograph of a young, beautiful and wistful Beatrice Webb (1858–1943).

Sidney Webb (1859–1947), indefatigable politician, writer and co-founder of the London School of Economics and the *New Statesman*.

IN THE MIDLANDS
"Mummer, why don't they forcibly feed us?"

A typically powerful cartoon by Will Dyson, Australian illustrator of the *Daily Herald*, refers to the forcible feeding of imprisoned suffragettes.

· LABOUR'S · MAY · DAY ·
DEDICATED · TO · THE · WORKERS · OF · THE · WORLD

The Labour Representation Committee beating on the doors of Parliament; inside the citadel after the 1906 election it now confronts the three evils of sweating, landlordism and monopoly.

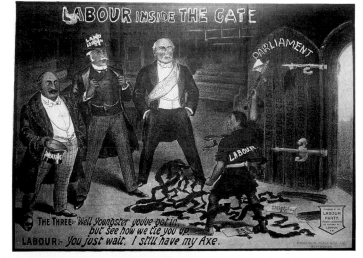

The twenty-nine Labour MPs after the 1906 election. Keir Hardie is in the centre, Ramsay MacDonald is second on Hardie's right and Philip Snowden is eighth from the right in the back row.

Philip Snowden (1864–1937) photographed just after he had vilified his former colleagues in the general election of October 1931. With him is his wife Ethel, herself a socialist pioneer.

The annual Durham Labour Women's Gala in the 1920s. Dr Marion Phillips, Labour's first Woman's Officer, is in the centre. On her left is a very elegant Jennie Lee, later wife of Aneurin Bevan and creator of the Open University.

A tank on patrol in London during the General Strike of May 1926: the iron fist inside the velvet glove?

Ramsay Macdonald (1866–1937) with Britain's first ever woman Cabinet minister, Margaret Bondfield (1873–1953), Minister of Labour between 1929 and 1931.

GREET THE DAWN:
GIVE LABOUR IT'S CHANCE

MEN & WOMEN WORKERS
YOUR CHANCE AT LAST!

POLLING BOOTH
OPEN

NO HANDS
WANTED

WORKS
CLOSED

THE WORKS ARE CLOSED!
BUT THE BALLOT BOX IS OPEN
VOTE
LABOUR
IN YOUR OWN INTERESTS!

WORDS
WORDS WORDS
WORDS WORDS
WORDS WORDS
WORDS WORDS
WORDS

MERE EMPTY WORDS
THE
CONSERVATIVE
BIG NOISE

VOTE
LABOUR
AND GET SOMETHING DONE
TO ENSURE
PROSPERITY FOR ALL

LABOUR

"WHEN THEY KEEP GIVING ME NEW TOYS
ISN'T IT NATURAL THAT I'D WANT TO PLAY
WITH 'EM?"

DON'T
TOUCH

Presents
from
PEACE LOVING
NATIONS

WAR

POISON GAS

CAN AND WILL MAKE
A LAND FIT FOR
HEROES TO LIVE IN

Examples of some of the
powerful visual propaganda
used by the Labour Party in
the 1920s.

Cripps, who was born in 1889, came from what was originally a Conservative background. His father, for many years a Tory MP, was ennobled but then shifted his political allegiance over to Labour and served in both Ramsay MacDonald administrations. Cripps was sent to Winchester and then won a scholarship to Oxford, although he actually studied at London University because the science facilities were much better there. In the 1920s he established a formidable reputation at the Bar and became the youngest KC in 1927. But whereas other barristers were usually happy to take the money and run, Cripps was always prepared to represent trade unions at little or no charge. For example, he argued the miners' case at the inquiry into the Gresford colliery disaster in September 1934 in which 265 men were killed. Cripps' summing-up lasted fourteen hours and extended over three days.

His undoubted talents marked him out for political office and in January 1931 he was elected MP for Bristol East at a by-election. Serving as MacDonald's Solicitor-General he was a moderate member of the administration and when in August 1931 MacDonald asked him to join the National Government it took Cripps twelve days of agonising before he turned down the offer. But then Cripps, like many other people who remained in the Labour Party, swung sharply leftwards in reaction to the collapse of MacDonald's government and the election catastrophe.

In October 1932 he helped set up the Socialist League which was a ginger group endeavouring to provide ideas and research for the use of the Labour Party. Its membership ranged from J. T. Murphy, a gifted writer and organiser who had been a founder member of the Communist Party but had since been expelled, to the young Michael Foot and Barbara Betts (later Castle), to the outstanding journalist H. N. Brailsford. Another recruit was Sir Charles Trevelyan, the park gates of whose mansion in Northumberland were decorated with the hammer and sickle. But it was Cripps who soon dominated the League, both intellectually and also financially, helping to support a body which never had more than 3,000 members.

In a series of pamphlets and lectures he argued that any future Labour administration must, on election, be prepared to take drastic emergency action if it was serious about introducing radical change in Britain. In *Can Socialism Come by Constitutional Methods?* he suggested that a socialist government might have 'to make itself temporarily into a dictatorship'. It should abolish the House of Lords and if necessary prolong the life of Parliament for a further term 'without an election'. He hinted too at electoral reforms 'to eliminate the power of money.' In one article he advocated passing a statute which would give the government the power to control all financial dealings in the City of London; this legislation would not be subject to judicial review. He then went on to demand that 'the whole financial machinery' of Britain and not just the City should be taken over by the state.

It was a bold series of proposals and in January 1934 Cripps aimed his fire at an even more controversial target. In what became known as his 'Buckingham Palace speech', he suggested there might be royal opposition to any radical government. The subsequent outcry caused Cripps to back down smartly.

If you read Cripps' writings today, several points emerge. Like his aunt, Beatrice Webb, he placed inordinate faith in 'experts'. At one point he claimed that the working of several measures 'is not a matter for submission to the electorate, [it] is a matter for the experts' – no doubt Cripps and the Webbs among them. He was often inconsistent, one moment calling for 'a temporary dictatorship', the next attacking the right wing for associating socialism with dictatorship.

Above all, like many of the British Left before and since, Cripps gave no indication as to how any future Labour government was to be achieved. In 1933 and 1934 such an eventuality appeared remote but Cripps just blithely assumes it would happen. The League had virtually no contact with the trade unions who were the power brokers in the labour movement. The General Secretary of the TUC, Walter Citrine, attended one League meeting and his account of what happened sums up the yawning gulf between power and posture:

> It was altogether an interesting meeting and in response to an invitation to meet the group again I wound up by saying that I thought we had come to discuss practical politics. What I had found, however, was that we were discussing ultimate Socialist objectives of a theoretical character. I did not propose to waste my time further in doing so.

Cripps' aggressive rhetoric often obscured the valuable work done by other members of the League. Its first chairman was an able civil servant, E. F. Wise, who died tragically young in November 1933. The list of League publications show the fruits of much more detailed thinking than that produced by Cripps. G. D. H. Cole, for instance, published study guides which dealt with the gold standard, the Bank of England, banking generally and credit control. Harold Laski was another regular contributor.

But the research side of the League's activities was often overlooked because of the confrontational stance favoured by Cripps. Ben Pimlott has noted that the League 'merely grouped together the party intellectuals in an inward-looking huddle which enabled them to reinforce their own convictions without the distasteful need for compromise.' He continued, in words which are relevant beyond the 1930s, 'the more the League kept its own company the more it became convinced of its own rightness.'

In early 1937 the League embarked on a suicidal joint campaign with the Independent Labour Party and the Communist Party in calling for a Popular Front, which led to its inevitable disaffiliation and closure. The impotence of the Labour Left was brought home in 1939 when both Cripps and Aneurin Bevan were expelled from the Labour Party. One permanent outcome of Cripps' efforts in the 1930s was the weekly newspaper *Tribune* which in years to come provided a rallying point for the Labour Left.

The Socialist League was a failure. How successful was the political organisation further to its Left, the Communist Party of Great Britain? Still mired in the foolish 'Third Period' which called for the vilification of all non-Communists, it was not able to take advantage of the collapse of MacDonald's government. Instead of offering a constructive alternative to the Labour Party it spent its time initiating breakaway unions such as the United Clothing Workers' Union and the United Mineworkers of Scotland, both of which challenged the idea of solidarity that was a touchstone of labour sentiment.

Internationally the Comintern completely misjudged events. It claimed that Hitler's accession to power in January 1933 was devoid of political significance and ordered that no Communist Party should discuss this decision. None did. Belatedly, the Comintern realised that it should be trying to build alliances rather than destroying them and gradually by 1935 it moved to a 'Popular Front' policy. Non-Communists now were to be flattered and, if possible, worked with.

The British party was slow to change tack. It had taken much effort to get it to fall in behind the previous 'Third Period' line and as late as 1935 its programme was called simply *For A Soviet Britain*, which shows how out of touch the Party was in that the electorate was hardly likely to welcome what was seen as a 'foreign' government. The difficulty for the Party when it did come around to a Popular Front approach was that the need for such a broad alliance was less immediately obvious in Britain than in say France or Spain where working-class organisations were split into a variety of often antagonistic factions. Here, as trade union leaders like Citrine argued, there already existed a united or Popular Front made up of trade unions, the Labour Party and the Co-operative movement.

Many members of the Labour Party and the trade unions were also well aware that just a few years before they had been abused as 'social fascists'.

The publisher Victor Gollancz who became a stalwart of the Popular Front apparently never knew that the Communists had ever had any other policy (Orwell commented in his usual acerbic way that 'It's frightful that people who are so ignorant should have so much influence'). Others were less ignorant, recalling that Communist candidates stood against Labour Party candidates at elections and that the Party had promoted breakaway unions.

The Popular Front campaign represented an attempt to heal the post-1917 split in the labour movement between moderates and militants. It proved a failure – it was eighteen years too late. When the Communist Party applied to affiliate to the Labour Party in 1935 the request was turned down on two grounds. First of all there was the argument that the Communist Party's call for 'the dictatorship of the proletariat' was in conflict with the Labour Party's 'defence of political democracy'. Secondly, the request stemmed from the Comintern's change of tactics and not from any principled stand.

The Communist Party challenged the National Council of Labour to scrutinise its accounts in order to disprove 'Moscow gold' accusations – the offer was never taken up – and in 1937 the Communist Party obligingly dropped the idea of the dictatorship of the proletariat. The *Daily Worker* omitted the Hammer and Sickle emblem and slogan 'Workers of the World, Unite!' from its front page. But still the Labour Party refused affiliation.

As it turned out, the Labour Party was correct in its assessment. If the Communist Party really had changed its spots it would have candidly faced up to its own past. It didn't. In 1937 the veteran Communist Tom Bell, another Scot, published a short history of the Party which dealt with the 'Third Period' in some detail. This was heresy. As the Party was now in favour of a Popular Front, then it must always have been in favour of a Popular Front. Bell's book was vitriolically reviewed in *Labour Monthly* by the journalist and typographer Allen Hutt. The Communist Party leadership quickly 'withdrew' Bell's book, writing to all individual members demanding that anyone who had bought a copy should return it immediately to Party headquarters – hardly an example of the tolerance and freedom of debate which should have characterised the Popular Front.

The myth of Party infallibility ensured that fresh Party recruits were frequently unable to understand the zig-zags in policy and soon left. The turnover of members in Brighton, for instance, was so rapid that the whole Party changed every two years. Even internal Party publications admitted that members were sometimes unable to answer criticisms when the 'line' was altered: '. . . it must be confessed that too often our Party comrades are baffled in their attempts to answer such questions and need to have recourse to others to help them out of their difficulties.' In the summer of 1939 the

Party line was to change once more, its third major reversal in less than a decade – and then again two years later in 1941.

Between 1935 and 1939 the Party was prepared to go to almost any lengths to curry favour. The Young Communist League announced that it welcomed recruits from members of religious groups, boy scouts and girl guides while on May Day 1938 leading Scottish Communists paraded in tartan bearing pictures of such unlikely early Communists as Robert Bruce, William Wallace, Robbie Burns and Robert Louis Stevenson. Membership did grow, reaching over 17,000 in 1939. Freed from the Comintern's shackles because Moscow during the Popular Front period now recognised the validity of 'national roads to socialism', Marxism for the first time established a significant presence in Britain.

Most historians still concentrate on the much-tilled and academically respectable soil of the Auden, Spender, Day Lewis, MacNeice grouping. This selectivity overlooks the many individuals whose commitment to the Left proved much more lasting and fruitful. The late 1930s saw a flowering of radical work. Apart from Marxist scientists like J. D. Bernal, J. B. S. Haldane, Hyman Levy and Joseph Needham there were Marxist musicians such as Alan Bush who founded the Workers' Musical Association in 1936. Francis Klingender and others set up the Artists' International Association. Many people, including Paul Robeson, were involved in Unity Theatre in London and its branches outside the capital.

Of the historians and critics, outstanding figures included Edgell Rickword, Montagu Slater, Ralph Fox, Christopher Caudwell, A. L. Morton, Jack Lindsay, Alick West, T. A. Jackson, Gordon Childe, Rex Warner, Randall Swingler, Dona Torr, James Boswell, A. L. Lloyd and Professor George Thomson. There were new magazines such as *Left Review* and *Modern Quarterly*, the Marx Memorial Library and Workers' School was founded, and the Communist Party publishers Lawrence and Wishart began to bring out English-language versions of Marx's works. Every single person mentioned above remained 'on the Left' for the remainder of their lives, displaying a resilience which has reminded E. P. Thompson of the tenacity of eighteenth-century dissenters. Many of them lived close to each other in north Essex and formed a kind of alternative left-wing community.

What is remarkable about this Marxism of the mid-1930s was that, unlike in the 1960s and 1970s, it was not primarily the work of academics. In the 1930s it was not always advisable for left-wing dons to publicise their opinions: historian Christopher Hill published his early work under the pseudonym C. E. Gore, Joseph Needham was also 'Henry Holorenshaw' and Cambridge economics don Maurice Dobb was the anonymous editor of the volume *Britain Without Capitalists*. This Marxist tradition was deliberately non-academic, avoiding jargon and impenetrable prose because it was aimed at a largely non-university educated audience.

It was noticeable that many other university socialists such as G. D. H. Cole and R. H. Tawney, however eminent, were heavily involved in the adult education movement. This meant they had to explain their ideas before very varied audiences. In the preface to one of his books, R. H. Tawney paid tribute to his adult education classes: 'The friendly smitings of weavers, potters, miners, and engineers, have taught me much about the problems of political and economic science which cannot easily be learned from books.'

One splendid example of how to write for a general readership without being patronising was provided by Professor J. B. S. Haldane, a scientist from a distinguished family (his sister was Naomi Mitchison) who was renowned for his courage in trying out experiments with himself as the guinea pig. Professor of Genetics and then of Biochemistry at London University, Haldane's academic credentials were impeccable. But he was not afraid of popularising his ideas, writing a book for children and from 1937 a weekly column in the *Daily Worker* which ran to 345 articles in all, each of them a lucid and concise summary of an often abstruse topic. The *Daily Worker* itself, although unable to see the Soviet Union as anything other than a workers' paradise, was on any subject non-Soviet a splendid and vigorous read. Claud Cockburn was one of its regular contributors. The newspaper reached a circulation of over 100,000 on Saturdays.

The Left Book Club was one of the most influential creations of the late 1930s. It was run by the publisher Victor Gollancz. The idea for a membership club had first been floated in the United States: members who signed up received a monthly choice and could then choose other titles at reduced prices. In the summer of 1936 the Left Book Club was formally established. The three people who chose and commissioned the books were Gollancz, Harold Laski and the writer John Strachey. Neither Gollancz nor Laski were members of the Communist Party; nor was Strachey, who was regarded as a more valuable asset if he didn't join.

Strachey, whose uncle was the writer Lytton Strachey, had been a Labour MP and initially flirted with the New Party set up by Sir Oswald Mosley after he had resigned from MacDonald's government. Strachey then swung sharply to the left, rather like Sir Stafford Cripps. In the 1930s he published three lengthy books that were Marxist in tone and were produced under the supervision of the Communist Party's chief ideologist, Palme Dutt. Even more successful was his shorter work *Why You Should Be A Socialist*, which sold over 300,000 copies.

Dutt and the Communist Party leadership saw the Left Book Club as a valuable recruiting ground. Dutt once wrote to Strachey claiming that the Club's success was 'probably the greater because it is recognised by the general public as an independent commercial enterprise on its own feet, and not the propaganda of a particular political organisation.' But Gollancz was less astute in the general message of the books, as his biographer has pointed out: '... his propaganda alienated from the outset all Tories and most Liberals and anti-communist Labour. Bereft of other friends, Victor was thrown into the arms of the Communist Party.' Of the Club's first twenty-seven books, fifteen were by Communists. But, in the context of the Popular Front, this did not prove to be a handicap. Membership climbed to 60,000, organised into 1,300 groups and kept informed by the monthly *Left News*.

Digesting the Left Book Club publications today is something of a slog. A. J. P. Taylor thought that the Club was a safety valve in which reading became 'a substitute for action, not a prelude to it'; Club members 'worked off their rebelliousness by plodding through yet another orange-covered publication.' The most accessible books are generally the less political volumes such as George Orwell's *The Road to Wigan Pier* and Wilf Macartney's *Walls Have Mouths* about British prison conditions.

The official historian of the Left Book Club presents the project as one of sweetness and light. It wasn't. The Labour Party in the shape of one of its leading figures, Hugh Dalton, began to manoeuvre for space in *Left News* and for places on the editorial board. The Communist Party also demanded official representation while local readers' groups campaigned for a measure of internal democracy. Gollancz vacillated between the various vested interests. He turned down Orwell's book about the Spanish Civil War, *Homage to Catalonia*, before a word had been written as he knew that Orwell would offend the Communists by his views. At the same time Gollancz planned to include two prominent Liberals on the selection committee and to rename the Club the Anti-Fascist Association in order to widen its appeal. Gollancz's energy did much to make the Club a success, but he was wildly over-optimistic in his aims: 'I believe, as I have always believed, that we shall eventually reach a quarter of a million [members].'

In fact any future plans for the Club were dashed by the signing of the Nazi-Soviet Pact in August 1939 which shattered Gollancz's faith in the Communist Party. The Left Book Club declined rapidly, although it was not, in fact, officially wound up until 1945. It is difficult to assess the power and influence of ideas; A. J. P. Taylor might have been rude about the Club, but there is no doubt that it played a part in liberalising the British middle classes – with results that became evident both during and after the war.

Within the mainstream labour movement fresh thinking was hampered, as it often still is, by the cumbersome institutional machinery set up by the Labour Party in 1918. Resolutions to conferences were cobbled together into 'composite' resolutions, which were then briefly and superficially debated at Conference (the 'debate' occurring among delegates who had usually made up their minds already or were mandated to vote in a certain way regardless of the excellence of the different arguments voiced). The resolutions next needed to be passed by the trade union block vote that was ideal for stopping new ideas or initiatives but feeble at promoting them. With so many interest groups at work inside the Labour Party and the larger trade unions – and Britain was renowned for the huge number of different unions it had, particularly when compared with Germany or France – then 'logrolling' made it easy for one group to scotch a proposal which was potentially threatening: 'I'll stop this resolution for you if you help stop that one for me.' Such practices persist to this day.

In addition, as G. D. H. Cole and many others pointed out, the Labour Party had no proper research facilities with which to formulate and discuss ideas or policies. In any case the labour movement had traditionally distrusted what it thought of as 'cleverness'. By contrast the Conservative Party, often dismissed as 'the stupid party', had established a research department in 1929. The bureaucratic shambles was all the more obstructive in the 1930s because the union response to '1931' was to tighten their grip on the Labour Party. Never again would a MacDonald dazzle and dominate the movement over the heads of union bosses.

A National Joint Council of trade union and Labour Party leaders was set up in 1932 which met the day before the Labour Party's own body, thus pre-empting and vetting contentious issues. Referring to the union hold over the Labour Party in this decade, historian Henry Pelling has called it 'the General Council's party'. The trade unions were not given to rigorous analysis of the current situation. Swiftly putting an end to the idea of renaming the Labour Party the Socialist Party, they put their weight behind professional and competent party leaders whom they could trust, such as Clement Attlee and Herbert Morrison.

In effect the trade unions still had to move away from the first phase of the British labour movement, namely that of foundation and consolidation. They were, understandably, concerned above all to protect their members' interests, mainly levels of pay and working conditions. These were essentially sectional and industrial concerns and it was often difficult for the unions to move on from them and develop broader political and national strategies. One telling demonstration of this: few if any of the trade unions in the 1930s possessed research departments.

Take the issue of unemployment which was at the heart of domestic politics in this decade. If the National Government had few suggestions about what might be done, the trade unions had even less. What in fact did the TUC do in the 1930s? What programmes did it hammer out, what publications did it issue? Nothing. Instead the TUC came up with the idea of creating unemployed clubs and issuing their members with . . . chess sets and footballs. The only controversial action with which the TUC was involved in this decade came when Walter Citrine accepted a knighthood in 1935, to the disgust of some in the labour movement.

The TUC's paralysis of nerve inevitably spread to the Parliamentary Labour Party, which was unduly cautious and timid. The only political success came in 1934 when Herbert Morrison led Labour to its first ever victory at the London County Council elections. Otherwise the National Government under MacDonald and then Baldwin was able to coast along undisturbed by its opponents. Looking back at this period, John Saville has delivered a bleak but accurate assessment:

> . . . the most striking political characteristic of the 1930s was the way in which successive Conservative governments were able to ignore, on all fundamental matters, the Labour Party inside Westminster and the political and industrial movements outside.

For some on the Left, subscribers to the 'betrayal thesis' which claims that trade union and Labour leaders are always traitors and cowards, this caution was just further evidence of personal weakness. It was not as simple as this. Weak leadership reflected a weak membership – or perhaps non-membership as the trade unions lost nearly half their total number between 1920 and 1933. Apathy and political demoralisation were widespread. Turnouts at elections dropped. Mass Observation's 1939 study *Britain* revealed a politically ignorant population, while in Scotland things were so bad that the authorities encouraged the playing of football not as an antidote to revolution but in an attempt to wake people up a bit. With his usual bluntness, Orwell pointed out that although a great deal of money was raised for the Republican side in the Spanish Civil War it probably represented less than 5 per cent of the sum spent on the football pools each week. He lamented that 'there is no turbulence left in England.'

Is that it then? The 1930s as a total write-off for the British left? In terms of immediate and practical results, yes. But, with hindsight, it is clear that the groundwork was being painstakingly laid for the political transformation of the 1940s and the creation of a consensus of opinion which dominated both Labour and Conservative thinking until the late 1970s.

Crucial to this 'middle way' opinion during the 1930s was its largely 'non-party political' character. Contributors to this mood – it was too vague to categorise as a movement – ranged from the Conservative Harold Macmillan to Liberal John Maynard Keynes and to socialists Hugh Dalton and Evan Durbin. All recognised the value of patience, appreciating that the National Government's huge majority ruled out the 'quick fix' in favour of the long haul'.

The most important influences were the measures of planning and state intervention used by the Soviet government as it embarked on its Five Year Plan in 1928, apparently completed within four years. The Soviet experience provided a fruitful example and not a rigid and doctrinaire blueprint which had to be followed down to the last detail. No one could accuse, say, Harold Macmillan or Hugh Dalton of being 'fellow travellers' and in any case the Soviet lesson was reinforced by the success of President Roosevelt's 'New Deal' in the United States.

The genesis of the British approach can be traced back to Macmillan's joint authorship of *Industry and State* in 1928 and the Liberal manifesto *We Can Conquer Unemployment* in 1929. The pace quickened in the 1930s when it became clear that neither orthodox Conservatism nor traditional ethical socialism could deliver the economic growth needed to reduce unemployment.

In 1931 *Weekend Review* published a National Plan for Britain, calling for state intervention, a series of Five Year Plans, 'economic democracy' and equality of sacrifice. The overwhelming response led to the foundation of PEP (Political and Economic Planning) in October 1931. Both this body's name and the title of its journal, *Planning*, indicated the 'big idea' of the 1930s progressives. The Next Five Years Group also issued several policy documents and its wide membership formed what was in effect a British Popular Front. Macmillan published *The Middle Way* in 1938, which called for a Minimum Wage Act, a National Investment Board and planning for full employment. Outside bodies like the Pilgrim Trust explored in a non-partisan way *Men Without Work*. John Boyd Orr studied the question of diet. The Women's Health Inquiry Committee researched into *Working-Class Wives*, journalists such as George Orwell and Fenner Brockway helped to publicise how the other half – or more – lived. On and on it went.

There could be no uniformity or 'party line' in this maelstrom of ideas, except that they recognised that the traditional economic orthodoxy of free trade, the gold standard and balanced budgets were now the discarded relics of the Victorian age. Always stimulating and provocative, none of the publications could be written off as the work of 'party hacks'. Taken as a whole they amounted to a body of material which was more impressive than anything produced by the Labour Party or the trade unions and more constructive too than the majority of Left Book Club publications.

Important contributions were, however, made by members of the Labour Party, often individuals sponsored by the domineering and noisy character of Hugh Dalton, possibly the most important left-wing figure of the 1930s. Not only did Dalton help shift the Labour Party's foreign policy away from a quasi-pacifism towards outright opposition to Hitler and Mussolini and the consequent need to accept rearmament, he also in the long-term developed the new economic and political thinking of the time, making it acceptable to the Labour Party.

On the face of it, Dalton was an unlikely recruit to the Labour Party, although as Kenneth Morgan notes the Labour Party has always been a 'remarkably generous refuge for social eccentrics'. Born in 1887, Dalton's father had been the personal tutor to the future King George V and was now a Canon at Windsor Chapel. Hugh was sent to Eton and then King's College, Cambridge, where he fell under the spell of the poet and Fabian Rupert Brooke. Another important influence was Keir Hardie who visited the university in February 1907 and whose character so impressed Dalton that he always regarded 'Keir Hardie Night' as 'his own, personal, Damascus Road': 'I admired his total lack of fear or anger, his dignified bearing, his simplicity of speech and thought and faith . . .'

After war service in Italy, Dalton was appointed a lecturer at the London School of Economics. An unhappy marriage and the tragic death of his young daughter meant that from the 1920s Dalton began to channel his formidable energies exclusively into the Labour Party. That he should have thrown in his lot with the Labour Party, and apparently faced no prejudice despite his privileged background, shows how the Party was expanding away from the predominantly working-class character of its early days.

Dalton was never an easy man to get on with, always gossiping and intriguing, and his personal antipathy towards his old tutor John Maynard Keynes perhaps delayed the acceptance of Keynes' ideas within the Labour Party. Keynes argued that 'The outstanding faults of the economic society in which we live are its failure to provide for full employment and its arbitrary and inequitable distribution of wealth and income.' Government intervention, if selective and planned, could help boost the economy by means of the multiplier and increase consumption when necessary. It was a mistake to try and balance the budget year by year. Instead of being a passive 'nightwatchman' adjudicating between rival claims, the government should adopt an energetic and active role – behave as a player rather than a referee or umpire.

Although his *General Theory* was not published in book form until 1936, the general direction of Keynes' ideas had been known for several years before that. Dalton and others realised that, in Stuart Holland's words, Keynes '. . . seemed to offer a middle way between over-centralised Soviet planning and an anarchic unplanned capitalist market.' Fascism and communism were not now the only political choices on offer. Keynes had provided the necessary economic justification for European social democracy, offering a framework for piecemeal progress as opposed to revolutionary upheaval.

What distinguished Dalton and his circle from Macmillan was the greater emphasis that they as left-wingers placed on the need for equality. But they shared a preference for detail over wild assertion and for the practical over the theoretical – which is why Dalton called his most important book *Practical Socialism for Britain*. The detail was not always very exciting. Just look at the titles of three of Evan Durbin's 1930s books: *Purchasing Power and Trade Depression*, *The Problem of Credit Policy* and *Socialist Credit Policy* – hardly bedside reading. Nevertheless it was significant that Durbin and his colleagues in the New Fabian Research Bureau, set up by the indefatigable Cole, and the XYZ Club of Labour sympathisers in the City of London were prepared to go into such topics in this depth. One of the founders of the XYZ Club, Nicholas Davenport, has explained that he launched the initiative because of his concern at the vague and woolly thinking of the Left Book Club:

> I was alarmed by this Marxist programme because the Labour Party was so ignorant of the workings of the financial system that it was bound to create havoc if it attempted to put it all under government control.

Not all their thinking was the product of library work. Although the Labour Party in Britain was out of office from 1931 onwards, it could still watch and learn from social democratic parties elsewhere that did gain office. In 1938 Hugh Gaitskell admitted that left-wing governments in the past had not always been very good at handling financial and monetary problems but that now they could point to the successful administrations in Sweden, in New Zealand and also to the 'New Deal' in America. The Swedish example was especially encouraging. After winning power in 1932 the Swedish Social Democrats had launched an ambitious economic programme of government intervention and public works. They won a further election in 1939.

Dalton and his group did begin to win the intellectual arguments on the Left. Their thinking can be seen in *Labour's Immediate Programme*, adopted by the Party in 1937 and which remarkably sold over 400,000 copies in a pictorial version, and by the change in, for instance, John Strachey's views. His three 1930s books breathe Marxist fire and brimstone; in 1940 his book *A Programme for Progress* is full of New Deal sweetness and light. From the small acorns of 1930s 'middle way' beliefs grew the post-war oak trees of British economics and politics. At last, the Labour Party now possessed a proper economic blueprint. Without one, Dalton knew that the Labour Party would never succeed in winning over the electoral support of the 'middle ground' of voters who were vital if it was ever to win a majority of seats in a parliamentary system.

The Labour Party's new economic 'realism' was matched by the gradual change in its foreign policy. The 1934 Peace Ballot organised by the Peace Pledge Union had shown a high level of support for the League of Nations. The difficulty was that the League of Nations proved powerless in the face of dictators such as Hitler and Mussolini bent on aggression. For much of the 1930s the official Labour Party attitude was to stand firm against rearmament under the National Government. Not until 1937 did Dalton, Bevin and others within the Party persuade the majority that, regrettably, pious hopes were not sufficient weapons with which to oppose fascism and that Prime Minister Neville Chamberlain's policy of appeasement must be opposed.

Socialism and the British Left are not, however, just about cerebral and intellectual commitment, an affair of footnotes and research references. One essential part – the heart – must be about human feelings and loyalty to one's family, friends and community. Despite the wasteland that the 1930s represented for the British Left there were campaigns which, if not always successful in themselves, kept alive the spirit of hope and resistance. One was the Hunger Marches, led by Wal Hannington's National Unemployed Workers' Movement (NUWM). Although initially founded in 1922, it was only in the early 1930s that a series of Hunger Marches ending in rallies in London attracted public attention. The NUWM's agitation was all the more important in view of the Labour Party's failure to mount a single campaign on this issue.

Wal Hannington was an engineer and a founder-member of the Communist Party but he never got involved in disputes within the Party, concentrating instead on his trade union activities and on building up the NUWM. He made sure the NUWM was firmly rooted in each community, handling the cases of people of all political persuasions and none as they appeared before the Public Assistance Committees which decided on levels of dole money.

By 1932 the NUWM had a membership nationally of 50,000, more than ten times that of the Communist Party. It was a thoroughly legal body, sometimes to the despair of the Comintern in Moscow which occasionally, depending on which 'line' was in operation at any one time, demanded more militant action. The Hunger Marches had a galvanising effect on the towns through which they passed, particularly in the south of England where residents suddenly found the human consequences of widespread unemployment passing by their front doors. The Lancashire contingent of the 1932 march had a memorably radicalising effect on Oxford University students, as did their counterparts in Cambridge.

The NUWM gave the unemployed themselves a feeling of human worth. As one contemporary remembers, 'the constant agitation preserved above all else the sense of dignity of the unemployed man and woman. They really felt that here was a struggle they could take part in, that they weren't just on the scrap heap.' In his memoirs Hannington noted the NUWM's value in preventing the growth of fascism – in Germany, for example, the Nazis had come to power on the backs of the jobless. On one occasion the NUWM's campaign forced the government to withdraw the meagre new rates of benefit introduced at the end of 1934.

The NUWM was not the only organisation which held unemployed marches in the 1930s. The most famous was the Jarrow March of 1936 led by the town's Labour MP, Ellen Wilkinson, a remarkable person not just because of her indomitable spirit but because she was a woman. Looking back over previous chapters of this book, it is clear that the history of the British Left had been largely a masculine preserve. There were exceptions – Eleanor Marx, Annie Besant, Beatrice Webb, Sylvia Pankhurst, Mary Macarthur – but generally Mrs Marx, Mrs Hardie, Mrs Morris, Mrs Maclean and so on are background figures. Little thought had been given to what we now call 'feminism'. In fact, one of the disappointing aspects of the Communist Party in the 1920s and 1930s was that instead of exploring such issues it just reproduced a male hierarchical form of organisation. Reading the biographies and autobiographies of male socialists, invariably one comes to a thowaway paragraph where tribute is paid to the wife on whom the domestic burden fell. The wife is usually credited with the words 'I understand' or 'I don't mind'. The wives of prominent trade unionists were commonly referred to as 'trade union widows'.

Margaret Bondfield had achieved Cabinet status in MacDonald's 1929–31 government, the first woman of any party to do so. But Ellen Wilkinson was unique in the fire and zeal which she brought to her political activities. Raised in a Methodist household in Manchester, she won a scholarship to Manchester University in 1910. She then joined both the Fabians and the Independent Labour Party – again demonstrating the flexibility and tolerance of these early socialist bodies – and acted as women's organiser for the shopworkers' union now known as USDAW.

Wilkinson was a founder member of the Communist Party in 1920 but she left four years later, the same year she was elected Labour MP for Middlesbrough East. Conditions were so bad that she claimed 'Middlesbrough is a book of illustrations to Karl Marx.' She lost her seat in the 1931 debacle but was returned to Parliament in 1935 as MP for Jarrow.

If Middlesbrough was run down and depressed then Jarrow was even worse. J. B. Priestley visited the town in the autumn of 1933 and was appalled at what he found:

> One out of every two shops appeared to be permanently closed. Wherever we went there were men hanging about, not scores of them but hundreds and thousands of them. The whole town looked as if it had entered a perpetual penniless bleak Sabbath. The men wore the drawn masks of prisoners of war. A stranger from a distant civilisation, observing the condition of the place and its people, would have arrived at once at the conclusion that Jarrow had deeply offended some celestial emperor of the island and was now being punished. He would never believe us if we told him that in theory this town was as good as any other and that its inhabitants were not criminals but citizens with votes.

A tiny woman – only 4 feet 10 inches tall – and with striking red hair, Ellen Wilkinson's energy and cockiness led some sections of the Press to dub her 'Little Miss Perky' and she was certainly determined that Jarrow would not suffer in silence. She always remained on the Left: her flat in London even had a portrait of Lenin over the bed.

Knowing that parliamentary action would bring no result because of the National Government's huge majority and as a skilled journalist aware of the value of publicity, she set out on 5 October 1936 with 200 Jarrow men (ironically women were discouraged) to march to London. Again, as with the Hunger Marches of the NUWM, the official labour movement disapproved and told local Labour Party branches not to offer aid or assistance. Most disobeyed. The impact of the Jarrow March was heightened by the book that Wilkinson later published under the striking title *The Town That Was*

Murdered, issued by the Left Book Club. Once again such initiatives were instrumental in helping to shift middle-class opinion towards the Left.

The day before Wilkinson set out on the march an event took place in the East End of London which possessed both a symbolic and a practical value. In the autumn of 1932 Sir Oswald Mosley had set up his British Union of Fascists, modelling it on its counterparts in Italy and Germany. He insisted on being called 'Leader' and coached his followers to give the fascist salute. He deliberately fostered anti-Semitism with the aim of attracting more members, particularly in the East End where Jewish people proved convenient scapegoats for the poor living conditions which were none of their making.

In the summer of 1936 Mosley announced that he would lead a BUF march through the East End. The Labour Party, erring on the side of timidity as was usually the case in the 1930s, advised its members to stay indoors on 4 October 1936. The *Daily Herald*'s advice was 'Keep Away'. Thousands of people of all creeds and beliefs ignored the suggestion and formed a massive human barrier through which Mosley's fascists, despite vigorous police efforts, could not penetrate. The march had to be rerouted along the empty and deserted City of London. The Battle of Cable Street showed that fascism would not take root in Britain as it had done on the continent.

The Communist Party was in the forefront of resistance to Mosley at both Cable Street and in Bermondsey in October 1937 when another BUF march was aborted. These activities showed just how successful it was when, as had been the case with the Hunger Marches, it started from grass-roots activity and organised from the bottom up, rather than obeying orders from above. There could indeed have been an important role within the British Left for a body distinct from the trade-union dominated Labour Party.

One of the shouts at Cable Street was 'They Shall Not Pass', a slogan publicised by the Republican government in Spain which in the summer of 1936 had been attacked by General Franco's Fascists. The campaign on behalf of the Republicans was one of the great causes of the 1930s, mainly because the issues seemed so clear: an elected government had been assaulted by men demonstrably from the same stable as those in power in Berlin and Rome. Not only were enormous rallies and demonstrations held in Britain – again in opposition to the wishes of the trade union and Labour leadership which called for a policy of non-intervention – but some 2,000 Britons went to Spain to fight for the Republic. One of them, the future leader of the Transport and General Workers' Union, Jack Jones, wrote of the volunteers' feeling that 'international solidarity required something more than reading about it at home.' The overwhelming majority of recruits came from working-class homes.

That the Republicans were defeated in Spain and Chamberlain's National Government recognised the new Franco regime with indecent haste, somehow sums up the frustration which was the dominant feeling of the 1930s for the British Left. Despite the huge commitment of activists – for example, J. D. Bernal was involved in no less than thirty-five different committees in addition to his own research and a complicated personal life, and memoirs and autobiographies depict a similar pace of activity led by many others – nothing could shift the complacency of the National Government. But, at the very least, the groundwork was laid for a new and different Britain that was to emerge from the crucible of the Second World War – and campaigns such as the Hunger Marches and the 'Aid Spain' movement kept alive the spirit of revolt.

There was, however, one other reason why the Left made little headway in the 1930s. On many issues it was socialists who held the moral cards. On one they didn't and therefore sections of the British Left found themselves defending the indefensible, with terrible consequences then and with an impact still significant today.

CHAPTER SEVEN

Grand Illusions: British Socialists and Stalin in the 1930s

'What matters it whom we kill . . .'
Hugh MacDiarmid *First Hymn to Lenin*, 1931

'Shoot the Reptiles!'
Editoral headline in the *Daily Worker*, 24 August 1936

'There is no crime of Stalinism that cannot be more than matched in this century's annals of Western behaviour, in or out of Europe.'
Professor V. G. Kiernan, *The Times*, 28 October 1987

EVEN HIS political opponents liked and respected Willie Gallacher, Communist MP for West Fife from 1935 to 1950. Coming from a poverty-stricken working-class family in Scotland, Gallacher's fierce independence first showed itself at the age of nine when he played truant from the local Catholic school in protest at the regular beatings he received for not attending Mass. At twelve he began work as a grocer's delivery boy before training as an engineer. In his spare time he worked loyally as John Maclean's lieutenant, trying to spread his Marxist beliefs.

In 1920 Gallacher was a founder-member of the Communist Party of Great Britain. Imprisoned four times during his career for uttering seditious and revolutionary views, in September 1939 he was the only Member of Parliament brave enough to oppose Chamberlain's 'Munich' trip to meet Hitler. He remained devoted to his wife Jean throughout their tragic married life. Their two sons died at birth and both the boys they adopted were killed fighting in the Second World War. The widespread love and devotion that Gallacher inspired was visibly demonstrated when thousands of people took to the Fife streets for his funeral in August 1965.

Was Gallacher then a paragon of left-wing virtue? In some ways, yes. But in one crucial respect, no. Gallacher visited the Soviet Union in 1937 at the height of Stalin's purges, but saw nothing and said nothing even though the scale of the slaughter taking place around him was immense. He published one of several volumes of autobiography after the Khrushchev revelations of 1956 had shown how devastating the purges were. Yet once again he simply ignored the facts. For Gallacher, Stalin's 'excesses' had not happened.

Ivor Montagu managed a similar kind of self-deception. He was a man of extraordinarily wide interests and great charm who made films with Alfred Hitchcock, founded the International Chess Federation and was for many years non-playing captain of the British table tennis team as well as the first chairman of the International Table Tennis Federation because he was the only delegate who could speak all the necessary languages. Such was his love for his wife Hell that on her death he simply lost the will to live and died a few weeks later. Yet Montagu spent much of the late 1930s defending the Moscow Trials and the purges, reviling Stalin's victims and abusing those who defended them.

Finally, consider the case of Sidney and Beatrice Webb. Sidney was ennobled as Lord Passfield after serving in MacDonald's two Labour governments but still found the time to work with Beatrice on writing several thoroughly researched historical volumes. During the 1930s the couple suddenly discovered the wonders of Stalin's Russia, and in 1936 they published a book of 1,257 pages called *Soviet Communism: A New Civilisation?* By the next year they knew the answer to their rhetorical question – subsequent editions of the book dropped the question mark from the title. The Webbs were open about their love affair with the Soviet Union. Beatrice once commented: 'Old people often fall in love in extraordinary and ridiculous ways – with their chauffeurs for example: we feel it dignified to have fallen in love with Soviet Communism.'

How on earth could individuals as humane, benevolent and gifted as Gallacher, Montagu and the Webbs support and condone mass murder? Scrupulously outraged by a single breach of civil liberty in Britain – Victor Gollancz whose firm published several apologia for Stalin was at the same time Vice President of the National Committee for the Abolition of the Death Penalty [in Britain] – they turned a blind eye to killing, torture and imprisonment on a huge scale in the Soviet Union. How can political commitment cause sane people to throw their senses to the winds and argue that black is red and tomorrow may well be white?

This is certainly the most tragic chapter in the book. It shows how quickly idealism and naivety can slip into brutal complicity. The results of this 'grand illusion' were to damage enormously the British Left. First of all, it tarred socialism in Britain and elsewhere with the 'Moscow Trials' brush and allowed the political Right then and since to make much capital out of the episode. Secondly, the growing realisation of how much special pleading went on over the excesses of the Soviet Union explains to some extent why the British labour movement has traditionally been suspicious of left-wing intellectuals. Not all the defenders of the purges were intellectuals, certainly, but a disproportionate and vocal number were.

Finally, 'grand illusions' reveals much about a state of mind to which political activists are peculiarly prone: that understandable allegiance to a cause can easily become 'My Cause Right or Wrong', no matter how blatant or evil the wrong. This is certainly *not* a state of mind confined to the Left. In the same 1930s, for example, a variety of British people threw in their lot with Hitler, travelling to Nazi Germany and expressing fulsome admiration for the new regime's achievements, discreetly overlooking or excusing the treatment of Jews, trade unionists and minorities. Others criticised Hitler's methods but contented themselves with the omelette and eggs argument. Winston Churchill, for instance, is usually portrayed as an almost lone voice in the 1930s wilderness, ceaselessly warning of the Hitler menace. And yet it was Churchill who wrote in an article of 1935, which he republished in October 1937:

> Although no subsequent political action can condone wrong deeds or remove the guilt of blood, history is replete with examples of men who have risen to power by employing stern, grim, wicked and even frightful methods, but who, nevertheless, when their life is revealed as a whole, have been regarded as great figures whose lives have enriched the story of mankind. So may it be with Hitler.

Many of the individuals discussed in this chapter used similar arguments, but for them it was Joseph Stalin and not Adolf Hitler whose life enriched mankind.

Perhaps this chapter holds lessons for the British Left today and in the future. It is vital to discriminate between different issues and to maintain a sense of proportion. There are degrees of injustice. Those who used to chant that Mrs Thatcher was a 'fascist' or who criticised the IRA after the Brighton bombing for not having done the job properly only undermine the very cause which they seek to promote.

Why was there such emotional commitment to the cause of the Soviet Union in the 1930s? There had, of course, been supporters ever since 1917, and the Communist Party championed the Bolsheviks since its foundation in 1920. But a conjunction of events at the end of the 1920s and the beginning of the 1930s stimulated a much greater identification with the Soviet Union. The first Five Year Plan, launched in 1928, seemed to offer a planned and ordered system of economic progress as well as full employment which contrasted with the anarchy and chaos of Western capitalism, particularly after the 'Great Depression' began in the autumn of 1929. Secondly, the ignominious collapse of MacDonald's Labour government in August 1931 seemed to reveal the defects of socialists relying on parliamentary progress. As one member of the 'intellectual Left' commented:

> The discredit of Labour made even staunch supporters of the Party in Bloomsbury mutter that perhaps far more radical measures of Marxism were necessary to defeat reaction and stop the drift towards a new war.

In his memoir *My Silent War*, Kim Philby claimed that it was the events of August 1931 that prompted him to throw in his lot with the Soviet Union.

Professor Paul Hollander has shown in exhaustive detail how political pilgrims of the Left who are hostile towards the system in their own country generally gravitate towards a compensatory and uncritical love of another. George Bernard Shaw visited Russia in the summer of 1931. On his last evening he wrote in the visitors' book of his Moscow hotel: 'Tomorrow I leave this land of hope and return to our Western countries of despair.' In his manuscript about this journey, Shaw called the Soviet Union 'this earthly paradise for professional men'.

For many socialists deeply critical of Britain and the National Government, the Soviet Union became the repository of their hopes and optimism; in one famous phrase, 'I have seen the future and it works!' Many scientists such as J. D. Bernal admired the USSR as an exemplar of rational and ordered progress; 'science is communism' he argued. There, it seemed, long-term planning prevailed over short-term considerations and Soviet scientists were treated with the respect and admiration that Bernal thought was lacking in Britain.

Writers and artists also found the Soviet Union a model society to be emulated and praised. In 1937 the Communist Cecil Day Lewis, later to be Poet Laureate between 1968 and his death in 1972, edited a volume of essays called *The Mind in Chains*. Naturally, the mind was in chains only in this country and not in Stalin's Russia. Anthony Blunt in his contribution claimed that 'In the present state of capitalism the position of the artist is hopeless' whereas in the USSR a thriving workers' culture was being built.

Musician Alan Bush praised Soviet music at the expense of British music, J. D. Bernal praised Soviet science at the expense of British science, critic Edgell Rickword praised the new Soviet constitution – of course, Britain didn't even have a written one which he could criticise. Novelist Rex Warner saw everything clearly: 'There is no longer any hope in capitalism . . .'

The conviction that everything 'over there' was better than it was 'over here' reached absurd and chilling depths. Bernard Shaw claimed that it was difficult to get Soviet prisoners to leave gaol because conditions inside were so pleasant. And in his book *Soviet Democracy*, published in 1937 by Victor Gollancz's Left Book Club, Pat Sloan noted:

> Compared with the significance of that term in Britain, Soviet imprisonment stands out as an almost enjoyable experience.

It is doubtful if the millions of people who passed through Stalin's Gulags or 'holiday camps' would have agreed with Pat Sloan.

Approval of the Soviet Union was reinforced by sycophantic praise of Stalin – enthusiasts could even purchase their own 'Stalin Calendars' – and by what has been called 'the techniques of hospitality' during which gullible visitors were gulled even more. The travel agency Intourist was set up in 1929 and its Soviet staff of hundreds specialised in arranging suitably impressive itineraries. Tourists were naturally shown only the best and most modern sights on their carefully planned routes. Schedules were made so hectic that little time was left for doubt or speculation. When visitors were allowed to choose where to go, it was only from a vetted list. Few of them could speak Russian in order to ask awkward questions, and in any case they were carefully kept away from 'ordinary' Russians. In 1924 when a TUC delegation visited an electricity factory, secret police members replaced the real workforce. When Bernard Shaw went into a restaurant he found to his immense surprise and gratification that both the waitresses were experts on his plays. Predictably enough he then announced the superiority of Russian waitresses over their British counterparts.

Anything primitive or inefficient was blamed on the disastrous legacy of the Czars. All visitors were swamped by books, handbooks and pamphlets that contained masses of statistics proving that things were getting better all the time. Dutifully, many British observers transcribed such information in their own works. Sir Walter Citrine visited Russia in 1935. Though often sceptical about what he saw, even he couldn't resist reproducing 'Rates of Wages of the Workers in the First National Kaganovitch Ball-Bearing

Works in Moscow' and even 'Earnings at Underwear Factor, No 6, Moscow'!

Copious supplies of alcohol and quantities of food greeted the visitors. Above all, they were fêted and flattered. When Shaw went to the theatre, proceedings were suddenly interrupted by the unfurling of a banner which read in English 'To the brilliant master, Bernard Shaw – a warm welcome to Soviet soil'. When Sidney and Beatrice Webb came the next year, they were delighted to find they were treated, in Sidney's words, like 'a new type of royalty'. The Webbs were, in fact, a joke among even Soviet officials because of their habit of uncritically writing down in notebooks everything they were told.

If anything untoward did happen during a visit, it was easy to fob off visitors until they went home. During Shaw's trip, he and Nancy Astor attended a function at the British Embassy. A telegram was unexpectedly handed to Lady Astor sent by a Professor Krynin, a political exile then based at Yale University. He begged Shaw and Astor to persuade their Soviet hosts to let his family leave the country. Astor badgered the authorities but they simply stalled for time. After her departure, Western journalists who tried to visit the Krynin family found they had 'disappeared'.

The Moscow Trials of August 1936, January 1937 and March 1938 were the climax of the purges unleashed by Stalin as he systematically imposed his dictatorship by exterminating any possible rivals or threats to his rule. Even today the scale of the slaughter is unknown. Robert Conquest in *The Great Terror* estimated that one million people died in 1937–38 alone. His book has been serialised in post-glasnost Russia and it is now accepted that Conquest's figures were too low.

Such figures are mind-boggling. To try and bring out what these massacres meant in personal terms: on one day alone in 1937, Stalin and his lieutenant Molotov signed 3,167 death warrants before going off to the cinema for the evening. Of the 139 members of the Central Committee of 1934, 98 were eventually shot. Old revered Bolsheviks were suddenly unmasked as longstanding traitors. Of the seven members of the 1924 Politburo, six were to be executed or murdered; the seventh was Joseph Stalin. In September 1989 the *Independent* newspaper carried a letter from Colonel-General Dimitri Volkgonov, Chief of the Institute of Military History in Moscow. He wrote about the effect of the purges on the Red Army:

> The situation in the Soviet armed forces was dire: in 1937–38 the army was 'purged' of over 40,000 men: out of the 108 members of the old military council only 10 retained their posts.

Did this carnage in the Soviet Union cause misgivings among British admirers? Far from it. Here was a country, they argued, whose leader really knew how to deal with opposition to socialism, overlooking that if they as the opposition had been so dealt with in Britain they would have had rather different reactions. Bernard Shaw was in no doubt about the justification for Soviet conduct:

> The plain truth is that all civilised governments exact minimum standards of conduct which they enforce by killing the people who do not attain them. Our question is not to kill or not to kill, but how to select the right people to kill.

This cold-blooded attitude is reminiscent of one strand in Fabian thought which was always rather impatient with fallible human beings and their regrettable tendency not to behave exactly as the Fabians desired. David Caute has observed: 'The Webbs were excellent examples of the type which prefers mankind to people; which originally intends to sacrifice a few to save everyone and ends by sacrificing everyone to save a few.'

Several distinguished British lawyers supported the conduct of the Moscow Trials. The eminent barrister D. N. Pritt KC, Labour MP for North Hammersmith and a member of the Party's National Executive, defended the proceedings and helped allay the qualms of people around the world. During the first Trial of August 1936 he does seem to have felt that the evidence against the accused was a little shaky, but then quickly recovered himself and assured the readers of his pamphlet that 'over nearly the whole of the case the available proof did not require to be brought forward.' It is unlikely that Pritt would have accepted this argument if he had been a defending counsel in Britain. And even Pritt regretted the absence of a jury in the Moscow Trials.

Another barrister, Dudley Collard, watched the 1937 Trial. In a widely circulated pamphlet he informed his readers that 'in the result the court was more merciful than I would have been!' As fourteen of the seventeen defendants at this trial were shot and the other three were imprisoned for long sentences, it is difficult to know quite how the court could have been less merciful.

A number of explanations have been advanced to exonerate those who defended the trials and the purges. The first is 'we didn't know what was going on'. The problem with this defence is that numerous writers *at the time* argued that the proceedings were faked and that widespread abuse of civil rights was endemic in the Soviet Union. Moreover, many of those critics were longstanding socialists and so could not be dismissed as typical anti-Soviet reactionaries.

For example, take Fenner Brockway, throughout his long life an independent socialist of honesty and integrity. As early as 1927 he wrote in unequivocal terms to the Russian Council of People's Commissars:

> ... Not even my admiration for your wonderful achievements, my realisation of the immense significance of the maintenance of the Workers' Republic for 10 years, can close my ears to the cry of the Socialists in prison and exile in Russia. I know what imprisonment means, and I cannot do other than associate myself with those who, for their convictions, are undergoing imprisonment now.

Critics of the Trials at the time and not with hindsight included Dr Friedrich Adler, Secretary of the Labour and Socialist International. His influential pamphlet of 1936 called *The Witchcraft Trial in Moscow* systematically analysed the judicial proceedings. He noted that the defendants were always convicted on 'voluntary' confessions and never on written documents; that there was no right of appeal; that supposedly crucial meetings of the conspirators had taken place at the Hotel Bristol in Copenhagen in 1932, even though this hotel had, in fact, been demolished in 1917; and that the indictment of the defendants, their trial, sentence and execution had all taken place in just eleven days. He emphasised the bizarre and hysterical language of prosecutor Vyshinsky whose concluding words were 'I demand that dogs gone mad should be shot, every one of them!'

Another critic was F. A. Voigt, a respected journalist on the *Manchester Guardian* which was itself critical of the proceedings. He published his articles in book form in 1938 under the title *Unto Caesar*. Condemning the 'massacres' which were taking place, he explained exactly how and why the defendants confessed:

> If there is any recalcitrance it is broken by a threat, often no more than hinted at, to wife or husband, child or friend. And who in the world will *not* 'confess' if the penalty for refusal be the liberty, or even the life, of a mother or child?

Voigt also gave clear evidence of the effects of sleep deprivation on the defendants.

The labour movement's own newspaper, the *Daily Herald*, which had a circulation of over two million copies a day, attacked the proceedings from the start. A typical editorial of 30 January 1937 said that 'Truly the

Revolution is devouring its own children'; and 'There remains horror at the deed [of execution], pity for the victims, and dismay at the condition of the Soviet Union after 20 years of Soviet rule.'

Also hostile was the veteran socialist Emrys Hughes, Keir Hardie's son-in-law, who used his small circulation but prestigious *Forward* to campaign against the trials. Walter Citrine in his account *I Search For Truth in Russia* was outspoken about the dictatorship of Stalin and the complete uniformity of opinion: 'To argue with a Russian Communist is to argue with a gramophone record of Stalin.' Some of the editorials in the *New Statesman* magazine were ambiguous on the trials, but many well-respected contributors, such as Leonard Woolf, were condemnatory.

Extraordinary in their wealth of detail about conditions in the Soviet Union were two books by Vladimir and Tatiana Tchernavin whose *Escape from the Soviets* (1933) and *I Speak for the Silent* (1935) were issued in Britain by the reputable publishers Hamish Hamilton. Both books still have a power to shock comparable with Solzhenitsyn's *One Day in the Life of Ivan Denisovich*, published over twenty-five years later. The Tchernavins seem to have aroused the special ire of the Soviet authorities because of their professional qualifications: she had been a senior assistant at the Hermitage, he was a lecturer at the Agronomical Institute. Their books tell of the sudden motiveless arrests, the forced labour, the harsh penal camps, the shootings without trial, the atmosphere of suspicion and mistrust. Huge letter boxes were installed on street corners into which people could drop denunciations of each other. Those who 'confessed' were called, in prison slang, 'novelists' and their confessions 'novels'. Tchernavin detailed exactly how and why people confessed so as to spare family and friends.

It would be easy to continue with this evidence here, but the point has been made. Such material was produced and publicised *at the time* by sympathetic observers. Certainly more evidence was available after the 'revelations' of 1956, but much information existed before then. How could Pritt, Collard, the Webbs and the others see things so wrongly? Malcolm Muggeridge, a journalist who went to Russia in the early 1930s as a sympathiser but had the integrity to see what was going on and change his mind, provides an effective summary:

> The people who came to the Soviet Union wanted so passionately to see certain things in being that they could not see anything different. They were not liars. You could just not change their minds with facts.

Muggeridge's words apply just as much to those 'believers' who never visited the Soviet Union but who read about it safely at home. His argument is implicitly endorsed by the recent Communist Party history of the period. Noreen Branson writes of the Party leadership that:

> Fundamental to their approach was the belief – held by all Communists – that all persecution, tyranny and injustice had their roots in the capitalist system, and in capitalist property relations. It followed that, where the capitalist system was abolished, tyranny and persecution would wither away; insofar as they still manifested themselves in Russia, this was a hangover from Tsarist days, soon to disappear.

Clearly such a belief could, and did, excuse anything.

A second defence advanced was that to have spoken out would only have helped the Soviet Union's enemies without necessarily helping the victims. The Welsh miners' leader Arthur Horner was aware of illegalities taking place but argued: 'I knew ... that if I publicly spread my doubts about some of the things that were going on I would not assist my friends, but would give a weapon to those who would stop at nothing to destroy the Soviet Union.' Some private representations were made to the Soviet authorities but with little evidence of success. And, in any case, by not speaking out in public much more damage was in the end inflicted on the Soviet Union. Most importantly, injustice and cruelty is injustice and cruelty wherever and under whoever it happens. Selective moral outrage destroys any case for socialism as a fairer and more just way of organising society.

A third possible defence is that in the circumstances of the 1930s, most notably the rise of fascism on the continent, people simply had to choose between two rival camps: fascism or communism. This is a more understandable argument. Wherever one looked, fascism seemed to be gaining power: Italy, Portugal, Germany, Poland, Hungary, Romania, Austria ... Denis Healey was a Communist at Oxford in the late 1930s. His autobiography puts the choice starkly:

> For the young in those days, politics was a world of simple choices. The enemy was Hitler with his concentration camps. The objective was to prevent a war by standing up to Hitler. Only the Communist Party seemed unambiguously against Hitler.

At the same time Eric Hobsbawm was a Communist at Cambridge and he has argued that:

> ... modern political choice is not a constant process of selecting men or

measures, but a single or infrequent choice between packages, in which we buy the disagreeable part of the contents because there is no other way of getting the rest, and in any case because there is no other way to be politically effective.

But at what point can the package be returned to the retailer: after a thousand deaths, ten thousand, a million? Should one really condone the 'disagreeable part' in order to get the rest of the menu? It was difficult in the 1930s to be against fascism without thereby falling into the Soviet camp, but millions of people managed it. Neither were Nazi Germany and the Soviet Union the only choices. This was also the time of Roosevelt's New Deal government in the United States and of social democratic administrations in Sweden and New Zealand.

The deep-rooted problem was that many on the British Left then were unable to distinguish between fascism, liberal democracy and communism. For some, Chamberlain was as 'bad' as Hitler. It took a world war for people who thought like this to see the crucial difference. As Louis MacNeice wrote in 1939 in his *Autumn Journal*:

> Our top-heavy tedious parliamentary system
> Is our only ready weapon to defeat
> The legions' eagles and the lictors' axes.

Looking back at this grand illusion, it is striking to see how many intelligent and otherwise acute individuals allowed themselves to be deceived, especially when they were often intellectuals trained to be critical and thorough. The explanation, other than sheer gullibility, lies in the way that the Utopian aspirations of many sincere socialists led to the worship of a system and a society at the expense of fellow human beings.

Harry Ferns was a young Canadian who studied at Cambridge in the 1930s and joined the Communist Party. Later, after the war, he became Professor of Politics at Birmingham University. His excellent memoir *Reading from Right to Left* (1983) examines the passions of the time. In the 1930s, Communists like him 'did not regard the spilling of blood in a good cause as wicked and forbidden'; '. . . we prided ourselves on the realism which enabled us not to shrink from the stern dictates of history.' In other words, back to the familiar 'you can't make an omelette without breaking some eggs'. But as Colin Welch has pointed out in his review of a book about Walter Durranty, an influential journalist who defended the purges, 'you could break every egg in the world without making an omelette.'

Ferns also comments on the arrogance of Marxism, which flatters men and women by making them the centre of everything. Stalin played up to this feeling when he remarked that Bolsheviks were 'engineers of the soul'. Cecil Day Lewis, a Communist in Cheltenham in the mid-1930s, gave a good summary of this feeling:

> Inoculated against Roman Catholicism by the religion of my youth, I dimly felt the need for a faith which had the authority, the logic, the cut-and-driedness of the Roman church – a faith which would fill the void left by the leaking away of traditional religion, would make some sense of our troubled times and make real demands on me. Marxism appeared to fill the bill.

This faith developed the rigidities of many other religious faiths, even down to instigating its own inquisition which sought out and punished heretics whose views differed from the current orthodoxy. The possibility of dissent, of contradicting 'Stalin infallibility' was not allowed. But just to make sure, the meetings of renegades were disrupted and broken up as one Communist of the time, Joe Jacobs, has admitted in his autobiography when he says that his colleagues systematically pursued a vendetta against J. T. Murphy, the former Communist leader who had been expelled from the Party.

Even to talk to 'heretics' was unwise. Edward Upward, a friend of Isherwood and Auden and a longstanding supporter of the Left, has provided a frightening picture of one party member being ostracised for suspected Trotskyist leanings. The main protagonist of Upward's novel, Alan Sebrill, exhibits extraordinary self-deception when justifying the treatment meted out:

> His sense that their behaviour towards Bainton had been deficient in ordinary human kindness gave place to a recognition that if the [Communist] Party were to disappear from the world there would be no hope for humanity. The showing of kindness to a few deviationist human individuals could lead to disaster for human beings in general.

Such an attitude excuses any personal inhumanity. And lest it be thought that such a scene was just a novelist's imaginings, Margaret McCarthy in her autobiography depicts an almost identical situation at a local Communist Party meeting:

> I sat among them, sensitive to the atmosphere of the meeting, furtive, shifty, thick with moronic bigotry, and it seemed to me that I could not breathe, that I was choked and blinded by the fog of imbecile, foul and unnecessary conspiracy, the conspiracy of comrade against comrade.

McCarthy defended the accused who had been charged with heresy, although she knew what it would mean for her: 'I was destroying myself, going out into the darkness and the blankness alone, an outcast, an untouchable, with neither hope, nor belief, nor comradeship, nor understanding.' She was so upset that she even considered suicide.

That such things could happen among people who sincerely believed themselves to be working for 'the greater good' shows how some ideologies and beliefs can end up destroying what they hope to create. A sense of individual human worth, of tolerance, understanding and humour – all these qualities must be at the heart of any concept of 'the Left', if only to prevent any more 'Grand Illusions'.

CHAPTER EIGHT

New Worlds for Old?: Labour's Brave New World

On the first day of the 1945 Parliament, Labour's new MPs celebrated their election triumph by singing *The Red Flag*. Here are two different reactions:

'My complacency melted in a minute. I began to fear for my country.'

Conservative MP Oliver Lyttelton

'mildly disturbed ... These youngsters still had to absorb the atmosphere of the House. But I recognised that it was largely first-day high spirits.'

Herbert Morrison, Labour Leader of the House of Commons

King George VI met President Truman on 2 August 1945 after the election:

Truman: 'I hear you've had a revolution.'

George VI: 'Oh no, we don't have those here.'

CLEMENT ATTLEE was one of the most unlikely individuals ever to lead a British political party. Quiet, unassuming and with the appearance of a suburban bank manager, he seemed to be, in Churchill's famous phrase, 'a sheep in sheep's clothing'. His great interests in life were cricket, his old public school Haileybury, detective stories and doing *The Times* crossword. From the moment he was elected leader of the Labour Party in 1935 his position was under attack from rivals, but he was still there twenty years later — and it was Attlee's party which trounced Churchill's in the 1945 general election and Attlee's government which shaped post-war Britain.

Like Keir Hardie, Attlee left behind few clues as to what made him tick. His memoirs are unrevealing, and a series of television interviews given just before his death in 1967 are bland and uninformative. A former colleague writes of Attlee that he 'would never use one syllable where none would do.' Television interviews and the whole paraphernalia of the media were anathema to him. One illuminating piece of film captures Attlee being greeted at an airport by a battery of cameras. Asked whether he would like to comment on some political controversy, he snaps 'No' and stalks off. A friend of Denis Healey's once remarked that a conversation with most people was like a game of tennis; with Attlee it was like feeding biscuits to a dog – all you got out of him was yup, yup, yup.

Attlee was born in middle-class and respectable Putney, London in 1883. His father, a solicitor, sent his son to Haileybury public school and then to Oxford after which he read for the Bar at the Inner Temple. But Attlee's life was to change in October 1905 when he visited Haileybury House, the settlement established by his old public school in the East End of London. As Attlee recalled many years later, this visit proved to be 'a decisive step in my life'.

Institutions such as Haileybury House introduced public schoolboys to social work in the poorer parts of London. They sometimes had a patronising air about them, a sense of missionaries penetrating the wilds to impart a little learning and culture to the natives before scampering back to civilisation. In his autobiography George Lansbury was critical of the men and women:

> who went to East London full of enthusiasm and zeal for the welfare of the masses, and discovered the advancement of their own interests and the interests of the poor were best secured by leaving East London to stew in its own juice while they became members of parliament, cabinet ministers, civil servants . . .

Lansbury's resentment of 'outsiders' who came, saw and left was understandable. But Attlee was different. Horrified by the poverty and deprivation he saw around him, he decided to go and live in the East End, not for a few weeks but for years, in order to campaign for political change. He soon joined the Stepney branch of the Independent Labour Party. In 1908 his father died, leaving him a comfortable private income of £400 a year; again he resisted the temptation to depart for middle-class suburbia.

Instead Attlee joined the Fabians and worked as a lecture secretary for the Webbs, explaining and arguing in support of Beatrice Webb's Minority Report on the Poor Law. He subsequently had a short spell as secretary of

Toynbee Hall and then in 1911 was appointed one of the official 'explainers' of Lloyd George's National Insurance Act. He also lectured at Ruskin College in Oxford and at the new London School of Economics. In the light of these posts it might be assumed that Attlee had a gift for oratory or public speaking – this was then the surest way to progress within the labour movement. In fact, he hadn't, relying instead on hard work and thorough attention to detail to carry him through.

When war broke out in 1914 he had no qualms about where his duty lay. A convinced patriot, he fought throughout the conflict, being twice wounded and finally reaching the rank of Major. On his return to the East End, he was elected Mayor of Stepney and then, in 1922, MP for Limehouse. That same year he married Violet Millar, the start of a happy and long-lived relationship. Violet was not at all interested in politics. In the 1920s Attlee was a dedicated backbench MP, briefly tasting office in 1924 as Under Secretary of State for War. In MacDonald's second administration he was again at the War Office. When this government collapsed in 1931 he had no doubts where he stood, regarding MacDonald's action as 'the greatest betrayal in the political history of the country.'

So far Attlee's political career had been steady if not spectacular; no one could have foreseen the momentous events ahead. When at the October 1931 election the Labour Party was almost destroyed as an effective parliamentary force, Attlee was one of the forty-six MPs returned, which confirmed the value of representing a solid working-class constituency. For want of anyone better and because more obviously suitable candidates like Herbert Morrison had lost their seats he was elected deputy to George Lansbury, standing in when the elderly Party leader was ill. Lansbury suddenly resigned in 1935 and Attlee, with the support of most MPs who had seen his dedicated efforts over the last four years, defeated Herbert Morrison and Arthur Greenwood in the leadership contest. Most observers still felt that this was merely a stopgap appointment until someone more appropriate and certainly more charismatic should take over. But once at the summit, Attlee was not to be budged.

That he did become leader of the Labour Party was not just due to good luck. His election could be said to symbolise the changes taking place within the labour movement. Broadly, the committee room was ousting the street-corner meeting and effective political administration was becoming more important than cloudy idealism or rhetoric. In short, the Attlees were displacing the Hardies. Between 1935 and 1940 Attlee was a largely anonymous figure, publishing two rather dull books called *The Will and the Way to Socialism* and *The Labour Party in Perspective*. He also made a few left-wing gestures such as welcoming the 1936 Hunger Marchers to Hyde Park and visiting the International Brigade in Spain.

Attlee took little interest in the intellectual work of men like Dalton, G. D. H. Cole and Evan Durbin that was to transform his own party. In fact, throughout his career he was suspicious of the 'thinkers', dismissing them in his memoirs as 'the intelligentsia who can be trusted to take the wrong view on any subject.' They in turn did not at that time have a high opinion of Attlee; at the beginning of the war Hugh Dalton privately referred to him as 'The Rabbit' and thought Attlee 'at no time ... big enough or strong enough to carry the burden'.

Attlee's chance to prove Dalton and the others wrong came in 1940 when the Labour Party joined Churchill's coalition government. Not only did his post as deputy Prime Minister from February 1942 concentrating on the domestic front bring to the fore his undoubted administrative talents, but the conflict itself prompted a groundswell of opinion from right to left. The anti-fascist war brought the Labour Party and the trade unions back to the centre of the political stage after nearly a decade in the wings. 'Total War' as the conduct of the war effort was called because it required the mobilisation of the entire population, brought with it massive social, economic and political upheaval. The 'old order' – or the *Guilty Men* as a contemporary diatribe co-authored by Michael Foot put it – proved incapable of building and sustaining a war effort which could combat the Germans on equal terms.

Whether it was evacuation, or the Blitz, or rationing, or conscription, everything shook up the traditional way of doing things. Suddenly the three main ideas that had underpinned the Labour Party's approach in the second half of the 1930s – government intervention, the need for planning, and welfare provision – became politically respectable and were now deployed by the Churchill administration with hardly a murmur of dissent. The *Daily Express* might have thought that food rationing was 'a dreadful and terrible iniquity' but everyone else knew that equality of sacrifice demanded nothing less. Market forces were patently irrelevant when it came to, say, medical treatment after an air raid: human need was more important than the size of a victim's bank account.

With hindsight, after their massive defeat at the 1945 election, Conservatives often looked back and tried to find scapegoats for their loss. They developed a 'demonology' which included ABCA, the army education service introduced during the war, as well as CEMA, the government-sponsored arts agency which grew into the Arts Council. Others blamed publisher Allen Lane and Penguin Books or else Sir William Beveridge for

his Report, issued in December 1942, advocating decent welfare and employment insurance and which marked a new acceptance by the state that it had
a responsibility for the well-being of its citizens. A shortened version of the
Report sold over 600,000 copies.

Reactionaries like Evelyn Waugh dated 'the fall' from the German attack
on the Soviet Union in June 1941 which led to an Anglo-Soviet alliance and
widespread admiration for the achievements of the Red Army. All these
factors reinforced what Asa Briggs has called the links between warfare and
welfare, confirming that 'in many respects the character of the war effort
provided the most important propaganda of all.'

It would be wrong to categorise this wartime mood as revolutionary or
even socialist. Looking now at, say, J. B. Priestley's short radio talks *Postscripts*
or the 'Plan for Britain' published in the influential magazine *Picture Post*, or
the ideas of the new Common Wealth party which ran candidates in protest
at the war's electoral truce and by 1944 had two MPs and 15,000 members,
one is struck by their call for solid, decent human values — values which
were as much humanitarian as they were political. After suitable adjustment
they could easily be accommodated within the established system. There
had been no invasion of Britain, no defeat, and no collapse of traditional
institutions such as parliament, the monarchy or the civil service. According
to contemporary surveys by Mass Observation as well as the eyewitness
accounts of writers who worked in war factories, many groups continued in
their largely apolitical way, untouched by and uninterested in the visions of
a New Jerusalem that some socialists were trying to conjure up.

Nevertheless, as the embryonic opinion polls revealed, the war did help
shift popular opinion towards the left not just 'on the ground' but also
among the 'élite'. Lord Annan's autobiography *Our Age* charts how and why
his generation moved into positions of power and influence in the 1940s.
Reacting against the horrors of, say, Jarrow revealed by J. B. Priestley or
Ellen Wilkinson, these opinion formers were much more progressive, humane
and idealistic than their predecessors. Socialists had traditionally favoured
state intervention and now, too, many Conservatives joined them, keen to
show they had taken to heart Disraeli's aphorism of the 'Two Nations'. Both
agreed that:

> . . . palpable injustices and differences in the life chances of the well-to-do and
> of the poor could be diminished by public expenditure and redistributive
> taxation; and the agents to bring about change were the bureaucrats of
> central and local government under the control of their elected ministers and
> councillors.

This new collectivist determination to help create a better society went hand in hand with the new post-war consensus, which lasted from the 1940s to the 1970s. It was heralded by the publication in the summer of 1944 of the White Paper *Employment Policy* accepting that post-war governments should have '. . . as one of their primary responsibilities the maintenance of a high and stable level of employment'.

Again, it should be emphasised that this was not a socialist consensus; two of the individuals who contributed to it, J. M. Keynes and Sir William Beveridge, were both Liberals, while it was the Conservative R. A. Butler who introduced the Education Act of 1944. During the 1945 election campaign, Westminster Conservative Association reprinted Harold Macmillan's book *The Middle Way* in order to prove that Labour's nationalisation proposals had been stolen from the Tories.

Several Labour politicians held vital posts in the war coalition. Apart from Attlee, Herbert Morrison was an able and energetic Home Secretary, Ernest Bevin was a formidable Minister of Labour and Hugh Dalton headed the Ministry of Economic Warfare. The Labour Party had indeed 'come in from the cold'. But much would depend on the outcome of the general election to be held at the end of the war, the first for ten years. Could the Labour Party, led by a comparatively little-known individual, possibly defeat a Conservative Party led by a world-famous statesman who in the eyes of many had won the war for Britain?

Few on the British Left fully realised what changes in the political climate had been wrought by the war. Although its membership had leapt to nearly 60,000 the Communist Party still thought that Churchill was bound to win and therefore argued for the coalition government to continue. Attlee and his colleagues were also apprehensive, fearing that Churchill's status would prove to be the Conservative Party's trump card just as the victorious Lloyd George had triumphed at the end of the First World War. The Conservatives certainly made the most of 'the Churchill factor', simply calling their manifesto *Mr Churchill's Declaration of Policy to the Electors*, even though he himself admitted privately: 'I have no message'. One commentator observed that Conservative candidates were sent into the electoral fray armed with little more than a photograph of Churchill.

The Labour Party manifesto *Let Us Face the Future* encapsulated the policies produced by Dalton and his circle in the 1930s, subsequently tempered by wartime events. These included nationalisation of the basic industries, development of a welfare state and in particular a national health service, the expansion of education and a commitment to full employment. The Labour Party stressed that it put 'the nation above any sectional interest', unlike the Conservatives who favoured the better off. Neutral observers such as Mass Observation pointed out that the Labour Party appeared to the voters as a united party and that their candidates were generally younger and more vigorous than their opponents.

The two parties fought very different campaigns. Churchill toured the country in semi-regal style. Attlee, by contrast, was driven around by his wife Violet in the family's battered old car. In later years behaviour like this would have been seen by party managers as a potential disaster – akin to Michael Foot's amateurish style as leader in the 1983 campaign – but in 1945 it fitted the mood of a thoughtful, eager electorate. For the first time since possibly the English Civil War in the 1640s, 300 years before, Britain possessed a culture in which a nascent political consciousness – albeit still in a minority – was reflected by the large meetings and the amount of literature bought and read.

Blackburn differed little from other constituencies in the popular excite-ment aroused by the general election – the first after all since 1935. The agent for the young Labour candidate, Barbara Castle, has remembered it being 'an election campaign with an evangelical flavour'. The final pre-election rally concluded with a crowd of 10–12,000 massed in the Market Square, Blackburn, singing *Jerusalem*.

In such a politically alert atmosphere crude ploys such as Churchill's silly suggestion that if Labour won they would eventually introduce 'some form of Gestapo' in order to implement their policies backfired badly. The London *Evening Standard* printed pictures of Labour's National Executive under the caption 'These People Want to be Dictators. Study Their Faces!' In 1945, for the first and so far last time, the national Press was fairly evenly divided in its support for the two major parties. The 1945 general election was like the old-style hustings contests – and it was Labour that had the better argu-ments.

As the counts took place all over the country it was evident that some groups of people in particular had been strongly radicalised by the war. Leah Manning was the Labour candidate in Epping, North London, and she has described what happened:

> The count took place in the Drill Hall at Epping, and when the constituency boxes were opened, I was well down – radiant smiles from the Tory candidate's wife. But when the soldiers' vote came to be counted, my pile crept up and up. I was well in, by a majority of over a thousand.

In fact, only 60 per cent of the servicemen voted due to difficulties of communication, but it was solidly Labour. Two-thirds of the new voters who had attained their majority since the last general election in 1935 also supported Attlee's party.

The result was announced to a mixture of public shock, disbelief and joy. The Labour Party under Attlee had won 393 seats to the Conservatives' 213, a huge majority. Some people lit bonfires and danced happily in the streets, but for others it was a disaster, a first step on the way to what novelist Angela Thirkell dubbed 'A Brave New Revolting World'. Evelyn Waugh recalled that, for people like him, it was almost as if Britain was now under occupation. Even in the 1990s one still hears bitterness in many Conservatives' voices as they recall how an ungrateful nation stabbed Churchill in the back. A Gallup poll showed that 56 per cent of the sample had voted for sweeping change and it was clear that Churchill, for all his undoubted prowess as a wartime leader, was not the politician who in peace would preside over such changes.

The Labour Party won seats all over the country, even in previously barren areas such as the south-east and the west Midlands as well as in rural districts. Having broadened its appeal beyond the working classes, the Labour Party attracted enough of the middle-class vote, which it had needed to win a majority. It was now indeed a national party. For so far the only time, the Labour Party won a majority of seats in England. Its strength was confirmed at local level by big gains in the municipal elections of November 1945, the county council elections of March 1946, and the urban and rural district elections in April 1946. As E. P. Thompson notes:

> Labour, which had advanced its position on a multitude of wartime committees, now emphatically consolidated its local and regional positions: on boards of school governors, hospital management boards, on the magistrates' bench, on Watch Committees, in the intricate networking of local authority and on the workshop floor and in industrial committees.

Labour Party membership doubled to almost half a million individual members in 1945 and then rose to 645,345 the next year. One graphic sign of the political tide was shown by the fate of the Foot family. Father Isaac and two sons stood as Liberal candidates in the general election and all three were defeated. Another son, Michael, was a Labour candidate – he was elected.

For most political leaders, such a triumph would have been a heady experience. For some of Attlee's colleagues it certainly was. Hugh Dalton wrote in his diary of 'That first sensation, tingling and triumphant, was of a new society to be built, and we had the power to build it. There was exhilaration among us, joy and hope, determination and confidence. We felt exalted, dedicated, walking on air, walking with destiny.'

Attlee, in contrast, just seemed mildly baffled at the electorate's verdict. King George VI noted in his diary that the new Prime Minister was 'very surprised that his Party had won . . .' His leadership was still under attack. Almost as Attlee was on his way to Buckingham Palace to see the King, Herbert Morrison proposed that the Parliamentary Labour Party should be allowed a vote on the leadership issue. Morrison was aided in his manoeuvrings by his lover Ellen Wilkinson and by the chairman of the Party, Harold Laski. Laski had, in fact, written a blunt letter to Attlee at the start of the election, claiming that his leadership lacked '. . . a sense of the dramatic, the power to give a lead, the ability to reach out to the masses . . .' But Morrison and his co-conspirators came up against Attlee's most powerful supporter, Ernest Bevin, who swiftly threw his considerable political weight behind Attlee and the attempted coup came to nothing. Even Morrison's generally sympathetic biographers have problems explaining away his conduct.

Attlee returned to No 10 Downing Street at the head of the first Labour government to have a clear majority. Here was the chance to build a New Jerusalem in England's green and pleasant land.

Despite the singing of the *Red Flag* in the House of Commons and the fears of Conservative MPs like Oliver Lyttelton, the keynote of Attlee's early days in office was continuity. Parliament met for two weeks and then broke up for six weeks' holiday, hardly the act of an administration planning drastic changes. The Cabinet had an average age of over sixty, though of course age is not everything: the vigorous Lord Addison, appointed Leader of the House of Lords at the age of seventy-six, was still going strong five years later.

The government certainly contained some remarkable individuals. There was Attlee himself who retained his down-to-earth way of doing things. When he went to open a new cinema in the East End in 1947, the Prime Minister arrived and left by bus. There was Herbert Morrison, a bouncy and energetic Cockney who had run the London County Council and for all his intriguing was a brilliant administrator. His obsession with politics rendered him oblivious to his appearance: 'On one occasion he came to a meeting of the [London County] Council's most important committee – the General Purposes Committee – without his dentures, persisted in speaking at the meeting and seemed quite unaware of what other members may have thought.'

There was the High Anglican Sir Stafford Cripps who had once been nicknamed 'The Red Squire' because he owned a mansion house in the West Country; the pugnacious Ernest Bevin, almost as broad as he was tall, the Old Etonian Hugh Dalton, and the fiery Welsh orator Anuerin Bevan. Among the junior ministers were the former Clydesider Manny Shinwell, the ex-Welsh miner Jim Griffiths, the Marxist guru of the 1930s John Strachey, and Ellen Wilkinson.

It was a formidable array of talents, which did not guarantee that they got on well personally. Morrison and Dalton were plotters; Bevin detested Morrison as 'a scheming little bastard' whom he wouldn't trust further than he could throw him while Bevan liked Cripps, who in turn was suspected by the others. On and on it went. Probably the greatest of Attlee's achievements was to keep the Cabinet pulling in roughly the same direction over the next six years: as Bevin put it, 'By God, he's the only man who could have kept us together.' When he failed to do so in 1951, there were acrimonious resignations from the Cabinet and the Labour Party was soon out of office. Nobody then or since has ever quite explained Attlee's success, but A. P. Herbert once had a good go in a poem, one verse of which reads:

> Yet by some shy mysterious art
> He rules the roost, if not the heart.
> It may be 'character' – it may
> Be just his clever, cunning way.

Despite the militant backgrounds of some Cabinet members – both Morrison and Bevin had once belonged to the old Marxist Social Democratic Federation – it was the Fabian influence that was strongest, itself a reflection of the administrative and bureaucratic demands of 'Phase Two' of the British labour movement. Fabian detail was now more important than ethical assertion. More than half the Party's MPs were Fabians, forty-five were in the government and ten in the Cabinet. The new administration concentrated on the three major issues of nationalisation, planning and the introduction of a welfare state.

The overriding difficulty was that though it had not suffered as badly as some countries, Britain was in a parlous state. One-quarter of its national wealth had been wiped out, as had two-thirds of its export trade. No less than 4 million houses had been destroyed or damaged by German bombing while essential services had run down. Watching films of the period, one always notices the bleak and derelict locations glimpsed in the background. This wartime legacy was made much worse by the sudden ending of Lend-

Lease, the system of American financial aid, by the Truman administration within days of the general election. The government was therefore always teetering on the edge of financial crisis.

The Attlee government's economic policy, as elsewhere in Europe, centred on the extension of public ownership. The mines and the railways were two basic utilities which by 1945 were thoroughly dilapidated, and not just because of the war. Britain's mines had operated at a loss for years, run by many different companies paying low wages and with an horrific accident record. By 1945 even the coalowners recognised the need for some form of centralised body; the *Economist* commented soon after the Labour administration took office: 'Support for the principle of public ownership of the mines is very wide, extending probably to two-and-a-half of the three parties.'

As for the railways, though the numerous companies had been reduced to the 'Big Four' in 1921 this led to little modernisation – for instance, the use of diesel engines was virtually unknown before the war. During the conflict itself, the four independent companies had proved unable to cope with the increased flow of freight and a system of centralisation was introduced from 1941. Here too, as with the mines, the desirability of public ownership had practically been settled already and there was little opposition to the idea. In fact, as Attlee later recalled in his memoirs, 'Of all our nationalisation proposals, only Iron and Steel aroused much feeling, perhaps because hopes of profit were greater here than elsewhere.'

But how exactly was nationalisation to be carried out? The famous Clause Four called for 'the common ownership of the means of production, distribution, and exchange, and the best obtainable system of popular administration and control of each industry or service.' This was admirable in intention but lacking in detail. In the past some had welcomed the idea of workers' control. Attlee himself had written in 1935 that 'workers' control is an essential part of the new order', but ten years on such ideas had been quietly shelved. This was mainly due to the influence of Herbert Morrison who favoured the public corporation approach and justified nationalisation on the grounds of economic efficiency, not as a step towards socialism. It was Morrison who was responsible for overseeing the passage of the new government's nationalisation bills.

Ministers went to the policy cupboard and found it empty of solid fare. Shinwell, the new Minister of Fuel, asked Transport House for its documents on coal nationalisation and discovered that though it had been party policy for years only two papers existed – and one of these was in Welsh. Similarly, when George Strauss, the Minister of Supply, began to handle steel nationalisation in the summer of 1947 he too found that no detailed planning had been carried out by the Labour Party or its sympathisers. Certainly no draft legislation had been drawn up.

Because of this omission the Labour government had little idea how much compensation should be paid to former owners for their assets. The sums turned out to be extremely generous: £164 million for the mines, nearly £1,000 million for the railways, and later on £540 million for electricity and £265 million for the gas industry, paid for out of general taxation. The owners were often glad to be rid of their loss-making ventures on these terms.

The 1946 Act nationalising the coal industry also established the National Coal Board (NCB). The composition of this board showed the continuing influence of the old coalowners – the new chairman Lord Hyndley had formerly been chairman of the largest private group of collieries – and there was no provision for direct miner representation on any of the NCB committees above pit level.

The Transport Act of 1946 transferred into state ownership the railways, canals and most long-distance road haulage, setting up the Transport Commission. Despite the protracted attempts of the National Union of Railwaymen to introduce some measure of industrial democracy, relations between management and workforce remained as it had been under private ownership. Nor did the government obtain a unified transport policy, primarily because separate boards administered the rail and road systems under a directive to compete against each other.

Other measures of nationalisation covered the Bank of England in 1946, electricity in 1947 and gas in 1948. Continuity of personnel seemed to be imperative here too. At the Bank the governor, the deputy governor and all the other leading officials were reappointed to their posts; eight of the heads of the gas boards had been former executives of private gas companies.

The Attlee nationalisation programme suffered from a number of defects: all the industries taken over were bankrupt and backward – the unprofitable 20 per cent of British industry. Extravagant compensation was paid to companies; and the old management structures and relationships were transferred unchanged from the private to the public sector. The editor of the *Economist*, Geoffrey Crowther, speaking to an American audience in 1949, summed up the whole experience:

> The ordinary resident in England, unless he happens to have been a shareholder in any of the expropriated companies, is unable to detect any difference whatever as a result of nationalisation.

The workforce in the various industries seem to have been disappointed too. Surveys in *Railway Review* showed that fewer than 15 per cent of the sample thought that as railwaymen they had any share in the running of their industry. In the mines the National Coal Board was as distant as, and acted no differently from, the old coalowners. Dissatisfaction flared at the 1948 TUC Conference, and both the managers and trade union leaders confessed themselves puzzled by the frequent number of unofficial strikes: over 8,000 between 1947 and 1951. A series of studies on the nationalised industries by the Acton Society, undertaken between 1950 and 1952, reported a widespread feeling among the rank and file that public ownership had merely provided 'jobs for the boys' with 'the same old gang' in power again.

The long-term consequences of the Attlee nationalisation measures were important. Because the industries nationalised had all been on the verge of bankruptcy a strong association was established in the public mind between socialism and bureaucratic inefficiency. It did not matter one iota that these public utilities provided a cheap infrastructure of services for the benefit of private industry. Company profits soared from £643 million in 1938 to £1,586 million in 1948 and £1,830 million in 1949.

As for the rest of the government's economic policy, much had been made at the 1945 election of the fact that the Labour Party was the natural 'planning' party in contrast to the Conservative reliance on 'market forces'. Planning was respectable as a result of the war and *Let Us Face the Future* dwelt on the prospects of a future national plan for Britain. If this was to be executed with any degree of success then an efficient economic staff was vital. But with only fifteen economists in the economic section of the Cabinet and the same number of statisticians in the Central Statistical Office, government planning could be little more than a rather desperate whistling in the dark. Not surprisingly – and this prefigured what happened in the 1960s under Harold Wilson's premiership – when the Attlee government faced a convertibility crisis for the pound in 1947, Washington turned out to know rather more about what was happening than Whitehall itself. The pound also had to be hurriedly devalued by 30 per cent in September 1949.

No national plan was ever produced and when an *Economic Survey* was finally published in 1947 it revealed that 'planning' was now effectively little more than piecemeal exhortation to private industry as was evident in the tentative and ineffective National Investment Board, though the Distribution of Industry Act certainly helped in locating industry in previously run-down areas. Exchange controls were never introduced, so that £645 million flooded out of the country between 1947 and 1949. The advisers and consultants appointed by the government often came from important private firms and were thus at least implicitly hostile to Labour's reliance on planning and controls. Unilever, for example, filled ninety posts in the Ministry of Food, twelve of them senior positions.

This problem of personnel was again one which the Labour Party had never really thought through. In 1920 Beatrice Webb had claimed that a socialist order would require '. . . a dedicated Order, something resembling the Society of Jesus, which should exact a high standard of training, discipline and self-control among its members, and which would furnish, therefore, a leadership of the élite to guide the mass of citizens to a Socialist State.' This proposal, which resembles the Leninist conception of a revolutionary vanguard, was certainly never implemented. Attlee's Minister of Fuel, Hugh Gaitskell, wrote despairingly in his diary that it was difficult to find suitable people to occupy high managerial positions in the newly nationalised coal industry.

The nadir of this disorganised style of government came with the fuel crisis in early 1947 when harsh weather brought a 25 per cent drop in coal supplies. February proved to be the coldest month in Britain so far this century. Manny Shinwell – of whom Kenneth Morgan has scathingly commented that 'Shinwell's amazing longevity and colourful personality over eight decades of political activity have masked his almost consistently disastrous record in office' – was unable to cope, although such a shortfall had long been forecast. Britain's exports were hit and her economic recovery was dented. Though Mass Observation reported that most people thought the government had muddled through the crisis reasonably successfully, there need not have been a crisis in the first place.

The Labour government's social reforms centred on the development of a welfare state. Although the Liberals had introduced old-age pensions in 1908 and a national health and unemployment insurance system in 1911, these represented little more than a patchwork provision of services.

During the 1920s and 1930s no administration displayed more than a passing concern in social welfare and it was not until the impact of 'total war' made itself felt that basic welfare services were created. The family means test was replaced, social security benefits were raised and family allowances were introduced. A sequence of White Papers on health, insurance and employment was published by the coalition government towards the end of the war, demonstrating official acceptance of the philosophy of the welfare state, and the Labour government was active in the fields of social security, health, education, housing and jobs.

There were three major pieces of legislation on social security: the Industrial Injuries Act 1946, which incorporated much of the Beveridge

Report; the National Insurance Act 1946; and the National Assistance Act 1948, which established a safety-valve for all those who did not fall within the scope of the 1946 acts. All three measures were an immense improvement on the situation in the 1930s and tried to introduce 'the idea of a national minimum', regarded by Sir William Beveridge as 'a peculiarly British idea'. They wiped away almost the last vestiges of the 'Poor Law' mentality which had thought that it was a crime to be poor.

However, a number of shortcomings were apparent. For instance, the National Insurance Act followed in the path of the Liberal legislation before the First World War in being founded on the contributory principle of insurance which meant that, unlike a non-contributory scheme funded out of general taxation, the labour force was already substantially paying for their benefits out of deductions from their wages. Levied at a flat rate, the contributions operated as a regressive form of taxation. Nor were the benefits tied to the cost of living.

The provisions of the National Assistance Act were soon being used by thousands of people because national insurance benefits were so meagre – reflecting a lingering bias against anyone getting 'something' for 'nothing' – that many men and women had also to resort to means-tested national assistance. Two writers estimated that:

> ... the National Insurance benefits are so inadequate both in scale and scope that already by 1951 no less than two-and-a-half million people were being submitted to a means test. This is no less than one in every twenty of the population.

During the war improvements in health care had been brought about by centralisation under the Emergency Medical Service, and the principle was securely established that medical provision should be supplied on the grounds solely of need. Building on this consensus, Aneurin Bevan, the new Minister of Health, pushed through the National Health Service Act of 1946, which came into force in July 1948.

The great virtue of the NHS was that it took this vital area of life away from market forces, although it still allowed the retention of some pay beds within the state system. Bevan found himself unable to create a full-time salaried service and unfortunately the new health centres – which were to have emphasised the value of preventive medicine within the community – were largely a victim of government cuts in the later 1940s. Nevertheless these defects should not obscure the central achievement of the NHS and fittingly the service has retained massive popular support ever since its introduction.

The Education Act of 1944 introduced by the Conservative MP R. A. Butler had provided the framework within which Ellen Wilkinson, the Minister of Education, was to work. She raised the school-leaving age to fifteen but never sixteen as promised, and made no attempt to discourage private schools. There was also little support for those local education authorities not producing plans on a tripartite system of grammar, technical and secondary modern schools. Instead Wilkinson and her successor George Tomlinson emphasised the virtues of the élitist grammar schools, thus ensuring that the secondary moderns would suffer from inferior resources and prestige. The Labour Party did, however, increase government expenditure on education.

Opinion polls showed that housing was regarded by the electorate as the most important issue of the 1945 election. Attlee immediately broke one promise by not setting up a separate Ministry of Housing, and Aneurin Bevan struggled to handle both this department and that of health. Hugh Dalton noted in his diary Bevan's supposed remark: 'I never spend more than an hour a week on housing. Housing runs itself.'

The relative failure of the government's housing programme is shown by considering just how many houses were, in fact, built. Some 230,000 houses were completed in 1948 compared with 350,000 in 1938, so the government fell a long way short of its own target of 400,000 houses a year. Cuts in the housing budget in 1948 and 1949 further reduced the numbers, and a survey of 1951 concluded that there were 750,000 fewer houses than households – a far cry from fulfilling Labour's election pledge that every family should have a good standard of accommodation. Shortages of material and manpower meant that this promise was wildly optimistic. But, despite all the economic problems, 1 million permanent houses were built during the years of the Attlee government.

Bevan was also responsible for section 132 of the Local Government Act of 1948 which allowed local authorities to spend up to the product of a 6d rate for the provision of entertainment, drama, music and so on. In Janet Minihan's words, 'Section 132 at last eliminated the need for special enabling legislation and gave local authorities uniform opportunities to encourage cultural activities throughout their districts.'

As for the pledge to introduce full employment, from 1945 to 1951 a high level of employment was indeed maintained with the number of jobless restricted to about 3 per cent of the labour force. This was a significant improvement on the situation in the 1930s. In fact, the Labour government's main complaint related to the shortage of labour available.

No one could doubt the energy with which Attlee and his colleagues tried to tackle the many problems facing the country. In 1946 alone, eight major pieces of legislation were placed on the statute book. Herbert Morrison in his book *The Peaceful Revolution* claimed that between 1945 and 1948 over 200 public Acts of Parliament were passed. By the end of 1946 the Indian Secretary Lord Pethick Lawrence was so exhausted by his efforts to secure a peaceful British withdrawal from India that it was only during Cabinet meetings he found the time to sleep. No one could bear to wake him up.

Such a pace brought problems in its wake, notably those of ill health — and it should be remembered that the key figures in the administration had been continuously in office since 1940. Attlee, Bevin, Morrison and Cripps all had spells in hospital. Matters were not helped by a hostile Press. Writing of these Attlee years, the veteran *Sunday Times* journalist James Margach concluded: 'I have never known the Press so consistently and irresponsibly political, slanted and prejudiced.' Eventually, the government was goaded into appointing a royal commission to investigate Fleet Street — which was to recommend the setting up of the Press Council — but by then the damage had been done.

Ill health and a prejudiced Press were compounded by the sheer bad luck of unfortunate events beyond the government's control. The world wheat shortage in 1946 meant that bread rationing had to be introduced, which it hadn't during the war. One unfortunate mistake was Hugh Dalton's unintended Budget leak in 1947. He spoke to a journalist on his way to the chamber and by chance parts of his speech appeared in the papers before he had finished speaking in the House. Dalton was obliged to resign.

The government was harried by an energetic right-wing group called the British Housewives' League, which organised rallies and marches. Nor was it helped by the way in which R. A. Butler shifted the Conservative Party away from what were now untenable attitudes towards a critical acceptance of the new consensus. Their *Industrial Charter* of 1947 insisted that they too were now committed to a welfare state and to full employment. Under the chairmanship of Lord Woolton Conservative Central Office was overhauled and modernised. Perhaps one major success of the Attlee administration was to force the Conservative Party to adapt to Labour ideas, just as in the 1980s it proved to be the other way around.

By 1948 the Labour government was running out of steam. Influential figures such as Morrison were calling for 'consolidation' rather than further reform. Chancellor Cripps' White Paper of February 1948 demanded wage restraint and his budget of that year shifted the emphasis from direct to indirect taxation which always bears more heavily on the lower paid. There was to be no widescale redistribution of wealth and economist Dudley Seers noted in his book *The Levelling of Incomes since 1938*, published in 1951: '. . . there has been no continuation after 1944 of the previous trend towards equality of distribution.'

The government cautiously proceeded with iron and steel nationalisation, proposing to set up an Iron and Steel Corporation that would own the assets and liabilities of the steel companies but otherwise undertake no change at all in their organisational and administrative structures. The existing management and even the identities and names of the companies were to be retained intact. It was little more than a cosmetic exercise but by 1948 business interests and industrialists felt confident enough to go on to the offensive against the government – public relations firms like Aims of Industry were active, particularly in the 'Mr Cube' campaign opposing government plans for Tate and Lyle's sugar empire. 'Tate not State' was the slogan adopted.

The Steel Bill fell foul of the Tory majority in the House of Lords and thus the government found itself embroiled in a constitutional battle as well. The result was the Parliament Act of 1949, which did not abolish either hereditary peers or introduce an elected second chamber but instead cut to one year its power to delay bills passed by the House of Commons. The Iron and Steel Act did not come into operation until February 1951 because the government had agreed that the result of the 1950 election should be regarded as a mandate.

Attlee's government won the 1950 election but with a majority of only six seats. The administration limped on until another general election was held in October 1951. The Labour Party received just under 14 million votes, the highest that any party has ever received in this country, but the vagaries of the electoral system and the collapse of the Liberal Party vote (they put up 109 candidates compared with 475 the year before) returned the Conservatives to power. After six years Attlee and the Labour Party left office. It was to be thirteen years before another Labour Prime Minister returned to Downing Street.

How should one rate the Attlee government? Mrs Thatcher's governments in the 1980s saw the attempted dismantling of, and hostility towards, the three main post-war assumptions: government intervention, planning and state welfare. But it is a testimony to the strength and appeal of this social-democratic consensus that so much of it has remained intact, and that Mrs Thatcher herself had to announce that the National Health Service was safe in Conservative hands.

Post-war Britain has seen not only a remarkable rise in living standards but also the creation of a society in which people are better fed, better housed, better cared for, better educated and more fully employed than in the 1930s. Much of this success is due to Attlee's 1945–51 governments and to the dedicated and practical work of the Prime Minister himself. To criticise aspects of this record is not to call into question its outstanding overall achievement.

The administration's main omission was to shy away from implementing major institutional changes. Attlee always prided himself on his empirical and pragmatic approach – 'We were not afraid of compromise and practical solutions. We knew that mistakes would be made and that advance would be often by trial and error.' He remained something of an Establishment man, albeit a more progressive and humane Establishment. Attlee described himself as 'basically a Victorian' and he took enormous pride in the success of 'My young Haileyburians in the House . . .' It is also true that the war had not brought the collapse or discredit of long-established institutions.

But there was something symbolic and revealing about Attlee's decision to rebuild the bombed House of Commons exactly as it had been before the war, even though this meant that the people's representatives could not attend at the same time as there was not room for them all. Similarly, the Labour government had no truck with the idea of Scottish Home Rule as expressed in 'the Covenant':

> By 1950, the Covenant had attracted well over a million signatures. The government, however, brushed it aside. It offered no new initiatives other than increasing the already large numbers of civil servants in the Scottish Office in Edinburgh.

The good things which the Attlee administration did, such as the introduction of legal aid and family allowances, were too often marred by unimaginative failures elsewhere – for instance, not introducing the principle of equal pay for women civil servants or schoolteachers. It was also telling that the Labour government provoked less constitutional conflict than either the 1906 Liberal government or the New Deal administration which came to power in the United States in 1933.

The government steered clear of far-reaching reform of, say, the voting system, the hereditary principle in the House of Lords, the secret services, the civil service, the monarchy, the armed forces, the public schools, the judiciary, the Press, the rating system, local government and indeed from any grand gestures other than the Festival of Britain held in 1951. In 1947 Mass Observation suggested that people were 'ready for radical action' but were disappointed by the lack of 'spectacular appeals' and 'wider explanation' from the government. Attlee and his colleagues also completely failed to understand the economic moves towards European integration taking place on the continent.

It was inevitable that the government, heavily influenced as it was by the trade union connection, would tend towards a system of corporatism involving government, employers and unions. This approach summed up the invariably 'top heavy' approach at the heart of Fabian philosophy. The civil servant or 'the man in Whitehall' was always thought to know best. The resentment displayed by 'ordinary people' explains in part the success of the Ealing comedy films of the time which often portrayed 'a little man' fighting back against inflexible bureaucracy.

Attlee once claimed that William Morris was the patron saint of his government, but Morris would surely have brought some much needed flair and imagination to the administration. Looking back on the Attlee years Aneurin Bevan observed that: 'Our name became identified with greyness and dullness, frugalities, shortages.' In France the Monnet Planning Commission efficiently restructured French industry after the war. In Britain, by contrast, nationalisation and planning became indelibly associated with incompetence and waste. The Conservative Party slogan for the 1951 election was 'Set the People Free'.

But the Attlee governments were also handicapped by what would become a permanent feature of the postwar world and which brought with it debilitating consequences both politically and economically: the Cold War.

CHAPTER NINE

With Us or Against Us?: The Cold War in Britain

'Either with Christ or against Christ: either with His Church or against His Church.'

Pope Pius XII, December 1946

'The opinion of the Trade Unions is that the Bevanite activities are a deliberate attempt to undermine the leadership in the same way as Hitler and the communists did. There is no difference whatever between them.'

Will Lawther, leader of the miners, writing in the *Daily Telegraph*, 29 January 1953

'Humanity, not only in the USSR but in all countries, will always be deeply in his [Stalin's] debt.'

Christopher Hill, 1953

ON THE afternoon of 8 January 1947, six Cabinet ministers met at 10 Downing Street to decide whether Britain should build its own nuclear weapon. The most powerful member of this committee, which was kept secret not just from the Labour Party but from the rest of the Cabinet, was the Foreign Secretary Ernest Bevin whose thick, bulky appearance embodied the pugnacity and strength with which he steamrollered friends, colleagues and enemies alike.

That Bevin was Foreign Secretary at all was a tribute to his personal determination. Born in Somerset in March 1881, he was the illegitimate son of a farmworker, Diana Bevin, and never knew who his father was. His mother died when he was eight and he was brought up by a half-sister. Bevin left school at eleven to work on a local farm scaring away the birds. This was still his job in 1894, the very year that Thomas Hardy published his last novel which begins with a small boy scaring away the birds. But if Hardy's Jude was to remain obscure, Bevin was to become a statesman who shaped the post-war world.

At thirteen Bevin moved to Bristol where he worked as a drayman and joined the Bristol Socialist Society, just as Ramsay MacDonald had done ten years before. He became a lay preacher and a union activist, making a local name for himself by forming the unemployed into a 'Right To Work' committee. One protest that he organised is still talked of in Bristol. His friend and biographer Francis Williams describes it:

> One Sunday shortly before morning service in Bristol Cathedral a great crowd of unemployed assembled in Horsefair. There they formed in orderly procession and, with Bevin at their head, marched to the Cathedral. As the service began they entered, and, with Bevin leading them, silently took up places along every aisle of the great church. They remained there without stirring throughout the service, many of them clearly in great distress from hunger, all of them poorly clad; a mute challenge to the Christian conscience of every worshipper. When the service ended they filed slowly and quietly out of the Cathedral and, without speaking a word, reformed into procession and marched back to the Horsefair. There after a few words from Bevin who told them to go back to their homes without disturbance they dispersed.

In 1914 Bevin became a full-time trade union organiser. He made his name after the war as 'the Dockers' KC'. At an inquiry into dockers' wages in February 1920 he showed the court plates of meagre food to demonstrate what a docker's wage actually meant in terms of privation. In 1922 he was the driving force behind the formation of the Transport and General Workers' Union, the largest in Britain. Bevin was elected its General Secretary, a powerful position which meant that for the next thirty years he was a dominant figure in the labour movement. He brooked no internal opposition within the union and earned the nickname 'Boss Bevin'.

In 1935 Bevin's fierce speech at the Labour Party Conference calling for British rearmament prompted the pacifist George Lansbury to resign as Labour Party leader. When Bevin was told by friends that he had dealt unnecessarily harshly with Lansbury, he replied even more brutally: 'Lansbury has been going about dressed in saint's clothes for years, waiting for martyrdom. I set fire to the maggots.'

During the Second World War Bevin moved from the trade union world on to the national stage. Elected MP for Wandsworth in 1940, he had been appointed Minister of Labour in the Churchill government and was responsible for mobilising all available man and woman power. When Labour won the general election in 1945 he was expecting to be made Chancellor of the Exchequer but to his surprise found himself appointed Foreign Secretary.

Bevin brought to this post a hearty dislike of communism, mainly because much of his time in the 1920s and 1930s had been spent combating what he regarded as communist infiltration of his union. He urged the West to stand up to the Soviet Union and his unyielding stance was crucial in the formation of the North Atlantic Treaty Organisation (NATO) in April 1949. He also pushed through the decision that Britain needed its own bomb, making sure that the huge £100 million cost of the project was concealed in the 'secret budget'. The Cold War became several degrees colder.

'Defence' has often been a problem for the British labour movement because of various conflicting strands of thought within it. Pacifism, internationalism, 'Little Englandism', 'John Bull-ism', Christian socialism, Quakerism – these traditions give different answers to the question of how Britain should defend itself. Labour leaders who agreed with each other on much else have sometimes taken opposing views on this topic: Attlee and Dalton, for instance, both fought in the First World War; Lansbury and Morrison were anti-war protesters.

During the Second World War the United States, the Soviet Union and Britain formed an anti-fascist alliance even though in peace the Soviet Union had been regarded as an enemy. As the hostilities came to an end, previously hidden tensions started to surface. The United States and the Soviet Union in particular began to jockey for position in the post-war world. Always the realist, Stalin coldly observed: 'This war is not as in the past; whoever occupies a territory also imposes on it his own social system. Everyone imposes his own systems as far as his army can reach. It cannot be otherwise.' Already communism and capitalism were carving up the world between them.

Traditionally, Labour and the Conservatives had operated a bipartisan policy under which both parties agreed on the objectives to be pursued. But there were sometimes differences in emphasis, and during the 1945 election campaign the Labour Party stressed that it alone was ideally suited to handling the Soviet Union. Its manifesto *Let Us Face the Future* had reminded the electorate:

> Let it not be forgotten that in the years leading up to the war the Tories were so scared of Russia that they missed the chance to establish a partnership which might well have prevented the war.

Within months of this statement, however, Attlee's Labour government had changed its mind on the possibility of partnership. Instead it became sucked in to a new 'war', the Cold War. 'We' were in the right, 'They' were, of course, in the wrong. The very existence of the Cold War showed the internationalism of the modern twentieth-century world: no country could now be an island. A series of events – the failure to hold free and fair elections in Eastern Europe, Marshall Aid, the coup in Czechoslovakia, the Berlin Airlift, the formation of NATO and the Warsaw Pact – led to bitter hostility. It was a tragedy of misunderstanding; in Denis Healey's words, 'We took too seriously some of the Leninist rhetoric pouring out from Moscow, as the Russians took too seriously some of the anti-Communist rhetoric favoured by American politicians.'

Much of this chapter deals with the effect of American interference in Britain and Western Europe, involvement which was often secret, furtive and anti-democratic. But it must be stressed that Soviet interference in the new Eastern European regimes was much more overt and far-reaching. It is vital to keep a sense of proportion. Arthur Koestler pointed out that it was foolish to equate an 'imperfect democracy' (USA) with an 'imperfect totalitarian regime' (USSR).

The extent of American involvement in Western Europe after 1945 is still little-known. Why? The Americans themselves are understandably reluctant to publicise their activities; British historians shy away from such a controversial topic – one journalist commissioned to write an article on this subject found that his material was rejected by the *Sunday Times*; and many on the Left have not raised the matter because the Soviet Union did not exactly have clean hands. Revelations about one side would inevitably lead to revelations about the other.

The foundations of American involvement were laid during the latter part of the war when several US trade union leaders established committees in order to help influence post-war labour affairs. Several of those involved such as Jay Lovestone had once been Communists but were now zealous anti-Communists. Lovestone remained a bachelor because, as he put it, he was 'married to the idea of preventing the Kremlin from dominating the world.' Another figure involved, Irving Brown, was nicknamed 'Scarface' which somehow sums up the sleazy, underhand tactics which were often employed. Lovestone, Brown and their circle paid most attention to Italy and France. Both countries possessed a formidable Communist Party that had benefited from the discrediting of indigenous right-wing organisations which, with a few notable exceptions, had been either fascist during the war or had collaborated with the Germans.

Elections held in 1945 and 1946 gave the Communist Parties in Italy and France scores of seats and also a share in government. American concern at this Communist electoral success turned to alarm in the winter of 1946–47 when impending European economic and political collapse seemed likely. Any chaos would certainly have been to the advantage of the Communists who would have claimed that the only viable system left was the Soviet one.

The Americans responded in two ways. First of all President Truman announced the so-called 'Truman doctrine' in March 1947 which established that his government was prepared to play an active role outside the United States: 'I believe that we must assist free peoples to work out their destinies in their own way.' This interventionist stance was backed up by material support. Following a plan drawn up by General George Marshall, the United States pumped economic aid into Western Europe in an attempt to stave off disaster: between 1948 and 1951 a massive 13,000 million dollars of assistance was made over to European governments.

Secondly, they tried to undermine the Communist challenge by setting up rival left-wing but distinctly non-communist parties and by splitting Communist-controlled unions; and they also financed various right-wing organisations. In Italy the Christian Democrats received one million dollars, in France it was General de Gaulle who was funded. The right-wing union Force Ouvriere in France was encouraged to break away from the Communist-dominated CGT. In Italy a split within the General Confederation of Labour was fomented by American money while right-wing Catholic unions were assisted. The Communist-organised World Federation of Trade Unions was torn in two when Western trade unions were persuaded to withdraw and to form the new International Congress of Free Trade Unions (ICFTU) in December 1949. Much of this was done to a chorus of anti-Communist frenzy: 'Reds' were here, there and everywhere.

In Britain there were some indications of this mood. Even Harold Macmillan called for a 'Christian crusade' against Communism and George Orwell, admittedly a sick man, began to keep lists of suspected Communist conspirators. But these signs were few and far between. The Labour Party of Attlee and Bevin had never been in danger from the small British Communist Party and the government's response to industrial unrest would have been robust enough for a Conservative administration. Troops were used in eleven disputes between 1945 and 1951; strike-breaking became almost a reflex action for this Labour government. The police were often asked to find evidence that strikes were Communist initiated, but invariably had to report that no such evidence existed.

Much of the running was made by the Foreign Office, still smarting from its disastrous policies of the decade before; as Anne Deighton has put it: 'The appeasement analogy became the worst form of abuse within the

Foreign Office, and to stand up to the Russians an expiation for not standing up to Hitler.' In January 1948 the Labour government set up an organisation under Foreign Offices auspices which was called, innocuously enough, the Information Research Department (IRD). Paid for out of the secret fund maintained by all governments, the IRD had its own publication called *Freedom First* which it distributed to British trade unions. It also 'placed' articles favourable to the United States and British view of international affairs in the domestic and foreign Press.

By 1951 more than 1,000 'items' a year were being placed here and abroad. The IRD financed a firm of publishers, Ampersand, which in the 1950s produced over 100 anti-Communist books. The IRD remained active until 1977 when it was closed down by the new Foreign Secretary, Dr David Owen. Information about the IRD is difficult to find; its files have been destroyed by government 'weeders' on the grounds, patently untrue, that the material was not 'of sufficient historical importance to be selected for permanent preservation'.

At times the Attlee administration flirted with wide-scale anti-Communist measures, drawing up plans to penalise 'subversive or misleading propaganda' with up to fourteen years' imprisonment and to outlaw 'attempts to disrupt the nation's economy'. In the event, however, the traditional British respect for civil liberties saved the day and the proposals were dropped by the Cabinet.

The trade union movement, reflecting the small role that Marxism had played in Britain and the botched zigzagging policies of the British Party, was also predominantly anti-Communist. The TUC issued two pamphlets *Defend Democracy* and *The Tactics of Disruption*, both of which attacked Communist activities. In 1949 the Transport and General Workers' Union began to dismiss its Communist officials in a series of actions reminiscent of the blacklisting used in the United States.

What did this international polarisation from the late 1940s mean in individual, personal terms? To place the British experience in perspective, it is important to glance at what was happening in the United States. In 1947 President Truman, leader of the Democrats, enacted a Loyalty Order which failed to make any distinction between being a socialist and being a spy and traitor. Worse still, it established the notion of 'guilt by association' under which past contact with a 'subversive', even if only on personal and non-political grounds, was sufficient in itself to make one 'a potential subversive'. There were no rules of evidence.

A recent book by the journalist Carl Bernstein, *Loyalties*, reveals the scale and scope of the surveillance of suspects. His parents, once members of the American Communist Party, were the subject of more than 200 separate surveillances over a four-year period. When researching his book Bernstein found that the intelligence procedures used had been so exhaustive that even the names of the guests at his own Bar Mitzvah in 1957 were meticulously recorded. His parents remained under FBI surveillance for no less than thirty-five years. Historian David Caute's book on the subject is aptly titled *The Great Fear*.

Were similar actions taken in Britain? The government introduced civil service 'vetting' under which none of the formalities or safeguards of a usual administrative hearing were observed – for example, no witnesses could be identified, no evidence was given and no legal representation allowed. On the other hand, 'suspects' were transferred to other posts rather than being dismissed outright; the attitude was 'we should not make any martyrs'. To compare the scale of this vetting with that in the United States: in 1952, 134,000 civil servants were subject to checks; in America, by 1955 the figure had reached 9 million. In Britain 25 civil servants were dismissed, 25 resigned and 88 were transferred; in America, 9,500 government employees were sacked and 15,000 resigned.

Some prominent Communists in Britain did suffer checks to their careers. Andrew Rothstein, a founder member of the Communist Party, was dismissed from his post at London University on the grounds of 'inadequate scholarship'. J. D. Bernal lost his place on several government committees and lists of his supporters were sent to the authorities. Similar events happened to Professor J. B. S. Haldane. A. J. P. Taylor was banned from the Third Programme because his talks were considered too pro-Soviet. Within the universities, as Eric Hobsbawm has recalled, it was difficult for a left-winger to find a post after the Berlin Airlift in the summer of 1948 but those in place were not sacked. Some left-wing actors found their work at the BBC dried up.

Nevertheless, of the forty-five Communists I have spoken to specifically about this period very few had experienced any direct harassment or even unpleasantness – traditional British a-politicism and the feeling that people's opinions were their own private affair had provided a reasonably tolerant atmosphere. David Caute has likewise pointed out that there was no Un-British Activities Committee, Parliament did not go witchhunting and there were no loyalty oaths. Nor were there more than a handful of 'Communist' election smears directed at left-wing candidates. At the height of the Cold War the Labour Party's Transport House still played its annual cricket match against the staff of the *Daily Worker*. British respect for civil liberties creaked and groaned during the Cold War but survived largely intact – unlike in Eastern Europe where political trials, purges and imprisonment were frequent.

Where the Cold War did prove devastating in Britain was in the broader political and economic spheres. The decision to create Britain's own nuclear weapon and then in April 1949 to become a founder-member of NATO meant that the country's shaky economy was committed to a financial burden it could not afford. By 1949 the Labour government was spending £750 million, or 10 per cent of its national income, on defence. The British Army was three times its 1939 size, despite the acknowledged fact that the economy was suffering from a shortage of manpower. Indeed, between 1945 and 1950 Britain spent a higher proportion of its national income on defence than the United States.

The Korean War, which broke out in 1950, only exacerbated the problem. Money which could have been spent on improving living standards at home was instead poured into an unpleasant and unnecessary war abroad. The either/or choice set up by the Cold War meant that Britain acquired some particularly unsavoury allies such as Syngman Rhee, the leader of South Korea. After the Czechoslovakian coup in February 1948 Hugh Dalton had thought this might well be what the future held in store. He wrote in his diary: 'We should have to drag ourselves back behind the USA ... we should have to line up with all the worst reactionaries and the Catholic Church! Ugh!'

Another damaging consequence of the Cold War was that Britain's 'special relationship' with the United States precluded any search for potentially more fruitful relationships. As early as the 1920s Ernest Bevin had wanted 'to inculcate the spirit of a United States of Europe at least on an economic basis ...' He called for an economic United States of Europe 'spreading from the borders of Russia right to the borders of France ...' At the 1945 Labour Party conference Bevin talked of the possibility of a 'Third Way' between the United States and the Soviet Union.

In the Cold War climate such aspirations went by the board as too did some of the internationalism dear to the hearts of earlier leaders like Keir Hardie and Ramsay MacDonald. Instead a rather belligerent insularity was more evident; as Denis Healey has pungently expressed it: 'The Labour Party has never been prepared to learn anything from the experience of foreigners.'

So-called 'special relationships' with both the United States and the Commonwealth meant that the Labour government was not interested in developments in mainland Europe. It opposed both the European Defence Community and the Coal and Steel Community set up in April 1951. The Party's two leading foreign policy experts, Bevin and Dalton, were both hostile to any European idea. Herbert Morrison's reason for opposing the

Coal and Steel Community was a classic demonstration of Labour Party insularity: 'It's no good, we cannot do it, the Durham miners won't wear it.'

It is easy with the benefit of hindsight to say that here was the moment when post-war Britain took the wrong turn, but there was at the time a substantial section within the Labour Party calling for the creation of a 'United Socialist States of Europe' (USSE). On behalf of the Labour Party's NEC Hugh Dalton endorsed the philosophy of the USSE but nothing further was done. In the Cold War atmosphere any middle way was squeezed out.

For the British Communist Party the onset of the Cold War was disastrous. Emerging from the war with its highest ever membership of over 58,000 and buoyed up by its association with the Soviet Union, a wartime ally, it had high hopes for the 1945 election. In the event the British electorate drew a distinction between admiration for the Red Army and the Soviet role in winning the war, and voting Communist here in Britain. Only two Communists were elected; Willie Gallacher retained his seat in Fife and Phil Piratin won in Mile End, East London. These victories neatly encapsulated the Scottish and Jewish contribution to British communism. But just two MPs in contrast to the 104 Communists elected in France in 1946 showed yet again how tenuous was the Party's position in Britain.

Party membership continued to rise, reaching a high of 60,000 in 1946 – although the French Communist Party numbered 800,000 and the Italians a gigantic 1.7 million. The leadership tried to make the Party more friendly and less 'alien': for instance, the 'Politburo' was now renamed the Political Committee. New offices for the *Daily Worker* were built on Farringdon Road in 1948 – a bleak 'Stalinist' building designed by Erno Goldfinger, the man responsible for the nasty DHSS building at the Elephant and Castle. Ian Fleming is supposed to have taken his name for the villain in *Goldfinger*. Saturday sales of the *Daily Worker* reached 120,000 and a Scottish edition of the paper was started.

But the impact of the Cold War meant that the peak of Communist expansion had been reached. Before the Cold War it had been to the Party's advantage to be linked with the Soviet Union; after the Berlin Airlift of 1948 it definitely wasn't. The Comintern had been killed off by Stalin during the war but in October 1947 the Communist Information Bureau (Cominform) was set up. The British party was too small to be invited to join but it unhesitatingly obeyed the new orders which signalled a return to the sectarian rigidities of the 'Third Period' between 1928 and 1935.

Dissent was once again heresy, as Tito and the Yugoslav Communists found out when they refused to nationalise their industries and collectivise their agriculture on Soviet lines. The trauma of breaking with Moscow comes through in the memoirs of one of Tito's associates, Milovan Djilas, who had to persuade himself that 'In any event – life is possible without Stalin's love', almost as if an excommunicated Catholic was talking about the Pope.

Throughout Eastern Europe one-party states were established and purge trials weeded out potential troublemakers. By 1951 there were 350 labour camps in Czechoslovakia alone, holding 100,000 prisoners; 278 senior Party officials had been killed for holding 'incorrect' political views. Just as they did in the 1930s, leading British Communists welcomed these measures. Willie Gallacher wrote *The Case For Communism* which was published by Penguin Books in 1949:

> . . . But what about the opposition [in Eastern Europe]? What opposition? The parties in the Government bloc represent the people, and carry forward a policy in the interests of, and for the welfare of, the people. Those who want to put the clock back are enemies of the people. There can be no toleration for such.

As Pope Pius XII put it, those who are not with us are against us.

Within the British Party, disagreement was met by denunciation and expulsion. To dissent from 'the line' handed down from above was to ensure not just political ostracism but often personal ostracism too because most Party members' best friends were also Party members. Investigation of a suspect's views bore all the hallmarks of a medieval inquisition. The young E. P. Thompson, later a distinguished historian, was a Party member in the 1940s and early 1950s and has recalled what took place:

> That time produced one of the sharpest mental frosts I can remember on the Left. Vitalities shrivelled up and books lost their leaves. It was about this time that the Party blocked the publication of Hamish Henderson's translation of Gramsci's prison letters – it had been discovered (we were told) that Gramsci was guilty of some nameless 'deviation'.

Thompson remembers attending Party meetings at which hacks publicly scolded and 'unmasked' various unreliable individuals, and notes too how people found it almost impossible to defy this God-like Party:

> It was a shameful episode and I shared in the shame, for, however 'youthful' I

was, I had allowed myself to be made use of as part of the team of uncultured yobboes and musclemen under the command of the elderly Burns. But I was sad and puzzled also that my heroes had not allowed me to fight on their side. They had at once lost all their customary confidence, wit and vitality when placed in the formal posture of receiving criticism from one of the Party's senior officers.

Excruciating and distinctly 'unMarxist' was the widespread 'Stalin worship'. Eric Heffer was then a Party member: 'We accepted all Stalin's actions . . . I remember Party meetings where speeches were littered with phrases like "As Comrade Stalin has said . . ."' Professor Hyman Levy also noted that the cult of personality, as the Soviet leaders later referred to it, was in fact the cult of just one personality: 'During the later years of Stalin's life, if his name was mentioned at a party meeting, the members stood up in silent reverence.' Alan Sebrill, the protagonist in Edward Upward's *The Rotten Elements*, suffers a nervous breakdown but found 'he could stop his trembling by thinking of Stalin and by speaking the name of Stalin, repeatedly but not quite aloud, much as a religious believer might have called on the name of God.'

In such a climate it is not surprising that the last vestiges of electoral support for the British Communist Party faded away. In 1950, 97 of its 100 election candidates lost their deposits (and Gallacher and Piratin their seats); in 1951, all ten candidates lost their deposits. That same year the Party launched a silly and negative crusade called simply 'Hate America'.

Who were the Party 'minders' or 'musclemen' responsible for carrying out the 'line'? The man E. P. Thompson refers to above was Emile Burns, a former Cambridge student who was in charge of the Party's intellectuals. Another 'apparatchik' was James Klugmann, one more Cambridge Communist of the 1930s whose name periodically surfaces in 'Third Man' books. However, he was, to his credit, openly Communist, making no secret of his views. His personal life shows the closeness of the British Communist Party 'family'. He married Kitty Cornforth, sister of yet another Cambridge Communist Maurice Cornforth who for twenty-five years was managing director of Lawrence and Wishart, the Party's publishing house.

Klugmann was a man of erudition and charm who over the years amassed a magnificent collection of material on the history of the British labour movement. During the Second World War he worked for SOE (Special Operations Executive) in Cairo, helping to parachute British soldiers into Yugoslavia to fight alongside Tito's Partisans. He was in his element and there is a good portrait of Klugmann in historian Basil Davidson's account of his experiences called *Special Operations Europe*.

But in 1948 Tito was expelled from the Soviet camp when Stalin now argued that he had all along been an agent of Trotsky, of the Nazis, in fact of anyone opposed to the Soviet Union. His past must therefore be exposed. European Communist Parties were expected to mount campaigns vilifying Tito, and who better in the British Party to expose him than James Klugmann? He duly produced a book called *From Trotsky to Tito*, even though he must have known he was writing fiction and not fact.

But those who live by the Party line can sometimes die by it too. When the 'line' changed a few years later and Tito came back to favour, Klugmann was left with egg on his face. His book had to be withdrawn: he had perjured himself for nothing. Most people would surely have resigned from an organisation that pressured its members into doing such things. He didn't. Instead he was commissioned by the Party to write its history and he duly produced two unreadable volumes distinguished more for what is left out than what is put in. Klugmann regretted writing both the Tito book and his two histories and promised that the next volume would be an honest account. He died in 1977 before he was put to the test.

If the Cold War severely damaged the Communists, then it was almost as disastrous for the non-Communist Left. Whereas the Communist Party had not challenged the either/or choice between 'Washington' and 'Moscow', the Labour Left did try. But if you didn't unequivocally choose one side or another then it was easy for political opponents to smear you as a 'fellow traveller'.

Early evidence of this technique in action was provided by the fate of the 'Keep Left' group, a body of Labour MPs which during the late 1940s tried to formulate a 'third way' (similar to what Bevin himself had suggested in 1945) between the two superpowers. But under the unrelenting pressure of the Cold War to choose one side or the other, the group was soon whittled down to just a handful of members. It was a foretaste of what was to happen in the 1950s to the Bevanites.

Like George Lansbury, Aneurin Bevan had a charismatic personality, making him one of the British Left's most attractive figures. He is rightly looked upon as the architect of 'the jewel in the crown' of the Labour Party, namely the National Health Service. Today, thirty years after his death, his name is invoked as frequently and as reverentially as that of Keir Hardie himself. This goes to show how reputations and opinions change: in his lifetime Bevan was hated even by supposed colleagues for, as they saw it, stirring up trouble and harming Labour's electoral chances – on one occasion Hugh Gaitskell even claimed to see 'extraordinary parallels between Nye and Adolf Hitler . . .' In the last few years of his life Bevan was attacked by former friends and supporters when he changed his mind over nuclear disarmament and opposed CND.

So far this book has pointed to the major contribution that both Scotland and the East End have made to the British Left. Bevan epitomised the Welsh connection, drawing as it did on a radical tradition centred on the working man's club, the library and adult education classes. Although Bevan received little formal education, the absence was more than made up for by this network of militant culture which produced outstanding miners' leaders such as A. J. Cook, Arthur Horner and Will Paynter. Much of this was due to the creative influence of the South Wales Miners' Federation. Will Paynter has explained what made it so special:

> The Fed was a lot more than a trade union; it was a social institution providing through its leaders an all-round service of advice and assistance to the mining community on most of the problems that could arise between the cradle and the grave. Its function became a combination of economic, social and political leadership in these single industry communities . . . The leaders of the local miners' lodges were very much more than representatives dealing with problems of wages and conditions of employment in the mines. They were acknowledged social leaders called upon to help and advise in all kinds of domestic and social problems; they were indeed the village elders to whom the people went when in any kind of trouble.

The Fed instilled in Bevan a love of discussion and of debating with friends and opponents; one of his favourite sayings was 'This is my truth; now tell me yours.' He was never afraid to admit that he might be wrong. Perhaps it should also be emphasised that this sense of community was rooted in mutual hardship and loss. Arthur Horner's grandfather was brought home in bits in a sack after an underground explosion; Aneurin Bevan's father died in his son's arms, choked to death by pneumoconiosis.

Bevan began work down the mines when he had just turned fourteen – the age when many of his future political opponents were in their first year at private school – but left the pits after a series of accidents. With his energy and gift for public speaking, despite a stammer, he soon made a name for himself as a town and then a county councillor. In 1929, at the age of only thirty-three, he was elected Labour MP for the safe seat of Ebbw Vale. He held it at the 1931 landslide.

Although Bevan was a fine parliamentary speaker, he was always critical of the way in which the House of Commons muffled debate and conflict. In his book *In Place of Fear* he provided a graphic description of the reactions of a new Labour MP arriving at the Commons for the first time:

His first impression is that he is in church. The vaulted roofs and stained-glass windows, the rows of statues of great statesmen of the past, the echoing halls, the soft-footed attendants and the whispered conversation, contrast depressingly with the crowded meetings and the clang and clash of hot opinions he has left behind in his election campaign. Here he is, a tribune of the people, coming to make his voice heard in the seats of power. Instead, it seems he is expected to worship: and the most conservative of all religions – ancestor worship.

Frustrated by the huge majority of the National Government in the 1930s, Bevan and his wife Jennie Lee, who had herself been an MP at twenty-four, supported several extra-parliamentary campaigns. His agitation for a Popular Front resulted in his expulsion from the Labour Party in 1939. But although Bevan was keenly aware of the deadening effects of Parliament he was sure that it was only through this institution that power could be won and exercised. He always scorned left-wing zealots afraid of the compromises of power. When Jennie Lee had voluntarily left the Labour Party some years before, Bevan was scathing: '. . . why don't you get into a nunnery and be done with it? Lock yourself up in a separate cell away from the world and its wickedness? . . . it is the Labour Party or nothing.' He was soon readmitted to the Labour Party. During the war he sniped at Churchill's policies, particularly his caution in launching a 'Second Front' against the Germans, and earned himself the rebuke that he was 'a squalid nuisance'.

The first sign that Bevan was going to be something more than 'a beloved rebel' like the Clydeside MP Jimmy Maxton, loved by all but essentially an impotent force in British politics, came in late 1941 when Bevan became editor of the weekly *Tribune*. His iconoclastic manifesto published in early 1942 claimed that 'Even the parties of the "Left" seem to be mentally muscle-bound and repeat old phrases with less and less conviction.' It was appropriate that George Orwell, another socialist who delighted in pointing out that the emperor sometimes wore no clothes, should be *Tribune*'s literary editor at this time.

Bevan's opportunity to create rather than to criticise came, as we saw in the last chapter, after the Second World War. Although his record in charge of housing was patchy, his work at the Department of Health drew on his earlier experiences with the Tredegar Medical Aid Society. Started by some miners and steelworkers in 1890, the Society had provided a form of communal medical aid and was a fine example of working-class self-help. As two historians have commented, 'His riveting, passionate championing of the new Health Service was but an extension of the collective and accumulated concerns of the South Wales miners, their communities and their own, often sophisticated, local medical schemes.' But he also needed other, very different skills to pilot the Act through Parliament – Field Marshal Montgomery once declared that Bevan's handling of the doctors deserved the attention of all students of strategy.

Although Bevan did have a tendency to let his mouth run away with him – as in 1948 when he called Tories 'lower than vermin' – he was a loyal and successful member of the Cabinet; he refused to join the manoeuvrings against Attlee in 1947, dismissing what he called 'palace revolutions'. He was understandably put out when Hugh Gaitskell was promoted over him to be Chancellor of the Exchequer.

The underlying friction between Gaitskell and Bevan came to a head over the 'teeth and spectacles' issue in April 1951. Gaitskell was in charge of an economy burdened by a huge £4,700 million defence programme deemed necessary in view of the Korean War. He began to look for economies and advocated levying a modest charge for National Health Service patients acquiring teeth and spectacles. The sum involved was small, just £23 million, but for Bevan this charge struck at the heart of the sacrosanct principle of free treatment. In the middle of the argument was the bulk of the Cabinet, worried about the rising cost of the welfare state but confident that the savings could be found elsewhere. At the end of the day, the majority decided to follow Gaitskell rather than Bevan and he, together with Harold Wilson and John Freeman, resigned from the government. The Labour Party lost the subsequent election.

> The trade unions' influence upon the Party is due to two reasons: 1) money, lots of it, and 2) votes, many of them. This money will be spent and these votes cast in the direction which will further trade union policy . . .

Trade union leader Sir Charles Geddes' remark epitomises the hold the unions have always maintained over the Labour Party. In the 1950s it was the right-wing stance of the major unions which ensured that the Bevanites would be defeated in the Party's internal civil war.

Bevan wanted to examine the record of the government with a view to finding a way forward in the future. Writing in 1951 Richard Crossman had warned that '. . . the Labour Party is in danger of becoming not the party of change, but the defender of the post-war status quo.' However, such a post-mortem was anathema to several powerful trade union leaders who, in the context of the Cold War, were only too ready to categorise unwelcome questions as being 'Communist inspired'.

E. P. Thompson and others have noted that anti-Communism has always provided a good excuse for inertia. Arthur Deakin had succeeded Ernest Bevin as leader of the mammoth Transport and General Workers' Union and his quarterly reports to his union executive have been referred to as 'a sustained commentary' on the dangers of Communist activity. Deakin's description of the, to him, troublesome dockers' leaders captures his blunderbuss style; he called them '. . . a moronic crowd of irresponsible adventurers who do not know how much they are being exploited by foreign elements for purposes they do not see or understand.'

Quite apart from the way in which Deakin ran his own union, he and his right-wing colleagues – Tom Williamson of the General and Municipal Workers, Will Lawther of the miners and William Carron of the Engineers – dominated the block vote which, under the Labour Party Constitution of 1918, was integral to the running of the party. They not only controlled the voting at each Party Conference but also in effect nominated eighteen members (the twelve trade union seats, the five places kept for women, and the Treasurer) of the twenty-five-seat Labour Party National Executive. This left only seven remaining seats, which were voted for and occupied by the constituency parties' representatives. The trade unions also sponsored between a third and a half of Labour's MPs. Barbara Castle claimed at the 1953 Conference that 'The Labour Movement is in danger of dying a death of three million cuts – the block votes of four men.' In addition, the trade unions provided five-sixths of the Labour Party's income – and then and since have known what tune they wanted the piper to play.

The heavy-handed methods of Deakin and the others were an uncanny mirror image of the 'democratic centralism' used by their hated Communist opponents and in effect replicated the Cold War inside the ranks of the British labour movement. William Carron of the Engineers deployed a series of underhand techniques to ensure that his union's vote was cast in favour of the leadership. When Will Lawther was interrupted while speaking at a Labour Party Conference, he replied clearly if inelegantly: 'Shut your gob.' Their control was reinforced by the workings of Transport House under the Labour Party's general secretary Morgan Phillips. This was 'labourism' at its worst, bureaucratic and unimaginative, reliant on frequent calls for 'loyalty' and downgrading such activities as socialist education for fear that individuals might think for themselves.

Bevan was in no way a Communist sympathiser. One has only to read his introduction to Denis Healey's book about Communist takeover techniques in Eastern Europe, *The Curtain Falls* (1951), to see how he hated these repressive regimes. Another prominent Bevanite, Richard Crossman, edited a famous series of essays called *The God That Failed* in which six former Communists or Communist sympathisers attacked their former beliefs.

Bevan was not, in fact, seeking to overturn Labour Party policy or to denigrate the record of the Attlee government of which he had been for nearly six years a loyal and hard-working member. Instead the Bevanites simply wanted to hold the party to its commitments. But how best to assemble themselves in the face of the party machine? As 'Keep Left' had found, if the dissidents organised then they were accused of being a party within a party; if they didn't, they were picked off one by one.

One further ingredient in the tragedy is that the Bevanites were not some crackpot grouping. They included forty-seven MPs and two peers and Ian Mikardo has listed their achievements:

> Those forty-nine people included five ex-Ministers, two future Leaders of the Party, fourteen future Ministers, nine current or future members of the Party Executive and nine who were to become peers out of merit, not patronage. We had among us six distinguished writers, and nine members who were in the front rank of parliamentary orators and debaters.

Bevan was not a conspirator nor even much of an organiser and in 1952 the Bevanite group, such as it was, was disbanded. But instead of this decision leading to a frank and fraternal exchange of views, the atmosphere worsened. The Bevanites were popular with the constituencies and won six out of seven of the constituency seats on the National Executive in 1952. The party machine then embarked on a policy of expulsions and even loyalty pledges — a grotesque parody of McCarthyism — and smears, as with Lawther and Gaitskell's remarks quoted above. Morgan Phillips even kept dossiers on the Bevanites and other Labour rebels which he filed under the heading 'Lost Sheep'. To their credit the Bevanites opposed all expulsions from the Labour Party, unlike the Communists and their supporters who actually ganged up with the Labour Right to expel Trotskyists.

Bevan's book, *In Place of Fear*, published in 1952, exemplifies all the virtues and flaws of the British Labour Left. Warm, generous and humane, it is a moral call to arms with several striking phrases: '... no society can legitimately call itself civilised if a sick person is denied medical aid because of lack of means.' He insisted too that democratic socialism 'accepts the obligation to choose among different kinds of social action and in so doing to bear the pains of rejecting what is not practicable or less desirable.'

But *Fear* completely fails to specify what this 'social action' might be and the book is by turns vague and verbose. The most feeble chapter, 'The

Transition to Socialism', should have been the strongest. 'Planning' is advanced as a virtue but is never discussed in any detail. Typically, there is nothing about economic growth. These absences reflect not just Bevan's own comparative lack of interest in the nuts and bolts of socialism but is also a perennial weakness of the Labour Left. The Bevanites were essentially a product of, and reaction to, the Cold War and lacked the resources or ability to rise above it.

The publications of Bevan's followers are rarely more illuminating in outlining any 'New Jerusalem' and sometimes startlingly wrong. Writing in 1959 after a decade of unparalleled economic growth in the West, Richard Crossman claimed that '. . . the planned Socialist economy, as exemplified in the Communist States, is proving its capacity to outpace and overtake the wealthy and comfortable Western economies.' The next year Crossman attacked the Labour Right's theorist Anthony Crosland for his '. . . failure to observe the terrifying contrast between the drive and missionary energy displayed by the Communist bloc and the lethargic, comfortable indolence of the Western democracies.'

For all his undoubted qualities Bevan himself was a difficult man to work with. Ian Mikardo suggests that 'The trouble with Nye was that he wasn't a team player . . .' and avoided or postponed decisions. Richard Crossman voiced a similar complaint: 'He dominates its [Bevanites] discussions simply because he is fertile in ideas, but leadership and organisation are things he instinctively shrinks away from.' In an assessment written after Bevan's death Crossman was even more critical:

> . . . his trouble was precisely he did not grow up and remained a man of immense promise which rarely bore fruit . . . His real weaknesses were, first and foremost, His indolence . . . his second defect was a streak of cowardice. To put it bluntly, at critical moments he was inclined not to be there – an attack of bronchitis, perhaps, or just a sheer disappearance to his house in the country to avoid an unpleasant meeting or postpone a decision.

Such criticism perhaps makes one glad not to have been a friend of Crossman's! Attlee once pointed out that Bevan wanted to be both rebel and leader but, in fact, it wasn't possible to combine the two. But whatever criticisms anyone can make about Aneurin Bevan, nothing can take away from him the fact that he was the prime instigator of the National Health Service.

The failure of the Bevanites was due to much more than the personal characteristics of Nye Bevan himself. It was the Cold War which ensured that many of the democratic and libertarian impulses of the anti-fascist Second World War were lost. Anything orthodox or radical could so easily be tarred with the Communist or 'fellow traveller' brush, and the Labour Left were never able to break this ideological and administrative stranglehold.

This defeat ensured that the Labour Left was unable to put forward any constructive rethinking. Instead it was the Labour Right, untainted by any possible 'pro-Communist' slur, which filled the vacuum.

Above all, perhaps, the 1950s exhibited a distinctly unattractive image of the British Left, squabbling, expelling, criticising. It showed only too clearly how the Cold War poisoned the political atmosphere. Herbert Marcuse, one of the intellectual influences behind the rise of 'the New Left' in the 1950s and 1960s, once claimed that:

> ... our goals, our values, our old and new morality must be visible already in our actions. The new human beings whom we want to help to create — we must already strive to be these human beings right here and now.

No matter what the validity of the 'Bevanite' or 'Gaitskellite' camps, both failed Marcuse's injunction. The 1950s teach the British Left one negative lesson: how not to conduct a political party or a political debate.

CHAPTER TEN

Expanding Horizons: New Lefts 1956–1963

'Take an aspirin, comrade.'
Communist Party leader Harry Pollitt's reported advice to a
colleague worried about the Soviet invasion of Hungary in 1956

'Eden, Murderer of Budapest.'
Placard seen in late 1956

'Total abstinence and a good filing-system are not now the right
sign-posts to the socialist's Utopia: or at least, if they are, some of
us will fall by the wayside.'
Anthony Crosland in *The Future of Socialism*, 1956

ANEURIN BEVAN and Tony Crosland disagreed
about many things. They were on opposite sides during the Labour Party's
internal civil war in the 1950s and never seem to have struck up much of a
personal relationship. But they did agree on one crucial point: any concept
of socialism had to be about the quality of life, about enhancing people's
ability to enjoy themselves. This 'pleasure principle' was at the root of both
men's socialist beliefs.

Both Bevan and Crosland were sometimes accused of frivolity and a lack
of seriousness. Bevan was called a 'Bollinger Bolshevik' and a 'lounge-lizard
Lenin' because of his liking for champagne and the high life, but he was also
a man whose private pleasures included writing poetry. The handsome
Crosland was never short of girlfriends and these relationships, in the
balanced judgement of his future wife, brought much enjoyment to both
parties. His holidays were spent alone exploring architecture all over the
world. In his influential book *The Future of Socialism*, Crosland criticised
Sidney and Beatrice Webb for 'their lack of temptation towards any of the
emotional or physical pleasures of life' and continued: '. . . it is not only dark
Satanic things and people that now bar the road to the new Jerusalem, but

also, if not mainly, hygienic, respectable, virtuous things and people, lacking only in grace and vitality.'

Bevan and Crosland were both 'Cavaliers', sometimes to their detriment in terms of political advancement. Until the 1950s it was the Roundhead tradition that largely dominated the British labour movement, reflecting the Nonconformist strand which had contributed much to the early days and provided a bedrock of support for the new Labour Party. Although individual Fabians enjoyed drama and music, the Fabian leadership was largely indifferent to the arts or to more personal issues. For instance, George Bernard Shaw found it impossible to persuade his fellow Fabians to publish either Wagner's *Art and Revolution* or Oscar Wilde's *The Soul of Man under Socialism*, or to do justice to William Morris' *News from Nowhere*.

The Communist Party too, certainly in the 1920s and for much of the 1930s, had also frowned upon culture as a diversion. It was something to be 'dealt with' after the Revolution. Instead, comrade, why aren't you out selling the *Daily Worker*? Following Lenin's example, the Party called for asceticism and orthodoxy in members' private lives. Morality was subservient to the dictates of the Party: as the Communist Benjamin Farrington, Professor of Classics at University College, Swansea, once put it: '. . . where there is a Communist Party and where there is Marxist guidance, there is a clear moral principle to guide our actions in the violent times in which we live.' The Communist Party warned members that 'Moral and personal weaknesses' could be 'seized upon by the enemy'. It tried to discourage one of its star recruits, Professor J. B. S. Haldane, from being divorced by his first wife.

To be fair, many Communist Party leaders in Britain such as Pollitt, Gallacher, Dutt and Campbell enjoyed happy and monogamous marriages and there was no doubt that some early Cavaliers, most notably Victor Grayson, came to unhappy ends. Drink in particular was a recurring temptation which damaged the political careers of, for example, J. H. Thomas, Arthur Greenwood and, later, George Brown. In private, trade union leaders might well have enjoyed their 'beer and sandwiches'; in public they embodied the virtues of working-class respectability.

If it was sometimes difficult for men like Bevan and Crosland to live their lives as they wished then it was much harder for women. In her autobiography *The Tamarisk Tree*, Dora Russell has shown how repressive both labourism and communism were towards libertarian impulses and how they shied away from such questions as birth control and abortion. When she tried to get a resolution on birth control debated at a Labour Party meeting in 1924, she was told by Marion Phillips, the Woman's Officer of the national party, that 'Sex should not be dragged into politics, you will split the Party from top to bottom.' Dora Russell rejected this advice and helped set up the Workers' Birth Control Group in 1924. The Abortion Law Reform Association was founded in 1936 but on the whole the Labour Party shied away from such campaigns in case they antagonised potential Catholic voters.

Of course, much depended on which class a woman belonged to. Naomi Mitchison's memoirs of the inter-war years have shown how the availability of effective contraception enabled her and her friends to live active lives which included husbands – in her case the Labour lawyer Dick Mitchison – lovers, families and a full working life. One of Mitchison's circle was Margery Spring Rice who in 1939 published a book called *Working-Class Wives, Their Health and Conditions* – and there a very different story is told.

Based on information collected from 1,250 women, the picture presented by Spring Rice is one of unending toil and anxiety. Half the women spent twelve hours or more a day on their feet while 65 per cent said that their two hours' of 'leisure' a day included shopping, mending, sewing and doing household jobs:

> ... the women whose poverty and consequent hard work demand the greatest measure of consideration and carefully planned reform [were not able to join outside organisations]. The poorest women have no time to spare for such immediately irrelevant considerations as the establishment of a different system, a better education, a more comprehensive medical service, of some sort of organised co-operation.

It should also be remembered that up to the 1950s any yearnings for individual freedom had to recognise that both abortion and homosexuality were still illegal, divorce was difficult, birth control was often primitive and a lack of money or anything resembling 'youth culture' limited the opportunities for meeting and for relationships. In addition, the Cold War from the late 1940s reinforced notions of caution and conformity; as Robert Hewison neatly puts it, 'The Cold War tended to freeze public attitudes, and counselled silence about private ones.'

From the mid-1950s, however, the taken-for-granted orthodoxies and certainties started to appear less immutable. Living standards began to rise in the post-Second World War boom and affluence offered people greater opportunities and widened their horizons. The arrival of 'the consumer society' was heralded by the ending of the rationing of most foodstuffs in 1954 and of meat in 1956. Commercial television, which was on the air from 1955, confirmed and stimulated the growth of the advertising industry.

New consumer durables such as telephones, cars and household appliances like fridges and ovens brought more leisure and increased people's mobility. There were $2\frac{1}{2}$ million cars and 1 million television sets in Britain in 1951; by 1964 there were over 8 million cars and 13 million television sets. The first supermarkets were built and in 1955 Mary Quant opened Bazaar on the King's Road, Chelsea, the first boutique aimed directly at the young. Quant's husband and partner Alexander Plunket Greene hoped that it would change 'the depressing and stultifying life young Londoners then led.' Bill Haley toured England in 1957 with his new rock and roll music. And there were few more potent signs of expanding horizons than the 4 million British people taking holidays abroad by 1961.

These trends and transitions inevitably provoked political stirrings. The stark and simplistic choice thrown up by the Cold War − either for Washington or for Moscow − and the division within the British labour movement between Labour and Communist began to seem less categoric.

The first signs that Eastern Europe, or 'the People's Democracies' as Communists called them, were not and never had been any such thing emerged in Berlin in June 1953 when a workers' rebellion caught the authorities off guard. The rising was put down but only after the rule in Eastern Europe was shown to be dependent on coercion and not on consent. Yet this was a minor storm when compared with the convulsions to come in '1956'. Eric Hobsbawm has remarked of that year: 'As far as I know most Communists in most countries lived for several months in the political equivalent of a nervous breakdown.'

After Stalin's death in 1953 there had been a relaxation of tension in the Soviet Union and therefore in Eastern Europe. The Great Dictator had gone; the purges and mass executions, if not the gulags, had stopped − although the East Germans found out how limited this tolerance was. But the new Soviet leadership under Khrushchev did begin to edge away from the Stalinist era. 'As Stalin said' was no longer an argument-clincher. However, no one who went to Moscow for the 20th Congress of the Communist Party of the Soviet Union in February 1956 had any idea what revelations were in store.

Fortunately, we have a non-Soviet eyewitness account of this Congress. The Italian Vittorio Vidali had been a longstanding Communist who endured imprisonment, torture and exile under Mussolini's regime. He was a loyal Party man even though by his own estimate no less than thirty-eight of his friends and comrades had perished in Stalin's purges. Most people would surely have asked themselves whether any cause which demanded human sacrifice on so massive a scale could possibly be deserving of support. Such a question never seems to have occurred to Vidali, which shows yet again how dedicated Communists identified completely with anything the Soviet Union, or at least Stalin, did.

Vidali's account of the Congress tells of the hurried meetings, the surveillance of foreign delegates by the KGB and the snatched conversations with survivors of the purges, one of whom bitterly told Vidali: 'It is terrible to die as a traitor after having faithfully served the cause; there is no greater sorrow!' As he sat through the Congress proceedings, Vidali gradually realised that none of the Soviet leaders could even bring themselves to mention Stalin's name. Something momentous was happening but, typically, the Khrushchev revelations were delivered at a 'secret session' from which non-Soviet delegates were excluded. Although leading non-Russian Communists found out within a couple of months what Khrushchev had said, the speech was only published in full in the summer of 1956 by the American State Department. Suddenly it was clear that the purges, trials and prison camps had not been figments of overheated Western reactionary imagination. Stalin's critics had, in fact, been right all along.

Within the British Communist Party responses to the speech varied. For hard-line Stalinists such as Rajani Palme Dutt nothing had altered. He wrote airily that even the sun – presumably Stalin – has spots, which was a strange way to dismiss the deaths of millions. Apologists for the Moscow Trials, such as the lawyer D. N. Pritt, later expressed a few grudging words in a single sentence in three volumes of autobiography and then passed on to other matters.

Others couldn't even manage that. In the official biography of Harry Pollitt published in 1976, page after page is devoted to political trials in South Africa and the United States yet there is not a single word about the Moscow Trials. But even if his biographer twenty years later couldn't bring himself to write about the Trials, Harry Pollitt himself, according to Jimmy Reid, never really recovered from the revelations of the 20th Congress.

The official Communist Party line – and the Party was already in severe difficulties because of impatience at its meagre size by the Soviet leaders who were considering closing it down and calling for some form of alliance with the Bevanites – was mealy mouthed. Apparently, some 'mistakes' had been committed – at first they could not bring themselves to use the word 'crimes' – but these should not detract from outstanding Soviet economic success and the construction of socialism. How hollowly this reads in view of the USSR's economic crisis today.

Scores of Party members began to complain to Party headquarters in King

Street that this was surely an inadequate response to mass slaughter. Slowly, the Party leadership steeled itself to talk about 'grave injustices' in the Soviet Union. But enough was enough. Party members then were ordered to get on with the task of bringing Bolshevism to Britain. The doctrine of democratic centralism, or of obedience to orders from above, meant that such a decision could be enforced.

But, of course, once a hole had appeared in the dyke wall, it grew bigger. Some Communists began to argue that these 'grave injustices' had arisen in part because of the authoritarian nature of each individual Communist Party and of the Communist movement in its entirety. They claimed that the Party's massive bureaucracy — and the Communist Party had more full-time officials to its membership than the Conservative or Labour Parties — led to an ossified and top-heavy organisation. In July 1956 the two Communist historians, E. P. Thompson and John Saville, produced the first number of an unofficial journal which they called *The Reasoner*. On its title page was a quotation from Karl Marx himself: 'To leave error unrefuted is to encourage intellectual immorality.'

Alarm bells sounded in King Street. Thompson and Saville were told to cease publication. Before 1956 they might well have done. But now, no. The Emperor had been seen to have no clothes. They published two more issues and were suspended from the Party, whereupon both resigned. Other members were also resigning in the wake of Khrushchev's secret speech. One was the miners' official Lawrence Daly who complained that the fact that the leadership had once been unanimously pro-Stalin and was now unanimously anti-Stalin showed that fundamentally nothing had changed. Further shocks were still to come.

In October 1956 the Hungarian people rose against their own Communist regime. The *Daily Worker* sent one of its journalists, Peter Fryer, to Hungary to report on events. Fryer was thought to be 'reliable': he had been a Communist for fourteen years and on the staff of the *Daily Worker* for the last nine. But when he arrived in Hungary Fryer could see with his own eyes what was happening: 'I saw for myself that the uprising was neither organised nor controlled by fascists or reactionaries . . .'

His reports to the paper back in London conveyed this message. He also analysed what this repressive Communist system had meant for the Hungarian people:

> To speak one's mind, to ask an awkward question, even to speak about political questions in language not signposted with the safe, familiar monolithic jargon, was to run the risk of falling foul of the ubiquitous secret police.

Fryer honestly went on to condemn himself and others for their tacit acquiescence in what had been going on: 'It is a tragedy that we British Communists who visited Hungary did not admit, even to ourselves, the truth about what was taking place there, that we defended tyranny with all our heart and soul.' Fryer had smashed his own 'Grand Illusions'.

His reports to the *Daily Worker* back in London were censored by the acting editor George Matthews because they contradicted the official Communist 'line' on Hungary — that this was a fascist rising. The official line was never wrong; Fryer was therefore unreliable and — despite Communist commitment to the freedom of the Press — his reports were not to be printed. The Soviet tanks rolled into Budapest and the rising was put down at the cost of 20,000 Hungarian lives.

Peter Fryer promptly resigned from the *Daily Worker* as did one in four of its entire staff and 7,000 individual Communists, which represented about 20 per cent of the entire Party. The enmity within the British Communist Party was so bitter that when Unity Theatre in London staged a dramatisation of the Hungarian events there were fist fights in the audience. The Communist Party leadership did what it always had done in a crisis; in the words of journalist Llew Gardner, who resigned, 'The party survived on its constant appeal to loyalty.' John Gollan, who had succeeded Harry Pollitt as General Secretary of the Party when the latter retired because of ill health, was complacent about people leaving the Party: 'They are not our best comrades, otherwise they would not have left.'

Hungarian Tragedy, the title of Peter Fryer's book about what had happened, destroyed any moral claims the Communist Party might still have possessed to represent the oppressed and downtrodden. Here had been a people rising against oppression and yet it was the Communists themselves who had been the oppressors. But if anyone in the West believed that '1956' proved 'we' were the angels and 'they' were devils, they were wrong. The West itself had not emerged unblemished from the events of that year. The 'either' of Communism had been tarnished — but then the Suez crisis during which Eden's Conservative government mustered a last imperial twitch had hardly demonstrated the attractions of the 'or' of Western capitalism.

Disturbing too was the degree of complicity between East and West; 'we won't interfere in your crisis (Budapest/Suez) if you don't interfere in ours (Suez/Budapest).' Eden's Suez venture destroyed any chance, admittedly small, of Western intervention to help the Hungarians, which explains the placards 'Eden, Murderer of Budapest'. Complicity between the superpowers has been confirmed by the publication of the diary kept by the Yugoslav Ambassador in Moscow in 1956, Veljko Micunovic:

Khrushchev said that British and French aggressive pressure on Egypt provided a favourable moment for a further intervention by Soviet troops. It would help the Russians. There would be confusion and uproar in the West and the United Nations, but it would be less at a time when Britain, France, and Israel were waging a war against Egypt. 'They are bogged down there, and we are stuck in Hungary,' Khrushchev said.

What did this upheaval mean to socialists in Britain? Paradoxically the Cold War had given individual Communists a sense of identity in what seemed to be a distinctly hostile world. The novelist Mervyn Jones has put it well:

> In a real sense, the Party was held together by the ferocity of the cold war, the pressure of enemies on every side, the incessant onslaughts on the Soviet Union and Communism in the press and in speeches by both Tory and Labour politicians – onslaughts which included some home truths, but also a torrent of distortion and slanders. It seemed cowardly, and even indecent, to withdraw from the battle.

The events of 1956 broke up this Cold War mentality: Suez and Hungary awoke people 'from a kind of political trance . . .' It also destroyed the traditional identification between the Marxist Left and the Communist Party. Before 1956, to be a Marxist in this country almost certainly meant that you were a member of the Communist Party. After 1956 the spell of the Communist Party was broken.

Out of 1956 came what commentators, always eager to find a new label (fresh from discovering 'Angry Young Men'), called 'the New Left'. In fact, the name was only suggestive and not a dogmatic straitjacket; it lumps together many different individuals and ideas. It was clear, however, that the 'New Left' varied in several important ways from the 'Old Left'. In one typology, the Old Left was authoritarian, centralised, philistine and puritan while the New Left was libertarian, decentralised, open and experimental; the New Left offered '. . . more the style of an encounter group than a vanguard cadre.'

In the 1930s the Communist Party had possessed, in the words of member Philip Toynbee, very definite views on everything: 'There was a "line" for love; there was almost a line for friendship.' The New Left discarded this approach and instead stressed the qualities of warmth, generosity, tolerance and humanity. Above all, there was a rediscovery of the moral basis of political activity, a recognition that individuals and their feelings were not something worth sacrificing for 'the Party' or any other body. Stuart Hall has recalled:

> From the beginning we said that politics, seen as having to do principally with formal political parties, elections, getting the vote out, parliamentarianism, was ideological, confining. We raised issues of personal life, the way people live, culture, which weren't considered the topics of politics on the left.

This New Left represented a return to some of the ideas explored in the 'Socialism and the New Life' chapter of this book, ideas that had characterised much of the British Left up to 1917 before the labour movement split into the two camps of labourism and communism.

It was no coincidence that one of the New Left's leading figures, E. P. Thompson, had been the author of a massive study of William Morris. Although originally published in 1953 during the Cold War when Thompson was still a Communist and therefore accepted, as some critics pointed out, the idea of the dictatorship of the proletariat, more than enough of Morris' insights remained in the book to emphasise the moral dimension of politics.

Official Communist Party reaction to the New Left was revealing. One of its few remaining intellectuals, English lecturer Arnold Kettle, was dismissive of 'middle-class people ... spouting a lot of pious generalisations about socialist humanism.' To Party believers, 'socialist humanism' was heresy because it turned its back on the rigid 'class warfare' approach. In practice it represented a welcome and long overdue enlargement of what 'politics' was and might be. The New Left's energy was to spawn a host of activities that ranged from single issue campaigns such as CND and Shelter to the idea of community politics.

To recognise some weaknesses of the New Left is not to denigrate its largely positive contribution. For almost the first time since the days of Morris, Carpenter and Blatchford, the moral dimension had been restored to political activity. But in rebelling against Communist Party rigidity, the New Left often went too far the other way and decried the need for any kind of formal organisation. Hostile to the Parliamentarianism of Hugh Gaitskell's Labour Party, which in the 1950s seemed to think electoral campaigning every five years or so was the be-all and end-all of politics, the New Left was never able to turn a mood into a movement.

The New Left was also unable to create any coherent idea of the future, unlike Crosland's *The Future of Socialism* which became the Bible of the Labour Right. As always, the Left poured forth books, pamphlets and magazines but invariably these preferred easy posturing or vague rhetoric to mapping out a possible way forward. At a conference held in Oxford in 1987, several individuals active in the 1950s looked back on the movement with characteristic honesty. Raphael Samuel noted that they had stood for 'comprehensive redevelopment' in housing and that the New Left had nothing to say about the family, women's rights or homosexuality.

One good example of the New Left's gap between rhetoric and reality, and wonderfully ironic in view of the author's later pronounced change in opinions, was Paul Johnson's essay 'A Sense of Outrage' published in 1958. Johnson calls for the abolition of the monarchy and of the House of Lords, the dispossession of the public schools and Oxbridge, the disestablishment of the Church and the end of the central law college and of the Honours List. What is more all these changes must take place simultaneously. The author omitted to give any inkling as to how this might be done.

The New Left also displayed a tendency, seen too in the 1930s, to focus heavily on international affairs. In one sense such internationalism is admirable; but it is less so if pursued at the expense of domestic or 'bread and butter' issues. This tendency was apparent too in its most successful offshoot, the Campaign for Nuclear Disarmament (CND).

> Gaitskell and Nye Bevan are preparing for a sell,
> They want to get the votes and keep the atom bomb as well,
> But NATO's going to send us all to shovel coal in hell,
> If we don't ban the H-bomb now.

This song was composed by some London medical students and was meant to be used on CND marches to Aldermaston in Berkshire. The surprise, perhaps, is that Aneurin Bevan's name is coupled with that of Gaitskell. As bitter political rivals they had disagreed on almost every political issue. But from the mid-1950s Bevan began to shift his stance, and in 1957 he shocked friends and colleagues at the Labour Party Conference by delivering a speech attacking unilateral disarmament, pleading with delegates not to send any Foreign Secretary 'naked into the conference chamber.' Even more woundingly, he remarked that his opponents were guilty of an 'emotional spasm'.

Bevan was strongly attacked for his apparent volte-face and accused of opportunism. In fact, his decision had been thought through. Bevan's international contacts with Soviet leaders like Khrushchev had convinced him that if Britain did unilaterally renounce the bomb it would make no difference to the behaviour of the two superpowers. He also felt that the Labour Party would never win a general election with a unilateralist defence policy – an argument that was often voiced in the 1980s.

Bevan's speech heightened the sense of public anxiety felt about the proliferation of nuclear weapons. Although British governments both Labour and Conservative had drawn a veil of secrecy over the subject, it was clear by the mid-1950s that Britain's defence rested largely on the nuclear deterrent and was locked in with that of the Americans, as was shown by the number of US bases located in this country. In 1957 the Conservative Defence Minister Duncan Sandys published a White Paper urging the modernisation of Britain's nuclear capabilities. Next year's Defence White Paper was candid about the dangers:

> It must be recognised that, however carefully the balance of armaments is held, or thought to be held, there always remains a possibility that some unforeseen circumstance or miscalculation might spark off a world-wide catastrophe.

As the careers of Keir Hardie and George Lansbury showed, the British Left has always contained a strong tradition of pacifism and anti-militarism. CND also attracted everyone who detested nuclear weapons in the wake of Hiroshima and Nagasaki as well as drawing upon the vein of idealism which had been submerged in the *Realpolitik* of the Cold War.

But it was Bevan's speech that gave the movement its impetus. Outraged by his remarks, the novelist J. B. Priestley wrote a vitriolic article in the *New Statesman* which scorned the 'VIP-Highest-Priority-Top-Secret-Top-People Class, men now so conditioned by this atmosphere of power politics, intrigue, secrecy, insane invention, that they are more than half-barmy.'

The reaction to Priestley's article was so massive that it was decided to form what was, ironically, a 'Top People' pressure group. Philosopher Bertrand Russell was its president, Canon Collins of St Paul's was chairman. Of the nineteen names on the first year's executive, no less than thirteen were to be found in *Who's Who*. CND's sponsors included John Arlott, Peggy Ashcroft, Benjamin Britten, Edith Evans and Henry Moore. CND also had good contacts with the media: both Kingsley Martin, the editor of the *New Statesman*, and Michael Foot, editor of *Tribune*, were leading figures in the campaign. CND had no formal membership nor was it intended to be a permanent organisation, but its leaders soon found that widespread public support almost took over the campaign and they had to condone such activities as the annual Easter march to Aldermaston, first held in 1958. By March 1959 CND had over 270 local groups and 12 regional committees.

Particularly noticeable was the attraction CND held for the young. Previously 'youth' had been regarded as a stage of life to be got through as fast as possible on the way to maturity. Now the social changes transforming Britain in the 1950s prompted young people to be more vocal and expressive, and political involvement in CND was one feature of this mood.

Although CND was sometimes dismissed as the 'duffle-coat brigade' it is interesting that twenty years before Saatchi and Saatchi marketed Mrs Thatcher, CND was well aware of the importance of 'image'. Its *Advice to Marchers* was explicit: 'Don't do anything or wear anything that will distract the attention of the world from the great issues with which we are concerned.' The Executive even recommended that a delegation to Moscow should include 'a young and photogenic mother'. The CND symbol itself, which as Peggy Duff noted was ideal for graffiti, became an international sign.

There is no doubt that CND was '. . . essentially a middle-class movement, and had relatively little working-class and trade union backing.' Or, as A. J. P. Taylor pithily expressed it, CND was 'a movement of eggheads for eggheads . . .' That its members were overwhelmingly middle-class reflected that from this point onwards most radical political campaigns were not exclusively aimed at the manual working class – a recognition of changing social trends. It also suggests why the campaign was generally peaceful and orderly with hardly any shouting on the annual march. However, CND did get the backing of the prominent trade union leader Frank Cousins who was General Secretary of the huge Transport and General Workers' Union. With his support and the acquiescence of other unions, the Labour Party Conference in 1960 narrowly passed a unilateralist motion.

CND was astute in the way it gave prominence to the 'stars' who supported the movement, but, as always, the hard graft was done by 'the poor bloody infantry' who remained out of the spotlight. Mervyn Jones has noted the important role that women played in the campaign, and CND's secretary was the formidable Peggy Duff. Her career symbolises much of the dedication and selfless commitment at the root of the British Left over the last century.

Her husband, a journalist, was killed at the end of the war while reporting on a bombing raid over Germany, leaving her with three small children to bring up alone. This tragedy did not prevent Duff from being involved in a number of campaigns, seeking the kind of idealism which had first drawn her to the Common Wealth party during the war. She worked for 'Save Europe Now' which was run by Victor Gollancz in an attempt to prevent starvation among the victims of the war and soon learnt to stand up to Gollancz. His socialism did not prevent him displaying distinctly autocratic tendencies – 'He used to make up for his extreme pacifism by extreme aggressiveness.

His daughter used to say, "you should hear him if the bath water is cold."'

Peggy Duff then became business manager of *Tribune* newspaper from 1949 to 1955 and a supporter of Nye Bevan as well as being a councillor in St Pancras, London, for fifteen years. After CND she worked for a number of organisations, including the campaigns to abolish capital punishment ('the only one we won') and against the Vietnam War. She died in London in 1981. Her autobiography *Left, Left, Left* is a record of a person without political ambition who was determined to live up to William Morris' phrase: 'To grumble and not to act, that is throwing away one's life.'

It is wrong to dismiss CND as of little importance because, ultimately, it failed to rid Britain of nuclear weapons. Cabinet papers of the time, for instance, show the extent of Prime Minister Harold Macmillan's alarm at its success. But one problem which CND never resolved was similar to that faced by the Left Book Club. Moral indignation is not sufficient in itself to generate political change and CND, like the New Left generally, was apolitical. Political power in Britain did not lie in the roads of Berkshire or at Aldermaston itself, and no one quite knew what to do after the March was over. The Committee of 100 organised 'sit-downs' outside the Ministry of Defence in Whitehall but the authorities cracked down on its leaders and some received prison sentences.

Mervyn Jones used to warn CND groups that 'You're up against professional politicians. They're in this business for a lifetime. They don't intend to argue with you – they're waiting for you to get tired.' Jones was absolutely right. CND may have won the day at the 1960 Labour Party Conference, but there was always next year, and the year after that ... In fact, it needed only twelve months for the Labour Right to organise the block vote and reject unilateralism. The moral fervour of CND was ultimately no match for the professional politicians.

External events also conspired against CND. The peaceful outcome of the Cuban Missile Crisis in October 1962 appeared to show that the superpowers could draw back from the edge. Next year the signing of the Partial Test Ban Treaty in July 1963 reassured many people that the nuclear deterrent, for all its awfulness, might never have to be used. With hindsight, however, it is clear that it was the forthright opposition to unilateralism of Hugh Gaitskell and his associates that doomed CND to defeat on the British political stage.

Assessments of Hugh Gaitskell differ wildly. For his opponents he was, in Bevan's jibe, 'a desiccated calculating machine', a lofty and arrogant

Hampstead intellectual who knew little and understood even less of the rank and file. His friends and colleagues, on the other hand, almost idolised him, complaining that his cold public image bore no relation to the warm individual whose passion for dancing into the late hours left his circle exhausted. One thing which everyone agreed on was Gaitskell's intellectual honesty, his scrupulous refusal to fudge or muddy issues.

In some ways his integrity is reminiscent of that of Keir Hardie. The difference was that Hardie created and led what was initially a very small organisation. By the 1950s, when Gaitskell became leader of the Labour Party, both its size and that of the trade unions meant that compromise, ambiguity and equivocation were often essential weapons in the leader's armoury. Attlee, for instance, knew the value of saying nothing, as Gaitskell himself once noted in his diaries: '. . . one of Clem's peculiarities is that of out-silencing people. It is a useful weapon. Nothing can be more embarrassing if you cannot get a man to talk.' Gaitskell, however, was always direct and uncompromising.

Educated at Winchester and Oxford, Gaitskell worked as an adult education tutor in the Midlands for the Workers' Educational Association before spending the 1930s as an economics lecturer at London University. He was one of Hugh Dalton's group which had drawn up detailed Labour Party policies for the future. During the war he worked as a civil servant at the Ministry of Economic Warfare, which taught him how to get round the corridors of power. Elected MP for South Leeds in 1945, within little more than two years he was Minister of Fuel and Power. Three years later Gaitskell was appointed Chancellor of the Exchequer. This meteoric rise was helped by Hugh Dalton who since his own resignation as Chancellor over a budget leak channelled his energies into promoting his protégés. As already seen, it upset rivals like Aneurin Bevan who felt that this 'johnny come lately' had leapfrogged over him. Bevan had spent sixteen years on the backbenches waiting for power, Gaitskell less than a year.

Gaitskell's short time as Chancellor was dominated by the need to finance Britain's part in the Korean War, a struggle which led to the dispute with Bevan and the latter's resignation from the Cabinet. Although ostensibly over 'teeth and spectacles', the fight between the two men was about more than this; as Gaitskell put it, 'It was a battle between us for power — he knew it and so did I.'

Gaitskell won in 1951, just as he did in 1954 when he defeated Bevan for the post of Labour Party Treasurer and, most importantly of all, in December 1955 when Gaitskell was elected leader of the party after Attlee's resignation. The problem for Gaitskell was that he led a political organisation torn apart by internal feuding and faced by a Conservative Party that had won the last two elections and was benignly in charge of a Britain where living standards were rising.

Gaitskell criticised the Bevanites for not recognising the social and political changes that were transforming the country, for wanting the Labour Party to remain a party of protest rather than a party of government. The two theorists who did try to analyse Britain in the 1950s, John Strachey and Anthony Crosland, were neither of them on the Left of the Labour Party. Both Strachey and Crosland published their most important books in 1956.

John Strachey was the former Marxist of the 1930s who had been a Minister in Attlee's governments. His *Contemporary Capitalism* was a dense book that grappled with the legacy of Karl Marx. He argued that Marxists were wrong to claim that the State was nothing but an instrument of the ruling class: 'The fact is that in the conditions of contemporary democracy the State and its vast powers are rather prizes for which all sorts of interests are struggling and competing.' Strachey also maintained that economic instability might well provoke a harsher Conservatism than Eden's and Macmillan's in the 1950s; as his latest biographer has put it, 'Few could have predicted the nature of "Thatcherism" with such deadly accuracy.'

But it was Anthony Crosland's book *The Future of Socialism* which proved the more significant of the two, partly because despite its 529 pages it is surprisingly well-written for a complex book of political theory. Today the book is sometimes dismissed because of its seeming complacency that British economic growth could virtually be taken for granted. This is a little unfair: in a new edition published only eight years later, Crosland in fact noted the comparatively poor performance of 'the Anglo-Saxon economies'.

But in any case *The Future of Socialism* was always intended to be more than just an economic forecast. First of all Crosland grappled with the realities of day-to-day power in Britain with a detail and knowledge absent from, say, the publications of the Left Book Club, Bevan's *In Place of Fear* or the future writings of the New Left. He also stressed the libertarian strand of socialism, claiming the mantle of William Morris and anticipating future developments on the Left. He attacked the divorce laws, the licensing laws, the illegality of homosexuality, the abortion laws, censorship of books and plays and so on: 'Most of these are intolerable, and should be highly offensive to socialists, in whose blood there should always run a trace of the anarchist and the libertarian, and not too much of the prig and the prude.'

Finally, Crosland recognised that British society was changing enormously – and the Labour Party had to face up to this future. What was called 'revisionism' was '. . . an explicit admission that many of the old dreams are either dead or realised ... now the certainty and simplicity are gone; and everything has become complicated and ambiguous.' In particular the British working class no longer constituted so clear-cut and definite a grouping as had been the case in Keir Hardie's day.

This working-class culture was, as we have seen, primarily defensive rather than offensive, moderate and not revolutionary. Between the late nineteenth century and the 1940s it had been relatively homogeneous and fixed but now, paradoxically, the very reforms which the Labour Party had helped bring about after the war were undermining this uniformity. To take just one indicator, in 1900 three-quarters of Britain's workforce had been manual labourers; the figure in the 1950s was now below two-thirds and still dropping. The changes introduced by the Attlee government seemed to suggest that gentle reformism rather than any energetic prosecution of the 'class war' offered the best way forward; as Elizabeth Durbin has succinctly put it, 'The essence of the revisionist case for socialism is that the capitalist market system can be transformed into a collectivist state without recourse to violent class struggle.'

The Labour Left, on the other hand, scorned rethinking in favour of moral condemnation of this new Britain. 'Our people have achieved material prosperity in excess of their moral stature' claimed Aneurin Bevan at the Labour Party Conference in 1949. Ten years later he returned to the same theme: '... it is a vulgar society of which no decent person could be proud.' At the same Conference Michael Foot echoed Bevan's remarks: '... we have to change the mood of the people in this country, to open their eyes to what an evil and disgraceful and rotten society it is.' Richard Crossman speculated that 'The luxuries, gadgets, entertainments and packaged foodstuffs which so many workers enjoy in our Affluent Societies may strike him [an outside observer] as irrelevant and even vulgar and immoral ...'

Bevan and Crossman both owned farms as well as residences in London while Michael Foot lived in a pleasant part of Hampstead. Evidently, material prosperity with all its luxuries and gadgets hadn't blunted their own moral stature. Gaitskell's circle, on the other hand, was emphatic about the virtues of this prosperity: 'We are glad to see people better-off, and have no patience with those who are comfortably off themselves yet seem to resent the prosperity of others.' Consumption of consumer goods per head in Britain in the 1950s rose by over 20 per cent.

The revisionists argued that to win power in a parliamentary democracy the Labour Party had to broaden its appeal, just as it had done in 1945. The Labour Party had to be a national body rather than an amalgam of sectional interests. Gaitskell's arguments were apparently confirmed by the behaviour of other European socialists. In West Germany, for instance, the Social Democrats dropped their old Marxist ideological baggage at their 1959 Bad Godesberg Conference. By accepting the need for private ownership and in 1960 membership of NATO, they demonstrated that for them progress would come about only through building on the foundation of social-democratic post-war Germany and not by its overthrow. Piecemeal and moderate change was preferable to revolutionary upheaval. Equality was considered more important than wholesale public ownership. If the West German Social Democrats were the forerunners of this important shift in political approach, colleagues in other countries followed suit. The French socialists in effect also started again in 1959.

Gaitskell was a man who valued integrity and clarity above anything else, and the fact that the recent manifestos of his own party had wanted to nationalise one group of industries in 1950, none in 1951, and a completely different group in 1955 was the kind of inconsistency which he thought weakened the Labour Party. His determination to update and modernise the Labour Party was strengthened by the result of the 1959 general election when despite a lacklustre and inefficient campaign Harold Macmillan's Conservatives still increased their majority, helped by engineering a pre-election boom. A Conservative Party poster had read, 'Life's better under the Conservatives: don't let Labour ruin it.' Gaitskell himself made an election campaign blunder when he promised that his Party would not raise taxes if they won – even though the proposed programme was expensive. Not surprisingly the electorate was doubtful if he had done his sums.

This result now meant that in the fifty-three years of its existence the Labour Party had enjoyed a parliamentary majority for just six of them. Gaitskell's response to this election defeat split the Labour Party almost as much as did the dispute over unilateralism and defence.

> Has the very name 'Labour' become a vote loser on balance? . . . It would be unthinkable to give up the name 'Labour', which holds the loyalty of millions. But might there be a case for amending it to 'Labour and Radical', or 'Labour and Reform'?

Douglas Jay's article in the small-circulation magazine *Forward* opened a contentious can of worms. Published just a few days after the October 1959 defeat, Jay, a minister in the Attlee governments after the war and one of Gaitskell's closest friends, speculated on how and why Labour had lost. He pointed to two handicaps, namely the Labour Party's 'class image' and the fear that it wanted to nationalise everything in sight. One thing Jay did not mention was Clause Four.

Hugh Gaitskell, however, seized on Jay's musings and pointed to Clause Four as an issue which needed to be settled urgently. This clause was, as we have seen, vague and uncertain. It appeared on members' cards but it is doubtful if more than a handful of non-Party members had ever heard of it. Few expected the Labour Party ever to force through the sweeping 'common ownership of the means of production, distribution, and exchange', in other words 100 per cent nationalisation. In which case, said Gaitskell, it was a symbol of an outdated Party and should be scrapped.

But however convincing the intellectual arguments were for the revisionists, what the supremely rational Gaitskell overlooked was that the Labour Party, like most other political bodies, is made up of both irrationality and rationality in equal proportions. Emotion is as important as intellect, and this was borne out by the ease with which antagonists in the drama reached for religious imagery. Harold Wilson, for instance, opposed Gaitskell and claimed that tampering with Clause Four was like denying the authority of Genesis: 'We were being asked to take Genesis out of the Bible. You don't have to be a fundamentalist to say that Genesis is part of the Bible.' Trade union leader Frank Cousins maintained that 'We can have nationalisation without socialism – we cannot have socialism without nationalisation.'

Gaitskell found that many in the labour movement, usually his supporters, distrusted this campaign as in some way unnecessarily rocking the boat. Even the wielders of the trade union block vote turned against him and he eventually had to back down. The leaders of the German Social Democrats at Bad Godesberg had had no block vote to contend with. Gaitskell shied away from reforming voting procedures in the Labour Party – primarily because the block vote was usually his surest support.

In addition, Gaitskell's arguments were regarded by some within the labour movement as being all too typical of the 'Hampstead set' of intellectuals. This attitude towards the Party's thinkers formed an indelible strand within labourism. It held that intellectuals were fine in their place but from time to time they needed bringing down to earth. Revisionism was suspect because of its members' addresses.

Gaitskell was soon embroiled in another dispute that struck at the heart of the new image he was trying to present and there is no doubt that his discomfort over one helped the other. In 1960 the Campaign for Nuclear Disarmament (CND) pushed through a resolution at the 1960 Scarborough Labour Party Conference calling for nuclear disarmament. Gaitskell responded with a famous speech which contained the much-quoted passage that, 'We will fight and fight and fight again to bring back sanity and honesty and dignity, so that our Party with its great past may retain its glory and its greatness.'

Over the next twelve months the Campaign for Democratic Socialism (CDS), set up by the Labour Right, organised to overturn this motion. Carefully cultivating the Press and having no membership or subscriptions so as not to break Party rules, CDS targeted groups and individuals with great success and at the 1961 Conference unilateralism was defeated. Ironically, CDS set the pattern for the various internal left-wing groups that were organised to change the Labour Party in the 1980s.

Clause Four, CND — but this was by no means the end of Gaitskell's battles. In the early 1960s Macmillan's Conservative government began to explore the possibility of entering the Common Market. Although Gaitskell had attacked CND for its narrow national concerns in believing that Britain could stop the world because it wanted to get off, he came out against a closer relationship towards Europe — even though the majority of CDS members were convinced 'Europeans'.

One continuing characteristic of the British labour movement has been its insularity. Gaitskell shared this view. His friend Michael Postan observed that 'He [Gaitskell] had reasoned himself into international socialism, but his vision of the future was one of England's Jerusalem.' Gaitskell's speech at the 1962 Labour Party Conference in Brighton rejecting the application for membership was couched in embarrassing 'Little Englander' language, decrying 'the end of a thousand years of history.' Perhaps the most telling criticism of Gaitskell's words as the leader of a supposedly radical body was voiced by R. A. Butler, a leading figure within the Conservative Party: 'For them a thousand years of history books. For us the future.'

Looking back at Gaitskell's political career it seems to read like one fight after another: with Aneurin Bevan, with the Bevanites, over Clause Four, with CND, over Europe. Aneurin Bevan died in July 1960, Hugh Gaitskell in January 1963, and somehow their premature deaths before either had a further chance to display their undoubted talents in office summed up the barrenness of the 1950s and early 1960s for the British Left.

It took a series of blunders by the Conservatives and the appearance of a seemingly new and dazzling Labour leader to revive the Left's fortunes.

CHAPTER ELEVEN

Harold Wilson's New Britain:
Britain in the 1960s

'We need men with fire in their bellies and humanity in their hearts. The choice we offer ... is between standing still, clinging to the tired philosophy of a day that is gone, or moving forward in partnership and unity to a just society, to a dynamic, expanding, confident and above all purposive New Britain.'

Harold Wilson launching the Labour Party's 1964 general election campaign

'... the insufferable, smug, sanctimonious, naive, guilt-ridden, wet, pink orthodoxy of that sunset home of the third-rate minds of that third-rate decade, the 1960s.'

Norman Tebbit, quoted in the *Independent*, 22 February 1990

FEW POLITICAL reputations have plummeted so swiftly as that of Harold Wilson since his resignation as Prime Minister in 1976. Despite the fact that as leader of the Labour Party he won four out of five general elections and transformed his party from the no-hopers of the 1950s to the natural party of government, few people today can find much good to say about the Wilson years. Conservatives argue that he accelerated Britain's economic decline by caving in to every interest group, particularly the trade unions; socialists look back in disappointment at the high hopes raised by Wilson and then seemingly dashed.

Born in Yorkshire in 1916, Wilson came from a Liberal background, although any interest in politics was subordinate to his desire for academic success. After winning a First at Oxford he stayed on as a junior don before working as a civil servant during the Second World War. He belatedly joined the Labour Party in 1940. Elected a Labour MP just five years later in the 1945 election landslide, Wilson enjoyed meteoric advancement and in 1947 at the age of only thirty-one was appointed President of the Board of Trade.

Harold Wilson made a name for himself with a catchy phrase, which must have alerted him to the power of the media, a power he subsequently used to great effect. In November 1948 he launched what he called 'a bonfire of controls' by scrapping various restrictions which had required the issuing of over one million licences on certain commodities. In 1951 he surprised most people by resigning alongside Aneurin Bevan over the 'teeth and spectacles' issue. But Wilson was too shrewd to throw in his hand completely with a group that because of the trade union block vote was doomed to defeat. He took Bevan's place in the Shadow Cabinet when the latter resigned in 1954.

Wilson kept his head well below the parapet when Gaitskell was trying to ditch Clause Four of the Party's Constitution with its commitment to wholesale nationalisation, and his views on nuclear disarmament were ambiguous. He stood against Gaitskell in 1960 in a leadership contest, not expecting to win but in order to put down a marker for the future. After Gaitskell's unexpected death early in 1963, he was elected leader of the Parliamentary Labour Party, defeating George Brown and James Callaghan who between them split the natural right-wing majority.

But Wilson was the leader of what? Not only was the Labour Party a dispirited organisation which had lost three general elections in a row, it was still fresh from a bitter internal civil war. Several of his own colleagues distrusted him for his supposed opportunism. How was he – never a socialist virgin who preferred the purity of impotence to the constructive compromise of office – to secure electoral victory in such unpromising circumstances?

Wilson was the first Labour leader to feel comfortable with the medium of television. Normally it was the Conservatives who pioneered new techniques of campaigning, being the first party to draw systematically on opinion polls, the first to use mass advertising and the first to commission market research. The Labour Party's traditional approach to political communication was demonstrated during Clement Attlee's one and only visit to the BBC studios. An observer remarked that he 'sat obstinately silent and disapproving and departed as coldly as he had come.' In 1955 Wilson himself had described the Labour Party machine as 'still at the penny-farthing stage in a jet-propelled era' and little reorganisation had taken place over the intervening eight years.

Aneurin Bevan had ignored the cameras, alleging that the paraphernalia of polls and advertising would '. . . take all the poetry out of politics'. Hugh Gaitskell had painstakingly taught himself to endure the new techniques of modern political life. Harold Wilson, in contrast, positively welcomed them. During the 1950s, with the help of a young television producer called Anthony Wedgwood Benn, he trained himself to be an excellent studio performer. He learnt the value of talking in natural tones, of speaking in short and memorable phrases, and of holding a pipe to stop him waving his arms about.

Still only in his mid-forties, Wilson's energy was conclusively demonstrated by the thirty-two major speeches and innumerable broadcasts he made in just three months following his election as Labour Party leader. But he knew that he needed more than this, a message or theme which would grab the electorate's attention yet not expose the cracks in his own party. And what better appeal to modern Britain could there be than the idea of modernity itself?

Under this banner Wilson could present himself and his party as vigorous and go-ahead when compared to the lofty grandeur of Harold Macmillan's administration, which was now being torn apart by the Profumo scandal. In particular, this modern image was calculated to appeal to sections of the middle class or 'the middle ground' whose support had been won in 1945 and needed to be regained in the 1960s if the Labour Party hoped to win a majority at a general election.

Such a stance seemed almost to make a virtue out of the Labour Party's thirteen years out of office, leaving it untainted by recent economic anxieties yet promising a fresh start. 'Thirteen Wasted Years' was the Labour Party slogan. Wilson also embraced the idea of scientific change and progress with enthusiasm. To be fair he had always been interested in this. His father had been an industrial chemist and at Oxford Wilson had specialised in the study of technological advance. In his preface to the Labour Party document *Science and the Future of Britain* he wrote: 'The central feature of our post-war capitalist society is the scientific revolution.' Needless to say, this revolution was infinitely more attractive to Wilson than any revolution involving barricades. It had the merit of distracting the voters' attention away from the unpopular subject of nationalisation.

Even more encouragingly, Wilson had only to look across the Atlantic to see the way in which John F. Kennedy had taken America by storm in 1960, largely because his youth and energy contrasted so vividly with the solid but dull Republican years of the 1950s. It did not matter that Wilson himself was fudging several issues – an expediency which Hugh Gaitskell, for example, would have rejected. Nor was it thought disturbing that Wilson's speeches sometimes displayed a flatulence reminiscent of Ramsay MacDonald at his worst. Take this passage from a speech about 'Science and Society':

Whoever could make two ears of corn or two blades of grass to grow upon a spot of ground where only one grew before would deserve better of mankind and do more essential service to his country than the whole race of politicians put together.

The crucial thing was to catch a mood and in this he succeeded. For Wilson, this was much more significant than details in manifestos or policy documents which hardly anyone read anyway. Some of the enthusiasm that he generated clearly comes across in Tony Benn's diaries. In May 1963, for instance, more than a year before the election took place, Benn was writing happily: 'There is all the excitement of a revolutionary movement, with plans for this and that already afoot – just as if we were partisans poised for a victorious assault upon the capital.'

Faced by the new, low-key Conservative leader Sir Alec Douglas-Home, Wilson's vigour helped the Labour Party in October 1964 to win 317 seats to the Conservatives' 304 and the Liberals' 9. After thirteen years out of office Harold Wilson had managed to take his party back to power – just.

On the face of it, Harold Wilson's 1960s Cabinets were the most academically brilliant of all time; that of 1966 contained no less than eight Oxford Firsts. But, of course, a high IQ is no guarantee of political success nor does it necessarily bestow the ability to get on well with one's colleagues. The Wilson governments from 1964 to 1970 are riven with extraordinary personal rivalry and dissension – the most internecine since . . . well, the last Labour government under Attlee. Conservative Cabinets don't seem so prone to this internal bickering – or at least their members pre-Mrs Thatcher didn't publish diaries which told us the sordid details. Hugh Gaitskell was right when he once wrote in his diary that 'Ambition certainly does seem to kill the pleasanter aspects of human nature.'

Like Attlee's Cabinet, Wilson's contained several powerful and conflicting personalities. Apart from the Prime Minister himself, there was George Brown, belligerent and forceful; the politically shrewd James Callaghan; two Lords in Lord Gardiner and Lord Longford; trade union leader Frank Cousins; and Richard Crossman, known from his schooldays as 'Double Crossman'. Also present were Douglas Jay who had been one of Hugh Gaitskell's circle, pugnacious Denis Healey and the dry, schoolmasterly Michael Stewart. Another former Oxford don, Patrick Gordon-Walker, lost his seat in the 1964 election when his Conservative opponent fought an unpleasant racist campaign. He failed to be elected at a Leyton by-election in 1965 and had to resign as Foreign Secretary. Barbara Castle was in the first Cabinet and later recruits included Tony Crosland, Roy Jenkins and Tony Benn.

Wilson emphasised his government's commitment to economic growth and technological advance. In *The Future of Socialism*, published less than ten years before, Crosland had claimed that '... the contemporary mixed economy is characterised by high levels both of employment and productivity and by a reasonable degree of stability ...' By the early 1960s, however, it was becoming clear that neither high employment nor productivity could be taken for granted any longer. Competition from the Third World was increasing, the EEC was turning into a formidable rival and Japan was forging ahead. Not only was the economy burdened by the legacy of Britain's imperial past which necessitated the financing of a military presence 'east of Suez' that could not be afforded, the Wilson government inherited a huge balance of payments deficit of over £500 million from the Conservatives.

There was much to be done and a neutral observer might have anticipated that with thirteen years in which to prepare, the new administration would have been armed with a mass of blueprints and plans. In fact, just as in 1945, there were no detailed strategies to hand, even for reforms as crucial as the shift towards comprehensive education, the abolition of the eleven-plus exam and the raising of the school-leaving age to sixteen. This characteristic lack of preparation was not a new failing; in his memoirs George Brown was blunt about the way the Party ran its '... administrative and research departments on the most ridiculous shoestring':

> In those vital days I, as Deputy Leader of the Party, Chairman of the Home Policy Committee and heaven knows what else, had to work in a tiny office in the House of Commons with just one secretary for all attempts at co-ordinating policy, plus my constituency work, plus my parliamentary work.

This omission was all the more ominous because Wilson had encouraged popular expectation to believe that a time of peace and plenty was assured under his administration. The Labour manifesto had featured such issues as increased pensions and better education, health and housing because these were the commitments that everyone in the Labour Party could agree about.

The new government acted swiftly to remove prescription charges and promised to raise the level of pensions in the immediate future. The 'money men', whose confidence or otherwise about the British economy was vital, regarded these actions as being all too typical of profligate socialism and within a few weeks of the election there was a damaging run on the pound which put both sterling and the government under pressure. In his own account of these years, Wilson notes how undemocratic these pressures were:

> We had now reached the situation where a newly-elected Government with a mandate from the people was being told, not so much by the Governor of

the Bank of England but by international speculators, that the policies on which we had fought the election could not be implemented; that the Government was to be forced into the adoption of Tory policies to which it was fundamentally opposed. The Governor confirmed that that was, in fact, the case.

Moreover, Wilson and his Chancellor of the Exchequer, James Callaghan, had already drastically reduced their options by deciding on day one not to devalue the pound. Wilson knew full well that Attlee's Labour administration had been the last to devalue in 1949 and he did not want to begin his time in office with a similar admission of economic weakness. He was concerned too that the higher cost of imports after any devaluation, particularly of food, would hit working-class families disproportionately hard and that devaluation would 'featherbed' British industry by artificially boosting the export trade. On the other hand, the pound was clearly over-valued and devaluation would have given the economy a welcome boost.

Wilson, Callaghan and the Deputy Leader George Brown decided not to devalue and also to forbid debate about the matter. Therefore this issue was and is shrouded in secrecy and the fog is unlikely to lift because, in typically British style, the papers of the devaluation lobby have been 'lost'. It is clear that the decision against devaluation was taken by three men who were tired out by the election campaign. Douglas Jay, for one, has regretted that, 'It is characteristic of our system that a senior minister takes on the job of running a great department and trying to govern the country when he is twenty-four hours away from utter physical exhaustion.'

Wilson's continuing hostility to devaluation was also influenced by the secret deal he concluded in July 1965 with Lyndon Johnson's administration in the United States. Clive Ponting's research has shown how the Americans, worried in case devaluation of the pound would increase pressure on the dollar, were prepared to shore up the Wilson government as long as the pound was not devalued. The deal seems to have been known only to Wilson and Callaghan. But why should Wilson have needed American support so badly? The explanation for this British servility is to be found in the delusions of overseas grandeur which influenced this new Labour government just as much as it had previous Conservative ones.

In the summer of 1947 George Orwell had put his finger right on the nub of the question: 'Britain can only get free of America by dropping the attempt to be an extra-European power.' In fact, Government spending on foreign aid and commitments had risen from just over £50 million in 1952 to more than £400 million by 1964. Yet, as Leslie Stone has observed:

... Britain's economic power in relation to its chief trading competitors had been steadily waning. By the late sixties, its Gross National Product was estimated at $109 billion – well behind West Germany ($150 billion), France ($140 billion) and Japan ($167 billion). However, Japan devoted less than one per cent (0.9 per cent) of its GNP to expenditure on defence, while West Germany spent only 4.3 per cent. The figure for Britain was a whopping 5.7 per cent – a proportion exceeded among West European nations only by Portugal, which had serious colonial problems in Angola and Mozambique on its plate.

The imperial past struck back by giving Britain's leaders an attachment to overseas commitments that could not be met without drastically weakening the economy. Harold Wilson only began to shed his 'East of Suez' illusions after 1967 when it was already too late to alter his government's economic plans.

The tragedy of the government's – or at least its leadership's – determination not to devalue and to regard the level of the pound as some kind of national virility symbol was that it inevitably found itself pushed into policies of deflation and harsh measures in an attempt to defend the pound. The swingeing cuts of July 1965 and July 1966 made a mockery of the so-called 'National Plan', which Wilson had proposed as the centrepiece of his modernising Britain strategy. The Plan was put together by George Brown and a new creation, the Department of Economic Affairs (DEA). By switching the emphasis from consumption to investment the Plan was meant to set targets for industry and, by constructive planning, to ensure that they were met.

The Labour Party had always been identified as the 'natural' party of planning, in contrast to the Conservatives who were thought to prefer reliance on free enterprise and the operation of the market. In fact, both parties, reflecting the mood of the post-war consensus, had paid lip service to the virtues of planning; in June 1947 Herbert Morrison claimed that '... the idea of planning is by now above and beyond party politics.' It was less clear what this might mean in practice. The Attlee government had introduced a new body called the National Investment Council which, as a purely advisory group, gently chided private industry to be more efficient, but to very little effect. Only four 'Development Councils' were set up and it is ironic that Harold Wilson himself, as we saw earlier, initiated a bonfire of the controls usually associated with planning.

In the 1950s the statements of thinkers such as Anthony Crosland echoed Morrison's remarks: 'The issue now is not whether but how much and to what purpose to plan.' France, in particular, seemed to exemplify exactly how governments could activate the economy. Immediately after the war Jean Monnet established his 'Commissariat au Plan':

> Each of its 'modernisation committees' brought together thirty, forty, or fifty people from business, industry, the trade unions, and the administration, to discuss production targets, supplies, shortages, productivity bottlenecks, and future investment plans – not just as representatives of this interest or that, but as members of a team. In a typical year, 3,000 people from all over France might gather in the Plan's headquarters at 18 rue de Martignac, while a single official there might handle the files of 500 separate firms.

France's growth rate throughout the 1950s was significantly higher than Britain's and the Labour Party under Harold Wilson pledged itself to escape from what were seen as the 'stop-go' policies of previous Conservative governments. These had led to a predictable series of events neatly summarised by Professor David Marquand: whenever there was full employment, demand rose and imports were sucked in. The balance of payments then came under pressure and sterling weakened. The government refused to devalue which left only the option of reducing demand by means of deflationary cuts in spending. These measures produced rising unemployment which in turn prompted the government to boost demand in an attempt to deal with it, whereupon the whole circle started again: stop-go, stop-go.

However, the Labour Party's resolution to plan its way out of the 'stop-go' cycle did not include any attempt to plan the planning while in opposition. The idea for the expansionary DEA, which would counter the influence of the parsimonious Treasury, is thought to have been hastily concocted by Wilson and George Brown on the back of an envelope during the course of a taxi journey. In his autobiography Brown confirmed the story:

> Harold Wilson and I travelled together in a taxi, and it was on that ride to the House that we decided firmly to set up a Department of Economic Affairs, and that I should head it.

When the DEA began work immediately after the election it possessed just one desk and one chair – Frank Cousins had a similar experience at the new Ministry of Technology: 'No headquarters, no staff, not even funds.' It also became clear that in part the creation of the DEA enabled Harold Wilson to play off his two rivals for the 1963 leadership contest against each other. With George Brown at the DEA and James Callaghan at the Treasury, both

EQUALITY OF
SACRIFICE?

THE MAN AT THE TOP:—
"Equality of Sacrifice—that's the big idea, friends! **Let's all step down one rung!**"

£10000 A YEAR MAN

£1000 A YEAR MAN

£250 A YEAR MAN

THE UNEMPLOYED MAN

J. F. HORRABIN

From "PLEBS," (Organ of the N.C.L.C.)

VOTE LABOUR

A fine cartoon by artist and politician J. F. Horrabin used in the 1929 general election campaign.

The formation of the National Government under Ramsay MacDonald in August 1931 and the 10 per cent cut in the dole showed that he for one had forgotten Horrabin's 1929 election poster.

News ⚜ Chronicle

Holbrook's
Worcestershire SAUCE
A mere suggestion helps digestion

O WASTE
LET
ESE

POSTAGE : in U.K., 1d. ; Canada, 1d. ; Abroad, 1½d.

No. 26,632   LONDON   WEDNESDAY, AUGUST 26, 1931   MANCHESTER   ONE PENNY

NATIONAL CABINET OF TEN
Cut in "Dole"; Children's Allowances Not Touched—Mr. MACDONALD

Lord Reading [Foreign Secretary].

Sir Samuel Hoare (India).

Mr. N. Chamberlain (Health).

Mr. Baldwin [Lord President of the Council].

Mr. Ramsay MacDonald broadcasting last night.

Mr. Snowden [Chancellor of the Exchequer].

Lord Sankey (Lord Chancellor).

Mr. J. H. Thomas (Dominions).

Sir P. Cunliffe-Lister (Board of Trade).

LORD READING AS NEW FOREIGN SECRETARY

SIR AUSTEN AS FIRST LORD WITHOUT SEAT IN CABINET

MR. BALDWIN TO LEAD THE HOUSE

After a day of interviews Mr. MacDonald went to Buckingham Palace last evening and submitted his list of new Ministers for the approval of his Majesty. The list was issued later as follows:—

IN THE CABINET

Mr. J. RAMSAY MACDONALD — Prime Minister and First Lord of the Treasury

Mr. STANLEY BALDWIN — Lord President of the Council (Leader of the House).

Mr. PHILIP SNOWDEN — Chancellor of the Exchequer.

Sir H. SAMUEL — Home Secretary.

LORD SANKEY — Lord Chancellor.

LORD READING — Foreign Secretary.

Sir SAMUEL HOARE — Secretary for India.

INDIA CONFERENCE

NO CHANGE IN THE ARRANGEMENTS

It was announced last night from No. 10, Downing-street, that arrangements made for the India Round Table Conference would not be affected by the change of Government.

The Prime Minister will be chairman, Lord Sankey will preside at the forthcoming meeting of the Federal Structure Committee, and Lord Reading will continue to lend assistance in its work.

GANDHI MAY COME

TO-DAY'S TALK WITH VICEROY

SIMLA, Tuesday.

It is now definitely anticipated in Congress circles that Mr. Gandhi will attend the Round Table Conference in London, and he is expected to sail either on Saturday this week or by next week's boat.

He will meet the Viceroy (Lord Willingdon) at 11 o'clock to-morrow morning.

To-day Mr. Gandhi had a long conversation with Mr. Emerson, the Home Secretary, regarding alleged breaches of the Delhi Pact, particularly in Gujerat, where it is understood that an inquiry will probably be held.

The Viceroy, who is recovering from

NAUTILUS 350 MILES FROM POLE

GOOD PROGRESS NORTHWARDS

MOUNTAIN RIDGES UNDER SEA

From Sir HUBERT WILKINS
(By Radio.)

Aboard Nautilus in Arctic Seas, Tuesday.

Our course is slightly East of North. We have made good progress to-day.

At 8 p.m. we are about 350 miles from the Pole.

The sun shines coldly, low on the horizon. High winds from the eastward continue, and we push through scattered ice-pack and considerable open water. The wind whips the tops of the waves into icy spray, and the pack, even far from the edge, heaves with the swell.

Soundings show that we passed over mountain ridges on the ocean bottom,

Summer Coming Back

A WARM SPELL EXPECTED

Weather Outlook : Cool at first, then sunny and warmer.

The recent storm area has passed away across France and there is now a prospect of a general and perhaps prolonged spell of warmer and brighter weather, writes the "News-Chronicle" weather expert.

An anti-cyclone is coming in from the Atlantic and the barometer is rising generally.

The sun shone in London yesterday for several hours. If summer had been far off self that would be an obvious statement. Instead it is a statement almost unbelievable after a month or so of misplaced winter.

Here are the temperature readings taken by Messrs. Negretti and Zambra in Holborn:—

	Yesterday.	Monday.
6 a.m.	55	50
1 p.m.	60	54
9 p.m.	60	55
Maximum	63	55

At Kew Observatory the temperatures for the past 11 days are the lowest since 1876.

L.S.D. OF BAD WEATHER

Insurance Loss

The world's insurance gamble against the weather is about £20,000,000 a year.

It is estimated (writes a "News-Chronicle") correspondent) that this is approximately the total liabilities in Europe and America which is covered by premiums.

This year, as the manager of an important weather insurance department admitted yesterday, the increase of claims has meant a loss on the year's working.

LATE NEWS

STEAMER SUNK IN COLLISION

TWO MEN MISSING

The steamer Mungo, Dublin coaster, was sunk off Liverpool last night after in a collision with the Mayflower [Liverpool], but eight of a crew of nine were picked up, Thomas Gannon (28), of Dublin, in hospital at Waldney and John Loughlin (48), of Kingstown.

Sword of Honour.—Senior Under-Officer M. M. J. Oswald was awarded the sword of Honour, the King's Medal and other prizes at the July passing out examination of gentlemen cadets of the third class at the Royal Military Academy.

IMPREGNABLE

FOR SOVIET BRITAIN...

The Truth about
TROTSKYISM:
Moscow Trial January 1937

by
HARRY POLLITT
R. PALME DUTT
and
The complete text of
THE INDICTMENT
2ᵈ.

Britain's Communist Party had no doubts about the Moscow Trials: 'We wholeheartedly support the measures taken by the Soviet Union against these enemies and terrorists.'

37A Clerkenwell Green, home of Britain's first socialist printing press, Lenin's office for eighteen months and since 1933 occupied by the Marx Memorial Library.

George Lansbury (1859–1940), pacifist, feminist, editor of the *Daily Herald*, Poplar councillor and leader of the Labour Party between 1931 and 1935.

Two of the posters used in the 1945 general
election campaign that emphasised the Labour
Party's peacetime aims: 'Homes fit for heroes'.

(*above left*) Sir Stafford Cripps (1889–1952), in the 1930s a rebel expelled from the Labour Party, in the 1940s a very austere Chancellor of the Exchequer.

(*above right*) Ernest Bevin (1881–1950), 'Dockers' KC', driving force behind the creation of the Transport and General Workers' Union in 1922 and of NATO in 1949.

Aneurin Bevan (1887–1960), orator, statesman, bon viveur, 'beloved rebel' and creator of the National Health Service.

At the microphone Clem Attlee (1883–1967) and next to him Herbert Morrison (1880–1965) at the 1954 Labour Party Conference; though three years the older, Morrison was still hoping to succeed Attlee.

Bevan and Ian Mikardo (with pipe) listen to Michael Foot (born 1913) speaking at
the annual *Tribune* rally in 1957.

Bevan and Foot fell out over CND, seen here gathering in Trafalgar Square in April
1958.

Labour posters appeal to the electorate during the 1959 election campaign.

With no success. A weary Hugh Gaitskell (1906–1963) and general secretary Morgan Phillips (1902–1963) concede defeat at a Press conference after the election

George Brown (1914–1985), ex-Gaitskellite, parts company with Barbara Castle (born 1911), ex-Bevanite.

Harold Wilson (born 1916), Prime Minister four times, with the man who never was, Denis Healey (born 1917).

Despite the personal popularity of Jim Callaghan during the 1979 general election campaign, the voters preferred the Conservative way.

The Three Musketeers of the Labour Left whose campaigns all met with limited success in the 1980s: the internal reforms of Tony Benn (born 1925), the miners' strike spearheaded by Arthur Scargill (born 1938), and the Greater London Council led by Ken Livingstone (born 1945).

Neil Kinnock (born 1942) faces the Militant challenge outside the Labour Party's new headquarters in Walworth Road, London.

Labour

In the 1980s the Red Rose replaced the Red Flag.

departments were soon engaged in fratricidal war over their respective roles and influence.

Callaghan's Exchequer moved quickly to isolate the upstart DEA. Despite Brown's energy and love of a fight, his department was continually producing plans and figures that forecast high rates of economic growth of around 4 per cent but which were then transformed into optimistic daydreams because of Chancellor Callaghan's deflationary cuts. The National Plan itself, published to fanfares in 1965, turned out to consist of 'little more than the printed replies to a questionnaire sent to industries about their estimates of inputs and outputs on the assumptions of 25 per cent real growth by 1970.'

The DEA was also hampered by the difficult personality of George Brown himself. Something of a 'raging bull', the diaries of Crossman, Castle and Benn reveal how Brown's demonic energy often deteriorated into drunken rantings and ravings. The DEA was never more than an irrelevance and after Brown moved to another post successive Ministers had even less impact on the British economy. The Department was quietly allowed to expire in 1969.

One vital flaw in the Wilson strategy was that although the Cabinet might well be bursting with dons and journalists, not one of them had any managerial experience. As Tam Dalyell has written of his friend Richard Crossman, 'He had never actually run anything.' None of the Cabinet had any practical experience of wealth creation. An economics don might well possess much theoretical expertise but these skills were not necessarily of much help when dealing with the pragmatism of an ICI or Unilever chairman. In May 1968 Crossman referred to '. . . the lack of success of the interventionist policies of Peter Shore and Tony Wedgwood Benn, young men who with carefree arrogance think they can enter the business world and help it to be more efficient.'

Some of these well meaning but ineffectual chickens were to come home to roost only in the future. In the first flush of his administration Harold Wilson's dynamism and seeming competence impressed many. Any difficulties could be explained away by blaming the Conservatives for leaving behind such a mess. Alternatively, Wilson could complain that his government was hamstrung by its tiny majority.

He called for a fresh election in March 1966 and throughout the campaign was careful to portray the Labour Party in national and patriotic terms in order to maximise support. In his two broadcasts Wilson apparently used the words 'Britain' forty-two times, 'government' thirty-nine times and 'Labour' not once. Helped too by the fact that the Conservatives had a new and largely unknown leader in Edward Heath, Wilson's strategy seemed to pay off when the electorate returned Labour to power with a gain of forty-eight seats. As in 1945, the Labour Party had now won a thumping majority. Attlee's government had introduced much of social democratic Britain. What could Wilson's achieve?

After the election Wilson could no longer rely on the 'small majority' excuse. Moreover it was now two years since the Conservatives had governed. Nor could he claim that his Cabinet was inexperienced in office. Yet, armed as they were with the full panoply of civil service resources, it was difficult to understand why the new Labour administration should yet again lack detailed and thought-through policies. One reason for this omission lies in the personality of the Prime Minister himself.

When Harold Wilson was elected leader of the Labour Party he knew full well that, like Margaret Thatcher in the following decade, only a small minority of his shadow and then full Cabinet had voted for him in the leadership contest. David Howell has pointed out that 'In office Wilson paid for his earlier independent strategy; his earlier isolation from any faction meant that he lacked a dependable basis of support. The result was a tendency to surround himself with advisers who acted as a necessary reassurance, but also as an insulator against disturbances from outside.' The most controversial member of this 'kitchen Cabinet' was Wilson's secretary, Marcia Williams, later Lady Falkender.

Always worried about his own position, Wilson continually moved ministers from department to department so that they would be unable to build up a permanent power base from which to challenge him. What one commentator has called this 'Artful Dodger' style of government meant that the civil service benefited from this high-powered game of musical chairs because no minister was really able to get on top of his job, apart from Denis Healey who remained as minister of Defence from 1964 to 1970. Anthony Crosland once claimed of ministers that:

> It takes you six months to get your head properly above water, a year to get the general drift of most of the field, and two years really to master the whole of a department.

Wilson rarely allowed anyone two years in the same post. The Wilson government also lacked a 'fixer' like Herbert Morrison who as Leader of the House of Commons in the Attlee administration had eased through legislation with a minimum of fuss.

Wilson's personalised approach to politics undermined any consistent strategy by elevating tactics above principle. Virtually every member of the government seems to have spent much of their time either 'leaking' to the Press or thinking about it, emulating Wilson's own conduct. Douglas Jay was a minister in both the Attlee and Wilson governments and has claimed that the latter was a much less happy affair than the former, while Tony Benn has recorded that 'Cabinets used to spend sometimes as long on discussing the leak after the last Cabinet as they did on the business on the agenda for that day.'

In such a poisonous atmosphere even Wilson's closest supporters began to doubt his qualities. Richard Crossman was, in his own words, 'an absolutely solid Harold man' yet his diaries reveal the Prime Minister's drift and inconsistency. As early as December 1964 Crossman notes, '. . . the Cabinet isn't very firm or very stable because the central leadership isn't there, the sense of priorities, the sense of grip that you need.' In June 1965 he laments, 'Here we are, drifting along, with our momentum halted and the Civil Service taking over more every day.'

In December 1966, after the second election, Crossman observes of Wilson that 'His main aim is to stay in office. That's the real thing and for that purpose he will use almost any trick or gimmick if he can only do it.' By April 1969 Crossman is berating: 'the muddle-headed incompetence of the central direction of the party . . . He is just a figure posturing there in the middle without any drive except to stay as Prime Minister as long as he can.' On and on it goes. Tony Benn, at the time one of Wilson's 'kitchen Cabinet', thought the Prime Minister was 'a manipulator who thinks he can get out of everything by fixing somebody or something.' Perhaps Tony Crosland, a former Gaitskellite, put it more succinctly: 'The trouble with Harold is that one hasn't the faintest idea whether the bastard means what he says even at the moment he speaks it.' No one doubted Wilson's drive and resilience, and other hard-working members of the Cabinet sometimes found it difficult to keep up with him. Nevertheless this energy so often failed to achieve results.

July 1966 saw yet another run on the pound and, once again, devaluation was ruled out in favour of a further bout of deflation. The modernising 'white heat' image of only two years before was now a very distant memory. Eventually, the pound had to be devalued by 14 per cent in November 1967. The bungling of this issue contrasts unfavourably with the well-managed and decisive devaluation of the franc carried through by Mitterrand and his newly-elected Socialist government in France in the summer of 1982.

The Wilson governments were marginally more successful with their taxation policies. Previous Labour governments had generally preferred to administer the existing system, and when they did introduce new taxes they were often swiftly replaced by incoming Conservative governments. Attlee, for instance, had introduced a 100 per cent development tax levied on unearned land value but this was discarded by the Churchill administration in 1953.

Three new taxes were introduced by the Wilson government, Selective Employment Tax, Capital Gains Tax and Corporation Tax. Additionally, in the absence of substantial economic growth, Labour was forced to raise taxes in order to pay for increased welfare spending. Between 1964 and 1970 taxes on personal income rose from an average of 10 to 14 per cent. However, one academic commentator has calculated that the net effect of Labour's financial policies was indeed to make the rich poorer and the poor richer.

But if the Wilson governments proved incapable of tackling economic weakness, they were responsible for a series of libertarian measures, associated with the Home Secretary Roy Jenkins, which helped humanise the country. In many ways the 'High Politics' of Cabinet reshuffles and departmental comings and goings pass the majority of people by. These social changes affected everyone.

The Labour administration initiated, or at least did not obstruct, homosexual reform, abortion reform, divorce reform, the end of theatre censorship, the abolition of capital punishment and the banning of corporal punishment in prisons. It supervised the introduction of equal pay legislation, redundancy payments, the Law Commission, the Ombudsman, legislation outlawing racial discrimination, the expansion of higher education and the publication of state papers after thirty years and not fifty.

The Lord Chancellor, Lord Gardiner, oversaw criminal law reforms, the establishment of the Family Division of the High Court and changes in property and matrimonial law. He also appointed the first ever woman High Court judge. The select committees introduced in 1969 helped provide additional much-needed scrutiny of the executive. The age of majority was lowered from twenty-one to eighteen and the Open University was set up through the efforts of Bevan's widow Jennie Lee, who had been given the completely new post of Minister of the Arts. She ensured that arts spending doubled. Jim Griffiths was appointed the first Secretary of State for Wales and by 1970, for the first time, Britain was spending more on education than it was on defence. These reforms, often emanating from backbench MPs and then supported by Roy Jenkins as Home Secretary, all helped to change the quality of people's lives for the better.

In many ways this avalanche of reform represented yet another area of the post-war consensus forged in the 1930s and 1940s — it was the social equivalent of the welfare state and full employment, which were recognised by virtually everyone as achievements. The measures marked a welcome return to some of the libertarian themes discussed in Chapter Three, 'Socialism and the New Life', and which can be traced through from Edward Carpenter to E. M. Forster and Bloomsbury to Noel Annan's *Our Age*. Personal relationships and friendships were paramount and anything that came in the way of them, especially if it related to outdated legal constraints, was suspect.

One Marxist critic of the Labour Party, David Coates, called the Wilson governments' record in the field of social reform 'appalling' — yet he fails to mention a single one of the above changes. Although the 1964–70 administrations did not solve Britain's economic problems (which government can claim it has?), its social reforms were a remarkable achievement. Today some right-wing commentators and politicians like Norman Tebbit castigate this supposedly permissive society — and undoubtedly some people did use their freedoms in selfish ways. But to claim that because, say, consenting male adults were now able to behave as they wished in private or theatregoers could see *Oh! Calcutta!* live on stage represented the start of some twentieth-century Sodom and Gomorrah is ridiculous and comes ill from people who usually make much of the philosophy that people should have as much freedom to choose as possible.

Although the social reforms of the Wilson government certainly matched the changes introduced by Gladstone's one hundred years before, it did not imitate the earlier administration's attack on institutional inertia. Needless to say, the monarchy was an issue that Wilson decided to tiptoe around; in his diaries, Richard Crossman describes with some disgust the time that a Cabinet minister had to spend rehearsing the ceremony of becoming a Privy Councillor:

> I don't suppose anything more dull, pretentious, or plain silly has ever been invented. There we were, sixteen grown men. For over an hour we were taught how to stand up, how to kneel on one knee on a cushion, how to raise the right hand with the Bible in it, how to advance three paces towards the Queen, how to take the hand and kiss it, how to move back ten paces without falling over the stools — which had been carefully arranged so that you did fall over them.

Crossman himself botched up reform of the House of Lords. What seemed to be all-party support for the measure that would have abolished the right of hereditary peers to vote in the Lords was torpedoed by the unlikely combination of Michael Foot and Enoch Powell. The latter felt the reforms went too far while the former considered they did not go far enough. When Crossman did attempt something innovative, such as advocating experimental closed-circuit televising of the Commons, he discovered that he was the only Cabinet minister who voted for the proposal.

The Fulton Committee found that the civil service was prejudiced against professional and technical experts and proposed some important changes. As Clive Ponting has put it:

> The crucial recommendation was the abolition of classes within the Civil Service. If this had been implemented then the generalist administrators (the public school-Oxbridge-educated arts graduates) would lose their key roles as amateur advisers to ministers to professionally qualified accountants, economists and statisticians.

This reform should have been near to the heart of Harold Wilson's determination to create 'a dynamic, expanding, confident and above all purposive new Britain.' Anyone who has watched the series *Yes, Minister* can imagine Sir Humphrey Appleby's reaction to these proposals. By leaving the implementation of the Fulton Report to the Applebys of the civil service, the Wilson government guaranteed that nothing would be done, as duly occurred. In both Germany and France at exactly the same time ministries were being reorganised and modernised.

The Official Secrets Act remained intact. Prescription charges, abolished with a flourish in 1964, were reimposed in 1968. Despite promises, the government – or at least three Ministers, namely Wilson, Healey and Gordon-Walker who omitted to inform their Cabinet colleagues of the decision – did not cancel the Polaris nuclear project. Again, despite promises, a wealth tax was never implemented.

Surrounded by his loyal kitchen Cabinet Harold Wilson became increasingly isolated and paranoid, hankering after an American 'Presidential style' form of leadership. Time and again, whether it was over arms sales to South Africa, or support for American involvement in Vietnam, or the introduction of the Commonwealth Immigration Act in 1968 denying Kenyan Asians who held British passports the right to enter the country, the policies of the Wilson government seemed to be shabby and opportunist, lacking any political, let alone ethical, principle.

One telling illustration of this moral vacuum occurred after the declaration of unilateral independence by Ian Smith's Rhodesian regime in November

1965. Sanctions were introduced against the rebel government but the major oil companies such as Shell and BP were determined to maintain the flow of oil into Rhodesia. They therefore introduced 'swap' arrangements with a French company by which they evaded the letter of the law. It is unclear how much the government knew about what was going on. At best they were guilty of carelessness and of not asking relevant questions; at worst, they were accomplices to the oil companies' behaviour.

One underlying weakness of the Wilson governments was that they never attracted good policy ideas whether it be from members of the Cabinet or from extra-parliamentary sources. The diaries of Crossman, Castle and Benn reveal ministers desperately coping with short-term departmental crises and therefore never able to stand back from the fray.

As for the other sections of the British labour movement, the Communist Party was declining inexorably in terms of both numbers and influence. It may have opposed the Soviet invasion of Czechoslovakia in 1968 but its protests would hardly have caused Moscow to lose any sleep. The other left-wing movements of the 1960s continued the trend, first established by CND, of no longer basing themselves exclusively on the manual working class. The most prominent of these movements was composed of students.

The 1960s saw a doubling of student numbers at universities, polytechnics and colleges of further education. Unlike the previous decade when students were docile and accepting, the new generation believed in voicing complaints as noisily as possible. Dissatisfaction with the teaching and conditions then spilled over into protest against American military involvement in Vietnam. Like CND members, the students were firmly anti-political, dismissing elections as charades and, similarly, they usually had no idea what to do after a demonstration was over. For want of anything better, the demo became an end in itself, full of sound and fury but signifying not a lot. E. P. Thompson once scathingly dismissed the events of 1968 as 'a rich kid's revolutionary farce'.

Perhaps one reason for Thompson's dismissive remark was that many of the students in the West had little sense of perspective. Tariq Ali was instrumental in organising several VSC (Vietnam Solidarity Campaign) marches. In his own words, 'We wished to transform Western civilisation because we regarded it as politically, morally and culturally bankrupt.' But in Czechoslovakia, where a real revolution was taking place, David Caute has observed that 'The Czechoslovak reform movement, students included, was working for precisely the freedoms which Western radicals were rejecting as bogus and manipulative . . .'

The Revolutionary Students Socialist Federation (RSSF) was brutally frank in its manifesto of November 1968, committing itself to '. . . the revolutionary overthrow of capitalism and imperialism and its replacement by workers' power, and bases itself on the recognition that the only social class in industrial countries capable of making the revolution is the working class.' The only problem with this declaration was that the RSSF had few contacts with, or influence among, the British working class.

In fact, the one truly working-class demonstration which did take place in 1968 showed how misguided some students were in romanticising the revolutionary potential of the British working class. In April 1968 Conservative MP Enoch Powell delivered his notorious 'rivers of blood' speech. A few days later he was sacked from the Shadow Cabinet by Edward Heath, whereupon 4,000 London dockers went on strike in support of his views. The dockers and the Smithfield meat porters also marched to the Houses of Parliament to voice their racist opinions. Some of the more thoughtful students were horrified by these actions. As David Widgery has expressed it:

> Here were workers doing what we International Socialists were recommending: rank-and-file activity, political struggle on an industrial basis — only they were doing it the other way round. So it was all blowing up in our faces . . .

Some students retreated into a sectarian isolation, setting up tiny little groups which then divided into even tinier groups. David Widgery has provided a thirty-eight-page glossary giving a split-by-split taxonomy of these left-wing bodies, among which were to be found the Microfaction and the snappily-titled 'Committee to Defeat Revisionism, for Communist Unity'.

One important section of this counter-culture turned away in despair from Britain towards European and Third World Marxism. The New Left dismissed the accepted socialist tradition that the Left should speak to everyone and not just to a few. The 'Old Left' had not always been successful in this, but it had at least tried. The Communist Party, for instance, had often insisted that intellectuals joining the Party should first undertake menial tasks, while the adult education tradition, which included men as gifted as G. D. H. Cole and R. H. Tawney, had always been an effective influence. In one striking phrase Cole once said that WEA tutors were the true missionaries of today, doing the kind of job which at one time the churches used to do.

This 'missionary' tradition was now discarded because some of the 'New New Left' contended that British socialism lacked a good healthy dose of 'theory', which could only be imported from abroad. There is no doubt that the British Left had and has often been overly wedded to a dull and insular pragmatism, but to condemn it in its entirety was to throw out the baby with the bathwater. In fact, it was clear that *New Left Review* knew little and cared a lot less about Britain's own radical heritage. In one essay, for instance, its editor Perry Anderson claimed that, 'The vast majority of those intellectuals who had briefly been on the Left [in the 1930s] swung to the right ...' A glance at this book's 1930s chapter shows how wrong Anderson's assertion is.

No matter, a series of 'rave' notices introduced the readers of *New Left Review* to the work of several European thinkers. This latest theory was usually couched in an arcane and inaccessible language understood only by those few in the know which displayed what Perry Anderson himself, in rather arcane language, later complained was 'its very surplus above the necessary minimum quotient of verbal complexity'. This seemed to demonstrate one of R. H. Tawney's maxims: 'It is possible to be learned and a fool.'

Such obfuscation camouflaged some of the more generous impulses manifested in the 1960s agitation which, at its best, represented a disgust with organised electoral politics in favour of a libertarian 'do-it-yourself' approach. Even Michael Stewart, Foreign Secretary in the Wilson government, remarked on the greater tendency towards 'group action' in the 1960s. Referring to his Fulham constituency he wrote:

> In 1945 I would receive letters which said, in effect, 'Conditions in this street are awful; please do something about it.' The 1970 version would be, 'We have formed a residents' association to deal with some problems in this neighbourhood; will you please come to the inaugural meeting.'

In later years these impulses resurfaced as a new concern for feminism, for the environment and for 'single issue' campaigns.

As Harold Wilson surveyed the political scene from his bunker at No 10 Downing Street, increasingly at odds with the Labour Party Conference — between 1964 and 1970 the Conference voted against government measures on no less than thirteen occasions — the Parliamentary Labour Party and even his own Cabinet, inevitably he began to look for explanations for the delayed appearance of his 'New Britain'.

The large Labour majority meant that the party whips found it increasingly difficult to dragoon backbenchers into voting for measures they did not support. In March 1967 a number of MPs abstained in protest at the White

Paper on Defence. A furious Wilson responded at the next meeting of the Parliamentary Labour Party:

> All I say is watch it. Every dog is allowed one bite, but a different view is taken of a dog that goes on biting all the time. If there are doubts that the dog is biting not because of dictates of conscience but because he is considered vicious, then things happen to that dog. He may not get his licence renewed when it falls due.

Not only was this an extraordinarily arrogant and tactless attitude to take towards MPs of his own party, it was bound to be counter-productive. Two months later thirty-six Labour MPs voted against the Government's proposal to apply for Britain to join the Common Market and a further fifty-one abstained. As it turned out, the application was vetoed by General de Gaulle.

At odds with much of his own party, Wilson started to turn his attention towards what he thought was trade union obstructiveness. During the seamen's strike of 1966, for instance, he tried to play the 'Communist bogey' card, blaming a handful of supposedly Communist agitators on the union executive and thereby hoping to pressure the union to call off the action. It is revealing that Edward Heath was unimpressed when Wilson showed him the evidence for his assertion. A damaging dock strike the following year was led by the Communist Jack Dash, nicknamed 'The Red Napoleon', whose men had benefited from the de-casualisation of dock work but whose militancy was beginning to drive employers to find other, cheaper and more reliable docks at which to unload.

The obvious difficulty facing any Labour government was that ever since Keir Hardie the link with the trade unions had been central to the very existence of the Labour Party itself and had ensured that it had successfully ousted the Liberal Party as the major rival to the Conservatives. It was the trade unions that provided party funds and therefore any attempt to interfere with the paymasters was bound to be provocative. In addition, post-war corporatism – the cosy alliance between government, employers and trade unions – had strengthened the hand of the unions, as too had full employment. One symbol of the unions' permanence and power was the opening in March 1958 of its new headquarters, Congress House in Bloomsbury. Decorated by two pieces of sculpture, the state trumpeters of the Royal Horse Guards sounded a special fanfare for the event. Throughout the 1950s the Conservative government was only too willing to discuss anything and everything with prominent trade unionists: 'beer and sandwiches' at the Ministry of Labour.

The trade unions had always been sectional bodies concerned, above all, with the welfare of their own members rather than national issues. Their concentration on wage bargaining meant that their actions were usually seen or experienced negatively. The unions' only power was to withdraw their labour, which almost always inconvenienced the public. There were few single industry unions. The motor car industry, for instance, contained men from twenty-two different unions. Between 1964 and 1966 there were thirty unofficial strikes for every one official strike sanctioned by a union.

The trade unions' narrow and defensive stance was illustrated by the fact that with the notable exception of Ernest Bevin the record of leading trade unionists drafted into Labour governments was often disappointing. For instance, Frank Cousins, the leader of the Transport and General Workers' Union, was brought in as Minister of Science and Technology in 1964 but was uncomfortable dealing with civil servants and the minutiae of administration. In July 1966 he resigned in protest at the Prices and Incomes Bill, which in effect banned all prices and wages increases for the next six months.

There had been few cases of union corruption, compared with the regular cases of business and company fraud. One bad instance had occurred in the 1950s when the Electrical Trades Union (ETU) was run by a handful of Communists who illegally fixed ballots in order to retain power. It took a court case to break their hold.

But the problem plaguing the Wilson government was the rash of unofficial strikes and the new ploy of 'working to rule', which had been pioneered by shop stewards who were the militant arm of the unions. For many people the image of the shop steward was synonymous with the rigid character of Brother Fred Kite, played by Peter Sellers in the film *I'm All Right Jack*. In the film the company's management is shown to be unscrupulous and incompetent, but it is the Sellers part which people tend to remember.

Now very much a part of the Establishment — its centenary in 1968 was marked by the issue of a commemorative stamp — the TUC frequently disapproved of 'wildcat' actions but found itself unable or unwilling to do anything about it. The prominence given to trade union behaviour by the right-wing Press meant that it was not easy to keep matters in proportion; the academic expert H. A. Turner recorded:

An effective anti-influenza serum would probably be of more measurable benefit to the economy than an effective anti-strike law — and perhaps be less difficult and costly to produce.

Crossman noted in his diaries the Prime Minister's musings on the effectiveness of the American Democratic Party, which had no formal links with the unions. Wilson waited for the report of the Donovan Commission, which had been set up to inquire into trade unions, hoping that it would recommend drastic measures. In fact, its modest advice was that pay bargaining should be operated on a more centralised basis but that otherwise, for want of a better alternative, labour relations should remain as they were. This was not good enough for Wilson. He asked Barbara Castle to tackle the union problem.

The daughter of a tax inspector who was a member of the Independent Labour Party, Barbara Betts was educated at Bradford Girls' Grammar School and Oxford where she was an active member of the Labour Club. In the late 1930s she was a journalist on the left-wing weekly *Tribune*. She married the journalist Ted Castle and in 1945 was elected MP for Blackburn. Sir Stafford Cripps appointed her his Parliamentary Private Secretary. In the 1950s she was a Bevanite but found opposition frustrating. Like Bevan, she welcomed the challenge of government: 'This is the real morality: having to choose, having not to choose. Anybody can be on the side of the angels when there's never a devil around.'

Harold Wilson appointed her Minister for Overseas Development in 1964 and then moved her to the Ministry of Transport. In the face of much opposition, it was Castle who in October 1966 introduced the Breathalyser in order to curb drunken driving. But the opposition she faced on this issue was as nothing when compared with the storm raised by her White Paper *In Place of Strife* issued in January 1969 when she was Minister of Employment and Productivity.

She decided to recognise the trade union position by introducing what she regarded as a charter giving the unions statutory rights:

> So, first and foremost, *In Place of Strife* was a charter of trade union rights: the right to belong to a trade union, safeguards against unfair dismissal, the right to the disclosure of information for bargaining purposes, the 'check-off' system of collecting trade union dues, protection for sympathetic strikes and steps towards industrial democracy: long-standing trade union demands, many of which have since been met.

Conversely Mrs Castle also thought that if trade union members had rights, they also owed duties: 'If power is to be shared so must responsibility.' *In Place of Strife* called for penal clauses to be levied against strikers taking part in unofficial action, a twenty-eight-day pause before a strike could begin and, in notable anticipation of the future, ballots of union members before industrial action could be called.

In effect, Barbara Castle was trying to reform the unions before someone else did it for them. But, unlike any post-war administration whether it had been Conservative or Labour, Castle and Wilson were proposing to introduce legal restraints on their own colleagues, allies and financial backers. Just as Gaitskell had done, they underestimated the entrenched interests that dominated the unions and their collective ethos of 'labourism' which valued solidarity above everything else – even economic efficiency.

There did seem to be popular support for *Strife* but this was no help in passing the proposals through the Cabinet and then Parliament where one in three Labour MPs was sponsored by the trade unions. What made it worse was that Wilson's highly personalised style over the last five years returned to haunt him. Few of his own Cabinet now trusted him. He had also miscalculated in introducing such an important measure towards the end of his term in office when his incomes policies had already exhausted the fund of political goodwill which the unions had originally had towards a Labour government.

In addition, several major unions had recently elected left-wing leaders. Hugh Scanlon was now President of the Engineers, Lawrence Daly General Secretary of the Mineworkers and Jack Jones of the Transport and General Workers' Union. In his autobiography Jones claims that 'Wilson and Castle were basically academics and it was difficult to persuade them to see things from a shop-floor angle.'

Wilson and Castle found themselves more and more isolated as everyone else in the Cabinet withdrew their support for the Bill. Tony Benn recorded their defeat:

> Harold and Barbara then became extremely bitter. Harold threatened to resign several times and said he wouldn't do what the Cabinet wanted him to do and they would have to look for a new Leader, and so on; people were completely unmoved by it. His bluff was called and he just looked weak and petty, he spoke too much, he interrupted, he was angry. Barbara was frantic in the usual Barbara sort of way.

The TUC came up with a face-saving device for Wilson and Castle, namely a 'solemn and binding' agreement that in cases of unofficial strikes the union would do their best to get members to return to work. But everyone knew that the unions had won. The *In Place of Strife* debacle showed that the

Labour Party was still essentially a trade union party. The fortunes of the two were inextricably linked. This was bound to cause problems if and when the trade unions, still growing, failed to move with the times and became unpopular with the public at large. As Barbara Castle had warned, their failure to adapt themselves meant that, in the 1980s, this job would be done for them in a much harsher way.

The mishandling of *In Place of Strife* somehow symbolised the cul-de-sac down which the Wilson government had manoeuvred itself. The hopes of a 'New Britain' had long gone. In June 1970 the Conservatives under Heath won the general election, to the surprise of many leading Labour figures. Tony Benn has noted how he felt when the first result came in, showing an enormous swing to the Conservatives: 'In a fraction of a second, one went from a pretty confident belief in victory to absolute certainty of defeat.' Somehow it signified the way in which the hopes of just six years before had been dashed.

Looking back at Harold Wilson's two governments of 1964–1966 and 1966–1970, the verdict must be that although much was done, especially in the social sphere, there was an inability to translate rhetoric into action, particularly over core economic issues. In Kenneth Morgan's words: 'In the end, public relations superseded public planning, tactics swamped strategy, and cosmetics dominated economics.' Two years of 'hard slog' between 1968 and 1970 did produce a balance of payments surplus, but this achievement was hardly the one that those enthusiasts for Wilson's 'New Britain' would have expected after six years of a Labour government. Average economic growth between 1966 and 1970 was no more than 1.8 per cent a year. Was there more to what Clive Ponting has called a 'breach of promise' than the personal failings of Harold Wilson?

Clearly there was. The Attlee governments after the Second World War had marked an end and not a beginning. A social democratic society had been created and in its wake both Conservatives and Labour had done little more than administer it. This consensus was sometimes dubbed 'Butskellism', a recognition that R. A. Butler's Conservative approach was very similar to that of Hugh Gaitskell's.

It was as if a sturdy and comfortable family car which had given excellent service over the years had now begun to develop a series of faults. Instead of scrapping the car and buying a new one, the Wilson administration confined itself to tinkering, with patching up here and there and hoping this would suffice. The Labour government very briefly sketched out a blueprint for a new model but this was soon scrapped. Wilson was therefore restricted to ad hoc repair work and 'crisis management'. If this failing undermined the

Wilson years of the 1960s when the car was still in relatively good shape, how much worse would the problems be in the late 1970s after yet further disrepair and bad treatment?

CHAPTER TWELVE

Endings: The British Left in the 1970s

'In all my dealings with the NUT [National Union of Teachers] at that time, I never once heard mention of education or children.'
Bernard Donoughue, Senior Policy Adviser at No 10 Downing Street between 1974 and 1979

'You know there are times, perhaps once every 30 years, when there is a sea-change in politics. It then does not matter what you say or what you do. There is a shift in what the public wants and what it approves of. I suspect there is now such a sea-change – and it is for Mrs Thatcher.'
James Callaghan, Labour Prime Minister, speaking in May 1979 just before the election result was known

THE CABINET MINISTER who had led the opposition to Barbara Castle's *In Place of Strife* proposals was James Callaghan, sometimes described by his colleagues as 'The Keeper of the Cloth Cap'; in other words, he was considered to be the individual who would fight the hardest to maintain the trade union-Labour Party link.

Having begun work in the 1930s as a clerk in the Inland Revenue and then being elected an MP in the landslide of 1945, Callaghan's subsequent political career was the familiar story of a man once on the Left – in 1945 he voted against Britain's financial arrangements with the Americans and resigned his junior ministerial post – who shifted gradually towards the Right of the Labour Party. In the 1950s he was a staunch Gaitskellite. He stood against Harold Wilson in the 1963 leadership contest, coming third behind Wilson and George Brown but gaining enough votes to ensure himself a senior post in any future Labour government.

Jim Callaghan eventually owned a farm in Sussex and liked to think he truly embodied what he called his 'God-given common sense'. His speeches often contained expressions like 'Bless my soul' and he sometimes acted as if he was the Labour Party's belated answer to Stanley Baldwin, though Harold Wilson also fancied this role. Callaghan was certainly like Baldwin in his keen sense of political power, and he is the only man to have occupied the offices of Chancellor of the Exchequer, Home Secretary, Foreign Secretary and Prime Minister.

It was less clear what political ideas motivated him. Back in 1956 Hugh Gaitskell commented in his diary: 'He [Callaghan] is a most talented Parliamentarian and a man of very considerable charm, but he seems to me to have absolutely no philosophical basis. You never know what he is going to say.' Jim Callaghan's two most permanent achievements have, in fact, nothing directly to do with politics; as Parliamentary Secretary at the Ministry of Transport at the end of the Attlee governments, it was he who resurrected two forgotten projects that led to the introduction of zebra crossings and cat's-eyes.

Callaghan was appointed Chancellor of the Exchequer in 1964. His most important and fateful decision was his first: not to devalue the pound. The next three years were spent trying to defend this position. The devaluation of November 1967 was seen as an admission of defeat and Callaghan was moved to the post of Home Secretary. In August 1969 he was responsible for sending British troops into Ulster. Working on the recipe for political success which he had supposedly outlined to George Wigg back in the 1940s of waiting for the trade unions to decide their line and then following them, he also successfully defeated Barbara Castle's proposals for trade union reform. Ten years later his actions would return to haunt him.

In March 1974 Callaghan was appointed Foreign Secretary in Harold Wilson's minority government, a post he continued to hold after the October election had given Labour a small majority. Most of his time over the next two years was spent renegotiating Britain's place in the EEC and he therefore missed much of the domestic drama caused by the struggle of the Wilson administration to cope with a multitude of problems ranging from rampant inflation to rising unemployment and zero economic growth.

Unlike the 1945 and 1964 Labour governments, Wilson's 1974 administration came to office armed with a formidable batch of programmes and plans. After 1970 the Labour Party had devoted much of its time to drawing up suitable blueprints for any future Labour government; at one point over 50 committees and nearly 1,000 people were hard at work on behalf of the National Executive Committee (NEC). The only problem was that Harold Wilson and most of his Cabinet were strongly opposed to the NEC's proposals. Wilson deliberately failed to turn up to many NEC meetings.

The Labour Party Constitution drawn up in 1918 by Sidney Webb and Arthur Henderson had reflected the variety of opinions and organisations that made up the British Labour Party. In particular, Webb and Henderson ensured that the Party had no single source of authority. Instead a balance was to be maintained between the Parliamentary Labour Party, the constituency Labour Parties and the Party's annual conference, which was dominated by the trade union block vote. Such an arrangement, admirable in theory and often in practice, nevertheless meant that the Party was prone to factionalism whereby different groups could wield influence in one or other of the three bodies.

The situation was made more complicated whenever there was a Labour government. Labour Prime Ministers and Cabinets argued that national concerns must take priority over party matters and sometimes felt justified in ignoring Conference decisions. A Labour Prime Minister is able to supplement his Party powers with that of national patronage. When the Labour Party is out of office, the National Executive Committee elected by the annual conference regains its influence. An early example of the friction between the NEC and the leader of the Parliamentary Labour Party came in 1945 when Chairman Harold Laski tried to prevent Clement Attlee from becoming Prime Minister. But it was in the 1970s that matters began to boil up when the NEC, partly in response to what were seen as the disappointments of the Wilson governments between 1964 and 1970, moved leftwards.

This shift in political position was exacerbated by the way in which the rank and file of the Labour Party was becoming much less deferential to the leadership. As Patrick Seyd has noted, the 1970s saw a growing radicalisation of three groups in particular within the Party: local councillors, local activists, and a number of prominent trade union leaders. In addition, women within the Party and, to a lesser extent, black people argued too that radical internal reforms were needed. In effect, it meant that the various shades of opinion within the Labour Party were strengthening and becoming almost factions or 'tendencies'.

The good thing about this diversity was and is that the Labour Party contains a vigour and excitement usually superior to that of its political rivals. The drawback is the image of disunity this turmoil conveys to the electorate and the fact that as much time is spent fighting internal battles as external ones. Harold Wilson once claimed that:

> This party is a bit like an old stagecoach. If you drive it rapidly, everyone aboard is either so exhilarated or so seasick that you don't have a lot of difficulty. If you keep stopping, however, then everyone gets out and starts arguing about which way to go.

Wilson's own governments of 1964–70 had brought the stagecoach to a halt, and now everyone was only too keen to discuss future directions.

In the past most successful pressure groups within the Labour Party had been created by its right wing; most notably the Campaign for Democratic Socialism which had helped Hugh Gaitskell reverse the 1960 Conference resolution in favour of unilateralism. Now, however, it was left-wing groups such as the Campaign for Labour Party Democracy (CLPD), formed in 1973, that brought disciplined pressure to bear on local constituency parties and then on the annual Conference by putting forward suggested resolutions and working to get them accepted.

This leftwards shift was reinforced by the changing political complexion of the unions such as the Transport and General Workers' Union and the Engineers. In the 1950s the Labour Party leadership could rely on the stolid and distinctly unradical support of leaders such as Arthur Deakin and William Carron in order to defeat the Bevanites. Now, in the 1970s, both unions were more left-wing and less inclined to offer unthinking support for Harold Wilson and his Cabinet colleagues.

In 1973 the decision was taken to scrap the old 'proscribed list', which had banned members of certain groups and bodies, usually Communist or Trotskyist, from joining the Labour Party. The attitude now seemed to be that the Labour Party was such a broad church that anyone, even 'atheists', were welcome. There were to be 'no enemies to the Left', there was a place for everyone. The Trotskyist Militant Tendency would later make the most of this opportunity. These organisational changes within the Labour Party were backed by a determination never again to have a government like Harold Wilson's between 1966 and 1970, which had clearly run out of steam and ideas as to how to create a new and fairer Britain. Industrial events in the early 1970s also seemed to confirm that militancy could sometimes pay off.

The Heath government had adopted a 'no lame ducks' policy under which industrial failures could no longer expect to be bailed out by the state. In the summer of 1971 the men in the yards of the Upper Clyde Shipbuilders organised a 'work in' to protest at forthcoming redundancies. Well led by their shop stewards, who included Jimmy Reid and Jimmy Airlie, the men won the support of the labour movement and the Scottish public. In February 1972 the Heath government announced that it would provide £17 million to write off old losses and a further £18 million for capital development. This volte-face was confirmed by the Industry Act of 1972, which supported intervention and effectively reversed the previous 'market forces' stance. United trade union action also defeated Heath's Industrial Relations

Act, which had attempted to reform the industrial movement, and the two miners' strikes of 1973 and 1974 seemed to show that whoever was running the country it certainly was not the man supposed to be in charge, namely Edward Heath himself.

The revival of interest in Marxism since the 1960s also prompted the Labour Left to scorn the idea of piecemeal political reform in favour of a much grander and wide-ranging approach. The failures of British capitalism were attributed to low productivity and an inefficient private sector. In particular, it was clear that for decades British investment in the public sector had lagged behind that of its rivals. Influential figures on NEC working committees urged Britain to emulate the Italian public corporation IRI (Instituto di Riconstuzione Industriale), which controlled not just ailing industries but also supervised thriving sectors of the economy.

The Attlee governments had nationalised run-down and bankrupt industries, so helping to give state enterprise a bad name because it was generally identified with failure. For economists like Stuart Holland, IRI's record, on the other hand, in '. . . promoting investment, countering recession caused by investment hesitation in the private sector, locating all employment from entirely new plant in the problem region of the Italian South, and directly or indirectly countering the challenge to national sovereignty from multinational companies' offered a refreshing contrast. Any future Labour government should create a body with rather more clout than Wilson's Industrial Reorganisation Corporation, which in the 1960s had lacked the resources to restructure British industry.

The NEC drew up plans which included the creation of a National Enterprise Board that would take a stake in up to twenty-five of the country's leading manufacturing firms. The leading banks and insurance companies would be nationalised. Planning agreements would ensure that economic targets would be met. Measures of industrial democracy would give the workforce a greater say in the running of each business and import controls would protect Britain's balance of payments. As these controls conflicted with EEC rules, it was essential that Britain should leave the Common Market. Finally, a wealth tax levied on the country's richest people would siphon off money, which could then be redistributed in favour of the poorest.

Overall these ideas represented a return to the fundamentalist Clause Four tradition of the Labour Party which had been in abeyance since the days of Gaitskell and which Wilson's 'New Britain' had not revived. They entailed a massive increase in the role of government, marking a break from the mixed economy which had been at the heart of the post-war consensus administered by both Labour and Conservative governments since 1945.

It is hardly surprising that the 'old guard' in the form of Tony Crosland, who had always argued that the issue of public ownership was largely irrelevant, opposed these new policies, which appeared in the Labour Party programme of 1973 and both its 1974 election manifestos. In 1971 he had claimed that 'No one can say the party is in sight of formulating a better set of policies than we had in June 1970, when we were dismissed from office.' He was to describe the new NEC proposals as 'idiotic' and 'half-baked'.

Looking back on these fierce debates, one striking feature is how inexperienced in economic matters most of the participants on both sides were. Take Denis Healey, for instance, who was appointed Shadow Chancellor of the Exchequer in 1972. He himself has candidly admitted his own lack of expertise:

> ... I had no ministerial experience in the field. Moreover, I had no more knowledge of economics than the average newspaper reader – and I had never bothered to look at the City pages. Now I had to engage the Government over every aspect of finance, taxation, industrial and economic policy.

Tony Benn, a leading figure in favour of the new approach, was hardly more economically literate. An MP since the age of twenty-five, he had only ever worked for the BBC and therefore possessed no direct experience of industry. Bernard Donoughue, who was to be the senior adviser at No 10 between 1974 and 1979, commented on meeting Benn and his advisers that '... none of them conveyed the impression that they had any direct experience of working life or had the least idea what made a factory or a service industry succeed or fail.' Joel Barnett, a trained accountant who for five years was Chief Secretary at the Treasury, has pointed out that some of his Cabinet colleagues could not even read a simple balance sheet.

But if Harold Wilson and his Cabinet faced internal pressure resulting from a series of radical manifestos, the external position was even worse. In the long term, the share of British manufactured goods in the world export market had declined from over 20 per cent in the 1950s to under 10 per cent in the 1970s. Competition from the Third World and fellow EEC countries was intensifying. The pound was overvalued and therefore sterling crises were always likely. Inflation was rising and, in fact, averaged 16 per cent a year between 1974 and 1978. Unemployment climbed inexorably past the one million figure. Finally, the oil crisis of 1973–74 saw a quadrupling in prices and plunged the world economy into prolonged recession.

If that wasn't enough, Wilson's government between March 1974 and

October 1974 was in a minority in the House of Commons, and even after the second general election of 1974 its majority was tenuous. As David Coates observes, 'A majority of three for a party in which two of its members were under police investigation [for alleged involvement in local government corruption] was not the strongest base from which to launch a busy legislative programme, and even that slender majority did not survive long.'

It is hardly surprising that, lumbered with Labour Party policies he disapproved of, facing a world recession and in charge of a country which had just been through the turmoil of strikes and three-day weeks, Wilson's approach as Prime Minister seemed to be one of 'do as little as possible'. He himself admitted to an adviser after taking office in 1974 that 'I have been around this racetrack so often that I cannot generate any more enthusiasm for jumping any more hurdles.' Even when the Government attempted to do something positive such as introducing the Northern Ireland Assembly, its policies were destroyed by the Ulster Workers' Council strike of May 1974 and direct rule had to be re-established.

Wilson's 'do nothing' stance prompted his decision to hold a referendum in 1975 over Britain's membership of the EEC. This was not taken on the grounds that the people should have a say in the matter but because it was the best way to hold the Labour Party together in the face of the 1973 Conference decision with which he disagreed, that any future Labour government should withdraw from Brussels. This resolution had been reaffirmed by a margin of 2–1 at a special conference in April 1975.

The question of Europe was one which caused much conflict within the Labour Party. It was not simply a Labour Right versus Labour Left issue nor one of 'nationalism versus internationalism'. Hugh Gaitskell, for instance, had been opposed to membership, as was his prominent supporter, Douglas Jay. On the other hand, Gaitskellites Roy Jenkins and Bill Rodgers were strongly in favour. Both Denis Healey and Tony Benn changed their minds on this issue. Some Labour leaders argued that links with the Commonwealth and the United States would be jeopardised by membership of the Common Market, others maintained that Britain's economic decline meant that any other policy would be suicidal.

As it turned out, the referendum result was decisive. The public voted 2–1 to stay within the EEC. In the aftermath of the result, Harold Wilson demoted Tony Benn from his crucial post at the Department of Trade and Industry to a less important job at the Department of Energy. This move demonstrated the way in which the Labour government was diluting and undermining the proposals initiated by the National Executive in the early

1970s. Remaining within the EEC was just one particularly massive reversal of policy. There were to be others.

The NEB, for example, when it was eventually set up, was given funds of only £1,000 million over four years. This was not nearly enough for the state to establish a significant role within the private sector let alone occupy 'the commanding heights of the economy'. Instead the NEB was forced to prop up uneconomic businesses like British Leyland and British Steel. It was left to deal with 'the walking wounded of the industrial collapse', thus reinforcing the link between public control and inefficiency first established by the Attlee government.

The Wilson adminstration backed off from nationalising the banks and the insurance companies and planning agreements proved to be a farce. Not a single agreement was signed with any company other than Chrysler and with the National Coal Board, which was a part of the government anyway. Companies did not have to disclose relevant information to the unions. Industrial democracy – co-opting members of the workforce on to the board and giving them a greater say in the running of the business – was explored in an inquiry headed by Professor Alan Bullock. Even his watered-down proposals aroused conflicting opinions within the trade union movement because some argued they would dilute and confuse the function of trade unions. The proposals were quietly shelved.

The government was even less successful when it came to dealing with the private sector because it was never able to bargain with multinational companies on equal terms. The companies knew only too well that the Labour administration was desperate not to increase unemployment and so in the last resort they could always threaten to close down their factories and move to another country. Chrysler was one organisation that shamelessly took the government for a ride, obtaining a large subsidy of over £160 million but eventually selling out to another company which then closed down its factories, despite the earlier state support.

To left-wing accusations that he was 'betraying' party policy, Wilson could always claim that the Parliamentary Labour Party (PLP) did possess the right to go its own way. The constitutional position was, in fact, confused. The 1907 Labour Party Conference had established that Conference resolutions were binding on the PLP: 'on the understanding that the time and methods of giving effect to these instructions be left to the Party in the House, in conjunction with the National Executive.' Wilson argued that, in his opinion, 'the time and methods' were not yet right for the NEC's policies to be implemented. His attitude was bound to result in a campaign for a new relationship between the various sections of the movement.

It was only to be expected that Harold Wilson should begin to tire of politics, and in any case he had always intended to resign in 1976 when he reached the age of sixty. That April, six contenders entered the ballot to elect not just a party leader but also a Prime Minister. Five of the contestants had been educated at Oxford University: Tony Benn, Denis Healey, Roy Jenkins, Anthony Crosland and Michael Foot. The sixth, James Callaghan, had left school at sixteen. The contest went to a third ballot in which Callaghan defeated Foot by a margin of 176 votes to 137. Voting was still confined to members of the Parliamentary Labour Party, a procedure which was beginning to face criticism from some sections of the Party. Jim Callaghan, the man who had helped sabotage Barbara Castle's *In Place of Strife* policy, now had to deal with both a severe economic crisis and the trade union movement on whose support his political career had rested.

The diaries of Richard Crossman, Barbara Castle and Tony Benn, which cover the Wilson governments of 1964 to 1970, all tell a story of hopes dashed and expectations frustrated. The 'inside' stories so far published of the 1974 to 1979 Labour governments – namely from Benn and Castle again, but also from Wilson's Press secretary Joe Haines, from Bernard Donoughue and from Joel Barnett – make even more gloomy reading. Each week seems to have brought a fresh crisis which was often mishandled just in time for the government to lurch into some other pitfall. In Donoughue's words, 'It was like being on the sinking Titanic, although without the music.'

Joel Barnett's account is dominated by the long search for cuts that repeatedly had to be made in the health, housing, education and social security budgets. There were no less than fourteen budgets between March 1974 and June 1978. Ministers developed all kinds of ploys in order to resist cuts being made to their own departments. During one session Peter Shore, the Minister for the Environment, thumped the table with such vigour that fellow members of the Cabinet began to fear for his health:

> . . . the moral for spending Ministers must be to behave in as prickly a manner as possible. Better still, leave the impression that if you lose, you might not only resign, but become so convulsed with the strength of your case as to push your blood pressure right up and collapse on the Cabinet table.

The main problem for the government was that the orthodox techniques propounded by Keynesianism for use in economic recession no longer seemed to work. When Denis Healey became Chancellor of the Exchequer in 1974 he acted as Chancellors had done before him, namely he increased demand. He therefore cut the rate of VAT, froze rents, increased food subsidies and raised pensions, a policy which one historian has since called 'Father Christmas economics'.

Unfortunately, Healey's policies resulted in raging inflation, which was fuelled by the indexed pay increases granted to certain employees by the Heath government. Unemployment rose while economic growth stagnated. One explanation for this was that because governments of all persuasions were nominally committed to full employment, public money was often diverted, as already mentioned, to propping up uneconomic businesses in run-down areas which the government could not allow to go bust for political reasons. This explained the Chysler debacle. Harold Wilson had not dared to let the firm fold with the loss of nearly 40,000 jobs. Martin Holmes has scathingly concluded that 'The artificial preservation of jobs in fossilised industries was the central feature, in practice, of the government's industrial strategy.'

The Labour government's interventionist hopes were undermined too by the lack of practical expertise to be found inside the Department of Industry. One of the Party's leading financial experts, Harold Lever, has complained that '. . . the civil servants in the Department of Industry were ill-equipped to make investment decisions. They had no background in industry and no experience.' According to Joe Haines, the Treasury was even less help, being completely devoid of new ideas and desperately wanting to rely on either a statutory incomes policy or huge expenditure cuts. But that wasn't the end of it, as Denis Healey has written:

> For my first budget, three weeks after I took office, the Treasury gave me an estimate of the PSBR [Public Sector Borrowing Requirement] in 1974/5 which – leaving aside all the fiscal changes later in the year – turned out to be £4,000 million too low. This was the equivalent of 5.4 per cent of that year's GDP. The magnitude of that one forecasting error was greater than that of any fiscal change made by any Chancellor in British history. Two years later, in 1976, the Budget estimate of the PSBR was £2,000 million too high; and in November that year I handed an estimate to the IMF [International Monetary Fund] which turned out to be twice as high as it should have been . . . If I had been given accurate forecasts in 1976, I would never have needed to go to the IMF at all.

In view of such incompetence it is remarkable that Britain did not go bust years ago. The best civil service brains are generally supposed to end up at the Treasury.

One further problem was that the financial markets, capitalist to the nth degree, have always distrusted socialist governments and often therefore panic, moving funds away from sterling. Harold Wilson, of course, knew all about this; in his history of the 1964–70 governments he wrote of the events leading to devaluation in November 1967: '. . . what strikes me now as then was the suddenness with which we had been overwhelmed by the operations of a speculative market.' Writing of his time as Prime Minister, Jim Callaghan was more descriptive: 'The markets behaved with all the restraint of a screaming crowd of schoolgirls at a rock concert.'

In such circumstances the pound was always under pressure and within weeks of his election as Prime Minister, Callaghan faced a major sterling crisis. It must have been horribly reminiscent of the crisis he had faced twelve years before when he was Harold Wilson's Chancellor of the Exchequer. Pressure on the pound coincided with a bungled attempt by the Bank of England to bring down the value of sterling when they committed the schoolboy error of selling on an already falling market. Suddenly the pound was plummeting fast. Denis Healey was forced to increase interest rates yet again and plan for the further cuts necessary if a loan from the IMF was to be obtained.

On 28 September 1976 things deteriorated so rapidly that Healey, on his way to an international conference, had to turn back at Heathrow. He decided to go instead to the Labour Party Conference and make a speech that would demonstrate the government had things in hand. He opened his speech with the words, 'I come from the battlefront.' The discrepancy between Government and Conference was shown by the fact that only the day before the annual conference had called for the nationalisation of the banks.

At this same Conference of 1976, Jim Callaghan's speech hammered the final nails into the coffin of Keynesianism:

> We used to think you could spend your way out of a recession and increase employment by cutting taxes and boosting spending. I tell you in all candour that this option no longer exists, and that insofar as it ever did exist, it only worked by injecting a bigger dose of inflation into the system.

But if Keynesianism was dead, that seemed to leave the Labour government with only one other option: resort to the IMF for aid. This was entirely in line with the thinking of the forceful Denis Healey. Educated at Bradford Grammar School and then Oxford, Healey headed the Labour Party's International Department after the war. He had moved a long way from his student Communist days at university and was a Gaitskellite during the

Labour Party's civil wars in the 1950s, although he did not always agree with Gaitskell's tactics:

> I never understood why Hugh Gaitskell made that tremendous fuss about Clause Four. If only he'd kept quiet about it no one would have noticed it, or even remembered it was there. I mean, can you remember the ten commandments?

He had been Minister of Defence from 1964–70 and although a formidable politician he had never built up a personal following in the Party, largely because of his bluntness towards colleagues. Ian Mikardo has described Healey as 'a political bully wielding the language of sarcasm and contempt like a caveman's cudgel.' Another reason becomes evident from Healey's autobiography *The Time of My Life* which testifies that for him there were and are more important things in life than just politics: family, books, travel, the arts, good food and drink. From the summer of 1976 he did not have much time for any of these passions as he and Callaghan struggled to save the economy from collapse.

The events of the next few months have been told in detail by two *Sunday Times* journalists, Stephen Fay and Hugo Young, whose account of the negotiations with the IMF reads like a high-powered thriller. Bankers check into hotels under assumed names. Telephones are bugged. The 'hot line' between Callaghan and President Ford in Washington gets hotter. Callaghan secretly tries to enlist the help of Chancellor Schmidt of West Germany. Meetings are held, at the end of which no one is quite sure who has said, or agreed to, what.

The upshot was that in early December 1976 the Cabinet met to decide if it was to support the strategy of the Chancellor who demanded immediate government spending cuts of £1 billion with a further £1 billion to come the following year if an IMF loan was to be secured. Different options were available. Tony Benn argued that the IMF terms should be rejected in favour of a retreat into a siege economy behind a wall of import controls; in effect a policy of 'socialism in one country'. Denis Healey ridiculed this argument: 'He [Tony Benn] wants us to withdraw into the citadel, but only so long as we can slip out occasionally to borrow the money to buy the bows and arrows we'll need to shoot at the besieging armies.'

Tony Crosland, the Foreign Secretary but also a trained economist, was unhappy with the prospect of further cuts in welfare but failed to come up with a viable alternative. One Cabinet colleague recalled what happened:

That was the day Croslandism died. He [Crosland] said to me: 'This is nonsense, but we must do it.' He knew it meant the abandonment of his position as revisionist theorist. He knew he was going up a cul-de-sac. It was a tormenting time for him. I watched him, torturing himself.

'Croslandism' had maintained that a greater measure of equality could be achieved by means of economic growth, planning and state intervention. Almost every variable in that equation no longer held true. The world recession had also underlined the fact that Britain's national sovereignty over her own economic affairs had been much reduced.

But if Croslandism was rejected then so too was the fundamentalist Clause Four approach of Tony Benn, though even his political opponents such as Joel Barnett have stressed how forcefully he argued his case. One important reason was that Benn's own experiments in funding various projects had been sadly unsuccessful and yet again underlined the Labour Left's deficiencies when it came to handling economic issues. He financed three workers' co-operatives which had grown out of 'sit-ins' held after management announced plans to close down the Meriden motorbike works, Kirkby Manufacturing and the *Scottish Daily News*. Always the realist, Joel Barnett has written that 'The three co-operatives had one thing in common: they all began life with just about the worst possible prospects for success.' Some £10 million was invested in the three, but all failed.

Much was made of these failures and although it should be emphasised that £10 million was a paltry sum when compared with the £800 million distributed to industry in 1974–75 alone, it demonstrated yet again that the Left has a very patchy record when it comes to creating wealth rather than distributing it. This valid point has often been levelled at the trade union movement – not that British management always proved very successful at the same thing.

By the mid-1970s it was evident that mounting wage costs lay at the heart of Britain's increasing uncompetitiveness. But in view of the historic and continuing link between the trade unions and the Labour Party – no less than 129 Labour MPs were sponsored by various trade unions – it was very difficult for the political arm of the movement to reform the industrial and financial arm, as Harold Wilson and Barbara Castle knew only too well. Neither the government, nor the employers, nor the unions themselves were anxious to rock the boat. Full employment had greatly increased trade union power because there was now no 'reserve army of the unemployed' for employers to call upon. It was often easier, and less costly, for employers to buy off union demands, thus stoking up wage inflation.

The leaders of the largest unions such as the engineers and the transport and general workers were very powerful figures and ever since the Conservatives had introduced the National Economic Development Council in 1962 they had been accustomed to dealing with governments and employers on equal terms. Between 1968 and 1978 Jack Jones was General Secretary of the 2-million strong Transport and General Workers' Union. Jones' autobiography *Union Man* testifies to his wide-ranging influence. Dubbed 'Emperor Jones' by his critics, he found that not only did his suggestions end up as government legislation – as with the arbitration and conciliation service ACAS and the employment protection statutes – but that he was also courted by Prime Ministers from Heath to Wilson and Callaghan, asked to be a minister and a peer, invited to address 500 top world businessmen in Switzerland and shared jokes with the Queen and Prince Philip. Apparently Jones was never self-conscious or nervous but always supremely confident that he, as leader of the country's biggest union, deserved nothing less.

It was, and is, true that the only way most workers can defend their interests is through collective bodies such as trade unions. But the only sanction they can impose is to withdraw their labour, work to rule or 'go slow', which automatically affects public opinion negatively. By the 1970s it was clear that the unions were becoming ever more unpopular. Even a sympathetic observer such as journalist Robert Taylor criticised both their anti-intellectualism and the 'insular outlook of many union leaders'. The unions did little to combat this difficult image; for instance, they rarely sponsored arts projects or other 'good will' initiatives. Few trade union leaders were ever associated with non-union issues – unlike Jack Jones who did much to try and raise the levels of pensions.

The unions focused exclusively on the question of wages, an approach that was sometimes dubbed 'economism'. It is revealing to read Cabinet minister Barbara Castle's reaction in her diary when Mrs Thatcher was elected leader of the Conservative Party in February 1975:

> . . . men have been running the show as long as anyone can remember and they don't seem to have made much of a job of it. The excitement of switching to a woman might stir a lot of people out of their lethargy. I think it will be a good thing for the Labour Party too. There's a male-dominated party for you – not least because the trade unions are male-dominated, even the ones that cater for women. I remember just before the February election last year pleading on the NEC for us not to have a completely producer-oriented policy, because women lose out in the producer-run society. The battle for cash wage increases is a masculine obsession. Women are not sold

on it, particularly when it leads to strikes, because the men often don't pass their cash increases on to their wives. What matters to women is the social wage. Of course, no one listened to me: even to suggest that the battle for cash wage increases might be a mirage is to show disloyalty to trade unionism! I believe Margaret Thatcher's election will force our party to think again: and a jolly good thing too. To me, socialism isn't just militant trade unionism. It is the gentle society, in which every producer remembers he is a consumer too.

Mrs Castle might also have noted the offputting 'male' language of trade unions and Labour conference – 'Brother this' and 'Brother that' which subtly excluded women. The Communist tradition that referred to fellow Party members as 'Comrades' was hardly more welcoming.

Most people's memories of the 1974–79 Labour governments are dominated by images of trade union unrest, secondary picketing and civil disorder, that culminated in 'the Winter of Discontent' of 1978–79. This is misleading because in reality for the first three and a half years of the government the so-called 'Social Contract' brought prolonged and peaceful wage restraint which helped to bring inflation down from a peak of nearly 30 per cent in the summer of 1975. The difficulty with any incomes policy was that not only did it have to challenge the strongest trade unions if it was to be effective, it also required the trade union leaders to 'do the government's dirty work' for them by imposing restraint on their own members. This could only be a short-term policy because, in the end, trade union leaders' loyalty was to their members rather than to a government, even a Labour one. If they lost contact with their members then the shop stewards, who were closer to the workforce on the shop floor, stepped into the vacuum.

Attlee's government had introduced formal wage restraint after the war, which had been rejected within two years by trade union leaders impeccably loyal to the Labour government. In the 1960s Harold Wilson had relied on a Prices and Incomes Board. His legislation had prompted the resignation of the most important trade union Cabinet member, Frank Cousins. Both experiences bore out only too well Michael Stewart's remark:

> Throughout the whole history of incomes policies, now stretching over a generation, the trouble has been that governments do not consciously embark on such policies until acute economic difficulty obliges them to do so. In consequence, the policy always takes the form of telling people that their standard of life must either remain stationary or go down; and this makes the whole idea unpopular.

At the beginning of the 1974 Labour government the trade union leadership proved thoroughly responsible in its attitude towards pay increases, especially when senior management showed no such restraint and the government's price controls were ineffective. They tried to make a go of the 'Social Contract' initiated by Jack Jones which went some way towards Barbara Castle's 'social wage' arguments. Speaking at the 1975 TUC Conference, General Secretary Len Murray could hardly have been more explicit:

> Some people, for a time, are going to have some reduction in their living standards. We are a low wage country. That is because our country's industrial performance has been low, below that of our competitors; because investment has been too low and too often in the wrong places and because in turn productivity has been too low. We cannot put that right in real terms merely by paying ourselves more money.

It was, however, unlikely that this stance could survive for ever, especially when price controls proved ineffective and those on salaries and higher incomes exercised no similar restraint in their demands. The Labour government did pass legislation strengthening the union movement and the rights of its members, such as the Trade and Union Labour Relations Acts of 1974 and 1976, a Health and Safety at Work Act, a Sex Discrimination Act and an Equal Pay Act. But even these measures were of secondary importance behind the issue of wage claims.

The perceived failure of Harold Wilson's 1964–70 governments had led many young socialists to leave the Labour Party in disgust. Some channelled their energies into single-issue campaigns such as Shelter, Child Poverty Action Group, the Anti-Apartheid Movement or even the Young Liberals. Others joined the various 'Far Left' groups such as International Socialism (who were to become the Socialist Workers' Party), the International Marxist Group or the Workers' Revolutionary Party. Few of these groups could boast hundreds let alone thousands of members and, as had been the case with Hyndman's earlier Social Democratic Federation or the Communist Party, the number of ex-members always outnumbered present recruits.

One interesting sidelight illustrates the way that although the British Communist Party has never been very successful in its own right, it has not been a negligible force. Three of the four key individuals discussing wage policy at this time – Denis Healey, Len Murray of the TUC and Hugh Scanlon of the Engineers – had all once been members of the Communist Party and a fourth, Jack Jones, had fought for the Communist-dominated International Brigade during the Spanish Civil War in the 1930s.

The 1970s witnessed a marked expansion in radical culture – there were at least twenty-five left-wing publishers together with a network of bookshops and dozens of journals and magazines. The ten radical bookshops open in 1970 had grown to 150 by 1980 and the use of the small photo-offset printing press and the IBM composer for typesetting ensured that the shops were always full to bursting with pamphlets and newspapers. With hindsight, if one reads through the material today one can't help marvelling at the revolutionary posturing which seemed to be *de rigueur*. The fight against Heath's Industrial Relations Act led some radicals to believe that the millennium was at hand. For instance, in 1972 Tariq Ali of the International Marxist Group published a book called *The Coming British Revolution*. It contains the prediction that:

> ... the coming decade will see the beginning of social upheavals and explosions which will totally shatter the complacency of the British bourgeoisie as it tries to adjust to the changed situation.

Few within the British labour movement paid more than lip service to women's issues. Robert Taylor observed that when 'female' matters came up for debate on Tuesday mornings at the annual TUC Conference there was always a stampede towards the bars. It was little different elsewhere on the Left, as Lynne Segal has recalled in terms reminiscent of the complaints recorded in Chapter Three, 'Socialism and the New Life':

> ... while women were active in all the campaigns that were going on, they were active in a subordinate way. So they were the ones licking the envelopes and making the cups of tea. They were the ones doing the background work while the men were in the foreground.

One important feature of the women's movement was that it stressed the value of personal feelings and experiences that both labourism and communism had tended to ignore as irrelevant. Not only was what you said and did important but also *how* you said and did things. There was no reason why people shouldn't say 'I don't know' or even – horror of horrors – 'I was wrong'. All this was very different from the dogmatism characteristic of parts of the British Left.

Many on the Left still failed to recognise that, in Beatrix Campbell's words, '... protest has only a limited life – it has to ferment into the politics of the possible'. At the same time the Right was showing how this could be done. The 1970s saw the establishment of institutions such as the Centre for

Policy Studies or the rejuvenation of older ones like the Institute of Economic Affairs. Unlike the left-wing groups, they made it their business to know their way around 'the corridors of power' and were fully aware of how best to present their proposals in a clear and concise way. Their publications became required reading for Conservative MPs. It is difficult to imagine that Labour MPs found much of use or even interest in the pages of *New Left Review* or *Socialist Worker*.

One area that this renaissance in right-wing thinking homed in on was the expansion of personal choice. There is no doubt that 'labourism' was vulnerable to the onslaught because it had traditionally been associated with controls, size and faceless bureaucracy. Collective action had so often been impersonal and therefore the 'anti-statist' mood played on this dissatisfaction.

Take the question of council house sales. There was no intrinsic reason why people shouldn't have the opportunity to own their homes, except that it went against the Labour Party's instinctive preference for 'mass' over individual choice. The Labour government, just like Labour councils, believed Douglas Jay, a minister in the Attlee and Wilson governments, when he claimed that 'the Gentleman in Whitehall is usually right'. This has been christened the 'We Know Best' tendency. Roy Hattersley has written of the rules and regulations laid down by the Labour council in Sheffield:

> There was a time when pigeon-keeping was prohibited on Sheffield council estates and when, in the same city, it was an offence (punishable with eviction) to paint a front door in anything except the stipulated colour, to fence in pieces of garden which were adjacent to individual houses but designated collective property, or to make structural changes inside or outside which, in private property, would have been unhesitatingly designated as improvements.

This prohibitive uniformity has always represented one powerful strand within Fabian thinking. Just as tower blocks were originally considered a beneficial exercise in social engineering — and if people didn't like being storeys up in the sky without a garden and with vandalised lifts, that was their problem, not 'ours' — so council house sales were ruled out. Tenants' rights were potentially subversive and therefore were also frowned upon. The preoccupation with 'mass' this or 'mass' that was where the two traditions of labourism and communism once again bore an uncanny resemblance to each other. Both exemplified what Colin Ward has called 'the ideological stranglehold of state worship on the left.'

The Labour government was also unable to tackle the problem of Britain's increasingly shabby and run-down public services, particularly that of transport. This ensured that the concept of nationalisation – something that had always been at the heart of labourism – was now an unpopular albatross around its neck. Theorists like Tony Crosland had regarded high public expenditure as morally praiseworthy and so the standard left-wing response was to call for more public money. This reaction ignored the objection that the rise in public expenditure – from 46 per cent of the gross domestic product in 1965 to 60 per cent in 1976 – was seen as threatening by many. As Robert Skidelsky once put it:

> Big Brother has crept up on us, not in the shape of a mad, bloodthirsty dictator, but in the far more insidious form of the Caring Expert, who claims knowledge of what a better future would look like, and uses taxpayers' money as well as regulations to bring it about.

It was also an inadequate response because in the harsh economic climate of the 1970s sufficient public money was never likely to be available. In an article in the *Guardian* Joel Barnett outlined the dilemma:

> All in all then, there are no miracles left. We have to face the unpalatable fact that with, at best, low rates of economic growth, and at worst, nil or even negative growth, public expenditure cuts will be necessary – not to create room for Conservative-style tax cuts, but to ensure that socialists' priorities in public expenditure are safeguarded and that vital public services are not deprived of essential additional funds. This seems self-evident, yet even to whisper that a future Labour Government will have to cut public expenditure brings forth serious charges and dire threats of expulsion, as I know to my cost.

The problem could not be solved by throwing money at it. The ethos of the nationalised industries was that they were run in favour of the producers themselves, primarily the trade unions, rather than the consumers. It was an attitude which contrasted unfavourably with the success of several large private companies. Take the Co-operative movement, once one of the pillars of the collectivist society on which the British labour movement had been built. By the 1970s it seemed more and more a relic of the past and certainly less attractive than its rivals. As a *Guardian* editorial asked after the May 1979 election: 'How many consumers today find it more liberating to do business with North Thames Gas than to shop at Sainsbury's or Marks and Spencer?'

By the 1970s it was clear that 'labourism' was in crisis. Keir Hardie had been right to base his new political party within the trade union movement. These roots had enabled it to oust the Liberal Party as the main opposition to the Conservatives and to allow Labour governments irregular spells in office. But, of course, society had moved on since Hardie's day: the problem was that labourism hadn't.

With no fresh ideas either of its own or any coming from outside to help revitalise it, the Callaghan government devoted its time to a frantic attempt to remain in office. Its majority was slowly being whittled down at by-elections and in March 1977 a deal was struck with David Steel's Liberal Party. This was the 'Lib-Lab Pact' from which the Liberals, eager to get their hands on power after decades in the political wilderness, got virtually nothing but won Labour the benefit of more time in office.

The Callaghan government fought desperately to maintain its pay norms that established a figure below which wage increases were meant to be kept. In November 1977 they defeated a firemen's strike called in support of a 30 per cent pay claim by sending in troops. But by the summer of 1978 the pay dam was beginning to burst. After three years of wage restraint, union members were starting to get restive, particularly among more skilled workers who had seen the pay differentials separating them from the less skilled being gradually eroded. The atmosphere was in any case made more acrimonious by the effects of deflation and of cuts in public expenditure. Unemployment was still rising, as too was the number of people below the official poverty line, from 1.4 million to 2.2 million.

Not only had Jack Jones and Hugh Scanlon, both of them personally committed to exercising their power responsibly in support of the Callaghan administration retired, but union conferences began to pass resolutions attacking continued wage restraint. Negotiations between the Government and the unions arrived at a suggested figure of 5 per cent for future wage increases; a figure which today Denis Healey and others consider was much too low. It appears, however, that most of those involved in the discussions felt that Callaghan would call an election for the autumn of 1978 and that the figure would be revised if Labour won.

In fact, Callaghan, to the surprise of most of his colleagues, put off an election and so the 5 per cent figure stood. From this point onwards, everything went wrong. The Labour Party Conference itself voted by a margin of 2–1 against any form of wage restraint. An avalanche of pay claims in the 20 to 30 per cent range came surging in, and the Government was defeated by its own backbenchers in December 1978 when it attempted to continue sanctions against private firms which awarded employees in excess of 5 per cent.

The problem with 'free collective bargaining' was that it was fine for members of strong unions with negotiating muscle but less so for anyone else, especially for those in no union at all. The pay claims put in by railwaymen, road haulage drivers, hospital workers and oil-tanker drivers were pursued aggressively by the employees involved, using secondary picketing if necessary. Callaghan called it 'free collective vandalism' and the government's special Cabinet Committee devoted to pay seemed, in Joel Barnett's words, 'to meet almost round the clock'.

Even the weather conspired against the government – the winter of 1978–79 was foul and cold. Jim Callaghan attended an international conference in sunny Guadeloupe and returned to find the country manifestly falling apart and an ever more vociferous right-wing Press quite prepared to make up remarks or stories if need be. The unpopularity of the industrial wing of the labour movement was bound to rub off on its political arm.

The government seemed almost powerless in the face of the actions of its own erstwhile supporters, the unions, and drifted hopelessly. In the 1960s the then General Secretary of the TUC, George Woodcock, boasted that the trade union movement had moved out of Trafalgar Square and into the committee rooms of power. In the winter of 1978–79 it looked as if it was going back to Trafalgar Square. At one point ministers even considered sending tanks into ICI's medical headquarters which was being blockaded by strikers in order to retrieve drugs and other essential equipment. A State of Emergency was nearly declared on several occasions. The Conservative Party's advertising agency, Saatchi and Saatchi, produced posters under the title 'Labour Isn't Working'. One particularly horrifying episode came when gravediggers on Merseyside refused to bury the dead. Seen widely on television, such incidents did enormous damage to the trade union movement. In his memoirs Jim Callaghan, a robust defender of trade union interests, remarked sadly that, 'Even with the passage of time I find it painful to write about some of the excesses that took place.'

The Liberals had pulled out of the pact with the government in July 1978 and Callaghan had to search around for alternative political allies. Devolution of power to Wales and Scotland raised its head and so once again the government began to curry favour, not on any principled grounds but simply in order to cling to office. The Ulster Unionists were promised more seats if they stuck with the government. This was labourism at its most top-heavy and unattractive.

James Callaghan called an election for May 1979. His Party's run-up to it was marked by a bitter row over the contents of the manifesto. Although the Government had not introduced its early 1970s proposals, the NEC was still some way to the left of the Prime Minister and his colleagues. The NEC's working committees had produced a series of radical plans that included the outright abolition of the House of Lords. This had been overwhelmingly passed at the 1977 Labour Party Conference and naturally the NEC expected to see the proposal included in the election manifesto.

In fact, Callaghan and his advisers at No 10 at the last moment rewrote the manifesto and excluded the more left-wing schemes. The NEC proved powerless to do anything about this reversal. The dispute was a portent of the internal rows which were to shake the Labour Party after it had lost the election to Mrs Thatcher's Conservative Party. The Labour campaign centred almost exclusively on Jim Callaghan, but despite his own personal popularity and the achievements of the previous five years such as higher real pensions and the introduction of the child benefit scheme, the Conservatives won a forty-three seat majority. One irony was that only one in two trade unionists voted in the election for their 'own' party.

The election defeat marked the end of the second phase in the history of the British labour movement. It was now clear that the Attlee governments between 1945 and 1951 had represented an end and not a beginning. Phase one – the pioneering or 'hearts' phase associated, above all, with Keir Hardie – had finished in 1931 with the collapse of Ramsay MacDonald's administration. Phase two – consolidation and administration – had seen the creation of a modern social democratic state based around the three principles of government intervention, public ownership and a welfare state. This, the 'minds' phase, was largely accomplished by 1951. Subsequent governments, Conservative and Labour, had basically just administered this machine.

But there was one important problem that the makers of British social democracy had not entirely solved, namely the provision of steady and sustained economic growth. As this flaw increasingly reared its head, governments began to resort to more drastic measures, such as Wilson and Castle's *In Place of Strife* plans, Edward Heath's free market policies of 1970–72 and his Industrial Relations Act, and the Callaghan government's 5 per cent pay policy. When economic growth faltered and the number out of work rose to $1\frac{1}{4}$ million, the relationship between government, employers and trade unions was bound to break down. A similar crisis faced social democratic parties all over Europe.

What is remarkable and worth emphasising is how successful this post-war consensus had been in raising living standards, in providing welfare and generally in creating a better and more humane Britain. One reason for these achievements was the width of the consensus that had grown out of the

1930s and 1940s. Compare, for instance, the autobiographies of two individuals from very different backgrounds, Will Paynter's *My Generation* and Noel Annan's *Our Age*.

Paynter began work on a farm at age thirteen, was sent down the mines the next year, took part in the Hunger Marches in the 1930s, was several times imprisoned for his views, was a member of the International Brigade in the Spanish Civil War and sat on the executive of the South Wales Miners' Federation between 1936 and 1968. Noel Annan, on the other hand, went to public school and Cambridge. At the age of only forty he was appointed Provost of King's College, Cambridge, and his career since has been full of glittering prizes and awards. Yet despite the obvious contrast in their careers, both Paynter and Annan would have agreed that modern Britain was an immeasurably more humane and civilised society when compared with inter-war Britain.

By the late 1970s, however, commentators such as Jeremy Seabrook began to publish books with titles such as *What Went Wrong?*, which bemoaned the way in which the British labour movement had lost its moral dimension. It had certainly proved unable to rise to the intellectual challenge of constructing a post-Keynesian order. Noel Annan has concluded that the greatest error of 'our age' was '. . . to neglect – and some even to despise – the need for their country to become more efficient and more productive in business and industry; and their greatest failure to persuade organised labour to join in that enterprise.'

The big question now was whether the British labour movement could move forward and create a new programme and new ideas that would build on the best of the two earlier phases and yet still adapt itself to a post-industrial Britain unsure of its role or its future.

Part Three

Into the Twenty-first Century?

'I ... PONDERED HOW MEN FIGHT AND LOSE THE BATTLE, AND THE THING THAT THEY FOUGHT FOR COMES ABOUT IN SPITE OF THEIR DEFEAT, AND WHEN IT COMES TURNS OUT NOT TO BE WHAT THEY MEANT, AND OTHER MEN HAVE TO FIGHT FOR WHAT THEY MEANT UNDER ANOTHER NAME.'

William Morris, *A Dream of John Ball* (1886)

CHAPTER THIRTEEN

The 1980s: Into the Crucible

'Like Germany after 1945, Britain after Thatcher will be a scene of destruction.'
Professor Eric Hobsbawm, the *Guardian*, 11 July 1988

'I got to be Leader of the Labour Party by being good on television.'
Neil Kinnock, quoted in Michael Cockerell, *Live from Number 10*

IN MAY 1979, James Callaghan's Labour government was comprehensively defeated by the Conservative Party led by Mrs Thatcher. Previous Tory administrations had displayed all the pragmatism and moderation thought to be characteristically British, but Mrs Thatcher dispensed with such niceties. She came to power armed with a radical agenda and – unlike Edward Heath's brief and unsuccessful 'free market' approach in the early 1970s – the political will to carry it through. Her targets included the three post-war assumptions up to now accepted by both Labour and Conservative governments: full employment, government intervention to boost the economy if necessary and the welfare state.

Much of the policy had been worked out while the Conservatives were in opposition between 1974 and 1979 so that the Tories were well briefed, unlike the largely unprepared Labour governments of 1945 and 1964. As one of Mrs Thatcher's then colleagues, John Biffen, has noted:

> What was distinctive about the Thatcher government was its determination to pursue relentlessly these objectives. There were to be no U-turns. Furthermore, the Thatcher Tories had undertaken massive and detailed work in opposition. From the outset, the government could present its objectives to the civil service aware of the difficulties and having the political will to discount them.

It was clear that Mrs Thatcher's victory represented, as Jim Callaghan had observed in May 1979, part of a wider sea-change in world politics that was not restricted to Britain. In both the United States and West Germany, right-wing governments were elected to office and retained power at subsequent elections. It was not inevitable, however, that socialists should lose elections. The French Socialists gained power in May 1981, the Spanish in October 1982.

The question, therefore, was how could the British Left emulate their French and Spanish colleagues? How should supposed radicals react to what was a distinctly radical administration that sold off council houses and privatised industries such as British Telecom?

In *The Lion and the Unicorn*, George Orwell criticised one characteristic of the British Left:

> The mentality of the English left-wing intelligentsia can be studied in half a dozen weekly and monthly papers. The immediately striking thing about all these papers is their generally negative, querulous attitude, their complete lack at all times of any constructive suggestion. There is little in them except the irresponsible carping of people who have never been and never expect to be in a position of power.

Orwell's essay was, in fact, first published in 1940, but he might just as well have been writing fifty years later.

For some, the Thatcher 'nightmare' could only possibly be brief. The Oxford don R. W. Johnson, for instance, commented that '. . . the [Thatcher] ship is heading due North for the Pole and will, ere long, encounter vast and fearsome icebergs; and that nothing is more certain than that the crew will ultimately, and not altogether unreasonably, mutiny.' This would have been a brilliant prediction if only Johnson's article had been published on 30 August 1989; but it appeared on 30 August 1979.

Others contented themselves with the thought that Mrs Thatcher's success was merely a temporary aberration on the part of the electorate and that she would be soundly defeated at the next election. Then, as the German Communists had said when the Nazis came to power in 1933, it will be 'our turn'. After the 1983 and 1987 elections, these optimists were still twiddling their thumbs and awaiting their now somewhat delayed turn.

Some thought political opposition meant chanting a single slogan – 'Thatcher Out' – but nothing more. Others, unable to wound Mrs Thatcher politically, resorted to personal sneers. In a notorious article published in the *Sunday Telegraph* on 10 January 1988, several critics of the Prime Minister were asked to give their considered opinions of her. Academic Mary

Warnock complained of Mrs Thatcher's appearance that she was 'packaged together in a way that's not exactly vulgar, just *low.*' Poet Peter Porter thought she was 'bullying, stupid and brutal'; the artist David Gentleman found her 'arrogant, tasteless and vain'. Jonathan Miller called her 'loathsome, repulsive in every way', Alan Bennett declared that Mrs Thatcher was a paid-up philistine, 'typical of the people who go to the Chichester Festival'. On and on it went. With friends like this, does the British Left need enemies?

Even more negative was the picture of 'Thatcher's Britain' conveyed in books, films and plays. The heroine of Margaret Drabble's novel *A Natural Curiosity* complains that 'England's not a bad country – it's just a mean, cold, ugly, divided, tired, clapped-out, post-imperial, post-industrial slag-heap covered in polystyrene hamburger cartons.' Playwright Hanif Kureishi disagreed with Miss Drabble's heroine; he thought England was not a 'slag-heap' but, rather, 'a rat-hole':

> England seems to have become a squalid, ugly and uncomfortable place. For some reason I am starting to feel that it is an intolerant, racist, homophobic, narrow-minded, authoritarian rat-hole run by vicious, suburban-minded materialistic philistines who think democracy is constituted by the selling of a few council houses and shares.

A few intellectuals completely lost their heads when faced with a political philosophy they did not like. Eric Hobsbawm is one of the shrewdest of all left-wing commentators, but to compare 1980s Britain, when living standards in real terms have risen by a third, to Germany in 1945 – cities razed to the ground, millions dead, no essential services – is paranoia. Like the little boy who cried 'wolf' once too often, it is difficult to know what words Professor Hobsbawm would use if fascism really were to come to Britain.

There seemed to be a damaging inability to discriminate, as was seen earlier in Chapter Seven, 'Grand Illusions'. Professor Ben Pimlott started a magazine that he called *Samizdat* after the name given to the illegal literature produced by dissidents in Communist countries. Both its title and that of another campaign called Charter 88 represented an attempt to cling on to the coat-tails of dissent in Eastern Europe. An editorial in the *Independent* noted that the title was 'making an extreme and unconvincing statement about the nature of the society in which we live.' *Samizdat* claimed that opinion in Britain 'is controlled not by fear of the gulag but more subtly through the persuasive powers of the deferential media.'

There is no doubt that the majority of the Press in Britain is right-wing, often squalidly and xenophobically so. It is also true that seven out of eleven national daily newspapers supported Mrs Thatcher at the 1987 election. But look at *Samizdat*'s editorial board and its contributors: Ben Pimlott, Eric Hobsbawm, Margaret Drabble, Peter Kellner, Jonathan Porritt, Roy Hattersley — who can claim that these individuals are denied access to the media? Their views appear regularly in *The Sunday Times*, the *Guardian*, on television and so on — as indeed they should. But then to turn around and talk of the deferential media's control of opinion is surely misplaced. To read Timothy Garton Ash's description of the purges and restrictions common in Czechoslovakia in 1984 also puts the complaints of some British left-wingers in some kind of perspective.

Orwell's point has been made. There were many good reasons to take issue with Mrs Thatcher's policies. There was the squandering of North Sea oil, the emphasis on consumption at the expense of investment, the dismantling of the welfare state, the human consequences of mass unemployment, the cavalier attitude towards research, development and training, the chronic underfunding of scientific research ... But so often the Left in the 1980s, consumed by a personal hatred of Mrs Thatcher, failed to make the arguments and the contest was allowed to go by default.

British labourism has usually been uncomfortable with 'intellectuals'. We saw in an earlier chapter that some of the hostility towards Gaitskell and his 'Hampstead set' arose from their seeming isolation from the working-class rank and file. Trade union leaders have traditionally been suspicious of people sitting round 'thinking', which explains why the educational facilities of most trade unions have always been so patchy. When Jack Jones stood for the post of Chancellor of the University of London it was in order to help 'bring the University down from the clouds and nearer to the people.'

This pragmatic, hard-headed attitude is fine as far it goes, which is not far. Sometimes it barely seems to extend beyond the 'We're here because we're here' stage. In fact, ideas and more general 'moods of opinion' do play a crucial part in how people vote. In the 1930s and 1940s the intellectual climate went Labour's way, in the 1970s it shifted towards the Conservatives. Richard Crossman, himself a tutor for the Workers' Educational Association (WEA) in the 1930s, was clear about this:

> The first essential for the election of a Left-Wing government in Britain is the creation of a favourable climate of opinion among non-political voters. And, although the practical politicians hate to admit it, the truth is that this favourable climate can never be created by the Labour Party itself, but only by the 'disloyal intelligentsia' — the journalists, writers, playwrights and critics who are able to discredit the Establishment and to air Left-Wing ideas when

they are still too novel for the practical politicians to adopt . . . The psychologi-
cal landslide to the Left [in the 1930s and early 1940s] was set in motion not
by party organisation or party propaganda, but by those who contributed to
the New Statesman, joined the Left Book Club, taught evening classes for the
WEA and, during the war, lectured for the Army Bureau of Current Affairs.

Even the most partisan British socialist could hardly claim that the 1980s
saw the creation of Crossman's 'favourable climate of opinion among non-
political voters'.

There were, however, two other responses to 'Thatcherism' which, though
almost diametrically opposed to each other, were more significant. The first
was led by Tony Benn, the other was the more cerebral response associated
with the monthly magazine *Marxism Today*.

Tony Benn has been subjected to much shameful personal abuse. Some right-
wing papers have been obsessed by his wish to be called Tony Benn and not
Anthony Wedgwood Benn, which revealed their devotion to trivia. Several
cartoonists have even compared him with Adolf Hitler. In fact, he stands
firmly in one tradition of English radicalism, particularly in his desire, as he
sees it, to take power away from the élite and restore it to the people
themselves.

He was born in 1925 next door to Sidney and Beatrice Webb's London
home. His father served in Attlee's post-war governments and was ennobled
as Viscount Stansgate. Tony Benn was educated at Westminster and Oxford
before working in television and becoming the Labour MP for Bristol South
East, Sir Stafford Cripps' old seat. In the 1950s he was heavily involved in
the Movement for Colonial Freedom. After his father's death in 1960 he
fought a long and eventually successful three-year battle to renounce his
peerage because he wanted to continue to sit in the House of Commons.

Benn's abilities and enthusiasm meant that he was soon a leading figure in
the Labour Party and he served in the Wilson governments in the 1960s. As
Postmaster-General he began the issue of commemorative stamps. In July
1966 he was promoted to the Cabinet as Minister of Technology and
brought to the post typical energy and thoroughness: when he changed his
mind over the Common Market he went out and bought all forty-four
volumes containing the EEC's rules and regulations. Because of his comparative youthfulness, it is likely that if he had just kept his head down he might
well in due course have been elected Leader of the Labour Party.

He didn't. Instead, as a result of his own experiences in office, he became
convinced that sweeping changes were required if a fairer and more just

society was to be established. In March 1973 he remarked that '. . . the Party without Karl Marx really lacks a basic analytical core' – though more than three years later a first reading of *The Communist Manifesto* prompted him to write in his diary: '. . . I found that, without having read any Communist text, I had come to Marx's view.' As Hugh Dalton had found out, hell hath no fury like the Establishment who sees 'one of us' defect to 'the other side' and he was virulently criticised. Unlike those of most socialists, Tony Benn's ideas became more left-wing and not less. The response of his colleagues was summed up by Harold Wilson's aside that 'He immatures with age'.

In the early 1970s he was a key figure in the leftwards shift of the Labour Party and he was appointed Secretary of State for Industry in 1974. However, he was a leading campaigner in the fight to take Britain out of the Common Market and when the referendum decided decisively to remain in it, Wilson took the chance to demote Benn to the Energy Department. In Neil Kinnock's words, 'Benn bought the move to Energy. All he could do was to visit oil-rigs. It was a walk-over for the Prime Minister.' Tony Benn ruminated sadly in his diary:

> . . . the Referendum campaign and the defeat on 5 June was a far bigger defeat for the Left – and me in particular – than I had realised. Like bereavement, it hits you but at first you don't really take it on board . . . the Department of Energy is really a side Department.

Inside the Cabinet he argued in vain for traditional left-wing measures of massive nationalisation and increased public spending. No matter how many times he was defeated he always came back off the ropes. His resilience reminded one critic of a squash ball. But despite his disagreements he did not resign, as Aneurin Bevan and Harold Wilson had done in 1951 and as Messrs Heseltine, Lawson and Howe were to do. It was an omission that Tony Benn later regretted.

After the 1979 election defeat, Tony Benn developed a strategy for the Labour Party which argued that the post-war consensus had finally come to an end. Mrs Thatcher's government represented the right-wing response, the labour movement in turn should match this with a tough left-wing programme. Much of his campaign rested on the need for 'accountability'. The following remarks were made in an interview of July 1977:

> I watch everybody else with power like a hawk and I say to myself, when I see other people with power, who are they accountable to? When I see the

head of an oil company, who is he accountable to? When I see the editor of *The Times*, who is he accountable to? When I see anyone with power, a banker, who is he accountable to? . . . I think the most terrible thing is when people give up their critical examination of those who exercise power and say, 'let us leave it all to the wise men at the top, they know.'

By these rigorous standards there was no doubt that the Labour Party leadership was barely accountable to anybody and Benn argued that its members, whether it was the Leader, the Cabinet or even individual MPs, had often been out of touch with grass-roots opinion, cynically calling on Party activists to do their bit when it came to winning elections but then ignoring them for the next five years. There was also a great deal of resentment at the way in which Harold Wilson and Jim Callaghan had completely ignored the policies laboriously drawn up by the NEC.

The reason why the Party leaders had got away with this casual attitude lay in the structure of the Labour Party Constitution. As already discussed, this had created a tripartite division of power between the constituency parties, the Parliamentary Labour Party and the annual Conference, which was in effect dominated by the trade unions. In practice, it was the constituency activists who had the worst of the deal because they had very little influence on MPs and could always be swamped by the block vote. When Sidney Webb helped draw up the Constitution he had complained that constituency parties 'were frequently unrepresentative groups of nonentities dominated by fanatics, cranks, and extremists'. In private, many other Labour leaders would have agreed with Webb.

Constituency activists had always been suspicious of their leaders who enjoyed luxurious life styles. In his definition of what Labour is for and against, quoted in the Introduction, 'Beginnings', Ben Pimlott cites 'personal wealth' as something to which Labour is opposed and often wealthy socialists have come in for criticism on this score. After his death in 1896, for instance, William Morris was attacked for leaving a will worth £55,000. More recently Aneurin Bevan, Richard Crossman and Jim Callaghan have all owned large farms. It was not so much wealth per se that was the complaint but rather the isolation which both it and Ministerial office brought. Richard Crossman typified what could happen when he left the Cabinet in 1970 and became the editor of the *New Statesman*. Mervyn Jones was an observer:

The trouble wasn't so much his age (he was sixty-two) as the fact that he had spent most of the intervening period in the rarefied atmosphere of the corridors of power. It was phenomenal to see how insulated he had been from life in the real world; he seemed to peer about, vainly seeking to pick up the threads, like Dr Manette after his release from the Bastille. There were many anecdotes about his ignorance of what anything cost – a round of drinks, the train fare to Brighton, the stamp on a letter.

After losing office in 1979 Tony Benn described in his diary catching the London tube to Heathrow: 'It is the first time for many years that I have travelled non-VIP, entirely on my own: being a Minister with chauffeur-driven cars and helicopters and police escorts makes you out of touch.'

Benn was therefore quite correct in much of this analysis. The Parliamentary Labour Party in the 1970s was on the whole dull, stodgy, middle-aged, male and, of course, white. New ideas, whether they were to do with feminism or the environment, workers' co-operatives or libertarian issues, had simply passed the higher echelons in the Labour Party by. He was right too in noting the familiar pattern whereby once left-wing Labour MPs eventually succumbed to the charms of parliamentary life and shed their radicalism. Looking back through this book, time and again one sees how 'militants' determined to resist the blandishments of 'the Establishment' soon settled down to a comfortable backbench existence and lost any contact with the Party outside Westminster. The autobiography of the former fiery Clydeside MP David Kirkwood, *My Life of Revolt*, depicts just such a process. It was Victor Grayson's refusal to let this happen to him before the First World War which makes him such a fascinating figure and, of course, Dennis Skinner also follows in this tradition.

In effect, Tony Benn was calling for a new-style Labour Party in which MPs were no longer to be the representatives at Parliament of all their constituents but were to be delegates answerable to the constituency activists at Labour Party meetings. This was not a novel demand – it had surfaced inside the Labour Representation Committee in 1902, but Keir Hardie had thrown his considerable political weight against the proposal and it had been defeated. Similarly, Tony Benn's plan to reduce any future Labour Prime Minister's powers of patronage had been foreshadowed by Stafford Cripps' call in his Socialist League days in the 1930s for the Cabinet to be elected by the Parliamentary Party as a whole.

Tony Benn's campaign was sustained by several well-organised groups such as the Campaign for Labour Party Democracy (CLPD), which targeted carefully-chosen MPs and constituencies. The CLPD was, above all, a grouping of activists and it was revealing that for all Tony Benn's talk in his two books *Arguments for Socialism* and *Arguments for Democracy* about giving power to the people, it was the unrepresentative activists who were calling the tune – they were bound to be unrepresentative in part because only a very small proportion of people in Britain take part in political activity. Much was made of the 'Silent Majority', although left-winger Ian Mikardo had a good riposte to this: 'The Good Samaritan was an activist: those who passed by on the other side were members of the Silent Majority.'

Helped by the defection of Reg Prentice who had claimed to be the victim of left-wing infiltration into his local Labour Party but then went off and joined not the Liberals but the Conservatives in October 1977, Benn and CLPD were able to make out a convincing case for their arguments. The lofty attitude taken by opponents is summed up in Roy Hattersley's dismissal of '. . . the army of political riff-raff who infiltrated the Labour Party in the late sixties and early seventies . . .' This 'army' was remarkably successful in its campaign and it was soon accepted that some form of electoral college should be set up in order to elect the Party leader.

Although CLPD stressed how much more democratic this system would be, in practice it was the trade union vote which yet again decided the end result. The unattractive wheeling and dealing culminated in a special conference held at Wembley in February 1981. It was these shenanigans that prompted the breakaway of some senior Labour Party figures, namely Dr David Owen, Shirley Williams, Bill Rodgers and Roy Jenkins, who formed the Social Democratic Party (SDP) which they considered to be the kind of party Labour should and would have been if only it too had experienced a 'Bad Godesberg' conversion like the Germans. From this point on, the anti-Conservative opposition was fragmented between the SDP, the Liberals and Labour.

The Benn campaign was strengthened by the changed fortunes of the Campaign for Nuclear Disarmament (CND) which attracted support again after a period of decline between the mid-1960s and the late-1970s. Once again, as in the aftermath of Hungary and Suez, it was international actions on both sides of 'the iron curtain' that provided the momentum. The Americans decided to install Cruise missiles in Britain, while the Soviet Union went ahead with their own SS-20s and also invaded Afghanistan. The Labour Party went unilateralist and, unlike in 1960, remained so. Well led by Monsignor Bruce Kent and Joan Ruddock, at its peak in 1984 CND could claim 90,000 national members with a further quarter of a million people belonging to local groups. Unilateralism was, of course, a policy irrevocably associated with the Labour Party's new leader, Michael Foot, who had been a leading figure in the earlier movement.

Michael Foot comes from a distinguished West Country Liberal family, but he himself has always been a socialist. He first made a name as a journalist and author. Colleagues always contrasted the savagery of Foot's writings with the private gentleness of the man himself. Jim Callaghan has written of Michael Foot that 'His absence of self-seeking is matched only by his optimistic belief that even the most unworthy colleague has some redeeming trait . . .'

After the Second World War he was elected an MP and became a committed Bevanite, writing for and then editing the weekly paper *Tribune*. His passionate commitment to international peace meant he was heavily involved in the 1950s with CND, which caused a falling out with Aneurin Bevan after Bevan's speech at the Labour Party Conference in 1957 when he renounced unilateralism. However, the two men were eventually reconciled and after Bevan's death in 1960 Foot inherited his parliamentary seat at Ebbw Vale as well as writing a two-volume biography of his hero.

Foot's passionate oratory with its call for traditional socialist policies earned him the label 'the darling of the Left' and he seemed little interested in the day-to-day practicalities of political power. In 1966 he had been asked to take his friend Frank Cousins' post in the Cabinet but on grounds of principle he refused. In 1974, however, he was unexpectedly invited to join the Cabinet as Minister of Employment and over the next five years was a loyal member of the Wilson and then the Callaghan governments. When James Callaghan resigned as leader in November 1980, Foot defeated Denis Healey in the leadership contest by 139 votes to 129. That Foot won in a straight Left versus Right contest whereas he had lost fairly easily against Callaghan just four years before showed how the Parliamentary Labour Party was changing its complexion.

Michael Foot's long-held unilateralism chimed in with the new CND movement which maintained that Britain should dismantle its nuclear weapons, whatever was happening elsewhere in the world. Since these weapons were immoral per se, it would be wrong to use them as bargaining counters. The moral force of this renunciation would supposedly be enough for other countries to follow Britain's lead. However admirable in theory, this was in practice an example of the Labour Left's often unrealistic attitude towards foreign affairs. National groups inevitably generate international tensions and antagonisms, the task is to contain and deal with these tensions. A policy of 'stop the world, I want to get off' is not the best or most practical way of doing this. Historian James Hinton, himself a CND activist, has written that 'Peace activists have been as prone to delusions of imperial grandeur as have Britain's rulers. The Pax Britannica bequeathed a legacy of "imperialist pacifism"'.

Foot and Benn agreed on unilateralism, as they did on another crucial issue, namely withdrawal from the EEC. This policy amazed Labour's fellow European socialists. When asked just what the subsequent 'siege economy' would mean for the living standards of the British people, let alone exactly who Britain would trade with, Labour's anti-EECers had no convincing answer. Furthermore, Tony Benn was not able to explain why he, one of those most responsible for Harold Wilson's decision to hold a referendum on this issue in 1975, did not accept and abide by the vote of the people.

But Michael Foot and Tony Benn, on the face of it brothers-in-arms, soon fell out dramatically. Foot could see that Tony Benn's campaign was causing much internal bitterness reminiscent of the 1950s. It also muted the Labour Party's response to Mrs Thatcher's government which by 1981 was faced by industrial recession and rising unemployment together with outbreaks of rioting in London, Liverpool and Bristol.

Foot's annoyance with what he considered diversions came to a head in 1981 when Tony Benn announced that under the new electoral college system he would challenge Denis Healey for the post of deputy leader of the Labour Party. The antagonism caused by this contest was evident at the 1981 Labour Party Conference at Brighton when hostilities were so bitter it was difficult to believe that this was the annual meeting of one fraternal body and not that of several antagonistic groups. At one fringe meeting, an MP who had not voted for Tony Benn was greeted by shouts of 'Judas'.

Tony Benn narrowly lost this contest to Denis Healey, but his influence and that of his supporters was evident in the 1983 general election when the Labour Party fought on the basis of its most radical manifesto ever, promising 'irreversible change' – which in a political democracy seemed alarmingly authoritarian. It certainly contained some startling inanities, such as the contradictory assertion that 'Unilateralism and multilateralism must go hand in hand if either is to succeed.'

One leading Labour MP, Gerald Kaufman, called it 'the longest suicide note in history' and the Conservatives, under the chairmanship of Cecil Parkinson, bought up copies of the manifesto so that they could publicise it themselves, knowing that this would only help their cause. They were bolstered too by the successful Falklands campaign of 1981.

The different ways in which the Conservatives and Labour fought the 1983 election showed how ossified and antiquated much of the British labour movement had become. The Labour Party conducted a campaign that would have done Keir Hardie proud. Their campaign committee was 'a rag, tag and bobtail affair'; 'people I had never seen before seemed to wander in and out giving advice and then vanishing.' So said Sam McCluskie, chairman of the campaign committee – although it doesn't say much for McCluskie's chairmanship that he allowed this to happen.

The special computer installed at Walworth Road headquarters broke down, the party's own pollster Robert Worcester had not been given the funds to start research until early 1983, and the advertising agency hired to present Labour's case – the first time the party had used such an organisation – began work only five weeks before the general election and even then was excluded from the actual running of the campaign. As the head of the agency Johnny Wright complained:

> We wouldn't think of launching a new brand of washing-up liquid or a can of soup in anything under nine months to a year and that's rather more trivial than advertising a major political party.

Symbolically enough, Michael Foot's own campaign focused predominantly on his supporters rather than those voters who needed to be won over. For example, no special facilities were provided for journalists accompanying his entourage. His speeches were not co-ordinated with those of other leading members of the Party. At one point the running of Foot's national tour was so inadequate that the police themselves had to request more forward planning. One journalist who travelled with the Labour leader concluded:

> In the end, the Labour leader was beaten by an unwieldy schedule, a speaking style that was too discursive for the television age, a manifesto that took an academic semester to explain and, finally, a too personalised and too personable approach to his own politics – one worthy of his heroes of the eighteenth century.

In his own account of the 1983 campaign published as *Another Heart and Other Pulses*, Michael Foot replied to the abuse and misrepresentations he had suffered throughout. But he also noted the puzzling contrast between 'the fighting spirit in our rank-and-file and the mood of the general electorate.' Although Foot claimed that this was an election fought out on television he concluded that with his 'inordinate list of public meetings', he saw less of what was happening in that television offensive than anyone else – which surely sums up the inadequacies of his campaign. For Michael Foot, as for many on the Left, the message was all and the medium was nothing.

The result was that Mrs Thatcher's Conservative Party won a sweeping 144-seat majority. Labour's share of the vote was a measly 28 per cent while its total of 8.4 million votes was only just ahead of the 7.8 million cast for Alliance candidates. The fact that the Labour Party had held its own in the local elections just a month before the general election clearly showed that there had been nothing 'inevitable' about the result.

The poor campaign run by the national Labour Party contrasted unfavourably with the populist if controversial flair shown by the Greater London Council (GLC) and its young leader Ken Livingstone who was quite prepared to use the GLC's resources to campaign against Mrs Thatcher's Government.

Ken Livingstone was a good example of the radicalisation that had swept across the Labour Party in the late-1960s following the disillusion felt with Harold Wilson's governments. He was elected a Lambeth councillor in 1971 and two years later won a seat on the GLC. Supported by his wife Christine who was a schoolteacher, Livingstone was able to devote himself full-time to local London politics. The Labour Party won a majority at the May 1981 GLC elections and the day after the result was known the thirty-five-year-old Livingstone ousted the previous Labour leader, Andrew McIntosh. The *Sun* newspaper greeted his victory with the banner headline, in capitals, 'Red Ken Crowned King Of London'.

The GLC's former headquarters, County Hall, stands just across the river from the Houses of Parliament and there is no doubt that Livingstone consciously put forward policies which were very different from Mrs Thatcher's. He helped introduce cheap fares on public transport in a programme named 'fares fair' until it was banned by the House of Lords. Livingstone turned down an invitation to attend the royal wedding in 1981 and, more controversially, he called for British troops to be withdrawn from Ireland. The GLC was also heavily criticised by some sections of the Press for funding several minority groups; by the end of 1983 the GLC had given grants to more than 1,000 voluntary organisations.

Throughout the 1980s the Labour Party generally did much better in local elections than it did nationally. In part this regional resistance was an attempt by grass-roots activists to make up for the Labour Party's inability to dent the Conservatives' Westminster dominance. The GLC, Liverpool, Sheffield, Glasgow and smaller London councils such as Islington, Camden and Lambeth all adopted policies that challenged the Government's insistence on privatisation and budgetary cuts. It must have been galling for Conservative ministers to be driven through 'nuclear free zones'.

The council that grabbed most of the headlines was Liverpool's and the influence there of the Militant Tendency caused almost as many headaches for Michael Foot as it did for Mrs Thatcher. The Far Left in Britain has always been unsure on the 'ideologically correct' attitude to be taken towards the Labour Party. An activist such as Gerry Healy dismissed it as irrevocably 'reformist' and therefore set up the Workers' Revolutionary Party (WRP); overwhelming self-confidence in his beliefs was expected to make up for the tiny membership. Most of these 'Far Left' groups managed to attract at least one 'star' name: actress Vanessa Redgrave joined the WRP, journalist Paul Foot belonged to International Socialism, later the Socialist Workers' Party, and Tariq Ali fronted the International Marxist Group.

Militant, however, argued that, like it or not, the Labour Party was the largest working-class organisation in Britain and that their members should pursue what was called 'entryism'. Their brand of Marxism was fundamentalist to the nth degree, wanting to nationalise the whole of British industry which would then presumably be run by the editorial board of the *Militant* newspaper. But it was Militant's energy and powers of organisation rather than their ideas that allowed them to take over run-down and apathetic Labour Party branches.

The GLC and several other councils tried to promote local economic recovery by setting up a network of enterprise boards and agencies. The Greater London Enterprise Board (GLEB), for instance, analysed the London economy in great detail but simply did not have the resources to buck the trend of world and British recession. Another flaw was not novel: looking back in 1987 at the 1950s New Left, economist Michael Barratt Brown noted that:

> ... we often appeared, except in the practice of writing and the arts, like a bunch of amateurs. We could not even run a coffee bar without losing money – how much less could we be trusted to manage the country's foreign trade. This lack of managerial skills became more obvious than ever when the Greater London Council and some other Labour authorities set up enterprise boards to manage business enterprises. The lessons have still not been learned. As yet there is still no Labour management college, nor even courses in management at the trade-union colleges.

Sadly, many of the new enterprises went bankrupt, just as the three co-operatives at Kirkby, Meriden and the *Scottish Daily News* had done under the last Labour government.

Finally, however powerful these local councils were on their own patch, they simply could not defeat the national government, which introduced rate-capping and surcharged individual councillors for overspending. In Liverpool, well-known individual members of Militant such as Derek Hatton were expelled from the Labour Party. Mrs Thatcher also decided to get rid of the GLC and the other metropolitan councils. The next elections scheduled for May 1985 were perfunctorily scrapped and the GLC was abolished. The powerlessness of the Labour Party, the GLC and the other councils in the face of the Conservative government's actions demonstrated just how centralised power had become in Britain. Local socialism had been defeated by national conservatism. Ken Livingstone himself ended up on the other side of the Thames when he was elected an MP in 1987.

Although Tony Benn was adamant in his calls for greater democracy throughout British society, one institution noticeably exempt from his strictures was the trade union movement. Paradoxically, Benn's attitude was echoed by the Labour Right which also seemed prepared to let sleeping dogs lie because the block vote had traditionally supported the leadership of the Party. The Labour Left was of a similar mind but in their case it was because they hoped that in the near future the block vote might well become left wing in character. Anyone who argued that this obsession with arithmetic — are we going to get the USDAW vote, and what about the firemen etc? — was distinctly undemocratic and unsocialist was given short shrift.

Another difficulty was that the industrial response to Mrs Thatcher was no more successful than the political or that of local government. By outlawing secondary picketing, curbing the closed shop, sequestrating union assets if necessary and calling for pre-strike ballots, the Conservative Party had reformed the unions in a much more drastic fashion than Barbara Castle's original *Strife* proposals had ever envisaged.

The unions were also under pressure from a falling membership that dropped from over 50 per cent of the workforce in 1979 to less than 40 per cent by 1989. But instead of offering potential members compelling reasons why they should join a trade union in the first place, most union leaders condemned the 'Tory laws' outright and called for their complete repeal, even though several of them proved popular with their own membership. In one case, however, Mrs Thatcher's government was directly challenged. This was during the miners' strike of 1984–85.

Sometimes likened to the Brigade of Guards in terms of its prestige, the National Union of Mineworkers (NUM) was regarded in a special light by the labour movement because of the unique dangers its members faced daily in their jobs. In the 1960s the Wilson governments were in favour of nuclear power and the pits began to be run down at the rate of one closure a week. The NUM initially offered little resistance to this policy.

In the 1970s the NUM's backbone stiffened and in both 1972 and 1974 the NUM went on strike in defiance of Edward Heath's Conservative government, winning each time. The 1972 dispute witnessed what was dubbed 'The Battle of Saltley Gate' when the picketing miners and their supporters managed by sheer weight of numbers to close down the Saltley coke works in the Midlands. The miners' official who had supervised this operation was Arthur Scargill of the Yorkshire NUM.

Arthur Scargill left school at fifteen and went down the mines. His father was a Communist and he himself joined the Young Communist League. He quickly moved up through the ranks of the Yorkshire NUM, earning the nickname of 'the miners' QC' when he worked as the compensation agent arguing his members' cases. He fully realised the importance of television and at the age of only thirty-five was elected President of the Yorkshire Miners in 1973. In December 1981 he was elected President of the NUM nationally, succeeding Joe Gormley. Scargill won 70 per cent of the votes cast.

If no one doubted Arthur Scargill's devotion to his members, no one doubted either his hostility towards the Conservative government or his hope that a national strike might bring down Mrs Thatcher, just as less than ten years before it had brought down Edward Heath. The difficulty Scargill faced was the NUM's long tradition of pit-head democracy under which strike action had to be approved by a substantial majority. Three times Scargill called for a ballot in favour of industrial action and each time he lost. Scargill faced not only the government but also a new head of the Coal Board, Ian McGregor, who had almost halved the workforce in the British steel industry.

In March 1984 the Coal Board announced the sudden closure of Cortonwood pit in Yorkshire. The Yorkshire miners came out on strike but Scargill refused to call a national ballot of his members, even though surveys suggested that this time he might well have won a majority for industrial action. Instead he adopted a policy of 'picketing out' other areas, notably in Nottinghamshire where many miners had refused to strike. This was bound to lead to scenes of violence as miner fought against miner. The NUM pickets tried but failed to close the coking works at Orgreave in the Midlands. The government had prepared carefully for just such a strike by keeping coal stocks deliberately high.

At its 1984 Conference the TUC promised the miners 'total support' but union leaders found that their members were unwilling to risk their own jobs when not all the miners were out on strike anyway. Despite the heroic sacrifices of individual miners and their families, more and more began to trickle back to work. Finally, after no less than a year, the NUM had to abandon the strike. Arthur Scargill's tactics contrasted unfavourably with the disciplined behaviour of the dockers in the 1889 strike when their leaders realised that public support for their action was imperative.

The failure of the strike accelerated the rate of pit closures. Deprived of the men who had joined the breakaway Union of Democratic Mineworkers, the NUM's membership fell below 100,000. Symbolic of the NUM's demise was the closure in December 1990 of Mardy Colliery, the last deep mine in the Rhondda Valley. The shaft had been sunk in 1875 at a time when Keir Hardie was still a miner and the Labour Party was not to be formed for another thirty years. At its peak no less than 100,000 miners worked in the Rhondda Valley. In a striking sign of the times, the pit at Mardy was closed and will eventually be grassed over, returning the valley to the state it was in in 1875. The Rhondda Heritage Park opened in May 1991.

So by 1985 the British Left was in a mess. Tony Benn's campaign had certainly brought changes within the Labour Party but had hardly captured widespread popular support. The Labour Party had been trounced at the last election. The unions had no idea what strategy to adopt and the defeat of the miners showed that an industrial challenge was unlikely to be effective. Ken Livingstone's GLC was about to be abolished. Far Left groups such as the Socialist Workers' Party and the International Marxist Group were numbered in just hundreds of supporters. CND had failed to win over a majority of the public. The intellectual left was not winning many arguments. The future looked very bleak.

This book has often been critical of the British Communist Party because of its failure to develop a useful, viable and provocative left-wing body outside of the Labour Party. Instead, by surrendering autonomy to an organisation based thousands of miles away in Moscow whose knowledge of and interest in socialism in Britain was sketchy, the Communist Party hindered the British Left. The only years in which the Party was allowed relative freedom to go its own way, between 1935 and 1939 and then 1941 to 1948, were, not surprisingly, the years in which the Party grew in size and influence.

By the 1970s the Communist Party was patently uncertain of itself and of its role in Britain. The *Daily Worker* had been renamed under what was thought to be the more friendly title the *Morning Star* while the Party's programme *The British Road to Socialism* accepted that parliamentary success offered the best way forward. That this was advocated by a party which had not had a single MP since 1950 was hardly an encouraging prospect. In any case the Communist Party was bound to lose out electorally to the Labour Party.

The Party's industrial influence, traditionally its strength, had declined along with traditional manual trades such as mining and overall it was in a parlous financial state. Disaster was staved off by selling its headquarters in

King Street, Covent Garden, for a useful sum and moving to a cheaper building in Smithfield, which had once been a pub called the Crossed Keys. The pub's Catholic sign depicting the keys of St Peter continued to adorn the front of the building.

Confusion among the British Communists was matched by that in their European counterparts. The Italian Communists had always boasted a tradition of relative pluralism, mainly because it had been an underground body under Mussolini and so had missed out on the full rigours of the 'Third Period'. The Spanish party was developing what it called 'Eurocommunism'. In other words, arguing that individual parties should work out their own programmes and policies free from Moscow's tutelage. Obvious surely, but it had taken sixty years before European Communists felt able to face up to this responsibility.

Slowly, British Communists began to think for themselves, to ask questions rather than to parrot some party line. They organised a series of successful study schools called 'Communist Universities of London' at which the emphasis was on pluralism and tolerance. Even more iconoclastic was the party's theoretical monthly *Marxism Today*. Founded in October 1957, it had been edited by James Klugmann and was full of long and dense articles read only by the very enthusiastic or the deeply committed. But when Klugmann died in 1977 his young assistant Martin Jacques took over and turned the magazine outwards away from the party faithful towards the less committed. The logo declaring that *Marxism Today* was the monthly journal of the Communist Party was discreetly removed from the front cover, a distribution deal was concluded with W. H. Smith, its range of contributors was widened to include prominent non-socialists, and the design was improved and updated.

In 1978 Eric Hobsbawm gave the annual Marx Memorial Lecture, which was later published under the title *The Forward March of Labour Halted?* Hobsbawm drew attention to a number of trends that had long been noted by non-socialist commentators but which now, because the eminent Hobsbawm had mentioned them, could be freely discussed on the Left. It was clear that the 'world of labour' on which Keir Hardie had helped build the modern British labour movement — on collectives, class, cities, factories — was dissolving.

Instead Hobsbawm pointed to certain trends, which if anything gathered pace during the 1980s. There was the shift away from jobs in manufacturing industry — from 7.2 million in 1979 to 5.2 million in 1989 — to service industries which in 1989 employed more than 15 million people. The number of homeowners had risen from 40 per cent in 1959 to 66 per cent in

1987. There was the growth of shareownership, stimulated by the Conservative government's 'privatisation' programme: today, 11 million shareowners outnumber the country's 8½ million trade unionists. Many more women were working and geographical mobility had increased. A graphic illustration of changing trends could be seen in the fortunes of the white-collar union ASTMS (Association of Scientific, Technical and Managerial Staff). In 1964 it had only 60,000 members; by 1988, renamed Manufacturing, Science and Finance, it had over 650,000 members and an annual income of £18 million a year.

It was striking how many of these points were reminiscent of the very similar arguments advanced by Tony Crosland, Hugh Gaitskell and the other Labour Party 'revisionists' back in the 1950s. But because of the success of Harold Wilson as a political campaigner in winning elections and the 'follow my intellectual leader' mentality prominent on the Left, no one had called attention to the force of these arguments. And some commentators like R. W. Johnson couldn't resist pointing out the irony that it was a member of the dwindling Communist Party, Eric Hobsbawm, who was providing intellectual sustenance for the Labour Party:

> It was strange indeed to think that Labour needed to take instruction in such areas from someone who was a lifelong member of quite another political party, one whose regular and vertiginous decline had in no way been stemmed by the wise counsel Professor Hobsbawm had been able to offer its leadership on such matters.

These social and economic trends did not in themselves automatically mean that socialism was outdated, but they did suggest much rethinking needed to be done.

One certainty was that this process was not going to be carried out by traditional Communists, often nicknamed 'tankies' because they had supported the sending in of Soviet tanks to Hungary in 1956 and Czechoslovakia in 1968. For them, Marxism was writ in stone and remained true and 'scientific' now and for ever. Jacques and his circle brushed aside such prejudices and tried to identity the British Left with the future and not, as had frequently been the case, with the past. They rejected completely the orthodox notion of 'party infallibility'. Instead, *Marxism Today* began to play the kind of gadfly role that the Communist Party should always have adopted but because of the Moscow connection had not.

There were, however, several issues from which the magazine shied away. For instance, although it certainly had an impact within the British Left

Marxism Today has so far been unable to reach large numbers of readers. Perhaps in recognition of this failure, it has never discussed the lack of political interest in Britain, an apathy which could clearly be seen in its own circulation figures. According to *Willings Press Guide 1989*, *Marxism Today*'s circulation was a minuscule 13,153 copies. This meant it lagged behind *Lancashire Today* (15,000), *Scottish Farmer* (25,050) and a long way behind *Flower Arranger* (57,000).

Marxism Today tried hard to get its contributors to write in more accessible language; although often successful in this, certainly when contrasted with many other left-wing publications, the tone and substance of what sometimes appeared showed how isolated the socialist tradition had allowed itself to become from ordinary English. Its *New Times* collection, for example, repeatedly uses language reminiscent of the worst of the old and exhibits such obscurantist gems as 'the most advanced flexible specialisation strategies', 'universal human-life realisation', 'the Brazilianisation of advanced capitalism' and 'Japanisation'. In their introduction to the book, Stuart Hall and Martin Jacques claim that 'The very proliferation of new sites of social antagonism makes the prospect of constructing a unified counter-hegemonic force as the agency of progressive change, if anything, harder rather than easier.' It is interesting to speculate what the human beings who might constitute a 'unified counter-hegemonic force' would make of all this.

Moreover, Martin Jacques, unable to run the magazine without financial assistance from the Communist Party, could do nothing about the magazine's biggest albatross: its own title. It was stuck with the word 'Marxism' when it was becoming more and more clear that 'Marxism' either meant nothing at all or else the repressive regimes of Eastern Europe and was therefore to be condemned.

Nevertheless *Marxism Today* did represent a much more thoughtful and less knee-jerk response to the Conservative administration than some of the responses noted at the beginning of this chapter – George Orwell could well have written for the magazine. It exemplified Martin Jacques' own attitude: 'I hate living in the ghetto. I like getting on with everyone. I like mixing with the right because they keep you on your toes and you learn things.'

And the magazine did have some influence on the new leader of the Labour Party.

At first glance, Neil Kinnock is very much a man of the Labour Left. A politician whose oratorical skills were instrumental in earning him a safe parliamentary seat at the age of just twenty-nine, he is an admirer of Nye Bevan and contributed a preface to Bevan's book *In Place of Fear* when it was republished in 1978. He is also Welsh, a former adult education tutor and was a passionate supporter of CND.

Associated with the emotional rather than the intellectual wing of British socialism, Kinnock was educated at Cardiff University. It seems that some Oxbridge socialists will never forgive him for this, although after the mess that Harold Wilson's Oxford Firsts got themselves into this is surely a recommendation rather than a stigma. For four years he worked as a tutor for the Workers' Educational Association in East Glamorgan before being elected MP for Bedwellty in 1970.

During the Callaghan government of 1976 to 1979 Kinnock had a a brief spell in the relatively minor role of Parliamentary Private Secretary to Michael Foot. He courageously campaigned against devolution for Wales and he helped organise Foot's successful leadership bid in 1980. Disturbed by what he saw as the fanaticism and intolerance of Tony Benn's supporters, Kinnock controversially abstained in the deputy leadership contest in 1981.

Like Bevan, Kinnock has always had a tendency to let his mouth run away with him. For example, his remark about Mrs Thatcher glorying in other people's guts during the Falklands War almost matched Bevan's 'lower than vermin' jibe. But a more important similarity is that Kinnock possesses a strong streak of pragmatism, just as Bevan did. When the Independent Labour Party (ILP) broke away from the Labour Party in 1931, Bevan sneered that they were political virgins going off into the wilderness. No doubt Kinnock felt the same way about the antics of some of Benn's supporters. For both Bevan and Kinnock, principles count for little without the political power to implement them. In modern Britain, political power still means victory at a general election.

When Neil Kinnock was elected leader in 1983, the Labour Party was in a mess. Badly beaten at the recent election, it had to face a Conservative government dominated by a confident and determined leader. In addition, there was still the threat of the Liberals and the SDP under David Owen, which had enticed away several Labour MPs and hundreds of thousands of votes as well as splitting the anti-Thatcher vote.

Trade union membership was plummeting almost as fast as individual Labour Party membership, which had collapsed from the total of 702,000 in 1972 and was to reach a nadir of 297,000 in 1986, facilitating the penetration of small constituency parties by groups such as Militant. The Party was committed to unilateralism in defence and to withdrawal from the EEC. Neil Kinnock himself agreed with both policies which, although they pleased party activists, were not so popular with the electorate.

The trade unions were showing little sign of adapting to the 1980s and their only consistent strategy seemed to be one of 'we are against'. When the *Economist* compared Labour's policies with those of its European counterparts, it found the British party had by far the most left-wing programme – this in a country that had elected Mrs Thatcher. And to cap it all, Arthur Scargill and the NUM were about to go on bitter and protracted strike without balloting their membership. Neil Kinnock could have been forgiven for shutting up shop and going home.

He didn't. First of all he surrounded himself with reliable and trusted advisers. Larry Whitty was put in charge of the Labour Party internally, tackling the chronic financial crisis. He reorganised the Walworth Road headquarters in South London, which was itself a sign that the move away from Transport House might lead to a decline in trade union influence. Kinnock also appointed advisers such as Patricia Hewitt, Charles Clarke and John Eatwell with experience in pressure-group and student politics. More controversially, Peter Mandelson was put in charge of communications and immediately encouraged the Labour Party to look outwards to the public and away from the activists. This totally ignored the Campaign Group from the Labour Left which as late as 1985 could still be found urging the Party to shun the use of opinion polls.

Kinnock realised that he must first sort out the Party itself. He carefully kept his distance from Scargill and even had his hair cut shorter to play down any physical resemblance between them. At the Labour Party Conference in 1985 he attacked Militant for its manipulations on Merseyside and, with growing control of the National Executive Committee (NEC), started to expel Militant supporters, implicitly reviving the proscribed list abolished in 1973. He successfully marginalised Tony Benn and gave local parties more leeway in their relationship with MPs so that the annual reselection procedure became less of a dogfight.

He also began to look for ways of increasing democracy within the Party and in particular of reducing both the power of the trade union block vote and of local activists. Somewhat belatedly, he edged towards the policy of one member, one vote. But he had to tread carefully because of this central dilemma: only the trade union block vote could, under party rules, reform the trade union block vote – and the trade unions accounted for 89 per cent of the votes cast at Conferences. Farcically, this block vote amounted to 6 million votes – yet only $3\frac{1}{2}$ million unionists had actually voted Labour at the 1987 general election.

But, of course, it was trade union money which supported the Labour Party and its financial needs were only likely to grow: the party spent £4,200,000 during its 1987 election campaign alone. The costs of new campaigning techniques – from direct mail shots to computer-aided telephone interviews – would increasingly require large sums of money. Over one-half of Labour MPs were sponsored by the unions. The problem was that the unions themselves were under pressure from declining membership.

Kinnock's relative success can be contrasted with the comparative failure of Hugh Gaitskell to get his way thirty years before. Left-wing critics argued that Kinnock was returning the Party to the bad old authoritarian days of Morgan Phillips, the General Secretary in the 1950s who had kept a strict hold over the party, but Kinnock knew that the images of extremism and disunity which had become associated with Labour were crucial in alienating support.

He began to abandon key longstanding policies. Withdrawal from the EEC was quietly dropped. Nationalisation was put on the back burner and the sale of council houses was accepted. Not all the new union laws would be repealed. Penal rates of taxation would not be introduced. The House of Lords would not be abolished outright. Much of the 1970s programme, whether it was import controls or planning agreements, was discarded.

And at the 1987 election the slick, new Labour Party was able to play the 'Neil and Glenys' card for all it was worth, just as Harold Wilson over twenty years earlier had played the 'modern party for a modern world' card. Music from Brahms introduced meetings and top director Hugh Hudson produced a glossy political broadcast about the leader and his family which improved Kinnock's personal rating in the polls by 19 per cent overnight. The Conservatives were rattled and although Labour lost, the government's majority was reduced.

What was worrying for Neil Kinnock and his advisers was that although it was generally accepted the Labour Party ran a better campaign than its opponents, the Conservatives still won a 102-seat majority. The Labour Party's share of the vote only inched up from 28 per cent in 1983 to 31 per cent in 1987, a long way behind the 37 per cent figure achieved as recently as 1979 – a sign of how inadequate the Left's response had been to Mrs Thatcher in the 1980s. In 1959 Hugh Gaitskell's Labour Party ran a superior campaign to the Conservatives and lost – but won just under 44 per cent of the vote.

The Labour Party continued its search to present a much softer image to the electorate; the Red Rose rather than the Red Flag. Unilateralism was discarded and the closed shop was no longer sacrosanct. One extraordinary irony is that here was the Labour Party being transformed into a moderate middle of the road party by a leader whom Hugh Gaitskell would have distrusted – and yet the changes amounted to no less than the Labour Party's own 'Bad Godesberg':

> The colour of Party membership books was changed from red to blue and Party members were expected to stop addressing each other as Comrade and to use the term 'party friend'. The flag of the Federal Republic was now flown alongside the traditional red flag above the party headquarters ... The overriding aim of the Party leadership in the years after Bad Godesberg was to participate in Government.

This description, in fact, refers to the changes which took place within the German Social Democrats in the 1950s, but there are obvious parallels with the Labour Party in the 1980s.

But despite the slaughter of sacred cows, it was not clear what the Labour Party actually stood for. After the 1987 election Peter Mandelson called for more changes if Labour was ever to win another election: 'I think this requires switching from a policy committee based process to a communications-based exercise.' Yet however good the communications might be, people still wanted to know where Labour stood on taxes, labour laws, the EEC and federalism, health, housing, education and so on.

The NEC initiated a series of seven 'Policy Reviews' which were, in Martin Jacques' words, 'an exercise in exorcism' and proved disappointingly insubstantial on just how Labour proposed to create 'Socialism with a Human Face'. Members of the committees were determined not to build up the £34 billion bill in pledges which the party's proposals were estimated to have amounted to at the 1987 election. It was also clear that the Labour Party had no distinctive economic approach. In the 1930s it had been able to use the work of J. M. Keynes; in the 1970s all it had had to offer was the gloomy and unpopular Alternative Economic Strategy (AES), which called for extensive public ownership and increased government expenditure.

Some critics argued that the Labour Party needed, as Mrs Thatcher had done, a 'Big Idea', but it seemed short of even good little ideas. One possibility put forward was that of 'market socialism'. As Bryan Gould, who had handled the 1987 election campaign, explained in his book *A Future for Socialism*: 'Our basic stance should therefore be that there is nothing inherently unsocialist about the market mechanism, if used for well-defined and properly understood purposes, and if properly regulated and monitored.'

The admission that market forces had a part to play in the Labour Party's economic strategy was a sign of how far Neil Kinnock's Labour Party had adjusted itself to the new political climate under Mrs Thatcher – just as in the 1940s it had been the Conservative Party that adjusted to the Labour Party. But so far market socialism has proved elusive when explaining what it would actually mean in practice.

Throughout 1989, 1990 and 1991 the Labour Party has continued to issue a whole range of position papers outlining its views and policies on any number of issues. One encouraging feature has been the recognition that the Party must be more keen to stimulate wealth creation in the first place, particularly in view of the apparent Conservative disinterest in the manufacturing industry – a recent cross-party report noted that there has been no net investment throughout the 1980s (it would be interesting to speculate what the Japanese would think of this) and that there have been no less than twelve Conservative Ministers at the Department of Trade and Industry since 1979.

The Labour Party has put forward many good suggestions, among them being proposed technology trusts, a National Investment Bank, regional development agencies, tax allowances for research and training, a Ministry for Women, and a Freedom of Information Act guaranteeing access to information. Some proposals such as the National Economic Assessment with its annual publication sound very much like Harold Wilson and George Brown's National Plan, which went horribly wrong.

Yet somehow this has not added up to the 'favourable climate of opinion' Crossman talked about. Eric Hobsbawm once declared that '. . . I don't actually believe that people vote for programmes. They vote for perspectives, they vote for hopes or against fears. I don't believe that most of the people who voted overwhelmingly for Labour in 1945 knew exactly what their programme was.' Admittedly, it is never easy for the opposition to generate such a shift in opinion but there is no sign of overwhelming public support for, or even interest in, the Labour Party's programme.

Why is there this sense of disappointment? The basic reason lies in the old and stultifying legacy of 'labourism' – admirable in its day but its day has now long since gone. Yet still it exercises a lingering hold. It is revealing that whereas the Conservatives needed only three years at most to adapt to the new post-war mood in the mid-1940s, Labour is struggling to adapt to a new Britain after ten. Take the composition of the Parliamentary Labour Party itself: of 229 MPs, less than one in ten are women, and only four are black or coloured. Looking at these proportions an outside observer would think that Britain was an all-white, 90 per cent male society.

Three things in particular are wrong. Firstly, typically, there is what Hobsbawm has called 'the terrible insularity' of the Policy Reviews. Anyone would think that it had been the British Labour Party and not its French, Italian, Spanish and Scandinavian colleagues who had successfully maintained their share of the electoral vote.

Secondly, there is the usual institutional timidity, a feeling that labourism is happy to work the system in which it grew up. Take proportional representation (PR), which Labour's leadership is opposed to and so will have to be dragged kicking and squealing behind the popular mood. In his lengthy restatement of modern democratic socialism, *Choose Freedom*, Roy Hattersley is unable to spare a single sentence in his 254 pages for this subject nor to a proposed Bill of Rights.

Thirdly, there is the sense that surveys and opinion polls have told the Labour leadership what the electorate is against – but have failed to tell them what it is for. Instead the Labour Party has become 'safe' to the point of dullness. You get the feeling that 'it's our turn next' and so we'll lie low, say nothing and hope that a tide of anti-Conservatism brings us safely to office.

This negative stance absurdly personalised the issues. It was always likely to be scuppered if Mrs Thatcher left office before the next election. And when this did, in fact, happen in November 1990, Labour's policy cupboard was left looking distinctly bare. Not only was some foolish abuse hurled at the departing Mrs Thatcher – Jack Straw, Shadow Minister of Education, called her 'an evil woman', which makes one wonder what adjective he would apply to Stalin or Hitler – but the Party's 'short-termism' had left it devoid of both Hardie-like ideals or Attlee-like administrative policies.

In their study of the 1987 election, David Butler and Dennis Kavanagh claimed that:

> Since 1979 the Conservatives had located a large constituency of 'winners', people who have an interest in the return of a Conservative government. It includes much of the affluent South, home-owners, share-owners, and most of those in work, whose standard of living, measured in post-tax incomes, has improved appreciably since 1979.

But they add a sting in the tail: 'The rub is that continued economic prosperity may be the necessary lubricant to maintain the coalition.'

What might a genuinely radical and progressive party be doing to build up its own coalition, which doesn't rely purely on the prospect and hope of Conservative economic failure?

CHAPTER FOURTEEN

The 1990s and Beyond:
Looking Backwards and Forwards

'"It's a poor sort of memory that only works backwards," the
Queen remarked.'
Lewis Carroll, *Through the Looking Glass* (1872)

'Most people couldn't care less about the future of socialism, but
almost everyone cares about the future of Britain.'
Paul Hirst, *After Thatcher* (1989)

'CERTAINLY we need to modernise our policies and
our image – but that is precisely what we are doing.'

'The Labour Party should get rid of the Militant Tendency, unite behind Neil
Kinnock and then we'll win the next election.'

'We have pulled back from the brink of 1983, we have seen off the Social
Democrats, now we'll do the same to the Tories.'

'The Labour Party leadership ought to spend less time looking at opinion
polls and more time campaigning for socialism.'

'Wasn't there a book published at the end of the 1950s called *Must Labour
Lose?* And what happened? We won the next two elections. It'll be the same
again.'

'East European socialism had nothing to do with British socialism.'

'Now more than ever people need an alternative to the Tories. The Labour
Party is that alternative – always has been and always will be.'

These are just a few representative views from a number of Labour MPs, parliamentary candidates and Labour Party members who I have talked to over the last few months.

Virtually every one of them seems certain that the Labour Party will play a significant part in the next century, even if they were to lose a fourth election in a row. Not one individual agreed with my suggestion that the Labour Party might change its name in order to demonstrate to the electorate that it was looking forward and not back. Only a handful thought that the formal link between the Labour Party and the trade union movement should be reduced let alone ended.

Yet the problems that face the British labour movement in the 1990s are surely more fundamental than the issues of Neil Kinnock's leadership, expelling Militant supporters or even winning a general election. With their roots in the past, the Labour Party and the trade unions are finding it difficult to respond to the expectations and values of a country very different from that known to Keir Hardie and H. M. Hyndman.

Nearly one hundred and fifty years ago Karl Marx wrote that 'The tradition of all the dead generations weighs like a nightmare on the brain of the living.' He could well have been describing the position of the British labour movement in the 1990s.

To Build A New Jerusalem shows how two important socialist traditions emerged in the late nineteenth century in the wake of industrialisation, the growth of cities and the development of collective organisations such as trade unions. One tradition was the militant or revolutionary strand generally associated with the various Communist Parties, the other was the moderate and gradualist approach embodied by Europe's Social Democrats. In Britain the latter tradition was dubbed 'labourism' and has been most visibly represented by the Labour Party.

The turmoil of the late 1980s and early 1990s in Eastern Europe and the Soviet Union has confirmed the defeat of the revolutionary tradition. It became increasingly clear that the 'Communist bloc' could not even offer its citizens an adequate standard of living in order to offset the repressive nature of the system under which they lived; state socialism, bloated bureaucracy and an ubiquitous secret police were undemocratic and unpopular.

In the West, most Communist Parties have disintegrated or are desperately trying to distance themselves from their former comrades in the Soviet Union. The Italian Communist Party has been renamed the Democratic Party of the Left, the French Communist Party is in decline and torn by dissension while in Britain the Party is expected to go into voluntary liquidation.

The revolutionary tradition was never very strong in Britain, even though the character of the Bolshevik Party was hammered out at meetings held in London before the First World War. The formation of trade unions in Britain predated and marginalised the influence of Marxism, and the willingness of the British Communist Party to chop and change its 'line' at the behest of the Soviet Union simply underlined its lack of independence and diminished its credibility in the eyes of many members of the labour movement.

Labourism proved much the stronger of the two traditions. In keeping with the general tenor of British life it was moderate, cautious, anti-theoretical, defensive, stable, happy to work within the system, generous, suspicious of ideologues, stolid, solid, patriotic, scrupulously constitutional and unreceptive to extremes whether they were fascist or communist.

Labourism was never a single entity. It encompassed several strands of thought – just as the Conservative tradition does. Particularly marked has been the tension between the ethical mood, characteristic of the labour movement up to the 1930s, and the bureaucratic approach that became dominant after the downfall of Ramsay MacDonald and the second Labour government in 1931. Labourism was unique to Britain because unlike its Social Democrat colleagues in Europe, the Labour Party was created by the trade union movement and maintained strong ties between the two bodies.

But just as the revolutionary tradition is now demonstrably at an end, so too is labourism. The disarray of the Callaghan government and its defeat in 1979 has been followed by two subsequent election losses and an inability to combat 'Thatcherism'. The policies of Mrs Thatcher's government also weakened labourism's customary strongholds; local government lost much of its autonomy, public sector industries such as steel, mining, transport and the docks were run down, the sale of more than a million council houses encouraged private rather than public ownership and a series of laws hamstrung the power of the trade unions, which had always been integral to labourism. The consumer has been exalted at the expense of the producer.

Why should both traditions have collapsed in the last decades of the twentieth century? Because they were created by a world that in its essentials no longer exists. The 'world of labour' known to Keir Hardie and H. M. Hyndman was one of manual labour, steam power, factories, a limited franchise, friendly societies, widespread poverty, virtually non-existent social services and comparatively primitive communications. Large numbers of people concentrated together sharing many of the same experiences naturally developed a collective identity, which in its turn led to the emergence of mass political parties claiming to speak for the working class.

But times have changed. Professor Charles Handy and others have noted the shift away from labour-intensive manufacturing towards knowledge-based organisations and service industries. Telephones, computers, 'smart cards', faxes and the other products of information technology and telecommunications allow individuals to work at home or wherever they wish, reducing the need for them to live in cities or to work in one place at offices and factories. Already two million people in Britain do part of their work by telephone. With the spread of faxes, of view-phones, of 'teleworking' and of shopping and banking by telephone, the Henley Centre for Forecasting predicts that this figure will rise to ten million by the year 2000. The solidarity of the work place has been dissolved by the microchip.

Women will comprise over half the workforce by the year 2000. Rises in the standard of living, home ownership, private shares, and the availability of foreign travel and consumer goods have broadened people's expectations. From 1992 Britain will be part of a single European market.

Taken as a whole these changes amount to a transformation comparable in scale to those that shaped the country a hundred years ago and created our 'Modern Britain'. They are certain to alter the character of political activity – for example, people are now less likely to take part in 'politics' so far as this comprises such tasks as canvassing, attending committee meetings, addressing envelopes and 'getting the vote out' at elections. The 'mass' political party is in decline and both Conservative and Labour Party membership has dropped dramatically since the 1950s. Despite recent campaigning, Labour Party membership is now 310,000 – less than one-sixth of that enjoyed by the National Trust.

These social and political changes are not confined to Britain. Throughout Europe electorates are proving much more volatile than in the past, increasingly concerned with 'issue voting' than with party packages. The power of the media allows party leaders to appeal directly to the public, bypassing the activists. New political organisations, often focused on a single issue, have sprung up. The growing influence of the European Community and its Parliament will stimulate further changes as political parties form alliances with colleagues from other countries.

Not only does it seem as if the labels 'Communist' and even 'Marxist' are now discredited beyond redemption, but 'socialism' itself is under attack. Conservatives argue that there is something inherent in the ideas and practice of socialism that inevitably leads to bureaucracy, conformity and even repression. These changes present both challenges and opportunities for the British labour movement as it tries to create a credible and popular alternative to conservatism.

So far the attempts to fashion such an alternative have met with mixed success only. It is clear what today's Labour Party is against – penal taxation, nationalisation, unilateral nuclear disarmament, old-style planning – but it is much more difficult to identify what it stands for. A suitable description of Neil Kinnock's party might be 'Not The Conservative Party'. Both during the 1987 general election campaign and since, the reliance of party managers on essentially PR techniques has left the Labour Party looking slick but lightweight.

Neil Kinnock himself has changed his mind on several issues, notably over unilateral disarmament. He has also slaughtered some 'sacred cows', particularly the contentious Clause Four of the Party Constitution which calls for 'the common ownership of the means of production'. When Hugh Gaitskell tried to ditch this clause after 1959 the consequent furore forced him to back down. Kinnock seems to have succeeded where Gaitskell failed, with barely a murmur of dissent. He claims that 'the huge majority of the Labour party' never believed in wholesale nationalisation in the first place: 'They were the tunes of glory coming out. Well, we've stopped that nonsense.' Despite Neil Kinnock's abilities as a party manager and the avalanche of policy papers and documents that have been issued, it is less clear what the new tunes might be.

This is not, of course, coincidence. The British labour movement drew much of its strength and resilience from its roots in 'the world of labour' created one hundred years ago. Labourism reflected precisely those concerns and aspirations. To create a new identity for the 1990s and beyond will necessarily entail the rejection of labourism.

Before discussing the defects of labourism, its achievements should be praised. The Labour Party has not been conspicuously successful as a national electoral force; as David Marquand points out, 'The seventy-odd years since Labour became the main anti-Conservative party in the state have seen only two decisive Labour victories. The governments produced by those victories have held office for a total of only nine years.' Nevertheless labourism has contributed enormously in creating a fairer and more just Britain, both in terms of full(er) employment, the welfare state, better work conditions and increased wages. The Attlee government of 1945–50 was undoubtedly the highpoint of this tradition, though some of the social reforms introduced by the Wilson government of 1966–70 were also significant. It would be wrong too to forget the dedicated and selfless work of countless Labour Party members and supporters who have struggled to help create a better world.

But today, in the 1990s, the 'nightmare on the brain of the living' represented by labourism holds back the labour movement on many issues and prevents it developing a viable alternative to the Conservatives. Take the following areas: the role of the trade unions; the importance of economic growth; labourism's traditional lack of interest in ideas; its preference for 'masses' and 'blocks' whether they be tower blocks or block votes rather than for more individualist values; its constitutional inertia; its style of politics; and, finally, its insularity. They are discussed separately below, yet all stem from the same root problem.

It is important to preface any discussion of the trade union movement with a tribute. For well over a century unions have been exemplars of British self-help. They would not have been needed if employers had treated their workforce more justly. Anti-unionists may associate them with industrial militancy and obstructiveness, but much of their work is carried out in areas never reported by the Press. In 1989, for instance, they secured about £150 million in compensation for people who had suffered industrial injuries.

Today, however, trade unions need to face up to the challenges presented by self-employment, 'home-working', decentralised pay bargaining, the spread of no strike deals and employers' demand for single unions, a more flexible workforce, service industries and the linking of pay to performance. The solidarity of the workplace is no longer self-evident: there are now four million less trade unionists in Britain than in 1979. Only one person in four employed in the private sector belongs to a union so that union representation is increasingly confined to the shrinking public sector.

Yet instead of responding to these changes, many union leaders have restricted themselves to calls ad nauseam for the 'Tory union laws' to be repealed, even when strike ballots and the election of officials have proved both popular and democratically essential. Sometimes these calls have been associated with an ostrich-like rejection of social change, as in Ron Todd's attack in 1988 on 'yuppies' and cordless telephones.

Cartoonist David Low invariably portrayed the TUC as a carthorse because of its inertia, and it is revealing to compare union attachment to the status quo with the enthusiasm for the future of industrialists such as Sir John Harvey-Jones: 'Management is about change, and maintaining a high rate of change.' Some union leaders are pinning their hopes of power and influence on the European Community's 'Social Charter' but to regard 'Europe' as the instant answer would be misguided. Employers are likely to play off the labour movements in different countries against each other and so far the attempts to establish links between national unions have come to virtually nothing. In any case, the British trade union movement is markedly different from its European counterparts, for example in its multitude of small unions. The German TUC, by comparison, contains only seventeen industrial unions and their approach is 'one plant, one union'; a practice to which most British unions are opposed.

Shadow Cabinet member David Blunkett has suggested that consumer organisations may turn out to be the 'trade unions' of the twenty-first century because of the shift away from the demands of the producer towards rights of the consumer. In order to be effective and popular representatives of the workforce, unions will need to go beyond their 'economistic' preoccupation with wage levels. They will have to follow the lead of unions such as the Inland Revenue Staff Federation and offer members such services as shopping discounts, credit cards, cheap car insurance, various forms of legal and financial advice and counselling services, especially if they wish to attract the skilled and managerial workforces of the new hi-tech industries.

Without economic growth there will be insufficient jobs and therefore trade unions should be in the vanguard of profit-sharing and co-ownership schemes. They will need to emulate the flexibility and entrepreneurial spirit of the shop stewards at Lucas who in the 1970s put forward a number of alternative plans to the company's armaments manufacture. These ranged from producing pacemakers and kidney machines to a special railroad car which could drive on and off a railway.

The transformation of the trade unions would inevitably change the Labour Party, but perhaps the link between them should be broken anyway? In the past this link could be justified on the grounds that the trade unions created the Labour Party in the first place because they wanted a political arm to supplement their industrial activity, and there is no doubt that it gave the Labour Party roots financial support and the resilience that allowed it to displace the Liberal Party. Today, however, the Labour Party is the only political organisation in Europe that gives the unions such an institutional role. A break would benefit the trade unions too, forcing them to develop strategies beyond their present Godot-like wait for the election of a Labour government.

The union hold on the Labour Party can be seen in the number of trade union-sponsored MPs – 155 out of a total of 230 – and in the block vote at Conferences. A system of 'one member, one vote' would eliminate the block vote, and because most individual members of the Labour Party are also unionists, the union voice would still be heard. In terms of finance, the Labour Party should call for the restriction of central party expenditure during elections and the state funding of political parties, as happens in several European countries. This would undermine the unhealthy reliance of the Conservatives and Labour on business and unions respectively as well as ridding people of the uncomfortable feeling that whichever party has most money to spend is more likely to win a general election.

Socialists have always been uncomfortable about the question of wealth creation. Marxists and others have endlessly condemned 'materialism' – other people's if not always their own. Traditionally, the electorate associates the Labour Party with 'hard times' or with disaster: the mishandling of the Great Depression by MacDonald's government, Cripps' austerity measures after the Second World War, devaluation and the collapse of the National Plan under Harold Wilson, the bailing out of Callaghan's Labour government in 1976 by the International Monetary Fund. At local level too, the actions of some Labour-controlled councils have meant that the Labour Party is often associated with 'big public spending' and mismanagement of resources.

Opinion polls today show that the Conservatives score much higher than Labour on the question of economic competence and there is a widespread feeling that socialists are often more concerned with the distribution of wealth rather than its creation. But it is economic prosperity that gives people the opportunity for choice and the ability to exercise more control over their own lives; as Beatrix Campbell puts it, 'All this anti-consumerist talk is so anti-mass pleasure . . .' Only future economic growth will allow us to destroy the inequalities which still disfigure our society. Unless the Labour Party can deliver a better quality of life it will become irrelevant because, as Bryan Gould reminds us, the early leaders of the labour movement did not say 'Join us and accept a lower standard of living.'

The economic mess caused by collectivisation in Eastern Europe ensures that the mixed economy is here to stay, by default if by nothing else. Yet the question remains as to the right mix between the private and public sectors in order to combine economic growth, full employment, social services and stable prices. In the 1970s and 1980s socialists were fond of interventionist bodies such as the National and the Greater London Enterprise Boards, but their patchy record hardly suggests that politicians and civil servants are better judges of investment and performance than businessmen. Few socialists now or in the past have had much practical experience of business or industry, which has not of course stopped them from airing their views at length. Manny Shinwell belatedly recognised this omission when he was Minister of Fuel in Attlee's administration:

> We are about to take over the mining industry. That is not as easy as it looks. I have been talking of nationalisation for forty years, but the complications of the transfer of property had never occurred to me.

Any future Labour government will be restricted in its plans to fund public spending from general taxation because of European Community harmonisation of VAT and duties, as well as the political costs of raising rates of company and personal taxes. It should concentrate on helping the private sector by maintaining an efficient infrastructure and providing assistance for research, development and training. For example, companies could devote a percentage of their payroll costs to training and there could be capital allowances for increased investment. Proposals need to be drawn up which would facilitate the funding of initiatives on a long-term basis rather than for short-term immediate profit. Apart from such measures, it would be better for a Labour government not to interfere with the private sector.

Labourism has usually distrusted 'ideas' and 'the socialist intelligentsia' as being potentially disruptive, and certainly some within the Labour Party, notably members of the Militant Tendency, have never progressed beyond the bludgeoning approach of Clause Four. The Labour Party's unwieldy policy-making system means that resolutions submitted to the annual conference are 'composited' into some unrecognisable form and then, after a perfunctory debate, passed or failed by the trade union block vote. This procedure is unlikely to produce the new public philosophy that the labour movement needs in the 1990s.

To start from fundamentals: what are politics for? A means to achieve a just and fair society that allows individuals the opportunity to develop to their full potential. If this is accepted then it seems to me that there should be greater emphasis on equality of opportunity. It would be unfair for any athletics race to start with some of the competitors already touching the finishing line. This leads to some radical questions: if state schools are not good enough for some children, then are they good enough for any? If the public health service is not good enough for Conservative politicians or members of the royal family, then why should it be good enough for anyone? There are certain areas of life — education, housing, health and transport — where public provision should take priority over private desires.

There is a personal reason why, for me, any philosophy of the 'I'm all right, Jack' school is to be condemned. Parts of my early life were spent in hospital undergoing a series of complex and no doubt very expensive operations. The cost of even one would have been beyond my parents' means and no medical insurance scheme would have taken me on. Left to the untender mercies of market forces I would have remained an invalid. But because there was a National Health Service everything turned out fine: in other words, because there was collective provision of health care. It is illuminating how survey after survey confirms that people would be prepared to pay higher taxes if this led to an improved welfare system. The Labour Party is right to stress the need for public control of the essentials of life —

health, housing, education, transport – and for the introduction of a national minimum income.

Any radical philosophy must contain a moral dimension because we live in a society where our actions matter and affect others. William Morris alluded to this when he made his character John Ball say: 'fellowship is life, and lack of fellowship is death.' The Morris tradition of 'personal priorities', explored in an earlier chapter, has often been marginalised or ignored by the British labour movement, which has generally preferred pragmatism to principle, but it has never entirely disappeared. For instance, R. H. Tawney developed a moral critique of modern society in his books *The Acquisitive Society* (1921) and *Equality* (1931). He argued that 'What a wise and good parent would desire for his own children, that a nation, in so far as it is wise and good, must desire for all children.' The humanist and ethical tradition of the labour movement also draws strength from the work of Christians such as William Temple, a friend of Tawney's who was briefly Archbishop of Canterbury during the Second World War and whose book *Christianity and Social Order* was a bestseller. Temple was clear that Christianity had moral, social and political responsibilities:

> Why should some of God's children have full opportunity to develop their capacities in freely-chosen occupations, while others are confined to a stunted form of existence, enslaved to types of labour which represent no personal choice but the sole opportunity offered? The Christian cannot ignore a challenge in the name of justice. He must either refuse it or, accepting it, devote himself to removal of the stigma.

This challenge still retains its force.

With its attachment to collectives and 'state worship', the British Left has often felt uncomfortable with individualism. Instead of thinking of people in 'chunks' or as suitable candidates for Fabian 'social engineering', the labour movement should accept the respect for individual values that still characterises much of British society. The good things in life such as family, friends, the arts, leisure and so on are rooted in the small-scale and the personal. William Morris once remarked that 'variety of life is as much the aim of true communism as equality of condition, and that nothing but a union of these two will bring real freedom.' Any future society, socialist or otherwise, which distrusts variety will deserve to fail.

This approach means that the Labour Party should welcome calls for industrial decentralisation. Both labourism and communism have usually behaved as if 'big is beautiful'. But today politics is about quality and not just quantity; it is not good enough for Labour politicians to throw taxpayers' money at a problem and hope the problem will go away.

The call for decentralisation and for different methods of production is not new. In 1864 Karl Marx himself wrote in glowing terms about the co-operative movement:

> The value of these great social experiments cannot be over-rated. By deed instead of by argument, they have shown that production on a large scale, and in accord with the behests of modern science, may be carried out without the existence of a class of masters employing a class of hands; that to bear fruit, the means of labour need not be monopolised as a means of dominion over, and extortion against, the labouring man himself . . .

In the last few years there has been some interest in experiments abroad that decentralise workplace power. In the United States, for example, there are ESOPs (employee share ownership plans) and in Sweden wage-earner funds. Much more work needs to be done both in this area and in ensuring that the collective provision of health, education and transport does not lead to bureaucratic rigidity.

One sign that the Labour Party may be edging away from thinking of people 'in the mass' is the recent interest in the notion of 'citizenship' and in plans to give individuals certain rights which will be enforceable against state and council bodies. This emphasis on the individual as a citizen was first developed during the Second World War in response to the barbaric ideas and actions of fascism. Like anything else radical or challenging, however, it was choked off by the Cold War, which invariably reduced political debate to a crude either/or. The idea of citizenship subsequently came to carry reactionary connotations: 'It was identified with control of immigration and the succession of Nationality Acts that placed conditions on aspiring (usually non-white) citizens.'

But recently every political party has tried to leap on to the 'citizenship' bandwagon, reflecting perhaps the less confrontational nature of British politics since Mrs Thatcher's resignation. Paddy Ashdown published a book in 1989 called *Citizens' Britain*, the Labour Party has produced several policy statements, and John Major wants to make his *Citizens' Charter* a centrepiece of Conservative thinking in the 1990s. Equally important have been the actions of councils such as that in York which has instigated a citizens' charter under which area committees allow residents to meet councillors face to face. Customer contracts have been introduced for services such as street cleaning, giving people redress if they experience problems.

Yet few people seem willing to discuss the obligations which must go hand-in-hand with such rights and, despite all the political huffing and puffing, the notion of citizenship or of 'empowerment' has hardly captured the public imagination. The Labour Party leadership acknowledged this apathy when it decided not to run a campaign on this particular issue. It must also be said that many citizens simply aren't interested in politics.

Labourism has always been scrupulously constitutional and deferential. This is somewhat ironic in view of Keir Hardie's pronounced republicanism – and it is interesting to imagine what his reaction would be to the news that hereditary titles still survive in Britain despite there having been several Labour governments. But much more hangs on this point than merely the existence or otherwise of the royal family. When dealing with the Establishment, Parliament, the civil service or the secret services, labourism has left these institutions virtually untouched. Any future radical administration will need to shake up the system with as much vigour as did Gladstone's between 1868–74.

The Labour Party should lead the campaign for constitutional and institutional reform. The stability and continuity of British life over the centuries has brought many blessings, but increasingly our heritage means we are obsessed with the past to the exclusion of the future; in E. P. Thompson's striking phrase, 'we lie upon our heritage like a Dunlopillo mattress and hope that, in our slumbers, those good, dead men of history will move us forward.'

Labour should examine 'the Westminster model' of government. This doctrine maintains that all power resides in the Houses of Parliament and any decision affecting British citizens must 'go through' Westminster. The notion of parliamentary sovereignty was once innovative and progressive, particularly when the labour movement was still fighting to extend the vote to all adults.

Today, however, it is a straitjacket, tying politicians to the idea of the nation state at a time when this concept is less and less relevant. Instead of facing up to a modern world of multinational companies and the European Community, Parliament stumbles on as before; this is how things were done in the past, therefore they will always be done like this. Often one has a sense of unreality when watching the House of Commons or, particularly, the House of Lords on television, a feeling of having stumbled on some semi-feudal relic which exists solely for its own members. Aneurin Bevan once remarked of Parliament that 'It is an elaborate conspiracy to prevent the real clash of opinion which exists outside from finding an appropriate echo within its walls.'

The sheer weight of Prime Ministerial patronage and the rigorous 'whip-ping' of MPs that takes place has further strengthened the power of the executive. Harold Wilson's 'dog licence' speech only put into words what most Prime Ministers feel and do. The role of the Cabinet has also declined; as Professor Richard Rose notes:

> Notwithstanding its formal importance, meetings of the Cabinet normally ratify rather than make decisions. One reason for this is pressure of time. The Cabinet usually meets only one morning a week, and its agenda is extremely crowded with routine business. A second reason is bureaucratic: the great majority of matters going up to Cabinet have normally been discussed in great detail beforehand in Whitehall committees.

There is an imperative need to 'shake up' the system. Some of the measures a radical administration would surely carry through include the introduction of fixed-term elections; the passage of a Freedom of Information Act; the creation of a Ministry of Law that would ensure everyone enjoyed quick and inexpensive access to the courts if necessary; the holding of local and national referenda; provision for the public election of Mayors; and the opening up of the civil service to non-career civil servants. Only drastic institutional change will bring about the 'open' and 'classless' society advocated by Conservative Prime Minister John Major.

One of the things that makes much left-wing propaganda deeply unappeal-ing is the attitude often taken towards those whose views differ. Labour politicians and trade union leaders should not continually carp at and criticise the Conservatives just for the sake of it. This only devalues the occasions on which criticism is truly justified. Pick up almost any issue of *Socialist Worker* or the *Morning Star* and life does indeed seem very depressing. Similarly, some members of the Shadow Cabinet – Gordon Brown, Gerald Kaufman, John Prescott – give the impression that they are only happy when things are going wrong so that they can then once more lambast the wicked Tory government.

The Labour Party should jettison its assumption that he or she who is not with us is against us. Why not explore issues with the Liberal Democrats? Why be afraid to discuss pacts and agreements? In the past it has often been Liberals such as Lloyd George, John Maynard Keynes and Sir William Beveridge who have 'thought the unthinkable' and come up with innovatory policies that were later adopted by the Labour Party.

Does it really matter if a programme of reforms which would benefit the country is labelled 'socialist' or not? Frankly, who cares? Brian Walden notes that when he was a member of the Labour Party:

> I used to be told that ... the clever thing to do was to call policies 'socialist' when talking to party members and something else when talking to the electorate. That begs the question: who is being fooled?

Is Mr Gorbachev 'right' or 'left'? Why are Soviet politicians who defend the communist regime described as 'conservatives'? Are the Green Parties 'right' or 'left'? What about the various nationalist movements? Have the changes in Eastern Europe been right- or left-wing? If socialism no longer entails the public ownership of the means of production or a major role for the state, does it mean anything at all? Our present political language finds it difficult to answer such questions.

Just eight years ago the Labour Party fought an election campaign promising that if successful it would take Britain out of the European Community. This short-sighted stance epitomised the 'Little Englander' mentality that was inseparable from labourism. Read the ever so slightly patronising tone of Tony Benn when he contrasts the attitude of European socialists with those in Britain: 'For them, the Treaty, with all its defects, is a step forward; for us it was a step back. Britain is, to that extent, a century ahead of them in democratic experience.'

Certainly the British labour movement is now firmly committed to Europe, but rather in the manner of a drowning man clasping at any life raft. And there are still occasional glimpses of the old, blinkered insularity as at the TUC Conference in September 1991 when speakers attacked the 'alien' consequences of Japanese investment in Britain.

To suggest that British radicals can learn from their European colleagues is not, of course, to argue that they have all or most of the answers. Everywhere the Left is finding it hard to develop a credible and distinctive identity. In Spain, Australia and France supposedly left-wing administrations have adopted seemingly 'Thatcherite' policies. The Swedish Social Democrats lost seats in the September 1991 elections while in Germany the Christian Democrats are firmly in power as too is a Republican President in the United States. But to compare the Labour Party with its counterparts does prompt a number of questions: should Labour emulate the French Socialists who have party conferences every two years and have developed links with other political groupings? Aren't there better ways of policy-making? Only 6 per cent of Britain's MPs are women; how and why does Denmark have 30 per cent and Norway 34 per cent?

The British labour movement needs to change drastically or it will die – but how many people are aware of the size of the challenge? Appeals either for 'loyalty' or not to rock the boat, the bland stage-managed conferences, the weight of vested bureaucratic interests in keeping things as they are and the professional optimism of politicians suggest that few are. The attitude of many in the labour movement is 'better the Devil we know than the one we don't'. This complacency and resistance to change suggests that labourism may well linger on. It might indeed win a general election, but if it is unable to transform itself then it is unlikely to transform Britain into a dynamic and progressive country fit for the twenty-first century.

The need for the Labour Party and a trade union movement is as great as ever. G. D. H. Cole once claimed that socialism was 'a broad, human movement on behalf of the bottom dog.' As long as we live in a society where there is injustice and inequality then a labour movement must represent 'the bottom dog' in order to argue for the value of collective concerns above self-interest.

To be an effective representative, however, the British labour movement must accept the challenges which now face it and move forward to help create a dynamic and progressive Britain. There have been and are encouraging signs that this will happen — which is why I feel optimistic about the future. As Shelley put it in the closing lines of *Promethus Unbound*:

> To suffer woes which Hope thinks infinite;
> To forgive wrongs darker than death or night;
> To defy Power, which seems omnipotent:
> To love and bear; to hope till Hope creates
> From its own wreck the thing it contemplates;
> Neither to change, nor falter, nor repent;
> This, like thy glory, Titan! is to be
> Good, great and joyous, beautiful and free;
> This is alone Life, Joy, Empire and Victory.

Select Bibliography

This select bibliography contains some of the books and articles that I found most helpful in writing *To Build A New Jerusalem*. Titles of particular use or interest are marked with an asterisk though this does not necessarily mean I agree with their arguments or interpretations. Further material can be found in the notes to the chapters.

General

R. Benewick, R. N. Berki and B. Parekh *Knowledge and Belief in Politics* (London: Allen and Unwin, 1973)

Asa Briggs *A Social History of England* (London: Weidenfeld and Nicolson, 1983)

Asa Briggs *Victorian Cities* (London: Pelican, 1969)

Asa Briggs *Victorian People* (London: Pelican, 1965)

*David Cannadine *The Pleasures of the Past* (London: Collins, 1989)

Michael Cockerell *Live From Number Ten* (London: Faber, 1988)

Andrew Gamble *Britain In Decline* (London: Macmillan, 1981)

A. H. Halsey *Change in British Society* (Oxford: University Press, 1981 ed)

J. F. C. Harrison *The Common People. A History from the Norman Conquest to the Present* (London: Fontana, 1984)

Christopher Harvie *No Gods and Precious Few Heroes* (London: Edward Arnold, 1981)

Christopher Hibbert *The English. A Social History 1066–1945* (London: Grafton Books, 1987)

E. J. Hobsbawm *Industry and Empire* (London: Pelican, 1969)

William Keegan and R. Pennant-Rea *Who Runs The Economy? Control and Influence in British Economic Policy* (London: Temple Smith, 1979)

Arthur Marwick *British Society Since 1945* (London: Penguin, 1982)

Arthur Marwick *Class: Image and Reality* (London: Collins, 1980)

Keith Middlemas *Politics in Industrial Society. The experience of the British system since 1911* (London: Deutsch, 1979)

Ferdinand Mount (ed) *The Inquiring Eye. The Writings of David Watt* (London: Penguin, 1988)

*George Orwell *The Collected Essays, Journalism and Letters in four volumes: An Age Like This; My Country Right or Left; As I Please; and In Front of Your Nose* (London: Penguin, 1970)

George Orwell *The English People* (London: Collins, 1947)

Alan Sked and Chris Cook *Post-war Britain* (London: Penguin, 1979)

Lytton Strachey *Eminent Victorians* (London: Chatto and Windus, 1928 ed)

A. J. P. Taylor *A Personal History* (London: Hamish Hamilton, 1982)

*E. P. Thompson *Writing by Candlelight* (London: Merlin Press, 1980)

Martin Weiner *English Culture And The Decline Of The Industrial Spirit 1850–1980* (Cambridge: University Press, 1981)

General History of the British Labour Movement

Perry Anderson and Robin Blackburn (eds) *Towards Socialism* (London: Fontana/New Left Review, 1965)

Perry Anderson *Arguments Within English Marxism* (London: Verso, 1980)

*Joyce M. Bellamy and John Saville (eds) *Dictionary of Labour Biography* (London: Macmillan, 1972 – series still in progress; eight volumes so far)

Asa Briggs and John Saville (eds) *Essays in Labour History* (London: Macmillan, 1967; volume two 1886–1923, Macmillan, 1971; volume three 1918–1939, Croom Helm, 1977)

John Callaghan *Socialism in Britain since 1884* (Oxford: Basil Blackwell, 1990)

David Coates *The Labour Party and the Struggle for Socialism* (Cambridge: University Press, 1975)

Ken Coates and Tony Topham *Trade Unions In Britain* (London: Faber, 1988 ed)

Margaret Cole *Makers of the Labour Movement* (London: Longmans, 1948)

Norman Dennis and A. H. Halsey *English Ethical Socialism. Thomas More to R. H. Tawney* (Oxford: Clarendon Press, 1988)

Donald D. Egbert *Social Radicalism and the Arts* (London: Duckworth, 1970)

*Hywel Francis and David Smith *The Fed* (London: Lawrence and Wishart, 1980)

James Hinton *Labour and Socialism. A History of the British Labour Movement 1867–1974* (Brighton: Wheatsheaf, 1983)

E. J. Hobsbawm *Labouring Men* (London: Weidenfeld and Nicolson, 1964)

E. J. Hobsbawm *Revolutionaries* (London: Quartet, 1977)

David Howell *British Social Democracy* (London: Croom Helm, 1980 ed)

T. A. Jackson *Trials of British Freedom* (London: Lawrence and Wishart, 1940)

Tony Lane *The Union Makes Us Strong. The British Working Class, Its Trade Unions and Politics* (London: Arrow, 1974)

*Jack Lindsay and Edgell Rickword (eds) *Spokesmen for Liberty* (London: Lawrence and Wishart, 1941)

David E. Martin and David Rubinstein (eds) *Ideology and the Labour Movement* (London: Croom Helm, 1979)

Ralph Miliband *Parliamentary Socialism* (London: Merlin Press, 1972 ed)

Ralph Miliband and John Saville (eds) *The Socialist Register* (London: Merlin Press, 1964 – still in progress)

*Kenneth O. Morgan *Labour People. Leaders and Lieutenants: Hardie to Kinnock* (Oxford: University Press, 1987)

Henry Pelling *The British Communist Party* (London: A. and C. Black, 1975 ed)

Henry Pelling (ed) *The Challenge of Socialism* (London: A. and C. Black, 1968 ed)

Henry Pelling *A History of British Trade Unionism* (London: Pelican, 1976 ed)

Ben Pimlott (ed) *Fabian Essays in Socialist Thought* (London: Heinemann, 1984)

Ben Pimlott and Chris Cook (eds) *Trade Unions In British Politics* (London: Longman, 1982)

Charles Poulsen *English Rebels* (London: Journeyman Press, 1984)

Andrew Rothstein *The House on Clerkenwell Green* (London: Marx Library, 1983 ed.)

Raphael Samuel (ed) *People's History and Socialist Theory* (London: Routledge and Kegan Paul, 1981)

John Saville 'The Ideology of Labourism' in R. Benewick, R. N. Berki and B. Parekh (eds) *Knowledge and Belief in Politics* (London: Allen and Unwin, 1973)

John Saville *The Labour Movement in Britain* (London: Faber, 1988)

Gareth Stedman Jones *Languages of class. Studies in English working class history 1832–1982* (Cambridge: University Press, 1983)

E. P. Thompson *The Making of the English Working Class* (London: Pelican, 1968)

E. P. Thompson *The Poverty of Theory and Other Essays* (London: Merlin Press, 1978)

Neal Wood *Communism and British Intellectuals* (London: Victor Gollancz, 1959)

Anthony Wright *Socialisms* (Oxford: University Press, 1986)

General on the International Labour Movement

W. Abendroth *A Short History of the European Working Class* (London: New Left Books, 1971)
Perry Anderson *Considerations on Western Marxism* (London: New Left Books, 1976)
*Timothy Garton Ash *The Uses of Adversity* (Cambridge: Granta Books, 1989)
Timothy Garton Ash *We The People* (Cambridge: Granta Books, 1990)
D. S. Bell and Byron Criddle *The French Socialist Party. The Emergence of a Party of Government* (Oxford: Clarendon Press, 1986)
David Caute *The Left in Europe since 1789* (London: Weidenfeld and Nicolson, 1966)
Fernando Claudin *The Communist Movement From Comintern To Cominform* (London: Peregrine, 1975)
Milovan Djilas *Conversations with Stalin* (London: Penguin, 1963)
Alfred Grosser *The Western Alliance. European-American Relations Since 1945* (London: Macmillan, 1980)
P. S. Gupta *Imperialism and the British Labour Movement, 1914–1964* (London: Macmillan, 1975)
Stephen Harding, David Phillips and Michael Fogarty (eds) *Contrasting Values in Western Europe* (London: Macmillan, 1986)
Paul Johnson *A History of the Modern World* (London: Weidenfeld and Nicolson, 1983)
*Richard Mayne *Postwar. The Dawn of Today's Europe* (London: Thames and Hudson, 1983)
Sonia Mazey and Michael Newman (eds) *Mitterrand's France* (London: Croom Helm, 1987)
Veljko Micunovic *Moscow Diary* (London: Chatto and Windus, 1980)
Keith Middlemas *Power and the Party. Changing Faces of Communism in Western Europe* (London: Deutsch, 1980)
Zdelnek Mlynar *Night Frost in Prague. The End of Humane Socialism* (London: C. Hurst, 1980)
Robin Okey *Eastern Europe 1740–1980* (London: Hutchinson, 1980)
William E. Paterson and Alastair H. Thomas (eds) *The Future of Social Democracy* (Oxford: Clarendon Press, 1986)
William E. Paterson and Alastair H. Thomas (eds) *Social Democratic Parties in Western Europe* (London: Croom Helm, 1976)
Donald Sassoon *The Strategy of the Italian Communist Party* (London: Frances Pinter, 1981)
Richard Scase (ed) *The State in Western Europe* (London: Croom Helm, 1980)
G. E. Smith, W. E. Paterson and P. H. Merkl (eds) *Development in West German Politics* (London: Macmillan, 1989)
Norman Stone *Europe Transformed, 1878–1919* (London: Fontana, 1983)
D. W. Urwin and W. E. Paterson (eds) *Development in Western Europe Today* (London: Longman, 1990)
Doreen Warriner *Revolution in Eastern Europe* (London: Turnstile Press, 1950)

CHAPTER ONE
Who Cares About Keir Hardie?

Robert Barltrop *Jack London* (London: Pluto Press, 1977)
Reg Beer *Matchgirls Strike 1888* (London: National Museum of Labour History, undated)
Ian Britain *Fabianism and Culture* (Cambridge: University Press, 1982)
H. H. Champion *The Great Dock Strike* (London: Swan Sonnenschein, 1890, reprinted 1988)
John Cockburn *The Hungry Heart* (London: Jarrold, 1956)
G. D. H. Cole *James Keir Hardie* (London: Victor Gollancz, 1941)
Margaret Cole *Beatrice Webb* (London: Longmans, Green, 1945)
Leonard Cottrell *Madame Tussaud* (London: Evans, 1951)

George Dangerfield *The Strange Death of Liberal England 1910–1914* (London: Constable, 1961 ed)

Hamilton Fyfe *Keir Hardie* (London: Duckworth, 1935)

A. G. Gardiner *Prophets, Priests and Kings* (London: A. Rivers, 1908)

J. Bruce Glasier *James Keir Hardie. A Memorial* (London: Labour Press, undated)

J. Bruce Glasier *Keir Hardie. The Man and the Message* (London: ILP, 1919)

J. Keir Hardie *From Serfdom to Socialism* (London: George Allen, 1907)

Emrys Hughes *Keir Hardie* (London: Allen and Unwin, 1956)

Emrys Hughes *Keir Hardie. Some Memories* (London: Francis Johnson, undated)

Jack London *The People of the Abyss* (London: Journeyman Press, 1978 ed)

David Lowe *From Pit to Parliament* (London: Labour Publishing Company, 1923)

A. M. McBriar *Fabian Socialism and English Politics, 1884–1918* (Cambridge: University Press, 1966)

*Norman and Jeanne MacKenzie *The First Fabians* (London: Weidenfeld and Nicolson, 1977)

James Maxton *Keir Hardie Prophet and Pioneer* (London: Francis Johnson, undated)

Kenneth O. Morgan *Keir Hardie radical and socialist* (London: Weidenfeld and Nicolson, 1975)

Henry Pelling *The Origins of the Labour Party, 1880–1900* (Oxford: Clarendon Press, 1966 ed)

Fred Reid *Keir Hardie. The Making of a Socialist* (London: Croom Helm, 1978)

Frank Smith *From Pit to Parliament* (Manchester: National Labour Press, undated)

William Stewart *J. Keir Hardie* (London: ILP, 1925)

Paul Thompson *The Edwardians* (London: Weidenfeld and Nicolson, 1975)

John Vincent *The Formation of the British Liberal Party* (London: Penguin, 1972)

Beatrice Webb *My Apprenticeship* (Cambridge: University Press, 1979)

Beatrice Webb *Our Partnership* (London: Longmans, Green, 1948)

CHAPTER TWO
The Mild-Mannered Desperadoes: Revolutionaries in Britain and British Revolutionaries

Rosemary Ashton *Little Germany: Exile and Asylum in Victorian England* (Oxford: University Press, 1986)

F. C. Ball *One of the Damned* (London: Weidenfeld and Nicolson, 1973)

Asa Briggs *Marx in London* (London: BBC, 1982)

David Clark *Victor Grayson. Labour's Lost Leader* (London: Quartet, 1975)

Henry Collins and Chimen Abramsky *Karl Marx And The British Labour Movement* (London: Macmillan, 1965)

Andrew Davies *Literary London* (London: Macmillan, 1987)

Isaac Deutscher *The Prophet Armed: Trotsky 1879–1921* (Oxford: University Press, 1970)

M. M. Drachkovitch (ed) *The Revolutionary Internationals, 1917–1943* (USA: Stanford University Press, 1966)

Mary Fels *Joseph Fels* (London: Allen and Unwin, 1920)

R. G. Gammage *History of the Chartist Movement 1837–1854* (London: Frank Cass, 1969 ed)

Reg Groves *But We Shall Rise Again* (London: Secker and Warburg, 1938)

Reg Groves *The Strange Case of Victor Grayson* (London: Pluto Press, 1975)

H. M. Hyndman *Further Reminiscences* (London: Macmillan, 1912)

H. M. Hyndman *Record of an Adventurous Life* (London: Macmillan, 1911)

Prince Kropotkin *Memoirs of a Revolutionist* (USA: New York, 1899)

Nadezhda Krupskaya *Memoirs of Lenin* (London: Lawrence and Wishart, 1970)

Wilhelm Liebknecht *Karl Marx* (1896; London: Journeyman Press, 1975)

David McLellan *Karl Marx. His Life and Thought* (London: Macmillan, 1973)

Ivan Maisky *Journey into the Past* (London: Hutchinson, 1962)

L. E. Mins (ed) *Founding of the First International* (Moscow: Co-operative Publishing House, 1935)

*S. S. Prawer *Karl Marx and World Literature* (Oxford: University Press, 1976)

**Reminiscences of Marx and Engels* (Moscow: Foreign Languages Publishing House, undated)

Donald Read and Eric Glasgow *Feargus O'Connor* (London: Edward Arnold, 1961)

Theodore Rothstein *From Chartism to Labourism* (London: Lawrence and Wishart, 1983 ed)

Andrew Rothstein *Lenin in Britain* (London: Communist Party, 1970)

John Saville *1848: The British State and the Chartist Movement* (Cambridge: University Press, 1987)

John Taylor *From Self-Help to Glamour* (London: History Workshop, pamphlet no 7, 1972)

Robert Tressell *The Ragged Trousered Philanthropists* (London: Panther, 1965 ed)

Chushichi Tsuzuki *H. M. Hyndman and British Socialism* (Oxford: University Press, 1961)

Barbara Tuchman *The Proud Tower* (London: Papermac, 1980)

Frances, Countess of Warwick *Afterthoughts* (London: Cassell, 1931)

Frances, Countess of Warwick *Life's Ebb and Flow* (London: Hutchinson, 1929)

Kirk Willis 'The Introduction And Critical Reception Of Marxist Thought In Britain, 1850–1900' in *The Historical Journal*, 20, 2, 1977.

CHAPTER THREE
Socialism and the New Life: Standards and Double Standards

R. Page Arnot *William Morris. The Man and the Myth* (London: Lawrence and Wishart, 1964)

Gilbert Beith (ed) *Edward Carpenter In Appreciation* (London: Allen and Unwin, 1931)

Annie Besant *An Autobiography* (Madras: Theosophical Publishing House, 1939)

Annie Besant *Autobiographical Sketches* (London: Freethought Publishing Company, 1885)

F. G. Bettany *Stewart Headlam: A Biography* (London: John Murray, 1926)

Robert Blatchford *English Prose And How To Write It* (London: Methuen, 1925)

Robert Blatchford *Merrie England* (London: Clarion, 1895 ed)

Robert Blatchford *My Eighty Years* (London: Cassell, 1931)

Ruth Brandon *The New Women And The Old Men* (London: Secker and Warburg, 1990)

Asa Briggs (ed) *William Morris: News from Nowhere and Selected Writings and Designs* (London: Penguin, 1984 ed)

Edward Carpenter *Edward Carpenter 1844–1929. A Restatement and Reappraisal* (London: Dr Williams Trust, 1970)

Edward Carpenter *My Days and Dreams* (London: Allen and Unwin, 1916)

G. D. H. Cole (ed) *William Morris, Prose, Verse, Lectures and Essays* (London: Nonesuch Press, 1946)

Andrew Davies *The East End Nobody Knows* (London: Macmillan, 1990)

Barbara Drake *Women in Trade Unions* (London: Allen and Unwin, 1921)

J. Bruce Glasier *William Morris and the Early Days of the Socialist Movement* (London: Longmans, Green, 1921)

Philip Henderson (ed) *The Letters of William Morris to his Family and Friends* (London: Longmans, 1950)

Peter d'A. Jones *The Christian Socialist Revival 1877–1914* (USA: Princeton, 1969)

*Yvonne Kapp *Eleanor Marx*, volume 1 Family Life (London: Lawrence and Wishart, 1972), volume 2 The Crowded Years (London: Lawrence and Wishart, 1976)

Jack Lindsay *William Morris: His Life and Work* (London: Constable, 1975)

Paul Meier *William Morris: The Marxist Dreamer*, two volumes (Brighton: Harvester, 1978)

Hannah Mitchell *The Hard Way Up* (London: Faber, 1968)

William Morris *The Beauty of Life* (London: Brentham Press, 1974 ed)

William Morris *The Novel on Blue Paper* (London: Journeyman Press, 1982)

George Orwell *The Road to Wigan Pier* (London: Penguin, 1962 ed)

Linda Parry *William Morris Textiles* (London: Weidenfeld and Nicolson, 1983)

M. B. Reckitt (ed) *For Christ and the People* (London: SPCK, 1968)

James Redmond (ed) *William Morris News from Nowhere* (London: Routledge and Kegan Paul, 1970)

W. Stephen Sanders *Early Socialist Days* (London: Hogarth Press, 1927)

A. H. Moncur Sime *Edward Carpenter. His Ideas and Ideals* (London: Kegan Paul, 1916)

Sheila Rowbotham *Hidden from History* (London: Pluto Press, 1973)

Sheila Rowbotham and Jeffrey Weeks *Socialism and the New Life: The Personal and Sexual Politics of Edward Carpenter and Havelock Ellis* (London: Pluto Press, 1977)

E. P. Thompson *William Morris: Romantic to Revolutionary* (London: Merlin Press, 1977 ed)

Laurence Thompson *Robert Blatchford: Portrait of an Englishman* (London: Victor Gollancz, 1951)

Laurence Thompson *The Enthusiasts* (London: Victor Gollancz, 1971)

John Trevor *My Quest for God* (London: Labour Prophet, 1897)

Chushichi Tsuzuki *Edward Carpenter 1844–1929: prophet of human fellowship* (Cambridge: University Press, 1980)

Oscar Wilde *De Profundis and other writings* (London: Penguin, 1973)

Stephen Winsten *Salt and his Circle* (London: Hutchinson, 1951)

CHAPTER FOUR

Tho' Cowards Flinch and Traitors Sneer: The Rise and Fall of Ramsay MacDonald

Robert Boothby, John Loder, Harold Macmillan and Oliver Stanley *Industry and the State* (London: Macmillan, 1927)

Noreen Branson *Britain in the Nineteen Twenties* (London: Weidenfeld and Nicolson, 1975)

Noreen Branson *Poplarism 1919–1925. George Lansbury and the Councillors' Revolt* (London: Lawrence and Wishart, 1979)

J. R. Clynes *Memoirs*, volume one 1869–1924, volume two 1924–1937 (London: Hutchinson, 1937)

Joe Corrie *The Road the Fiddler Went* (Glasgow: Forward Publishing Company, undated)

R. E. Dowse *Left in the Centre* (London: Longmans, 1966)

Lord Elton *The Life of James Ramsay MacDonald* (London: Collins, 1939)

John Gorman *Banner Bright* (London: Penguin, 1976)

M. A. Hamilton *J. Ramsay MacDonald* (London: Jonathan Cape, 1929)

Bob Holton *British Syndicalism 1900–1914* (London: Pluto Press, 1970)

George Lansbury *The Miracle of Fleet Street* (London: Labour Publishing Company, 1925)

Keith Laybourn *Philip Snowden: A Biography* (London: Temple Smith, 1988)

V. I. Lenin *Lenin on Ramsay MacDonald* (London: Modern Books, 1934)

David Lusted (ed) *Raymond Williams: Film TV Culture* (London: British Film Institute, 1989)

J. Ramsay MacDonald *Margaret Ethel MacDonald* (London: Hodder and Stoughton, 1912)

J. Ramsay MacDonald *Wanderings and Excursions* (London: Jonathan Cape, 1925)

Norman and Jeanne MacKenzie (eds) *The Diary of Beatrice Webb* volume four, 1924–1943 (London: Virago, 1985)

Ross McKibbin, *The Evolution of the Labour Party 1910–1924* (Oxford: University Press, 1974)

David Marquand *Ramsay MacDonald* (London: Jonathan Cape, 1977)
C. L. Mowat *Britain Between the Wars* (London: Methuen, 1956 ed)
Kingsley Martin *Father Figures* (London: Hutchinson, 1966)
*Jeffrey Richards and Anthony Aldgate *British Cinema and Society 1930–1970* (Oxford: Blackwell, 1983)
Robert Skidelsky *Politicians and the Slump: The Labour Government of 1929–1931* (London: Macmillan, 1967)
Viscount Snowden *An Autobiography*, volume one 1864–1919, volume two 1919–1934 (London: Ivor Nicholson and Watson, 1934)
Howard Spring *Fame Is The Spur* (London: Collins, 1940 ed)
Julian Symons *The General Strike* (1957; London: Cresset Library, 1987 ed)
Herbert Tracey *From Doughty Street to Downing Street* (London: Maclone, Savage, 1924)
*Egon Wertheimer *Portrait of the Labour Party* (London: G. P. Puttnam, 1929)

CHAPTER FIVE
British Revolutionaries in the 1920s

Guy Aldred *John Maclean* (Glasgow: Bakunin Press, 1932)
Tom Bell *John Maclean. A Fighter for Freedom* (Glasgow: Communist Party, Scottish Committee, 1944)
Tom Bell *Pioneering Days* (London: Lawrence and Wishart, 1941)
Jack and Bessie Braddock *The Braddocks* (London: Macdonald, 1963)
Noreen Branson *History of the Communist Party of Great Britain 1927–1941* (London: Lawrence and Wishart, 1985)
William Campbell *Villi the Clown* (London: Faber, 1981)
Raymond Challinor *John S. Clarke* (London: Pluto Press, 1977)
Raymond Challinor *The Origins of British Bolshevism* (London: Croom Helm, 1977)
John S. Clarke *Pen Pictures of Russia Under The 'Red Terror'* (Glasgow: National Workers' Committee, 1921)
Hugo Dewar *Communist Politics In Britain: The Communist Party of Great Britain From Its Origins To The Second World War* (London: Pluto Press, 1976)
R. M. Fox *Smoky Crusade* (London: Hogarth Press, 1937)
William Gallacher *Revolt On The Clyde* (London: Lawrence and Wishart, 1978 ed)
James Hinton and Richard Hyman *Trade Unions and Revolution. The Industrial Politics of the Early British Communist Party* (London: Pluto Press, 1975)
David Howell *A Lost Left. Three Studies in Socialism and Nationalism* (Manchester: University Press, 1986)
P. M. Kemp-Ashraf and Jack Mitchell (eds) *Essays in Honour of William Gallacher* (Berlin: Humboldt University, 1966)
Walter Kendall *The Revolutionary Movement in Britain, 1900–1921* (London: Weidenfeld and Nicolson, 1969)
George Lansbury *The Miracle of Fleet Street* (London: Labour Publishing Company, 1925)
L. J. Macfarlane *The British Communist Party* (London: Macgibbon and Kee, 1966)
Stuart Macintyre *Little Moscows: Communism and Working-Class Militancy in Inter-War Britain* (London: Croom Helm, 1980)
Stuart Macintyre *A Proletarian Science. Marxism in Britain 1917–1933* (Cambridge: University Press, 1980)
Iain McLean *The Legend of Red Clydeside* (Edinburgh: John Donald, 1983)
Harry McShane and Joan Smith *No Mean Fighter* (London: Pluto Press, 1978)

Roderick Martin *Communism and the British Trade Unions 1924–1933* (Oxford: University Press, 1969)

Francis Meynell *My Lives* (London: Bodley Head, 1971)

J. P. M. Millar *The Labour College Movement* (London: NCLC Publishing, 1979)

Nan Milton (ed) *In the Rapids of Revolution* (London: Allison and Busby, 1978)

Nan Milton *John Maclean* (London: Pluto Press, 1973)

Dora B. Montefiore *From a Victorian to a Modern* (London: E. Archer, 1927)

Vivien Morton and Stuart Macintyre *T. A. Jackson A Centenary Publication* (London: Our History pamphlet 73, undated)

Harry Pollitt *Serving My Time* (London: Lawrence and Wishart, 1940)

B. J. Ripley and J. McHugh *John Maclean* (Manchester: University Press, 1989)

Sheila Rowbotham *A New World for Women: Stella Browne Socialist-Feminist* (London: Pluto Press, 1977)

Leon Trotsky *Where Is Britain Going?* (London: Allen and Unwin, 1926)

Michael Woodhouse and Brian Pearce *Essays on the History of Communism in Britain* (London: New Park, 1975)

CHAPTER SIX
The 1930s: A New Beginning

Robert Blake *The Conservative Party from Peel to Churchill* (London: Fontana, 1972)

Noreen Branson and Margot Heinemann *Britain in the Nineteen Thirties* (London: Weidenfeld and Nicolson, 1971)

Lord Citrine *Men and Work* (London: Hutchinson, 1964)

Ronald Clark *JBS. The Life and Work of J. B. S. Haldane* (Oxford: University Press, 1984)

G. D. H. Cole *A History of the Labour Party from 1914* (London: Routledge and Kegan Paul, 1948)

Sir Stafford Cripps *Can Socialism Come by Constitutional Methods?* (London: Socialist League, 1933)

Sir Stafford Cripps *The Choice for Britain* (London: Socialist League, 1933–34)

Margaret Cole and Charles Smith (eds) *Democratic Sweden* (London: Routledge, 1938)

Judith Cook *Apprentices of Freedom* (London: Quartet, 1977)

Hugh Dalton *Practical Socialism for Britain* (London: Routledge, 1935)

Nicholas Davenport *Memoirs of a City Radical* (London: Weidenfeld and Nicolson, 1974)

Isaac Deutscher *The Prophet Outcast, Trotsky 1929–1940* (Oxford: University Press, 1970)

*Elizabeth Durbin *New Jerusalems. The Labour Party and the Economics of Democratic Socialism* (London: Routledge and Kegan Paul, 1985)

Ruth Dudley Edwards *Victor Gollancz* (London: Victor Gollancz, 1987)

Eric Estorick *Stafford Cripps* (London: Heinemann, 1949)

Michael Foot *Aneurin Bevan 1897–1945* (London: Paladin, 1975)

St John B. Groser *Politics and Persons* (London: SCM Press, 1949)

Carmel Haden Guest (ed) *David Guest. A Memoir* (London: Lawrence and Wishart, 1939)

Wal Hannington *Never On Our Knees* (London: Lawrence and Wishart, 1967)

*Bob Holman *Good Old George. The Life of George Lansbury* (Oxford: Lion Publishing, 1990)

Hazel Holt and Hilary Pym (eds) *A Very Private Eye* (London: Macmillan, 1984)

Arthur Horner *Incorrigible Rebel* (London: Macgibbon and Kee, 1960)

Douglas Hyde *I Believed* (London: Heinemann, 1950)

Joe Jacobs *Out of the Ghetto* (London: J. Simon, 1978)

Alan Jenkins *The Thirties* (London: Heinemann, 1975)

James Jupp *The Radical Left in Britain 1931–1941* (London: Frank Cass, 1982)
Edgar Lansbury *George Lansbury* (London: J. Sampson Low, 1934)
George Lansbury *My Life* (London: Constable, 1928)
S. W. Lerner *Breakaway Unions and the Small Trade Unions* (London: Allen and Unwin, 1961)
John Lewis *The Left Book Club* (London: Victor Gollancz, 1970)
John Lucas (ed) *The 1930s. A Challenge to Orthodoxy* (Brighton: Harvester Press, 1978)
Charlotte Haldane *Truth Will Out* (London: Weidenfeld and Nicolson, 1949)
D. E. McHenry *The Labour Party in Transition 1931–1938* (London: Routledge, 1938)
Kingsley Martin *Harold Laski 1893–1950* (London: Jonathan Cape, 1969 ed)
Naomi Mitchison *You May Well Ask* (London: Flamingo, 1986)
*Ben Pimlott *Hugh Dalton* (London: Jonathan Cape, 1985)
George Orwell *The Lion and the Unicorn* (London: Penguin, 1982 ed)
D. Pennington and K. Thomas (eds) *Puritans and Revolutionaries: Essays Presented to Christopher Hill* (Oxford: Clarendon Press, 1978)
Ben Pimlott *Labour and the Left in the 1930s* (Cambridge: University Press, 1977; new edition, Allen and Unwin, 1986)
Raymond Postgate *The Life of George Lansbury* (London: Longmans, Green, 1951)
J. B. Priestley *English Journey* (London: Penguin, 1977 ed)
Kathleen Raine *The Land Unknown* (London: Hamish Hamilton, 1975)
Philip Rieff (ed) *On Intellectuals* (USA: New York, 1969)
John Ramsden *The Making of Conservative Party Policy* (London: Longmans, 1980)
Margery Spring Rice *Working-Class Wives, Their Health and Conditions* (London: Penguin, 1939)
C. H. Rolph *Kingsley* (London: Victor Gollancz, 1973)
Marion Slingova *Truth Will Prevail* (London: Merlin Press, 1968)
Pat Sloan (ed) *John Cornford. A Memoir* (London: Jonathan Cape, 1936)
John Stevenson *Social Conditions in Britain Between the Wars* (London: Penguin, 1977)
A. J. P. Taylor *English History 1914–1945* (London: Pelican, 1970)
Hugh Thomas *John Strachey* (London: Eyre Methuen, 1973)
Ernie Trory *Between the Wars: Reflections of a Communist Organiser* (Brighton: Crabtree, 1974)
Froom Tyler *Cripps* (London: Harrap, 1942)
Betty D. Vernon *Ellen Wilkinson* (London: Croom Helm, 1982)
Gary Werskey *The Visible College. A Collective Biography of British Scientists and Socialists of the 1930s* (London: Free Association Books, 1988 ed)

CHAPTER SEVEN
Grand Illusions: British Socialists and Stalin in the 1930s

Dr Friedrich Adler *The Witchcraft Trial in Moscow* (London: Commission of Enquiry Into The Conditions Of Political Prisoners, 1936)
David Caute *The Fellow Travellers. A Postscript to the Enlightenment* (London: Weidenfeld and Nicolson, 1973)
Sir Walter Citrine *I Search for Truth in Russia* (London: Routledge, 1936)
Dudley Collard *Soviet Justice and the Trial of Radek and Others* (London: Victor Gollancz, 1937)
Robert Conquest *The Great Terror: A Reassessment* (London: Hutchinson, 1990 ed)
John Costello *Mask of Treachery* (London: Collins, 1988)
*H. S. Ferns *Reading from Right to Left* (Canada: University of Toronto Press, 1983)
William Gallacher *The Last Memoirs of William Gallacher* (London: Lawrence and Wishart, 1966)

William Gallacher *The Rolling of the Thunder* (London: Lawrence and Wishart, 1947)

Victor Gollancz (ed) *The Betrayal of the Left* (London: Gollancz, 1941)

Ian Grey *Stalin* (London: Abacus, 1982)

Richard Griffiths *Fellow Travellers of the Right. British Enthusiasts for Nazi Germany 1933–39* (London: Constable, 1980)

Paul Hollander *Political Pilgrims. Travels of Western Intellectuals to the Soviet Union, China and Cuba 1928–1978* (Oxford: University Press, 1981)

Robert Rhodes James *Churchill: A Study in Failure* (London: Pelican, 1973)

John Lehmann *The Whispering Gallery* (London: Longmans, 1955)

Cecil Day Lewis *The Buried Day* (London: Chatto and Windus, 1969)

Cecil Day Lewis (ed) *The Mind in Chains* (London: Muller, 1937)

Margaret McCarthy *Generation in Revolt* (London: Heinemann, 1953)

Sylvia R. Margulies *The Pilgrimage to Russia. The Soviet Union and the Treatment of Foreigners 1924–1937* (USA: University of Wisconsin Press, 1968)

Ivor Montagu *The Youngest Son* (London: Lawrence and Wishart, 1970)

Kim Philby *My Silent War* (London: Panther, 1969)

D. N. Pritt *The Zinoviev Trial* (London: Victor Gollancz, 1937)

George Bernard Shaw *The Rationalization of Russia* (USA: Indiana University Press, 1964)

Pat Sloan *Soviet Democracy* (London: Gollancz, 1937)

Survey: issue no 41, April 1962, articles by Hugo Dewar, Alfred Sherman etc

Tatiana Tchernavin *Escape from the Soviets* (London: Hamish Hamilton, 1933)

Vladimir Tchernavin *I Speak for the Silent* (London: Hamish Hamilton, 1935)

Edward Upward *The Spiral Ascent. A Trilogy* (London: Heinemann, 1977)

F. A. Voigt *Unto Caesar* (London: Constable, 1938)

CHAPTER EIGHT
New Worlds for Old?: Labour's Brave New World

Acton Society Trust *The Men on the Boards* (London: Acton Society Trust, 1951)

Acton Society Trust *The Worker's Point of View* (London: Acton Society Trust, 1952)

*Paul Addison *The Road to 1945* (London: Jonathan Cape, 1975)

Charles Barr *Ealing Studios* (London: Cameron and Tayleur, 1977)

*Noel Annan *Our Age. Portrait Of A Generation* (London: Weidenfeld and Nicolson, 1990)

Clement Attlee *As It Happened* (London: Heinemann, 1954)

Sir William Beveridge *The Pillars of Security* (London: Allen and Unwin, 1943)

Robert A. Brady *Crisis In Britain – Plans and Achievements of the Labour Government* (London: Cambridge University Press, 1950)

Susan Briggs *Keep Smiling Through* (London: Weidenfeld and Nicolson, 1975)

Trevor Burridge *Clement Attlee. A Political Biography* (London: Jonathan Cape, 1985)

T. D. Burridge *British Labour and Hitler's War* (London: Deutsch, 1976)

Angus Calder *The People's War. Britain 1939–1945* (London: Panther, 1971)

Virginia Cowles *No Cause for Alarm* (London: Hamish Hamilton, 1949)

Bernard Crick *George Orwell. A Life* (London: Secker and Warburg, 1980)

Hugh Dalton *High Tide and After* (London: Muller, 1962)

Andrew Davies *Where Did The Forties Go?* (London: Pluto Press, 1984)

Bernard Donoughue and G. W. Jones *Herbert Morrison. Portrait of a Politician* (London: Weidenfeld and Nicolson, 1973)

Granville Eastwood *Harold Laski* (Oxford: Mowbray, 1977)

Roger Eatwell *The 1945–1951 Labour Governments* (London: Batsford, 1979)

T. R. Fyvel *George Orwell. A Personal Memoir* (London: Weidenfeld and Nicolson, 1982)

William Harrington and Peter Young *The 1945 Revolution* (London: Davis-Poynter, 1978)

Kenneth Harris *Attlee* (London: Weidenfeld and Nicolson, 1982)

James Harvey and Katherine Hood *The British State* (London: Lawrence and Wishart, 1958)

Ian McLaine *The Ministry of Morale* (London: Allen and Unwin, 1979)

Leah Manning *A Life for Education* (London: Gollancz, 1970)

James Margach *The Abuse of Power* (London: Star, 1979)

Mass Observation *Peace and the Public* (London: Longmans, 1947)

Janet Minihan *The Nationalization of Culture* (London: Hamish Hamilton, 1977)

Lord Moran *Churchill* (London: Constable, 1966)

Kenneth O. Morgan *Labour in Power 1945–1951* (Oxford: University Press, 1984)

Herbert Morrison *An Autobiography* (London: Odhams, 1960)

Herbert Morrison *The Peaceful Revolution* (London: Allen and Unwin, 1949)

J. T. Murphy *Victory Production!* (London: Bodley Head, 1942)

D. Stark Murray *Why A National Health Service?* (London: Pemberton, 1971)

Leo Panitch *Social Democracy and Industrial Militancy* (Cambridge: University Press, 1976)

Henry Pelling *The Labour Governments, 1945–1951* (London: Macmillan, 1984)

D. N. Pritt *The Labour Government 1945–1951* (London: Lawrence and Wishart, 1963)

J. B. Priestley *Margin Released* (London: Heinemann, 1962)

A. A. Rogow with Peter Shore *The Labour Government and British Industry 1945–1951* (Oxford: Blackwell, 1955)

David Rubinstein *Socialism And The Labour Party: The Labour Left And Domestic Policy, 1945–1950* (Leeds: ILP Square One, undated)

Dudley Seers *The Levelling of Incomes Since 1938* (Oxford: Blackwell, 1951)

Emmanuel Shinwell *Lead With The Left* (London: Cassell, 1981)

Michael Sissons and Philip French (eds) *The Age of Austerity 1945–1951* (London: Hodder and Stoughton, 1963)

William Temple *Christianity and Social Order* (London: Penguin, 1942)

Richard M. Titmuss *Problems of Social Policy* (London: HMSO, 1950)

*James D. Wilkinson *The Intellectual Resistance in Europe* (USA: Harvard University Press, 1981)

Elizabeth Wilson *Only Halfway to Paradise* (London: Tavistock Publications, 1980)

CHAPTER NINE
With Us or Against Us? The Cold War in Britain

V. L. Allen *Trade Union Leadership* (London: Longmans, Green, 1957)

Daniel Bell (ed) *The Radical Right* (USA: New York, 1964)

Carl Bernstein *Loyalties* (London: Macmillan, 1989)

Aneurin Bevan *In Place of Fear* (London: Quartet, 1978 ed)

Philip Bolsover *America over Britain* (London: Lawrence and Wishart, 1953)

Eleanor Bontecou *The Federal Loyalty-Security Program* (USA: Cornell University Press, 1953)

Alan Bullock *Ernest Bevin: Foreign Secretary 1945–1951* (Oxford: University Press, 1983)

*John Campbell *Nye Bevan and the Mirage of British Socialism* (London: Weidenfeld and Nicolson, 1987)

David Caute *The Great Fear. The Communist Purge Under Truman and Eisenhower* (London: Secker and Warburg, 1978)

Richard Crossman *Planning for Freedom* (London: Hamish Hamilton, 1964)

Basil Davidson *Special Operations Europe* (London: Gollancz, 1980)

Anne Deighton (ed) *Britain and the First Cold War* (London: Macmillan, 1990)

Michael Foot *Aneurin Bevan 1945–1960* (London: Paladin, 1975)

William Gallacher *The Case for Communism* (London: Penguin, 1949)

Lord Gladwyn *The European Idea* (London: Weidenfeld and Nicolson, 1966)

Roy Godson *American Labor and European Politics* (USA: Crane, Russak, 1976)

Maurice Goldsmith *Sage: A Life of J. D. Bernal* (London: Hutchinson, 1980)

Martin Harrison *Trade Unions And The Labour Party Since 1945* (London: Allen and Unwin, 1960)

Douglas Hill (ed) *Tribune 40* (London: Quartet, 1977)

Fred Hirsch and Richard Fletcher *The CIA and the Labour Movement* (Nottingham: Spokesman Books, 1977)

David Howell *The Rise and Fall of Bevanism* (Leeds: ILP Square One, undated)

Leslie Hunter *The Road to Brighton Pier* (London: Arthur Barker, 1959)

Mark Jenkins *Bevanism. Labour's High Tide* (Nottingham: Spokesman, 1979)

Bill Jones *The Russia Complex: the British Labour Party and the Soviet Union* (Manchester: University Press, 1977)

Jennie Lee *My Life With Nye* (London: Jonathan Cape, 1980)

Jennie Lee *Tomorrow is a New Day* (London: Cresset Press, 1939)

David Leigh *The Frontiers of Secrecy* (London: Junction, 1980)

*Ian Mikardo *Back-bencher* (London: Weidenfeld and Nicolson, 1988)

Lewis Minkin *The Labour Party Conference* (Manchester: University Press, 1980 ed)

Janet Morgan (ed) *The Backbench Diaries Of Richard Crossman* (London: Hamish Hamilton and Jonathan Cape, 1981)

Dora Russell *The Tamarisk Tree. Challenge to the Cold War* (London: Virago, 1985)

Anthony Sampson *Macmillan* (London: Penguin, 1968)

Gordon Stewart *The Cloak and Dollar War* (London: Lawrence and Wishart, 1953)

Don Thomson and Rodney Larson *Where were you, brother?* (London: War on Want, 1978)

Francis Williams *Ernest Bevin* (London: Hutchinson, 1952)

CHAPTER TEN
Expanding Horizons: New Lefts 1956–1963

R. Benewick and T. Smith (eds) *Direct Action and Democratic Politics* (London: Allen and Unwin, 1972)

Vernon Bogdanor and Robert Skidelsky (eds) *The Age of Affluence 1951–1964* (London: Macmillan, 1970)

G. D. H. Cole *William Morris as a Socialist* (London: William Morris Society, 1960)

The Communist Answer to the Challenge of Our Time (London: Thames Publications, 1947)

C. A. R. Crosland *The Future of Socialism* (London: Jonathan Cape, 1956)

Tom Driberg *Ruling Passions* (London: Quartet, 1978)

Christopher Driver *The Disarmers. A Study in Protest* (London: Hodder and Stoughton, 1964)

Peggy Duff *Left, Left, Left* (London: Allison and Busby, 1971)

Peter Fryer *Hungarian Tragedy* (London: Dennis Dobson, 1956)

Hugh Gaitskell *Britain and the Common Market* (London: Labour Party, 1962)

Stephen Haseler *The Gaitskellites. Revisionism in the British Labour Party 1951–1964* (London: Macmillan, 1969)

Robert Hewison *In Anger: Culture in the Cold War* (London: Weidenfeld and Nicolson, 1981)

*James Hinton *Protests and Visions. Peace Politics In Twentieth-Century Britain* (London: Hutchinson Radius, 1989)

Douglas Jay *Change and Fortune. A Political Record* (London: Hutchinson, 1980)

*Mervyn Jones *Chances. An Autobiography* (London: Verso, 1987)

Norman Mackenzie (ed) *Conviction* (London: Macgibbon and Kee, 1958)

John Mahon *Harry Pollitt* (London: Lawrence and Wishart, 1976)

Michael Newman *John Strachey* (Manchester: University Press, 1989)

Kenneth Newton *The Sociology of British Communism* (London: Allen Lane, 1969)

Oxford University Socialist Group *Out of Apathy. Voices of the New Left Thirty Years On* (London: Verso, 1989)

D. N. Pritt *Brasshats and Bureaucrats* (London: Lawrence and Wishart, 1966)

W. T. Rodgers (ed) *Hugh Gaitskell* (London: Thames and Hudson, 1964)

*Dora Russell *The Tamarisk Tree. My Quest for liberty and love* (London: Paul Elek, 1975)

The Socialist Register 1976 (London: Merlin, 1976 – essays on 1956 by John Saville, Malcolm MacEwen, Margot Heinemann and Mervyn Jones)

John Strachey *Contemporary Capitalism* (London: Victor Gollancz, 1956)

Richard Taylor and Colin Pritchard *The Protest Makers. The British Nuclear Disarmament Movement of 1958-1965 Twenty Years On* (Oxford: Pergamon Press, 1980)

Richard Taylor and Nigel Young (eds) *Campaigns for peace: British peace movements in the twentieth century* (Manchester: University Press, 1987)

E. P. Thompson (ed) *Out of Apathy* (London: Stevens, 1960)

Philip Toynbee *Friends Apart* (London: Macgibbon and Kee, 1954)

Vittorio Vidali *Diary of the Twentieth Congress of the Communist Party of the Soviet Union* (London: Journeyman Press, 1984)

Philip M. Williams (ed) *The Diary of Hugh Gaitskell 1945–1956* (London: Jonathan Cape, 1983)

Philip M. Williams *Hugh Gaitskell* (London: Jonathan Cape, 1979; new, shortened edition, Oxford: University Press, 1982)

Lord Windlesham *Communication and Political Power* (London: Jonathan Cape, 1966)

Nigel Young *An Infantile Disorder? The Crisis and Decline of the New Left* (London: Routledge and Kegan Paul, 1977)

CHAPTER ELEVEN
Harold Wilson's New Britain: Britain in the 1960s

Martin Bailey *Oilgate* (London: Coronet, 1979)

Wilfrid Beckerman (ed) *The Labour Government's Economic Record: 1964–1970* (London: Duckworth, 1972)

Tony Benn *Office Without Power: Diaries 1968–72* (London: Hutchinson, 1988)

Tony Benn *Out of the Wilderness: Diaries 1963–67* (London: Hutchinson, 1987)

Robin Blackburn and Alexander Cockburn (eds) *Student Power* (London: Penguin, 1969)

Muriel Box *Rebel Advocate: A Biography of Gerald Gardiner* (London: Victor Gollancz, 1983)

George Brown *In My Way* (London: Victor Gollancz, 1971)

John Callaghan *The Far Left in British Politics* (Oxford: Basil Blackwell, 1987)

Barbara Castle *The Castle Diaries 1964–70* (London: Weidenfeld and Nicolson, 1984)

*David Caute *Sixty-Eight. The Year of the Barricades* (London: Hamish Hamilton, 1988)

Ken Coates *The Crisis of British Socialism* (Nottingham: Spokesman Books, 1972)

*Susan Crosland *Tony Crosland* (London: Jonathan Cape, 1982)

Richard Crossman *The Diaries of a Cabinet Minister*, volume one 1964–66 (London: Hamish Hamilton and Jonathan Cape, 1975); volume two 1966–68 (1976); volume three 1968–70 (1977)

Tam Dalyell *Dick Crossman. A Portrait* (London: Weidenfeld and Nicolson, 1989)

Wilfred De'Ath *Barbara Castle. A portrait from life* (London: Clifton Books, 1970)

Paul Foot *The Politics of Harold Wilson* (London: Penguin, 1968)
Ronald Fraser *1968. A Student Generation in Revolt* (London: Chatto and Windus, 1988)
Geoffrey Goodman *The Awkward Warrior. Frank Cousins: His Life and Times* (London: Davis-Poynter, 1979)
*Anthony Howard *Crossman. The Pursuit of Power* (London: Jonathan Cape, 1990)
Edward G. Janosik *Constituency Labour Parties in Britain* (London: Pall Mall Press, 1968)
Peter Jenkins *The Battle of Downing Street* (London: Charles Knight, 1970)
Gerald Kaufman (ed) *The Left* (London: Anthony Blond, 1966)
David McKie and Chris Cook (eds) *The Decade of Disillusion* (London: Macmillan, 1972)
Clive Ponting *Breach of Promise. Labour in Power 1964–1970* (London: Hamish Hamilton, 1989)
Michael Stewart *Life and Labour* (London: Sidgwick and Jackson, 1980)
Tariq Ali *Street Fighting Years* (London: Collins, 1987)
David Widgery *The Left in Britain 1956–1968* (London: Penguin, 1976)
Lord Wigg *George Wigg* (London: Michael Joseph, 1972)
Raymond Williams (ed) *May Day Manifesto* (London: Penguin, 1968)
Harold Wilson *The Labour Governments 1964–1970. A Personal Record* (London: Weidenfeld and Nicolson and Michael Joseph, 1971)

CHAPTER TWELVE
Endings: The British Left in the 1970s

Tony Benn *Against the Tide: Diaries 1973–76* (London: Hutchinson, 1989)
*Tony Benn *Conflict of Interest: Diaries 1977–80* (London: Hutchinson, 1990)
Joel Barnett *Inside the Treasury* (London: Deutsch, 1982)
Nick Bosanquet and Peter Townsend (ed) *Labour And Equality. A Fabian Study of Labour in Power, 1974–1979* (London: Heinemann, 1980)
David Butler and Dennis Kavanagh *The British General Election of 1979* (London: Macmillan, 1980)
*James Callaghan *Time And Chance* (London: Collins, 1987)
Barbara Castle *The Castle Diaries 1974–76* (London: Weidenfeld and Nicolson, 1980)
David Coates *Labour In Power? A Study of the Labour Government 1974–1979* (London: Longman, 1980)
Ken Coates (ed) *What Went Wrong* (Nottingham: Spokesman, 1979)
*Bernard Donoughue *Prime Minister: The Conduct of Policy under Harold Wilson and James Callaghan* (London: Jonathan Cape, 1987)
Stephen Fay and Hugo Young *The Day The £ Nearly Died* (London: Sunday Times Publications, 1978)
Joe Haines *The Politics of Power* (London: Jonathan Cape, 1977)
Michael Hatfield *The House The Left Built. Inside Labour Policy Making 1970–1975* (London: Victor Gollancz, 1978)
*Denis Healey *The Time Of My Life* (London: Michael Joseph, 1989)
Stuart Holland *The Socialist Challenge* (London: Quartet, 1975)
Martin Holmes *The Labour Government, 1974–1979* (London: Macmillan, 1985)
Robert Jenkins *Tony Benn. A Political Biography* (London: Writers and Readers, 1980)
Jack Jones *Union Man* (London: Collins, 1986)
Peter Kellner and Christopher Hitchens *Callaghan: The Road to Number Ten* (London: Cassell, 1976)
Will Paynter *My Generation* (London: Allen and Unwin, 1972)

Jimmy Reid *Reflections of a Clyde-built Man* (London: Souvenir Press, 1976)
Jeremy Seabrook *What Went Wrong?* (London: Victor Gollancz, 1978)
Patrick Seyd *The Rise And Fall Of The Labour Left* (London: Macmillan, 1987)
Robert Skidelsky (ed) *The End Of The Keynesian Era* (London: Macmillan, 1977)
Tariq Ali *The Coming British Revolution* (London: Jonathan Cape, 1972)
*Robert Taylor *The Fifth Estate. Britain's Unions in the Modern World* (London: Pan, 1980 ed)
Philip Whitehead *The Writing On The Wall. Britain in the Seventies* (London: Michael Joseph, 1985)

CHAPTER THIRTEEN
The 1980s: Into the Crucible

*Martin Adeney and John Lloyd *The Miners' Strike* (London: Routledge and Kegan Paul, 1986)
Michael Ball, Fred Gray and Linda McDowell *The Transformation of Britain. Contemporary Social and Economic Change* (London: Fontana, 1989)
Tony Benn *Arguments for Democracy* (London: Jonathan Cape, 1981)
Tony Benn *Arguments for Socialism* (London: Jonathan Cape, 1979)
Ian Bradley *Breaking The Mould? The Birth and Prospects of the Social Democratic Party* (Oxford: Martin Robertson, 1981)
David Butler and Dennis Kavanagh *The British General Election of 1983* (London: Macmillan, 1984)
David Butler and Dennis Kavanagh *The British General Election of 1987* (London: Macmillan, 1988)
*Beatrix Campbell *Wigan Pier Revisited* (London: Virago, 1984)
John Carvel *Citizen Ken* (London: Chatto and Windus, 1984)
Michael Crick *Scargill and the Miners* (London: Penguin, 1985)
Francis Cripps et al *Manifesto. Radical Strategy for Britain's Future* (London: Pan, 1981)
Michael Foot *Another Heart and Other Pulses: The Alternative to the Thatcher Society* (London: Collins, 1984)
David Graham and Peter Clarke *The New Enlightenment. The Rebirth of Liberalism* (London: Macmillan, 1984)
Stuart Hall and Martin Jacques (eds) *The Politics of Thatcherism* (London: Lawrence and Wishart, 1983)
Robert Harris *The Making of Neil Kinnock* (London: Faber, 1984)
Simon Hoggart and David Leigh *Michael Foot: a portrait* (London: Hodder and Stoughton, 1981)
Colin Hughes and Patrick Wintour *Labour Rebuilt* (London: Fourth Estate, 1990)
Martin Jacques and Francis Mulhern (eds) *The Forward March of Labour Halted?* (London: Verso, 1981)
Peter Jenkins *Mrs Thatcher's Revolution. The Ending of the Socialist Era* (London: Jonathan Cape, 1987)
R. W. Johnson *The Politics of Recession* (London: Macmillan, 1985)
Frank I. Luntz *Candidates, Consultants and Campaigns* (Oxford: Basil Blackwell, 1988)
Richard Rose *Politics in England* (London: Faber, 1980 ed)
Sheila Rowbotham et al *Beyond the Fragments* (London: Merlin Press, 1980)
Robert Skidelsky (ed) *Thatcherism* (London: Chatto and Windus, 1988)
*Hugo Young *One Of Us. A Biography of Margaret Thatcher* (London: Macmillan, 1989)

General: Britain is fortunate in the quality of the political commentators working for the 'serious' Press. It seems to me that writers like Hugo Young, Peter Kellner, Peter Jenkins, Martin Jacques, Robert Harris, Ferdinand Mount, R. W. Johnson, Bernard Crick, Ben Pimlott, Neal Ascherson and Anthony Howard conduct what are, in effect, public adult education sessions.

CHAPTER FOURTEEN
The 1990s and Beyond: Looking Backwards and Forwards

Geoff Andrews (ed) *Citizenship* (London: Lawrence and Wishart, 1991)
Paddy Ashdown *Citizens' Britain* (London: Fourth Estate, 1989)
Report of the Commission on Citizenship *Encouraging Citizenship* (London: HMSO, 1990; additional papers presented to the Commission by Raymond Plant, Brian Barrie, Ralf Dahrendorf and David Halpern are available from the Secretary to the Commission, 237 Pentonville Road, London N1 9NJ)
Bryan Gould *A Future for Socialism* (London: Jonathan Cape, 1989)
Stuart Hall and Martin Jacques (eds) *New Times. The Changing Face of Politics in the 1990s* (London: Lawrence and Wishart, 1989)
Charles Handy *The Age of Reason* (London: Business Books, 1989)
John Harvey-Jones *Making It Happen* (London: Collins, 1988)
Roy Hattersley *Choose Freedom* (London: Michael Joseph, 1987)
*Paul Hirst *After Thatcher* (London: Collins, 1989)
Eric Hobsbawm *Politics for a Rational Left* (London: Verso, 1989)
*Mary Kaldor (ed) *Europe from Below. An East-West Dialogue* (London: Verso, 1991)
Ken Livingstone *Livingstone's Labour: A Programme for the Nineties* (London: Allen and Unwin, 1989)
David Marquand *The Progressive Dilemma* (London: Heinmann, 1991)
*David Marquand *The Unprincipled Society. New Demands and Old Policies* (London: Jonathan Cape, 1988)
Giles Radice *Labour's Path to Power. The New Revisionism* (London: Macmillan, 1989)
J. R. Williams, R. M. Titmuss and F. J. Fisher (eds) *R. H. Tawney, A Portrait by Several Hands* (London: Shenvall Press, undated)
A. W. Wright *G. D. H. Cole and Socialist Democracy* (Oxford: Clarendon Press, 1979)

Notes

Publication details of all titles cited in the notes are given in the bibliography.

Beginnings

p. 1 *Workers of world*: Raymond Plant 'Servant or Master?' in *The Times*, 2 October 1990.

p. 1 *A third not knowing party*: *Daily Telegraph*, 14 May 1987.

p. 1 *Institute of Directors study*: *Daily Telegraph*, 3 September 1986.

p. 1 *Election holidy boom*: for example, *Evening Standard*, 26 May 1983.

p. 1 *Less than one-twentieth*: Stephen Harding, David Phillips, Michael Fogarty *Contrasting Values in Western Europe* p. 77.

p. 2 *37 Clerkenwell Green*: see Andrew Rothstein *The House on Clerkenwell Green*.

p. 4 *Jargon*: George Orwell *The English People* p. 34.

p. 4 *Reverse snobbery*: Anthony Barnett in Channel Four's tribute to Raymond Williams, *A Journey of Hope*, 19 June 1990.

p. 5 *Cult of personality*: Kenneth O. Morgan *Labour People* (Oxford: University Press, 1989) p. 1.

p. 6 *Explorer of the past*: Lytton Strachey *Eminent Victorians* vii.

p. 6 *1,600 files*: David Marquand *Ramsay MacDonald* (London: Jonathan Cape, 1977) p. 797.

p. 6 *Dalton's diaries*: see the article by his editor, Ben Pimlott, in the *Listener*, 17 July 1980. By piling together the diaries of Dalton, Crossman, Castle and Benn you don't prop up a table so much as make one.

p. 6 *Benn's letters*: *Daily Telegraph*, 16 November 1990.

p. 7 *Labour is known*: Ben Pimlott 'The Future of the Left' in Robert Skidelsky (ed) *Thatcherism* p. 83.

p. 7 *Pleasures of past*: David Cannadine *The Pleasures of the Past*.

CHAPTER ONE
Who Cares About Keir Hardie?

p. 15 *Right thing*: G. D. Cole *James Keir Hardie* p. 8.

p. 15 *Abstraction*: David Lowe *From Pit to Parliament* p. 36.

p. 16 *Hardie's 'garb'*: Frank Smith *From Pit to Parliament* p. 7.

p. 16 *Gardiner*: A. G. Gardiner *Prophets, Priests and Kings* p. 217.

p. 17 *Alone*: J. Bruce Glasier *James Keir Hardie. A Memorial* p. 65.

p. 17 *Hardie's illegitimacy*: Fred Reid *Keir Hardie. The Making of a Socialist* pp. 185–92.

p. 18 *Shorthand*: Frank Smith, p. 4.

p. 18 *Daylight*: G. D. H. Cole, p. 8.

p. 18 *Men with no property*: Henry Pelling *A History of British Trade Unionism* p. 32.

p. 19 *Applegarth*: Asa Briggs *Victorian People* p. 186.

p. 20 *Man made*: James Maxton *Keir Hardie Prophet and Pioneer* p. 9.

p. 20 *Not democrats*: John Vincent *The Formation of the British Liberal Party 1857–68* p. 35.

p. 21 *Damn charity*: William Temple *Christianity and Social Order* p. 14.

p. 22 *Trevelyan meeting*: William Stewart *J. Keir Hardie* p. 44.

p. 23 *Country of workers*: E. J. Hobsbawm *Industry and Empire* p. 154.

p. 23 *Without violence*: Henry Pelling (ed) *The Challenge of Socialism* p. 9.

p. 23 *Human sentiment*: Hamilton Fyfe *Keir Hardie* p. 71.

p. 23 *Labourism*: John Saville 'The Ideology of Labourism' in R. Benewick, R. N. Berki and B. Parekh *Knowledge and Belief in Politics* pp. 213–26.

p. 24 *Ethics*: J. Keir Hardie *From Serfdom to Socialism* p. 35.

p. 24 *Toynbee Hall Report*: Reg Beer *Matchgirls Strike 1888* p. 41.

p. 25 *Order and calm*: H. H. Champion *The Great Dock Strike* p. 6. One shouldn't overplay the popularity of the strikers. The attendants at Madame Tussaud's used to find needles stuck in the heart of John Burns' effigy: Leonard Cottrell *Madame Tussaud* p. 174.

p. 26 *European parties*: Norman Stone *Europe Transformed, 1878–1919* pp. 48–9.

p. 26 *Word masses*: see the sparkling essay by Asa Briggs 'The Language of 'Mass' and 'Masses' in Nineteenth-Century England' in D. Martin and D. Rubinstein (eds) *Ideology and the Labour Movement* pp. 62–83.

p. 26 *Personal influence*: Asa Briggs *Victorian Cities* p. 65.

p. 27 *Nation yours*: Hamilton Fyfe, p. 119.

p. 27 *Major and miner*: Kenneth O. Morgan *Keir Hardie radical and socialist* p. 51.

p. 28 *Wings clipped*: J. Bruce Glasier *Keir Hardie. The Man and the Message* p. 10.

p. 28 *Howling*: William Stewart, pp. 93–4.

p. 29 *Rueful countenance*: A. G. Gardiner, p. 216.

p. 29 *Few friends*: David Lowe, p. 36.

p. 29 *Vicious tastes*: J. Keir Hardie, p. 100.

p. 29 *Dress shirt*: A. G. Gardiner, p. 214.

p. 30 *Mrs Glasier*: Kenneth O. Morgan, p. 11.

p. 30 *Annie Hines*: Fred Reid, pp. 170–1.

p. 30 *Sylvia Pankhurst*: Kenneth O. Morgan, pp. 164–6.

p. 30 *Agitator*: Hamilton Fyfe, p. 61.

p. 31 *Old romance*: J. R. Clynes *Memoirs volume one 1869–1924* p. 34.

p. 31 *Twenty-three trade unionists*: see David Martin 'The Instruments of the People?' in D. Martin and D. Rubinstein *Ideology and the Labour Movement* pp. 125–46.

p. 31 *1906 MPs*: H. M. Hyndman quoted in Lord Elton *Ramsay MacDonald* p. 133.

p. 31 *Survey of MPs*: *Review of Reviews*, June 1906, vol XXXIII, pp. 568–82.

p. 31 *No manual labourers*: W. H. Mallock 'The Political Powers of Labour' in *The Nineteenth Century*, vol 60, August 1906, p. 211.

p. 32 *Child dies*: Jack London *The People of the Abyss* pp. 121–2; also see Robert Barltrop *Jack London* pp. 80–2.

p. 32 *Race of seers*: Emrys Hughes *Keir Hardie* pp. 3–4.

p. 33 *Adult organisation*: Margaret Cole *Beatrice Webb* p. 136.

p. 33 *Webbs' loo*: Kingsley Martin *Father Figures* p. 115.

p. 33 *The Potters*: Margaret Cole, p. 13.

p. 34 *Absorbed*: Norman and Jeanne MacKenzie *The First Fabians* p. 127.

p. 34 *Death*: MacKenzies, pp. 129, 134.

p. 34 *Fabian journalists and writers*: E. J. Hobsbawm essay 'The Fabians Reconsidered' in his *Labouring Men* p. 250.

p. 35 *Head only*: MacKenzies, p. 155.

p. 35 *One and one*: Margaret Cole, p. 43.

p. 35 *Babies*: quoted in Ruth Brandon *The New Women and the Old Men* p. 109.

CHAPTER TWO
The Mild-Mannered Desperadoes

p. 37 *'Marxists'*: Wilhelm Liebknecht *Biographical Memoirs* p. 71.

p. 37 *Against wall*: Lenin quoted in Paul Johnson *A History of the Modern World* p. 67.

p. 37 *Fight to knife*: Charles Poulsen *The English Rebels* p. 179.

p. 38 *Government preparations*: Reg Groves *But We Shall Rise Again* pp. 180–1.

p. 38 *Gunsmiths and telegraph system*: John Saville *1848: The British State and the Chartist Movement* p. 112.

p. 38 *Gagging Act*: Theodore Rothstein *From Chartism to Labourism* p. 143.

p. 38 *Vault of heaven and Feargus Rex*: R. G. Gammage *History of the Chartist Movement 1837–1854* pp. 45, 292.

p. 39 *Loss of nerve*: Donald Read and Eric Glasgow *Feargus O'Connor* p. 131.

p. 40 *Chelsea mob*: Andrew Davies *Literary London* p. 30.

p. 40 *Railway clerk*: Asa Briggs *Marx in London* p. 53.

p. 40 *Kinkel*: Rosemary Ashton *Little Germany* p. 153; see also S. S. Prawer *Karl Marx and World Literature* pp. 186–96.

p. 41 *One hundred organisations*: Jacques Freymond and Miklos Molnar 'The Rise and Fall of the First International' in M. M. Drachkovitch *The Revolutionary Internationals, 1864–1943* p. 14.

p. 41 *Pistol*: reminiscences of Theodore Cuno in *Reminiscences of Marx and Engels* p. 211.

p. 41 *Lack of money*: Yvonne Kapp *Eleanor Marx* volume one p. 36.

p. 42 *Prussian spy*: Yvonne Kapp, p. 290.

p. 42 *Marxes' humour*: Eleanor Marx-Aveling in *Reminiscences* p. 254.

p. 42 *Pub crawl*: Wilhelm Liebknecht, pp. 150–1.

p. 43 *Rule Britannia*: James Hinton *Labour and Socialism* p. 55.

p. 43 *Non-participatory*: eg Arthur Marwick *British Society Since 1945* pp. 164, 276.

p. 44 *Marx and melodrama*: Wylie Sypher 'Aesthetic of Revolution: the Marxist Melodrama' in *The Kenyon Review*, summer 1948, pp. 431–44.

p. 44 *Start a business*: Yvonne Kapp, p. 45.

p. 44 *Marx and importance of clarity*: S. S. Prawer, pp. 159, 357.

p. 45 *Brainless*: Wilhelm Liebknecht, p. 82.

p. 45 *Lack of translation*: Kirk Willis 'The Introduction and Critical Reception of Marxist Thought in Britain, 1850–1900' in *The Historical Journal*, 20, 2, (1977) pp. 423, 442.

p. 45 *Cricket blue*: H. M. Hyndman *Record of an Adventurous Life* p. 20.

p. 46 *Workers' universities*: John Taylor *From Self-Help to Glamour: the Workingman's Club, 1860–1972* p. 93.

p. 46 *Millennium*: Edward Carpenter *My Days and Dreams* p. 246.

p. 46 *Revolutionary cabinet*: Francis Williams *Ernest Bevin* p. 23.

p. 46 *Monday morning*: Barbara W. Tuchman *The Proud Tower* p. 360.

p. 46 *Hyndman's business activities*: Chushichi Tzusuki *H. M. Hyndman and British Socialism* pp. 140–44.

p. 47 *Desperadoes*: Beatrice Webb, diary, 6 March 1924, quoted in Neal Wood *Communism and British Intellectuals* p. 75.

p. 47 *SDF membership*: P. A. Watmough 'The Membership of the Social Democratic Federation, 1885–1902' in *Bulletin of the Society for the Study of Labour History*, no 34, Spring 1977, pp. 35–40.

p. 47 *Marxism and unions*: see excellent essay by E. J. Hobsbawm 'Karl Marx and the British Labour Movement' in his *Revolutionaries* pp. 95–108.

p. 48 *Pedantic tone*: William Morris letter to J. Bruce Glasier, 9 March 1892, in William Morris Gallery, Walthamstow.

p. 48 *Sectarianism*: H. M. Hyndman, p. 444.

p. 48 *Support for institutions*: Ross McKibbin 'Why was there no Marxism in Great Britain?' in *English Historical Review*, vol XCIV, no 391, April 1984, p. 329.

p. 48 *The election*: Robert Tressell *The Ragged Trousered Philanthropists* pp. 526ff.

p. 49 *New SDF methods*: T. A. Jackson *Trials of British Freedom* p. 180.

p. 49 *Charles Booth*: H. M. Hyndman, pp. 331–2; for a spirited defence of the SDF and its influence, John Foster 'The Merits of the SDF' in *Bulletin of the Marx Memorial Library*, No 105, Autumn 1985, pp. 25–37.

p. 49 *100,000*: Bernstein quoted in Walter Kendall *The Revolutionary Movement in Britain, 1900–21* p. 323.

p. 49 *Connell's appearance*: Viscount Snowden *An Autobiography* volume one 1864–1919 p. 72.

p. 49 *Poachers' union*: J. R. Clynes *Memoirs* volume one 1863–1924 p. 87.

p. 50 *Spirit of revolt*: Mike Pentelow 'Early fighter in a tough game' in *Land Worker*, May 1990.

p. 50 *100 guinea dress*: Frances, Countess of Warwick *Afterthoughts* p. 161.

p. 50 *Meeting with Blatchford*: Frances, Countess of Warwick *Life's Ebb and Flow* p. 91.

p. 50 *Warwick's train*: E. J. Hobsbawm 'Hyndman and the SDF' in his *Labouring Men* p. 233.

p. 50 *Coronation*: Gareth Stedman Jones *Languages of Class* p. 211.

p. 51 *House of murderers*: Reg Groves *The Strange Case of Victor Grayson* p. 69.

p. 51 *Comments on Grayson*: Edward Carpenter, p. 260; and Laurence Thompson *Robert Blatchford* p. 202.

p. 51 *Grayson's disappearance*: David Clark *Victor Grayson. Labour's Lost Leader* pp. 125ff.

p. 51 *Lenin on Grayson*: David Clark, p. 3.

p. 52 *Union jack*: Prince Peter Kropotkin *Memoirs of a Revolutionist* p. 377.

p. 52 *British tolerance*: Colin Holmes 'Immigrants, Refugees and Revolutionaries' in special issue of *Immigrants and Minorities*, 'From the Other Shore', vol 2, no 3, November 1983, pp. 8–14.

p. 52 *Lenin and Nadia*: Nadezhda Krupskaya *Memories of Lenin*

p. 53 *Lenin and morality*: quoted in Anthony Wright *Socialisms* pp. 53–4.

p. 53 *Iskra*: Andrew Rothstein *Lenin in Britain* pp. 12–13.

p. 53 *Communist Club*: see Ivan Maisky *Journey into the Past passim*.

p. 53 *Mental dynamite*: Chushichi Tsuzuki, p. 56.

p. 54 *Brotherhood Church*: Marx Library Bulletin, July/September 1957, no 3, p. 4.

p. 54 *Long speeches*: Angelica Balabanoff quoted in Isaac Deutscher *The Prophet Armed: Trotsky 1879–1921* p. 140.

p. 54 *The 5th Congress*: Arthur P. Dudden and Theodore H. von Laue 'The RSDLP and Joseph Fels' in *American Historical Review*, vol LXI, no 1, October 1955, p. 26ff.

p. 54 *Daily Mail*: Dudden and von Laue, p. 27.

p. 55 *Webb on Fels*: Beatrice Webb *Our Partnership* p. 291.

p. 55 *Fels loan*: Mary Fels *Joseph Fels* p. 237.

p. 55 *Loan paid back*: Dudden and von Laue, p. 47.

CHAPTER THREE
Socialism and the New Life

p. 56 *1883 letter*: Philip Henderson (ed) *The Letters of William Morris to his Family and Friends* p. 176.

p. 56 *Ours*: Reg Groves *The Strange Case of Victor Grayson* p. 111.

p. 56 *Hyndman*: Stephen Winsten *Salt and his Circle* p. 64.

p. 56 *Marjorie Davidson*: Norman and Jeanne MacKenzie *The First Fabians* p. 95.

p. 56 *Oliviers*: Ruth Brandon *The New Women and the Old Men* p. 99.

p. 57 *Uncomfortable*: John Trevor *My Quest for God* p. 223.

p. 57 *Victorian age*: A. H. Moncur Sime *Edward Carpenter. His Ideas and Ideals* p. 140.

p. 58 *Socialism as religion*: MacKenzies p. 159; also see Stephen Yeo 'A New Life: The Religion of Socialism in Britain, 1883–1896' in *History Workshop*, issue 4, Autumn 1977, pp. 5–56.

p. 58 *Shining eyes*: Laurence Thompson *Robert Blatchford. Portrait of an Englishman* p. 101.

p. 58 *Christ and communism*: J. Keir Hardie *From Serfdom to Socialism* p. 217.

p. 59 *Other-worldliness*: F. G. Bettany *Stewart Headlam· A Biography* p. 217.

p. 59 *First socialist organisation*: Kenneth Leech 'Stewart Headlam, 1847–1924, and the Guild of St Matthew' in M. B. Reckitt (ed) *For Christ and the People* p. 64.

p. 59 *Trafalgar Square*: F. G. Bettany, p. 83.

p. 59 *Guild numbers*: Peter d'A. Jones *The Christian Socialist Revival 1877–1914* p. 129.

p. 60 *Socialist Salvation Army*: John Trevor, p. 242.

p. 60 *Socialist Ten Commandments*: Fred Reid 'Socialist Sunday Schools in Britain 1892–1939' in *International Review of Social History*, vol XI, 1966, pp. 18–47. There was also a Proletarian School Movement with its 'Ten Proletarian Maxims', a Proletarian Flute Band etc: see the monthly *Proletcult* published between March 1922 and July 1924 (copies in the British Library).

p. 60 *Singing*: Francis Meynell *My Lives* p. 111.

p. 60 *Labour Party hymn*: David Clark *Victor Grayson. Labour's Lost Leader* p. 35.

p. 60 *Religious movement*: Philip M. Williams *Hugh Gaitskell* p. 333.

p. 60 *Genesis*: report in *The Times*, 16 December 1989.

p. 61 *Great change*: see chapter 'How The Change Came' in G. D. H. Cole *William Morris* pp. 96–121.

p. 62 *Angry*: Asa Briggs (ed) *William Morris: News from Nowhere and Selected Writings and Designs* p. 13.

p. 62 *University education*: J. Bruce Glasier *William Morris and the Early Days of the Socialist Movement* p. 38.

p. 62 *Three Musketeers*: Jack Lindsay *William Morris: His Life and Work* p. 296.

p. 62 *Epilepsy*: Penelope Fitzgerald's introduction to William Morris *The Novel on Blue Paper* x.

p. 62 *Frightful ignorance*: 'William Morris's Socialist Diary' in *History Workshop*, issue 13, Spring 1982, p. 23.

p. 63 *Dreading quarrels*: Morris letter to J. Bruce Glasier, 5 December 1890, at William Morris Gallery, Walthamstow.

p. 63 *Poet Laureate*: E. P. Thompson *William Morris. Romantic to Revolutionary* p. 603.

p. 64 *£50 guarantee*: Andrew Rothstein 'William Morris at Clerkenwell' in *The Times*, 11 April 1966.

p. 64 *May Morris*: Edward Carpenter *My Days and Dreams* p. 218.

p. 64 *Engels on Morris*: R. Page Arnot *William Morris, The Man and the Myth* p. 57.

p. 64 *Fascist Weekly*: R. Page Arnot, p. 120.

p. 64 *Snowing paper*: William Morris *The Beauty of Life* p. 17.

p. 64 *Dream of London*: William Morris *The Earthly Paradise* (1868–70).

p. 65 *Most effective*: entry on Blatchford by Judith Fincher Laird and John Saville in Joyce Bellamy and John Saville (eds) *Dictionary of Labour Biography* volume 4, p. 37.

p. 66 *Manchester slums*: Robert Blatchford *My Eighty Years* pp. 186–7.

p. 66 *Pint of bitter*: Margaret Cole *Makers of the Labour Movement* p. 195.

p. 66 *Everything else*: Laurence Thompson, p. 114.

p. 66 *'Clarionese'*: Judith A. Fincher *The Clarion Movement: A Study of a Socialist Attempt to Implement the Co-operative Commonwealth in England 1891–1914* (Manchester: MA Thesis, 1971) p. 178.

p. 67 *Reader's comfort*: Robert Blatchford *English Prose And How To Write It* p. 18.

p. 67 *Least attention*: Robert Blatchford *Merrie England* pp. 104, 109.

p. 68 *Grayson quote*: Reg Groves, p. 80.

p. 68 *Hardie quote*: Laurence Thompson, p. 117.

p. 68 *Chartist women*: R. G. Gammage *History of the Chartist Movement 1837–1854* p. 77.

p. 68 *Male bonding*: Raphael Samuel in the *Guardian*, 4 October 1984.

p. 68 *Male trade unionists*: Iris Minor 'Working-Class Women and Matrimonial Law Reform 1890–1914' in D. Martin and D. Rubinstein *Ideology and the Labour Movement* p. 103.

p. 68 *Six sisters*: Edward Carpenter, p. 32.

p. 69 *Paddington Station*: Ruth Brandon, p. 178.

p. 69 *Aveling*: H. M. Hyndman *Further Reminiscences* p. 142.

p. 69 *Besant's enthusiasms*: Yvonne Kapp *Eleanor Marx* volume one p. 268.

p. 70 *Fifty-one books*: MacKenzies, p. 53.

p. 70 *A priest*: Annie Besant *Autobiographical Sketches* p. 39.

p. 70 *High ideas*: Annie Besant *An Autobiography* p. 177.

p. 70 *Prevent conception: Autobiographical Sketches*, p. 122.

p. 71 *Bradlaugh photographs*: 'Introduction' by Dr George Arundel to *An Autobiography* p. 14.

p. 72 *Belfort Bax*: Sheila Rowbotham *Hidden from History* p. 95.

p. 72 *Absolute equality*: William Morris letter to J. Bruce Glasier, 24 April 1886, at William Morris Gallery, Walthamstow.

p. 72 *Average wages*: Sheila Rowbotham, p. 108.

p. 72 *Six obstacles*: Barbara Drake *Women in Trade Unions* pp. 198–202.

p. 73 *Men not single-minded*: Hannah Mitchell *The Hard Way Up* p. 149.

p. 73 *Broken pane*: Mrs Pankhurst quoted in George Dangerfield *The Strange Death of Liberal England* p. 170.

p. 73 *Shaw and Headlam*: Andrew Davies *The East End Nobody Knows* p. 82.

p. 73 *Ideas of authority*: Oscar Wilde *De Profundis and other writings* p. 24.

p. 73 *Gross vices*: Sheila Rowbotham and Jeffrey Weeks *Socialism and the New Life* p. 21.

p. 73 *Shaw's letters*: Edward Carpenter *Edward Carpenter 1844–1929. A Restatement and Reappraisal* p. 23.

p. 74 *Cambridge*: Edward Carpenter, *My Days and Dreams*, p. 72.

p. 74 *Rigid vegetarians*: Gilbert Beith (ed) *Edward Carpenter In Appreciation* p. 220.

p. 74 *Forster*: Gilbert Beith, p. 76.

p. 75 *Crusaders*: Clement Attlee *As It Happened* p. 35.

p. 75 *Rank and file*: W. Stephen Sanders *Early Socialist Days* p. 98.

p. 76 *Magnetic force*: George Orwell *The Road to Wigan Pier* p. 152.

CHAPTER FOUR
Tho' Cowards Flinch And Traitors Sneer

p. 77 *Feel proud*: Howard Spring *Fame is the Spur* p. 262. Film and novel have different endings. Spring is more sympathetic towards Shawcross than Nigel Balchin, the writer of the screenplay. There is an excellent discussion of the film by Raphael Samuel in David Lusted (ed) *Raymond Williams: Film TV Culture* pp. 57–66; also see J. Richards and A. Aldgate *British Cinema and Society 1930–1970* pp. 75–86.

p. 77 *Mass meeting*: James Hinton *Labour and Socialism* p. 113.

p. 77 *The god*: *J. Ramsay MacDonald – Centenary Commemoration*, held at the House of Commons, 12 October 1966, p. 3.

p. 77 *Legendary being*: Egon Wertheimer *Portrait of the Labour Party* p. 176.

p. 78 *Eyes plucked*: Gwyn Williams in John Gorman *Banner Bright* p. 16.

p. 78 *Watchmaker*: Lord Elton *The Life of James Ramsay MacDonald* p. 28.

p. 78 *Bristol SDF*: Lord Elton, pp. 45, 47.

p. 78 *Cyclists' Club*: M. A. Hamilton *J. Ramsay MacDonald* p. 25.

p. 79 *Work on DNB*: M. A. Hamilton, p. 29.

p. 79 *Wanting to be Prime Minister*: Ruth Brandon *The New Women and the Old Men* p. 97.

p. 79 *Election address*: Lord Elton, p. 74.

p. 79 *Lincoln's Inn Fields*: Herbert Tracey *From Doughty Street to Downing Street* p. 58.

p. 80 *Churchill's remark*: J. R. Clynes *Memoirs* volume two 1924–1937, p. 200.

p. 80 *Economic creeds*: Ramsay MacDonald's foreword to Joe Corrie *The Road the Fiddler Went*.

p. 81 *Any interpretation*: Viscount Snowden *An Autobiography* volume one, p. 216.

p. 81 *Leave economics to Snowden*: Kenneth O. Morgan *Labour People* p. 23.

p. 82 *Rail strike violence*: Bob Holton *British Syndicalism 1900–1914* pp. 104–5.

p. 82 *Blue Book*: J. Ramsay MacDonald *Margaret Ethel MacDonald* p. 136.

p. 83 *Heart in grave*: David Marquand *Ramsay MacDonald* p. 135.

p. 83 *Cannot go back*: Ralph Miliband *Parliamentary Socialism* p. 44.

p. 83 *Danger of being outlawed*: W. Abendroth *A Short History of the European Working Class* p. 59.

p. 84 *Wells' remark*: Lord Elton, p. 248.

p. 84 *Plumstead Common*: M. A. Hamilton, p. 72.

p. 84 *Held party together*: Ross McKibbin *The Evolution of the Labour Party 1910–1924* p. 243.

p. 84 *1918 Act*: Ross McKibbin, xv.

p. 84 *Henderson influence*: Kenneth O. Morgan, p. 80.

p. 85 *Number of unions*: David Caute *The Left in Europe* p. 139.

p. 85 *Building of Transport House*: information from Regan Scott, Librarian, 6 March 1991.

p. 85 *Trade union influence*: David Coates *The Labour Party and the Struggle for Socialism* p. 13.

p. 86 *MacDonald's Welsh meeting*: description by Jim Griffiths quoted in David Coates, ix.

p. 86 *Maximisation*: David Howell *British Social Democracy* p. 32.

p. 87 *Change from bottom*: J. Ramsay MacDonald *Wanderings and Excursions* p. 285.

p. 87 *1919 strike*: quoted in Aneurin Bevan *In Place of Fear* pp. 40–1.

p. 88 *Label on coat*: Charles Loch Mowat *Britain Between The Wars* p. 147.

p. 88 *Free love*: Charles Loch Mowat, p. 169.

p. 88 *At Buckingham Palace*: J. R. Clynes, volume one, pp. 343–4.

p. 88 *Red Flag*: David Marquand, p. 304.

p. 88 *Webb's club*: Margaret Cole *Beatrice Webb* p. 141.

p. 88 *Constituents*: Viscount Snowden, volume two, pp. 662–3.

p. 89 *Shaw's peerage*: J. R. Clynes, volume two, p. 46.

p. 89 *18 million leaflets*: Keith Middlemas *Politics in Industrial Society* p. 202.

p. 90 *1924 broadcasts*: John Antcliffe 'Politics of the Airwaves' in *History Today*, March 1984, pp. 4–10.

p. 90 *Right improvisation*: Egon Wertheimer, p. 195.

p. 90 *Economic democracy*: Robert Boothby, John Loder, Harold Macmillan and Oliver Stanley *Industry and the State* p. 143.

p. 91 *Striking railwaymen*: Noreen Branson *Britain in the Nineteen Twenties* p. 181.

p. 91 *Consequences of victory*: Julian Symons *The General Strike* p. 143.

p. 91 *700 meetings*: R. E. Dowse *Left in the Centre* p. 128.

p. 91 *War-weary*: Julian Symons, *ibid*, X.

p. 92 *Recovery around corner*: Aneurin Bevan, p. 47.

p. 93 *Selfish ambition*: quoted in Henry Pelling (ed) *The Challenge of Socialism* p. 147.

p. 93 *Knapsack*: Egon Wertheimer, p. 175.

p. 93 *Backbenchers*: Robert Skidelsky *Politicians and the Slump* p. 392.

p. 93 *Earthly paradise*: Keith Laybourn *Philip Snowden: A Biography* p. 167.

p. 94 *Raised in atmosphere*: Keith Laybourn, p. 97; Churchill, p. 97.

p. 94 *Accumulated material*: Viscount Snowden, volume one, p. 103.

p. 94 *Not much chance*: Robert Skidelsky, p. 393.

p. 95 *No clear advice*: David Marquand, p. 792.

p. 95 *Snowden's broadcast*: Ralph Miliband *Parliamentary Socialism* p. 191.

p. 95 *Colne Valley*: J. Ramsay MacDonald – *A Centenary Commemoration*, p. 11.

p. 95 *Rubber stamp*: Lord Citrine *Men and Work* p. 288.

p. 96 *Lenin's comment*: Lenin on Ramsay MacDonald p. 19.

CHAPTER FIVE
British Revolutionaries in the 1920s

p. 97 *Lenin's name*: Harry Pollitt *Serving My Time* pp. 123, 129.

p. 97 *Not killing*: George Orwell *The English People* (1947) p. 40.

p. 97 *Maclean stamp*: Robert Chesshyre 'The Man Who Brought Britain To The Brink of Revolution' in *Observer* Magazine, 13 July 1980, p. 24.

p. 98 *Scots and Irish*: Leon Trotsky *Where Is Britain Going?* p. 44.

p. 98 *1,000 an acre*: Iain McLean *The Legend of Red Clydeside* p. 18.

p. 98 *Cricket on Sunday*: William Joss in P. M. Kemp-Ashraf and Jack Mitchell (eds) *Essays in Honour of William Gallacher* p. 44.

p. 98 *Gambling*: Guy Aldred *John Maclean* p. 33.

p. 98 *Little humour*: B. J. Ripley and J. McHugh *John Maclean* p. 2.

p. 99 *Blatchford and Marx*: Tom Bell *John Maclean. A Fighter for Freedom* p. 8.

p. 99 *Lecture notes*: Tom Bell, pp. 128–30.

p. 99 *Weekly attendance*: Nan Milton (ed) *In the Rapids of Revolution* p. 11.

p. 99 *Maclean's oratory*: Nan Milton *John Maclean* pp. 83–4.

p. 100 *Impact of October 1917*: Harry McShane and Joan Smith *No Mean Fighter* p. 94.

p. 100 *Poison and breakdown*: Ripley and McHugh, pp. 96, 102.

p. 100 *Churchill and mutinies*: Walter Kendall *The Revolutionary Movement in Britain 1900–21* p. 189.

p. 101 *Director of Intelligence*: James Hinton *Labour and Socialism* p. 134.

p. 101 *Newspaper reports*: Walter Kendall, p. 138; troops firing, p. 139.

p. 101 *No plan*: William Gallacher *Revolt on the Clyde* p. 226.

p. 102 *1918 election*: Christopher Harvie *No Gods and Precious Few Heroes* p. 22.

p. 102 *German waiters*: Chushichi Tsuzuki *H. M. Hyndman and British Socialism* p. 243.

p. 102 *Role of Theodore Rothstein*: hostile accounts in Raymond Challinor *The Origins of British Bolshevism*, Nan Milton and Walter Kendall; favourable in David Burke 'Theodore Rothstein, Russian Émigré and British Socialist' in *Immigrants and Minorities*, vol 2, no 3, November 1983 and John Saville's introduction to Theodore Rothstein *From Chartism to Labourism*.

p. 103 *£15,000*: Andrew Rothstein in *Labour Monthly*, vol 51, no 12, December 1967, p. 567.

p. 103 *£85,000*: Jack and Bessie Braddock *The Braddocks* p. 44.

p. 103 *Bickering delayed formation*: L. J. Macfarlane *The British Communist Party* pp. 47–56, 279.

p. 103 *Less interference*: Nan Milton, *Rapids*, p. 225.

p. 103 *Rothstein argument*: David Howell *A Lost Left* p. 200.

p. 104 *Maclean of England*: Nan Milton, *John Maclean*, p. 243.

p. 104 *Pankhurst episode*: Henry Pelling *The British Communist Party* pp. 19–20.

p. 104 *Got to learn*: Walter Kendall, p. 228.

p. 105 *Desire for peace*: Fernando Claudin *The Communist Movement: From Comintern to Cominform* p. 60.

p. 105 *Soviet idea*: Monty Johnstone 'Early Communist Strategy for Britain: An Assessment' in *Marxism Today*, September 1978, p. 287

p. 105 *Letter to Pravda*: Martin Durham 'British Revolutionaries and the Suppression of the Left in Lenin's Russia, 1918–1924' in *Journal of Contemporary History*, vol 20, no 2, April 1985, p. 214.

p. 105 *Imported ideas*: John S. Clarke *Pen Pictures of Russia Under The 'Red Terror'* pp. 188, 194.

p. 105 *Lion tamer*: Raymond Challinor *John S. Clarke* p. 14.

p. 105 *Telegram*: Betty D. Vernon *Ellen Wilkinson* p. 36.

p. 106 *Intellectuals and Communist Party*: Gary Werskey *The Visible College* p. 150; also Neal Wood *Communism and British Intellectuals* p. 24.

p. 106 *Mental wreck*: Dora B. Montefiore *From a Victorian to a Modern* p. 201.

p. 106 *Jamaican's letter*: Iain McLean, p. 244.

p. 106 *Learning off by heart*: Stuart Macintyre *A Proletarian Science, Marxism in Britian 1917–1933* p. 87.

p. 106 *Postage stamps and catechisms*: A. L. Morton in *Bulletin of the Marx Memorial Library*, no 106, spring 1985, p. 21.

p. 107 *Lenin's language*: Paul Johnson *A History of the Modern World* p. 55.

p. 107 *King Street*: Walter Kendall, p. 436 note 13; also on financial assistance, see Roderick Martin *Communism and the British Trade Unions 1924–1933* p. 44 and Hugo Dewar *Communist Politics in Britain* pp. 43, 87.

p. 107 *Pollitt and Internationale*: William Campbell *Villi the Clown* p. 21.

p. 108 *Bolshevik discipline*: George Lansbury *The Miracle of Fleet Street* p. 41.

p. 108 *Politburo*: Henry Pelling, p. 189; almost half were Scots. However Pelling's figures don't square with the lists of Central Committee members provided in Noreen Branson *History of the Communist Party of Great Britain 1927–1941* pp. 339–41.

p. 109 *Quarter in Labour Party*: Noreen Branson, p. 5.

p. 109 *Lenin Corners*: Harry McShane and Joan Smith, p. 213.

p. 109 *Recruits to Moscow*: for example, twenty Welsh miners were sent between 1928 and 1933, see Hywel Francis in *Journal of Contemporary History*, vol 5, no 3, 1970.

p. 109 *Pollitt to Moscow*: Henry Pelling, pp. 54–5.

p. 109 *Saklatvala censure*: *Worker's Life*, 5 August 1927; and *Dictionary of National Biography* p. 778.

p. 110 *Scruples*: David Marquand *Ramsay MacDonald* p. 19.

p. 110 *Racing tips*: see for example, *Daily Worker* 3 January 1930; 16 January 1930; 10 February 1930. The *Daily Herald* had faced the same problem ten years before: Raymond Postgate *The Life of George Lansbury* pp. 142–3.

p. 110 *Culture after revolution*: Andrew Rothstein 'The Workers' Culture' in *The Plebs*, February 1922, p. 41.

p. 110 *Young Pioneers*: Hywel Francis and David Smith *The Fed* p. 161; also see Stuart Macintyre *Little Moscows*.

p. 110 *High votes*: Stuart Macintyre *A Proletarian Science*, p. 32.

p. 111 *Spoiling ballot papers*: Michael Woodhouse and Brian Pearce *Essays on the History of Communism in Britain* p. 188.

p. 111 *Toilet paper*: Wal Hannington in Kemp-Ashraf and Mitchell, p. 32.

p. 111 *Jane Austen*: Vivien Morton and Stuart Macintyre *T. A. Jackson A Centenary Publication* p. 23.

p. 111 *Snowden on Mann*: Viscount Snowden *An Autobiography*, volume one 1864–1919, pp. 75–6.

p. 111 *1,000 arrests*: James Hinton and Richard Hyman *Trade Unions and Revolution* p. 47.

p. 111 *Communist Party's devotion to Moscow*: confirmed by John Saville *The Labour Movement in Britain* p. 53.

CHAPTER SIX

The Thirties

p. 115 *Fruitful conception*: A. L. Rowse 'The Significance of Marx' in *The Plebs*, March 1933, vol xxv, No 3, p. 61.

p. 115 *Enjoying a richer life*: A. J. P. Taylor *English History 1914–1945* p. 396.

p. 115 *Practical politics*: Hugh Dalton *Practical Socialism for Britain* p. 27.

p. 116 *20 million cinema-goers*: John Stevenson *Social Conditions in Britain Between the Wars* p. 43.

p. 116 *Jubilee celebrations*: George Orwell 'Patriots and Revolutionaries' in Victor Gollancz (ed) *The Betrayal of the Left* p. 244; fatalism of 1930s, A. H. Halsey *Change in British Society* p. 156.

p. 116 *Wrongs and remedies*: James Jupp *The Radical Left in Britain 1931–1941* p. 125.

p. 117 *Touching coat*: Naomi Mitchison *You May Well Ask* p. 185.

p. 117 *Brick through window*: St John B. Groser *Politics and Persons* pp. 22–3.

p. 117 *Lansbury's home*: Raymond Postgate *The Life of George Lansbury* p. 104; also Edgar Lansbury *George Lansbury* pp. 50, 67.

p. 117 *'John Bull of Poplar'*: entry by M. A. Hamilton in *The Dictionary of National Biography, 1931–1940* (Oxford: University Press, 1949) p. 525.

p. 118 *Rating value*: St John B. Groser, p. 25.

p. 118 *Contempt of court*: Noreen Branson *Poplarism, 1919–1925* p. 46.

p. 118 *Lansbury in Brixton*: Edgar Lansbury, pp. 73–5.

p. 118 *Lansbury's health*: Raymond Postgate, p. 291.

p. 118 *Christ Himself*: quoted in Bob Holman *Good Old George* p. 76.

p. 119 *Lovable figure*: A. J. P. Taylor, p. 191 fn. 3.

p. 119 *Not to be a Marxist*: Kathleen Raine *The Land Unknown* p. 92.

p. 119 *Intellectually disreputable*: Robert Blake *The Conservative Party from Peel to Churchill* p. 255.

p. 119 *Daily Express*: Alan Jenkins *The Thirties* p. 62.

p. 120 *Guest*: Carmel Haden Guest (ed) *David Guest. A Memoir*; for Madge, see his excellent article in *The Times Literary Supplement*, 14 December 1979; for Cornford, Pat Sloan (ed) *John Cornford. A Memoir*

p. 120 *Pym*: Hazel Holt and Hilary Pym (eds) *A Very Private Eye* p. 35.

p. 120 *October Club*: Stuart Samuels 'English Intellectuals and Politics in the 1930s' in Philip Reiff (ed) *On Intellectuals* pp. 213–4.

p. 120 *Queues for Laski*: Kingsley Martin *Father Figures* p. 157.

p. 120 *Cripps' diet*: Froom Tyler *Cripps* p. 12; and cold bath, Kenneth O. Morgan *Labour People* p. 163.

p. 121 *Gresford*: Froom Tyler, p. 23.

p. 121 *Twelve days' agonising*: Ben Pimlott 'The Socialist League: Intellectuals and the Labour Left in the 1930s' in *Journal of Contemporary History*, vol 6, no 3, 1971, p. 17.

p. 121 *Trevelyan's gates*: Philip M. Williams (ed) *The Diary of Hugh Gaitskell 1945–1956* p. 76, fn. 69.

p. 121 *Cripps' financial aid*: Ben Pimlott *Labour and the Left in the 1930s*, pp. 34–5.

p. 121 *Dictatorship*: Sir Stafford Cripps *Can Socialism Come by Constitutional Methods?* p. 5.

p. 122 *Financial controls*: Sir Stafford Cripps 'Democracy and Dictatorship' in *Political Quarterly*, October–December 1933, p. 478; and Sir Stafford Cripps *The Choice for Britain* p. 7.

p. 122 *Buckingham Palace*: Eric Estorick *Stafford Cripps* pp. 124–5.

p. 122 *Experts*: Sir Stafford Cripps, *The Choice for Britain*, p. 8.

p. 122 *Interesting meeting*: Lord Citrine *Men and Work* p. 300.

p. 123 *Huddle*: Ben Pimlott, The Socialist League, pp. 37, 38.

p. 123 *United Clothing Workers' Union*: S. W. Lerner *Breakaway Unions and the Small Trade Union* pp. 85–143.

p. 123 *Idea of solidarity*: Roderick Martin *Communism and the British Trade Unions 1924–1933* p. 189.

p. 123 *Comintern and Hitler*: Isaac Deutscher *The Prophet Outcast. Trotsky 1929–1940* p. 201.

p. 123 *European Popular Fronts*: D. E. McHenry *The Labour Party in Transition 1931–1938* p. 256.

p. 123 *United front*: Sir Walter Citrine *I Search for Truth in Russia* p. 286.

p. 124 *Orwell on Gollancz*: Ian Angus and Sonia Orwell (eds) *An Age Like This* p. 580.

p. 124 *Labour Party affiliation*: *Daily Worker*, 30 January 1936; Labour Party Conference Report 1936, 'British Labour and Communism' pp. 296–300.

p. 124 *Dropped dictatorship*: Hugo Dewar *Communist Politics in Britain* pp. 123–4.

p. 124 *Scrutinise books*: Noreen Branson *History of the Communist Party of Great Britain 1927–1941* p. 154.

p. 124 *Hammer and sickle*: see *Daily Worker*, 1 January 1938.

p. 124 *Hutt's review*: *Labour Monthly*, July 1937, pp. 382–6.

p. 124 *Withdraw book*: information from two Communist Party members of the 1930s, both of whom wish to remain anonymous.

p. 124 *Brighton turnover*: Ernie Trory *Between the Wars: Reflections of a Communist Organiser* p. 107.

p. 124 *Baffled*: Tom Campbell on 'Party education' in *Party Organiser*, no 1, July 1938, p. 22.

p. 125 *Girl Guides*: see 'Who can be a Member of the League?' in *Our Youth*, June 1938, no 3.

p. 125 *Scottish May Day*: Christopher Harvie *No Gods and Precious Few Heroes* p. 102.

p. 125 *Dissenters*: see the splendid article by E. P. Thompson 'Organising the Left' in *Times Literary Supplement*, 19 February 1971.

p. 125 *Rickword*: for information on Rickword, Slater, Swingler etc, John Lucas (ed) *The 1930s. A Challenge to Orthodoxy*

p. 125 *Hill as Gore*: Rodney Hilton in D. Pennington and K. Thomas (eds) *Puritans and Revolutionaries: Essays Presented to Christopher Hill* p. 6.

p. 125 *'Holorenshaw'*: Gary Werskey *The Visible College* p. 169.

p. 126 *Tawney's weavers*: quoted in *R. H. Tawney. A Portrait By Several Hands* p. 7.

p. 126 *Haldane popularising*: Charlotte Haldane *Truth Will Out* p. 21.

p. 126 *100,000 sales*: James Jupp, p. 93.

p. 127 *Dutt and Strachey*: see letters inside Dutt's personal copies held at the Marx Memorial Library, London.

p. 127 *Independent enterprise*: Hugh Thomas *John Strachey* p. 155.

p. 127 *Propaganda alienating*: Ruth Dudley Edwards *Victor Gollancz* p. 232.

p. 127 *Official history*: Dr John Lewis *The Left Book Club*.

p. 127 *Internal friction*: Stuart Samuels 'The Left Book Club' in *Journal of Contemporary History*, vol 1, no 2, 1966, pp. 71–2.

p. 127 *Anti-Fascist Association*: Hugh Thomas, p. 179.

p. 127 *250,000*: Victor Gollancz editorial in *Left News*, no 31, November 1938.

p. 128 *Lack of research*: G. D. H. Cole *History of the Labour Party from 1914* pp. 123–4.

p. 128 *Against intellectuals*: David Howell *British Social Democracy* p. 56; for the Conservatives, see John Ramsden *The Making of Conservative Party Policy*.

p. 128 *National Joint Council*: Roger Eatwell and Anthony Wright 'Labour and the Lessons of 1931' in *History*, February 1978.

p. 128 *Name change*: Roger Eatwell *The 1945–1951 Labour Governments* p. 26.

p. 129 *Chess sets*: Henry Pelling *A History of British Trade Unionism* p. 207.

p. 129 *Bleak assessment*: John Saville 'May Day 1937' in Asa Briggs and John Saville (eds) *Essays in Labour History 1918–1939* p. 239, a judgement repeated in Saville *The Labour Movement in Britain* pp. 72–3.

p. 129 *Loss of membership*: Tony Lane *The Union Make Us Strong* p. 131.

p. 129 *Scottish football*: Christopher Harvie, p. 120.

p. 129 *Pools*: George Orwell *The Lion and the Unicorn* p. 48 fn.

p. 130 *Middle way*: see Arthur Marwick 'Middle Opinion in the Thirties: Planning, Progress and Political "Agreement"' in *English Historical Review*, April 1964, pp. 285–98; and more recently, Elizabeth Durbin *New Jerusalems*

p. 130 *Soviet influence*: L. P. Carpenter 'Corporatism in Britain, 1930–1945' in *Journal of Contemporary History*, 1976, p. 10.

p. 130 *National Plan*: *Week-End Review*, 14 February 1931.

p. 130 *PEP*: Kenneth Lindsay 'Early Days of PEP' in *Contemporary Review*, February 1973, pp. 57–61.

p. 130 *For these publications generally*: John Stevenson *op cit*, pp. 227 ff.

p. 131 *Better than Labour Party*: Arthur Marwick 'The Labour Party and the Welfare State in Britain 1900–1948' in *American Historical Review*, vol LXXIII, no 2, 1967, p. 395.

p. 131 *Generous refuge*: Kenneth O. Morgan, p. 121.

p. 131 *Keir Hardie Night*: Ben Pimlott *Hugh Dalton* pp. 44–5.

p. 131 *Dalton and Keynes*: Ben Pimlott *Hugh Dalton* p. 160.

p. 132 *Keynes and middle way*: Stuart Holland 'Keynes and the Socialists' in Robert Skidelsky (ed) *The End of the Keynesian Era* p. 68. Also see the excellent article in the same collection by Robert Skidelsky, 'The Political Meaning of the Keynesian Revolution'.

p. 132 *I was alarmed*: Nicholas Davenport *Memoirs of a City Radical* p. 75.

p. 132 *Left-wing governments*: Hugh Gaitskell in Margaret Cole and Charles Smith (eds) *Democratic Sweden* p. 96.

p. 133 *400,000 copies*: Ben Pimlott *Hugh Dalton* p. 238.

p. 133 *1934 ballot*: James Jupp, p. 5.

p. 133 *Labour Party not campaigning*: John Saville, May Day 1937, p. 241.

p. 134 *NUWM 50,000*: John Callaghan *The Far Left in British Politics* p. 40.

p. 134 *Constitutional NUWM*: Chris Cook and John Stevenson 'Historical Hide and Seek' in the *Guardian*, 25 August 1978: Henry Pelling, pp. 64–5.

p. 134 *NUWM in Oxford*: Marion Slingova *Truth Will Prevail* p. 19; in Cambridge, Gary Werskey, p. 217.

p. 134 *Constant agitation*: A. L. Morton 'The 1930s' in *Bulletin of the Marx Memorial Library*, no 106, spring 1985, p. 23.

p. 134 *Barrier against fascism*: Wal Hannington *Never On Our Knees* pp. 330–1.

p. 134 *Withdrawal of regulations*: Ralph Miliband *Parliamentary Socialism* p. 215.

p. 135 *Book of illustrations*: Betty D. Vernon *Ellen Wilkinson* p. 76.

p. 135 *Jarrow*: J. B. Priestley *English Journey* p. 298.

p. 135 *Women discouraged*: Betty D. Vernon, p. 141.

p. 136 *BUF and Bermondsey*: Noreen Branson, pp. 168–71.

p. 136 *International solidarity*: Jack Jones foreword to Judith Cook *Apprentices of Freedom* viii.

p. 137 *Thirty-five committees*: Kingsley Martin, p. 111; for similar activity, for example Joe Jacobs *Out of the Ghetto* p. 214 and Douglas Hyde *I Believed* p. 58.

CHAPTER SEVEN

Grand Illusions

p. 138 *Opposing Chamberlain*: Dictionary of National Biography, 1961–1970 p. 416.

p. 139 *Gallacher's memoirs*: in the USSR 1937, William Gallacher *The Rolling of the Thunder* pp. 190–1; *The Last Memoirs of William Gallacher*

p. 139 *Spoke languages*: Ivor Montagu *The Youngest Son* p. 357.

p. 139 *Defending Trials*: see for example *Left Book Club News*, October 1936 and *Left News*, April 1937.

p. 139 *Chauffeur*: Margaret Cole *Beatrice Webb* p. 173.

p. 139 *Capital punishment*: Ruth Dudley Edwards *Victor Gollancz* p. 244.

p. 140 *Those who supported Stalin*: 'Nearly all moneyed people who enter the left-wing movement follow the "Stalinist" line as a matter of course.' – George Orwell writing in July 1938, *An Age Like This* p. 381.

p. 140 *Admirers of Nazis*: Richard Griffiths *Fellow Travellers of the Right*.

p. 140 *Churchill's article*: Robert Rhodes James *Churchill: A Study in Failure* pp. 291–2.

p. 141 *Discredit of Labour*: John Lehmann *The Whispering Gallery* p. 178.

p. 141 *Philby*: Kim Philby *My Silent War* p. 15.

p. 141 *Rejecting own society*: Paul Hollander *Political Pilgrims* p. 231.

p. 141 *Land of hope*: introduction by Harry M. Geduld to Bernard Shaw *The Rationalization of Russia* p. 31; earthly paradise, p. 82.

p. 141 *Future that works*: David Caute *The Fellow Travellers* p. 24.

p. 141 *Science is communism*: Gary Werskey *The Visible College* p. 176.

p. 141 *Blunt*: C. Day Lewis (ed) *The Mind in Chains* p. 108; Rickword, p. 245; Warner, p. 30 etc.

p. 142 *Prisoners not leaving*: Bernard Shaw, p. 91.

p. 142 *Enjoyable experience*: Pat Sloan *Soviet Democracy* p. 111.

p. 142 *Intourist*: Sylvia R. Margulies *The Pilgrimage to Russia* p. 63.

p. 142 *Waitresses*: Bernard Shaw, p. 16.

p. 142 *Statistics*: Sir Walter Citrine *I Search for Truth in Russia* pp. 92–3, 100.

p. 143 *Banner*: Bernard Shaw, p. 19.

p. 143 *Royalty*: Norman and Jeanne MacKenzie *The First Fabians* p. 407.

p. 143 *Krynin affair*: Harry M. Geduld introduction to Bernard Shaw, pp. 21–3.

p. 143 *Stalin at cinema*: see Robert Conquest *The Great Terror* p. 235.

p. 143 *98 of 139*: Ian Grey *Stalin* p. 276.

p. 143 *Military purges*: Volkogonov letter in the *Independent*, 19 September 1989.

p. 144 *Who to kill*: Bernard Shaw, p. 112.

p. 144 *The Webbs*: David Caute, p. 69.

p. 144 *Pritt's influence*: Joe Jacobs *Out of the Ghetto* p. 226.

p. 144 *Available proof*: D. N. Pritt *The Zinoviev Trial* p. 9.

p. 144 *More merciful*: Dudley Collard *Soviet Justice and the Trial of Radek and Others* p. 79.

p. 145 *Brockway's letter*: quoted in the obituary of Brockway by Raphael Samuel in the *Independent*, 2 May 1988.

p. 145 *Hotel Bristol*: Dr Friedrich Adler *The Witchcraft Trial in Moscow* p. 14.

p. 145 *Manchester Guardian*: Hugo Dewar 'The Moscow Trials' in *Survey*, no 41, April 1961, p. 93.

p. 145 *Recalcitrance*: F. A. Voigt *Unto Caesar* p. 344.

p. 145 *Daily Herald and New Statesman*: see Peter Deli 'The Image of the Russian Purges in the Daily Herald and the New Statesman' in *Journal of Contemporary History*, vol 20, no 2, 1985, pp. 261–82.

p. 146 *Emrys Hughes*: Hugo Dewar, p. 94.

p. 146 *Gramophone record*: Sir Walter Citrine, p. 256.

p. 146 *Street corners*: Tatiana Tchernavin *Escape from the Soviets* p. 65.

p. 146 *Novelists*: Vladimir Tchernavin *I Speak for the Silent* pp. 178–85.

p. 146 *Muggeridge*: quoted in Sylvia R. Margulies, p. 187.

p. 147 *All persecution capitalist*: Noreen Branson *History of the Communist Party of Great Britain 1927–1941* p. 247.

p. 147 *Not spreading doubts*: Arthur Horner *Incorrigible Rebel* pp. 214–15.

p. 147 *Private representations*: for example by J. D. Bernal, see Gary Werskey, pp. 209–10.

p. 147 *Simple choice*: Denis Healey *The Time of My Life* p. 34.

p. 147 *Modern political choice*: E. J. Hobsbawm 'Intellectuals and Communism' in his collection *Revolutionaries* p. 27.

p. 148 *Spilling blood*: H. S. Ferns *Reading from Right to Left* p. 129.

p. 148 *Breaking eggs*: Colin Welch 'Or the greatest liar?' in the *Spectator*, 22 September 1990.

p. 149 *A faith*: Cecil Day Lewis *The Buried Day* p. 209.

p. 149 *Breaking up meetings*: Joe Jacobs, p. 87.

p. 149 *Alan Sebrill*: Edward Upward *In the Thirties*, 1962, published as part of the trilogy *The Spiral Ascent* pp. 176–7.

p. 149 *Bigotry*: Margaret McCarthy *Generation in Revolt* p. 253; suicide, pp. 254–5.

CHAPTER EIGHT
New Worlds for Old?

p. 151 *Complacency*: quoted in Henry Pelling 'The 1945 General Election Reconsidered' in *Historical Journal*, 23, 2, 1980, p. 414.

p. 151 *Mildly disturbed*: Herbert Morrison *An Autobiography* p. 251.

p. 151 *George VI*: William Harrington and Peter Young *The 1945 Revolution* p. 207.

p. 152 *One syllable*: Douglas Jay quoted in Peter Hennessy 'The man who built the welfare state' in the *Economist*, 11 November 1989, p. 26.

p. 152 *Biscuits to dog*: Wilfred Fienburgh in Denis Healey *The Time of My Life* p. 153.

p. 152 *Haileybury House*: Clement Attlee *As It Happened* p. 19.

p. 152 *East London visitors*: George Lansbury *My Life* p. 130.

p. 153 *Violet Millar*: Trevor Burridge *Clement Attlee: A Political Biography* p. 55.

p. 153 *Greatest betrayal*: Clement Attlee, p. 74.

p. 154 *Intelligentsia*: Clement Attlee, p. 86.

p. 154 *'The Rabbit'*: Dalton quoted in T. D. Burridge *British Labour and Hitler's War* p. 42.

p. 154 *Wartime shift*: massively chronicled in Angus Calder *The People's War*, more briefly in Andrew Davies *Where Did the Forties Go?*

p. 154 *Iniquity*: Susan Briggs *Keep Smiling Through* p. 153.

p. 155 *Warfare, welfare*: Asa Briggs 'The Welfare State in Historical Perspective' in *Archives Europeennes De Sociologie*, 1961, no 2, p. 227.

p. 155 *Character of war*: Paul Addison *The Road to 1945* p. 129.

p. 155 *Factory feeling*: J. T. Murphy *Victory Production!* p. 82; Mass Observation *War Factory* p. 45; R. P. Lynton 'Factory Psychology in the Transition' in *Pilot Papers*, vol 1, no 1, January 1946, p. 68.

p. 155 *Palpable injustices*: Noel Annan *Our Age* p. 12.

p. 156 *Westminster Conservatives*: Paul Foot *The Politics of Harold Wilson* p. 341, fn.1.

p. 156 *No message*: Lord Moran *Churchill* p. 183.

p. 156 *Only a photograph*: Virginia Cowles *No Cause for Alarm* p. 72.

p. 157 *United Labour Party*: Charles Madge (ed) *Pilot Guide to The General Election* pp. 91–2.

p. 157 *Age of candidates*: Mark Abrams 'The Labour Vote in the General Election' in *Pilot Papers*, vol 1, no 1, January 1946, pp. 17–18.

p. 157 *Blackburn*: Wilfred De'Ath *Barbara Castle* p. 65.

p. 157 *Dictators*: Granville Eastwood *Harold Laski* p. 130.

p. 157 *Hustings*: William Harrington and Peter Young, p. 157.

p. 157 *Press equal*: Roger Eatwell *The 1945–1951 Labour Governments* pp. 41–2.

p. 157 *Epping count*: Leah Manning *A Life for Education* p. 164.

p. 157 *Servicemen's vote*: see Penny Summerfield 'Education and Politics in the British armed forces in the Second World War' in *International Review of Social History*, vol XXVI, 1981, part two, p. 133.

p. 158 *Two-thirds Labour*: Mark Abrams, p. 7.

p. 158 *Sweeping change*: Roger Eatwell, p. 50.

p. 158 *Labour's position*: E. P. Thompson 'Mr Attlee and the Gadarene Swine' in the *Guardian*, 3 March 1984.

p. 158 *First sensation*: Hugh Dalton *High Tide and After* p. 3.

p. 159 *Attlee's surprise*: Henry Pelling, p. 408

p. 159 *Sense of dramatic*: Kenneth O. Morgan *Labour in Power 1945–1951* p. 37.

p. 159 *Morrison's attempted coup*: Bernard Donoughue and G. W. Jones *Herbert Morrison* pp. 339–44.

p. 159 *Average age*: Anthony Howard 'We are the Masters now' in Michael Sissons and Philip French (eds) *The Age of Austerity 1945–1951* p. 20.

p. 159 *Attlee on bus*: Andrew Davies *The East End Nobody Knows* p. 98.

p. 159 *Morrison's dentures*: Bernard Donoughue and G. W. Jones, p. 175.

p. 160 *Scheming*: Bevin quoted in Bernard Donoughue and G. W. Jones, p. 346.

p. 160 *Kept us together*: quoted in Maurice Shock's entry on Attlee, *Dictionary of National Biography 1961–1970* p. 55.

p. 160 *Herbert's poem*: quoted in Trevor Burridge, p. 3.

p. 160 *Number of Fabians*: Norman and Jeanne MacKenzie *The First Fabians* p. 409.

p. 160 *Films*: for example, Ealing's *Hue and Cry* (1946) and *Passport to Pimlico* (1948).

p. 161 *Nationalisation proposals*: Clement Attlee, p. 165.

p. 161 *Workers' control*: Robert S. Dahl 'Workers' Control Of Industry And The British Labour Party' in *American Political Science Review*, vol XLI, October 1947, pp. 875–900.

p. 161 *Two papers*: Alan Sked and Chris Cook *Post-war Britain* p. 31; also Emmanuel Shinwell *Lead With The Left* p. 131.

pp. 161–2 *Iron*: Godfrey Hodgson 'The Steel Debates' in Michael Sissons and Philip French, p. 305.

p. 162 *No draft legislation*: Roger Eatwell, p. 49. Also see Richard Crossman's complaint that the Attlee government failed '. . . to do its homework in the years before it achieved power' in his essay 'The Lessons of 1945' in P. Anderson and R. Blackburn (eds) *Towards Socialism* p. 153.

p. 162 *Compensation figures*: see Robert A. Brady *Crisis in Britain* pp. 110–14; 146–7; 162–3; 245–51.

p. 162 *Ordinary resident*: Geoffrey Crowther 'British socialism on trial' in *Atlantic Monthly*, May 1949, p. 27.

p. 163 *Railway Review*: David Rubinstein *Socialism and the Labour Party: the Labour Left and Domestic Policy, 1945–1950* p. 6.

p. 163 *Jobs for boys*: for example, Acton Society Trust *The Men on the Boards* p. 12 and Acton Society Trust *The Worker's Point of View* pp. 7–8.

p. 163 *Company profits*: Dudley Seers *The Levelling of Incomes since 1938* p. 72.

p. 164 *Unilever figures*: A. A. Rogow with Peter Shore *The Labour Government and British Industry 1945–51* p. 62.

p. 164 *Dedicated Order*: Rodney Barker 'The Fabian State' in Ben Pimlott (ed) *Fabian Essays in Socialist Thought* p. 34.

p. 164 *Lack of suitable people*: Philip M. Williams (ed) *The Diary of Hugh Gaitskell 1945–1956* p. 89.

p. 164 *Shinwell's longevity*: Kenneth O. Morgan 'Britain in the Dark' in the *Guardian*, 24 April 1987.

p. 164 *Fuel crisis*: Tom Harrisson 'British Opinion Moves Towards a New Synthesis' in *Public Opinion Quarterly*, vol 11, no 3, Fall 1947, p. 336.

p. 165 *British idea*: Sir William Beveridge *The Pillars of Security* p. 143.

p. 165 *National Insurance benefits*: James Harvey and Katherine Hood *The British State* p. 237.

p. 165 *Salaried service*: D. Stark Murray *Why A National Health Service?* p. 80.

p. 165 *Health centres*: Arthur Marwick 'The Labour Party and the Welfare State in Britain' in *American Historical Review*, December 1967, p. 402.

p. 166 *Debate on education*: see conflicting views of D. Rubinstein and W. Hughes in *History Workshop Journal*, no 7, Spring 1979, pp. 156–69.

p. 166 *One hour*: Hugh Dalton, p. 352.

p. 166 *Section 132*: Janet Minihan *The Nationalization of Culture* p. 242.

p. 167 *200 Acts*: Herbert Morrison *The Peaceful Revolution* p. 90.

p. 167 *Pethick Lawrence*: William Golant 'Clem and Ernie' in *The Times*, 29 November 1980.

p. 167 *Hostile Press*: James Margach *The Abuse of Power* p. 86.

p. 167 *Housewives' League*: Elizabeth Wilson *Only Halfway To Paradise* p. 167.

p. 168 *Equality of distribution*: Dudley Seers, p. 72.

p. 168 *Mr Cube*: A. A. Rogow with Peter Shore, pp. 142–5; also Henry Pelling *The Labour Governments, 1945–1951* pp. 217, 233.

p. 169 *Compromise*: Clement Attlee, p. 163.

p. 169 *Basically Victorian*: Trevor Burridge, p. 10.

p. 169 *Young Haileyburians*: Kenneth Harris *Attlee* p. 406.

p. 169 *Covenant*: Kenneth O. Morgan, p. 308.

p. 169 *Equal pay*: Kenneth O. Morgan, p. 56.

p. 169 *Lack of constitutional conflict*: David Marquand *The Politics of Nostalgia*, University of Salford inaugural lecture, 25 October 1979, no pagination.

p. 169 *Ready for radical action*: Mass Observation *Peace and the Public* p. 13.

p. 170 *Ealing and bureaucracy*: films include *Passport to Pimlico* (1948), *Whisky Galore* (1949) and *The Lavender Hill Mob* (1951).

p. 170 *William Morris*: E. J. Hobsbawm 'Morris on Art and Socialism' in *Our Time*, April 1948, p. 176.

p. 170 *Greyness*: John Campbell *Nye Bevan and the Mirage of British Socialism* p. 365.

CHAPTER NINE

With Us or Against Us?

p. 171 *Pope Pius*: quoted in Donald Sassoon *The Strategy of the Italian Communist Party* p. 59.

p. 171 *Lawther*: Mark Jenkins *Bevanism. Labour's High Tide* p. 180.

p. 171 *Humanity*: Christopher Hill 'Stalin and the Science of History' in *Modern Quarterly*, vol 8, no 4, autumn 1953, p. 212.

p. 172 *Bristol Cathedral*: Francis Williams *Ernest Bevin* p. 20.

p. 172 *'Boss Bevin'*: Francis Williams, p. 116.

p. 173 *Stalin and imposing system*: Roger Pethybridge 'The Soviet Union' in *History Today*, vol 33, October 1983, p. 30.

p. 174 *Taking too seriously*: Denis Healey *The Time of My Life* p. 101.

p. 174 *Koestler*: Bill Jones *The Russia Complex* p. 185.

p. 174 *Sunday Times*: Richard Fletcher *The CIA and the Labour Movement* p. 5.

p. 174 *Lovestone unmarried*: see his obituary in the *Guardian*, 12 March 1990.

p. 174 *'Scarface'*: obituary of Brown in the *Daily Telegraph*, 17 February 1989.

p. 175 *Details of US finance*: Trevor Barnes 'The Secret Cold War' in *The Historical Journal*, vol 24, no 2, 1981 and vol 25, no 3, 1982; Don Thomson and Rodney Larson *Where were you, brother?*; Roy Godson *American Labor and European Politics*.

p. 175 *Crusade*: Anthony Sampson *Macmillan* pp. 88–9.

p. 175 *Orwell's lists*: Bernard Crick *George Orwell. A Life* p. 388.

p. 175 *Strike-breaking*: Peter Hennessy and Keith Jeffrey 'How Attlee stood up to strikers' in *The Times*, 20 November 1979.

p. 175 *Appeasement analogy*: Anne Deighton 'Introduction' in Anne Deighton (ed) *Britain and the First Cold War* p. 5.

p. 176 *IRD*: David Leigh in the *Guardian*, 27 January, 1978; and *Frontiers of Secrecy* pp. 218–24; 'The Ministry of Truth' in *The Leveller*, March 1978, no 13, pp. 11–13; Richard Fletcher in the *Observer*, 29 January 1978.

p. 176 *Outlawing CP*: Peter Wilby '"Conspiracy" obsessed the Attlee Cabinet' in *The Sunday Times*, 4 January 1981.

p. 176 *200 surveillances*: Carl Bernstein *Loyalties* p. 151.

p. 177 *Great Fear*: David Caute *The Great Fear*

p. 177 *Civil service vetting*: Eleanor Bontecou 'The English Policy' in *The Federal Loyalty-Security Program* pp. 251–73.

p. 177 *Martyrs*: Peter Hennessy 'Successful cold war purge without hysteria' in *The Times*, 6 January 1981.

p. 177 *Comparison USA/UK*: Herbert H. Hyam 'England and America: Climates of Tolerance and Intolerance' in D. Bell (ed) *The Radical Right* pp. 269–306.

p. 177 *Bernal*: Gary Werskey *The Visible College* p. 278 and Maurice Goldsmith *Sage* p. 189.

p. 177 *Taylor*: A. J. P. Taylor *A Personal History* p. 234.

p. 177 *Summer 1948*: interview with E. J. Hobsbawm in *Radical History Review*, no 19, winter 1978–79, pp. 111–31.

p. 177 *Actors*: see, for example, the obituary of Alex McCrindle in the *Independent*, 10 May 1990.

p. 177 *Cricket match*: Ivor Montagu *The Youngest Son* p. 60.

p. 178 *Defence figures*: P. S. Gupta *Imperialism and the British Labour Movement, 1914–1964* p. 284

p. 178 *Ugh*: Bill Jones, p. 176.

p. 178 *United States of Europe*: Francis Williams, pp. 152, 153.

p. 178 *Foreigners*: Denis Healey, p. 353.

p. 178 *Bevin v Europe*: Lord Gladwyn *The European Idea* pp. 45, 50; also Richard Mayne *Postwar* p. 304.

p. 179 *Durham miners*: Bernard Donoughue and G. W. Jones *Herbert Morrison. Portrait of a Politician* p. 481.

p. 179 *Drawing distinction*: Iain McLaine *Ministry of Morale* pp. 208–9.

p. 180 *Stalin's love*: Milovan Djilas *Conversations with Stalin* p. 82.

p. 180 *Czechoslovakia*: see Karel Kaplan *The Short March* pp. 133–47.

p. 180 *Opposition*: William Gallacher *The Case for Communism* pp. 134–5.

p. 180 *Party meeting*: E. P. Thompson 'Edgell Rickword' in *PN Review*, vol 6, no 1, supplement, XXVI–XXVII.

p. 181 *Comrade Stalin*: Eric Heffer 'Joseph Stalin' in *The Independent Magazine*, 30 December 1989.

p. 181 *Standing up*: Gary Werskey, p. 311.

p. 181 *Sebrill and trembling*: Edward Upward *The Spiral Ascent* p. 470.

p. 181 *Hate America*: Neal Wood *Communism and British Intellectuals* p. 181.

p. 181 *Klugmann in Cairo*: Basil Davidson *Special Operations Europe* pp. 83–7.

p. 182 *Cold War pressure*: David Rubinstein *Socialism and the Labour Party: The Labour Left and Domestic Policy, 1945–1950* p. 14.

p. 182 *Nye and Hitler*: Janet Morgan (ed) *The Backbench Diaries of Richard Crossman* p. 410.

p. 183 *The Fed*: Will Paynter *My Generation* p. 110.

p. 183 *My truth*: Jennie Lee *My Life with Nye* p. 211.

p. 183 *Grandfather in sack*: Arthur Horner *Incorrigible Rebel* p. 11; Bevan's father, Aneurin Bevan *In Place of Fear* p. 45.

p. 184 *First impression*: Aneurin Bevan, p. 26.

p. 184 *Nunnery*: Jennie Lee *Tomorrow is a New Day* p. 151.

p. 184 *Bevan's manifesto*: Douglas Hill (ed) *Tribune 40* p. 27.

p. 184 *Tredegar*: Michael Foot *Aneurin Bevan 1897–1945* p. 66.

p. 184 *Riveting championing*: Hywel Francis and Dai Smith *The Fed* p. 434.

p. 185 *Montgomery*: Michael Stewart *Life and Labour* p. 71.

p. 185 *Palace revolutions*: Michael Foot *Aneurin Bevan 1945–1960* p. 92.

p. 185 *Trade unions' influence*: Geddes quoted in Martin Harrison *Trade Unions And The Labour Party Since 1945* p. 195.

p. 185 *Labour Party and change*: Richard Crossman *Planning for Freedom* p. 40.

p. 186 *Anti-communism*: E. P. Thompson 'The Peculiarities of the English' in *The Poverty of Theory* p. 75.

p. 186 *Deakin's sustained commentary*: Kenneth O. Morgan *Labour in Power, 1945–1951* p. 76.
p. 186 *Moronic crowd*: Leslie Hunter *The Road to Brighton Pier* p. 85.
p. 186 *Death of cuts*: Castle quoted in Christopher Driver *The Disarmers* p. 84.
p. 186 *Carron's techniques*: see Lewis Minkin *The Labour Party Conference* pp. 185–7 for a hilarious description.
p. 186 *Shut your gob*: Michael Foot, p. 377; to be fair to Lawther, he then went on to say, 'If your wisdom were commensurate with your clamour, you would be wise' – Leslie Hunter, p. 54.
p. 187 *Forty-seven Bevanites*: Ian Mikardo *Back-bencher* p. 120.
p. 187 *Bad atmosphere*: see, for example, Jack and Bessie Braddock *The Braddocks* p. 203.
p. 187 *Lost Sheep*: Kenneth O. Morgan, p. 67.
p. 187 *Versus expulsions*: Mark Jenkins, p. 182.
p. 187 *No society*: Aneurin Bevan, p. 100; obligation, pp. 201–2.
p. 188 *Not interested in policy*: Barbara Castle 'Crossman's last diaries' in *The Listener*, 5 March 1981.
p. 188 *Planned economy*: R. H. S. Crossman 'The Affluent Society' in *Planning for Freedom* p. 96; terrifying contrast, p. 120.
p. 188 *Not a team player*: Ian Mikardo, p. 151; avoided decisions, p. 109.
p. 188 *Dominates discussions*: Janet Morgan (ed) p. 53.
p. 188 *Didn't grow up*: Anthony Howard *Crossman* pp. 162–3.
p. 188 *Rebel and leader*: Janet Morgan (ed), p. 406.
p. 189 *Labour Left squeezed*: David Howell *The Rise and Fall of Bevanism* p. 35.
p. 189 *Labour Right*: Bill Jones, p. 213.
p. 189 *Our goals*: Marcuse quoted in Nigel Young *An Infantile Disorder?* p. 40.

CHAPTER TEN

Expanding Horizons

p. 190 *1956 placard*: Alfred Grosser *The Western Alliance* p. 145.
p. 190 *Abstinence*: C. A. R. Crosland *The Future of Socialism* p. 524.
p. 190 *Lounge lizard*: John Campbell *Nye Bevan and the Mirage of British Socialism* pp. 64ff.
p. 190 *Bevan's poetry*: Jennie Lee *My Life with Nye* p. 309.
p. 190 *Crosland's girlfriends*: Susan Crosland *Tony Crosland* p. 64.
p. 190 *Dark Satanic things*: C. A. R. Crosland, p. 522.
p. 191 *Fabians and arts*: I. M. Brittain *Fabianism and Culture* pp. 177–80, 209, 210, 212.
p. 191 *Shaw's complaint*: D. D. Egbert *Social Radicalism and the Arts* p. 44.
p. 191 *Moral principle*: B. Farrington in *The Communist Answer to the Challenge of Our Time* p. 47.
p. 191 *Warning members*: Mark Jenkins *Bevanism. Labour's High Tide* p. 210.
p. 191 *Haldane divorce*: Charlotte Haldane *Truth Will Out* p. 176.
p. 191 *Not dragging in sex*: Dora Russell *The Tamarisk Tree* p. 172.
p. 192 *Effective contraception*: Naomi Mitchison *You May Well Ask* p. 69; see the whole chapter 'Patterns of Loving' pp. 69–81.
p. 192 *Twelve hours*: Margery Spring Rice *Working-Class Wives, Their Health and Conditions* passim.
p. 192 *Freezing attitudes*: Robert Hewison *In Anger: Culture in the Cold War 1945–60* p. 122. It should also be noted that a homosexual such as the Labour MP Tom Driberg never gained even junior ministerial office; in his memoirs Driberg claimed that this was due to Clement Attlee and Harold Wilson being 'deeply prejudiced puritans': Tom Driberg *Ruling Passions* p. 198.
p. 193 *Cars and television*: Michael Pinto-Duschinsky 'Bread and Circuses? The Conservatives

in Office, 1951–1964' in Vernon Bogdanor and Robert Skidelsky (eds) *The Age of Affluence 1951–1964* p. 56.; also see Arthur Marwick *British Society Since 1945* pp. 18, 114ff.

p. 193 *Depressing life*: obituary of Plunket Greene in the *Daily Telegraph*, 9 May 1990.

p. 193 *Nervous breakdown*: Miriam Gross 'An Interview with Eric Hobsbawm' in *Time and Tide*, Autumn 1985, p. 54.

p. 193 *Thirty-eight friends*: Vittorio Vidali *Diary of the Twentieth Congress of the Communist Party of the Soviet Union* p. 18.

p. 194 *Sun spots*: Dutt quoted in Henry Pelling *The British Communist Party* p. 170.

p. 194 *Pritt*: See D. N. Pritt *Brasshakts and Bureaucrats*, p. 189.

p. 194 *Pollitt*: John Mahon *Harry Pollitt*.

p. 194 *Pollitt not recovering*: Jimmy Reid *Reflections of a Clyde-built Man* p. 40.

p. 194 *Closing down CP*: Vittorio Vidali, p. 63.

p. 195 *Reactions*: G. W. Grainger 'The Crisis in the British Communist Party' in *Problems of World Communism*, vol VI, no 2, March–April 1957, pp. 8–14; also see the essays in Ralph Miliband and John Saville (eds) *The Socialist Register 1976*.

p. 195 *CP officials*: Kenneth Newton *The Sociology of British Communism* p. 11, n.11.

p. 195 *Daly's complaint*: Douglas Hill (ed) *Tribune 40* p. 114.

p. 195 *Saw for myself*: Peter Fryer *Hungarian Tragedy* p. 7; speak one's mind, p. 8; a tragedy, p. 9.

p. 196 *Appeals to loyalty*: Llew Gardner in the *New Statesman*, 29 October 1976.

p. 196 *Best not leaving*: Henry Pelling, p. 180.

p. 197 *Khrushchev*: Veljko Micunovic *Moscow Diary* p. 134.

p. 197 *Party held together*: Mervyn Jones *Chances. An Autobiography* p. 117.

p. 197 *Political trance*: Mervyn Jones 'Days of Tragedy and Farce' in Ralph Miliband and John Saville (eds) *The Socialist Register* 1976 p. 82.

p. 197 *Typology*: Nigel Young *An Infantile Disorder?* p. 310; encounter group, p. 53.

p. 197 *Line on love*: Philip Toynbee *Friends Apart* p. 61.

p. 198 *From beginning*: Hall quoted in Ronald Fraser *1968* p. 30.

p. 198 *Morris*: E. P. Thompson foreword to revised edition *William Morris Romantic to Revolutionary* ix–xi.

p. 198 *Dictatorship of proletariat*: G. D. H. Cole *William Morris as a Socialist* p. 16.

p. 198 *Arnold Kettle*: quoted in E. P. Thompson *The Poverty of Theory* p. 75.

p. 199 *Comprehensive redevelopment*: Raphael Samuel 'Born-again Socialism' in Oxford University Socialist Group *Out of Apathy* p. 41; the family etc, p. 52.

p. 199 *Johnson's proposals*: Paul Johnson 'A Sense of Outrage' in Norman Mackenzie (ed) *Conviction*, pp. 202–17.

p. 199 *Gaitskell song*: Christopher Driver *The Disarmers* p. 61.

p. 199 *Bevan and election*: Philip M. Williams *Hugh Gaitskell* p. 297.

p. 200 *Who's Who*: Christopher Driver, p. 44.

p. 201 *Advice to Marchers*: David Widgery *The Left in Britain 1956–1968* p. 104.

p. 201 *Graffiti*: Peggy Duff *Left, Left, Left* p. 116.

p. 201 *Middle-class*: Richard Taylor 'The Labour Party and CND: 1957–1964' in R. Taylor and N. Young (eds) *Campaigns for Peace* p. 115.

p. 201 *Not working class*: John Callaghan *The Far Left in Britain*, X.

p. 201 *Orderly*: Peter Cadogan 'From Civil Disobedience to Confrontation' in R. Benewick and T. Smith (eds) *Direct Action and Democratic Politics* p. 169.

p. 201 *Role of women*: Mervyn Jones *Chances*, pp. 150–1.

p. 201 *Duff*: *Left, Left, Left*; also Hugh Hebert 'Unarmed combat' in the *Guardian*, 18 January 1980.

p. 202 *Macmillan's concern*: David Walker 'Macmillan ordered secret nuclear campaign' in *The Times*, 1 January 1990.

p. 202 *Moral indignation*: Robert Taylor 'The Campaign for Nuclear Disarmament' in Vernon Bogdanor and Robert Skidelsky (eds) pp. 250–1.

p. 202 *Professional politicians*: Mervyn Jones *Chances* p. 180.

p. 202 *Calculating machine*: it is possible Bevan was in fact referring to Attlee, see John Campbell *Nye Bevan and the Mirage of British Socialism* p. 293.

p. 203 *Attlee silence*: Philip M. Williams (ed) *The Diary of Hugh Gaitskell 1945–1956* p. 333.

p. 203 *Dalton's help*: Stephen Haseler *The Gaitskellites* p. 36.

p. 203 *Battle for power*: Williams *Hugh Gaitskell*, p. 183.

p. 204 *The State*: John Strachey *Contemporary Capitalism* p. 246 fn.

p. 204 *Predicting Thatcherism*: Michael Newman *John Strachey* p. 146.

p. 204 *Criticism of Crosland*: for example, Anthony Arblaster 'Anthony Crosland: Labour's Last Revisionist' in *Political Quarterly*, 48 (4), 1977, pp. 416ff.

p. 204 *Anglo-Saxon economies*: C. A. R. Crosland *The Future of Socialism* xi.

p. 204 *Anarchist and libertarian*: C. A. R. Crosland, 1956 edition, p. 522.

p. 204 *Old dreams dead*: C. A. R. Crosland, 1956 edition, p. 99.

p. 205 *Revisionism*: Elizabeth Durbin *New Jerusalems* p. 280.

p. 205 *Bevan and wealth*: John Campbell, xv, p. 363.

p. 205 *Change mood*: Vernon Bodganor 'The Labour Party in Opposition, 1951–1964' in Bogdanor and Skidelsky (eds), p. 95.

p. 205 *Luxuries and gadgets*: R. H. S. Crossman *Planning for Freedom* p. 100.

p. 205 *Glad to see people better-off*: quoted in Lord Windlesham *Communication and Political Power* p. 266.

p. 205 *Broaden appeal*: David Rubinstein *Socialism and the Labour Party: The Labour Left and Domestic Policy 1945–50* p. 22.

p. 206 *Bad Godesberg*: William E. Paterson 'The German Social Democratic Party' in William E. Paterson and Alastair H. Thomas (eds) *Social Democratic Parties in Western Europe* p. 185.

p. 206 *Different manifestos*: Williams, *Hugh Gaitskell* p. 273.

p. 206 *Name Labour*: Jay's article is reprinted in Douglas Jay *Change and Fortune* pp. 273–5.

p. 207 *Rationality*: Roy Jenkins on Gaitskell in W. T. Rodgers (ed) *Hugh Gaitskell* p. 126.

p. 207 *Genesis*: Vernon Bogdanor in Bodganor and Skidelsky (eds) p. 100.

p. 207 *Nationalisation*: Geoffrey Goodman *The Awkward Warrior* p. 242.

p. 208 *CDS and Europe*: Stephen Haseler, pp. 227–36.

p. 208 *England's Jerusalem*: Michael Postan in W. T. Rodgers (ed), p. 62.

p. 208 *A thousand years*: Hugh Gaitskell *Britain and the Common Market* p. 12.

p. 208 *History books*: John Barnes 'The Record' in David McKie and Chris Cook (eds) *The Decade of Disillusion*, p. 17.

CHAPTER ELEVEN

Harold Wilson's New Britain

p. 209 *Men with fire*: Clive Ponting *Breach of Promise* p. 15.

p. 210 *Conservative techniques*: Keith Middlemas *Politics in Industrial Society* pp. 338, 354–5.

p. 210 *Attlee's visit*: Michael Cockerell *Live from Number 10* p. 40.

p. 210 *Bevan and poetry of politics*: Roy Hattersley 'New Blood' in G. Kaufman (ed) *The Left* p. 158.

p. 210 *Gaitskell and TV*: Philip M. Williams *Hugh Gaitskell* p. 248.

p. 210 *Wilson and TV*: Michael Cockerell, pp. 87ff, 117.

p. 211 *Wilson's speeches*: John Barnes 'The Record' in David McKie and Chris Cook (eds) *The Decade of Disillusion* p. 19.

p. 211 *Industrial technology*: Paul Foot *The Politics of Harold Wilson* p. 148.

p. 211 *Ears of corn*: Lewis Minkin *The Labour Party Conference* p. 232.

p. 212 *Excitement*: Tony Benn *Out of the Wilderness: Diaries 1963–67* p. 13.

p. 212 *Eight firsts*: Denis Healey *The Time of My Life* p. 345.

p. 212 *Cabinet dissensions*: the bitterness was nothing compared with the venom among Wilson's own staff: for just one (extended) example, see Joe Haines, Wilson's Press secretary, and his diatribe against Marcia Williams in *The Politics of Power* pp. 156ff.

p. 212 *Ambition*: Philip M. Williams (ed) *The Diary of Hugh Gaitskell 1945–1956* p. 46.

p. 213 *Ridiculous shoestring*: George Brown *In My Way* p. 96.

p. 213 *Manifesto and social issues*: Michael Hatfield *The House The Left Built* pp. 28–9.

p. 213 *Governor of Bank*: Harold Wilson *The Labour Governments 1964–1970* p. 37.

p. 214 *Devaluation papers*: Peter Kellner and Christopher Hitchens *Callaghan: The Road to Number Ten* p. 50.

p. 214 *Characteristic of system*: Douglas Jay *Change and Fortune* p. 296.

p. 214 *Secret US agreement*: see chapter 'The American Connection' in Clive Ponting, pp. 40–60.

p. 214 *Get free of America*: George Orwell *Collected Essays, Journalism and Letters, volume 4* p. 426.

p. 215 *Britain's economic power*: Leslie Stone 'Britain and the World' in David McKie and Chris Cook (eds), p. 127.

p. 215 *Idea of planning*: Herbert Morrison *The Peaceful Revolution* p. 85.

p. 215 *Issue now*: C. A. R. Crosland *The Future of Socialism* p. 501.

p. 216 *Modernisation committees*: Richard Mayne *Postwar* p. 162.

p. 216 *Stop-go*: David Marquand *The Unprincipled Society* p. 44.

p. 216 *DEA in taxi*: George Brown, p. 97, though Brown says this was not 'the whole truth'.

p. 216 *No headquarters*: Geoffrey Goodman *The Awkward Warrior* p. 403.

p. 217 *Questionnaire*: Peter Sinclair 'The Economy – A Study In Failure' in David McKie and Chris Cook (eds), p. 103.

p. 217 *Hadn't run anything*: Tam Dalyell *Dick Crossman: A Portrait* p. 48.

p. 217 *Lack of success*: entry for 11 June 1968 in Richard Crossman *The Diaries of a Cabinet Minister*, Volume Three 1968–70, p. 57.

p. 217 *Britain forty-two times*: Clive Ponting, p. 160.

p. 218 *Independent strategy*: David Howell *British Social Democracy* p. 250.

p. 218 *Artful Dodger*: R. W. Johnson *The Politics of Recession* p. 270.

p. 218 *Takes six months*: Crosland quoted in Richard Rose *Politics in England* p. 183.

p. 218 *No Morrison*: Kenneth O. Morgan *Labour in Power 1945–1951* p. 51.

p. 219 *Unhappy government*: Douglas Jay, p. 411.

p. 219 *Cabinet and leaks*: Tony Benn quoted in Philip Whitehead *The Writing On The Wall* p. 15.

p. 219 *Crossman on Wilson*: entries for 6 December 1964, 13 June 1965, 11 December 1966 and 27 April 1969 in Richard Crossman *The Diaries of a Cabinet Minister*, Volume One 1964–66, pp. 88, 249; Volume Two 1966–68 (1976), p. 169; and Volume Three 1968–70 (1977), p. 459 respectively.

p. 219 *Manipulator*: Tony Benn, p. 391.

p. 219 *Trouble with Harold*: Susan Crosland *Tony Crosland* p. 184.

p. 219 *Wilson's energy*: Muriel Box *Rebel Advocate* p. 200; this book contains an appendix detailing the seventy-eight different subjects on which the Lord Chancellor, Lord Gardiner, spoke to the House of Lords between April 1966 and November 1967 alone, pp. 234–5.

p. 220 *Rich poorer*: Michael Stewart in Wilfred Beckerman (ed) *The Labour Government's Economic Record* pp. 110–11.

p. 221 *Appalling social record*: David Coates *The Labour Party and the Struggle for Socialism* p. 115.

p. 221 *Etiquette*: entry for 22 October 1964 in Richard Crossman, Volume One, p. 29.

p. 222 *Televising Commons*: Anthony Howard *Crossman The Pursuit of Power* pp. 281–2.

p. 222 *Fulton Committee*: Clive Ponting, p. 262.

p. 222 *German and French reorganisation*: see the essays by Pierre Birnbaum and Joachim Hirsch in Richard Scase (ed) *The State in Western Europe*.

p. 223 *Rhodesia and oil*: the whole sorry story is told in Martin Bailey *Oilgate*.

p. 223 *Rich kid's farce*: E. P. Thompson 'An Open Letter to Leszek Kolakowski', reprinted in *The Poverty of Theory* p. 99.

p. 223 *Transform civilisation*: Tariq Ali *Street Fighting Years* p. 226.

p. 223 *Czech reform movement*: David Caute *Sixty-Eight* viii.

p. 224 *RSSF manifesto*: David Widgery *The Left in Britain 1956–1968* p. 339.

p. 224 *Powell march*: Widgery quoted in Ronald Fraser *1968* p. 245; also see David Caute, pp. 74–6.

p. 224 *Glossary*: David Widgery, pp. 477–505.

p. 224 *Missionaries*: see Hugh Gaitskell's recollections of Cole in Asa Briggs and John Saville (eds) *Essays in Labour History* p. 15.

p. 225 *Vast majority*: Perry Anderson 'Components of the National Culture' in Robin Blackburn and Alexander Cockburn (eds) *Student Power* p. 223.

p. 225 *Very surplus*: Perry Anderson *Considerations on Western Marxism* p. 54.

p. 225 *Group action*: Michael Stewart *Life and Labour* pp. 256–7.

p. 225 *Thirteen conference defeats*: David Howell, p. 246.

p. 226 *Dog licence speech*: Edward G. Janosik *Constituency Labour Parties in Britain* p. 197.

p. 226 *Congress House opening*: Henry Pelling *A History of British Trade Unionism* p. 254.

p. 226 *Conservatives and unions*: V. L. Allen *Trade Union Leadership* p. 150; Tony Crosland called this 'a peaceful revolution' in his *The Future of Socialism* p. 32.

p. 227 *Number of unofficial strikes*: Robert Taylor *The Fifth Estate* p. 40.

p. 227 *Serum*: Turner quoted in Peter Jenkins *The Battle of Downing Street* xii.

p. 228 *American Democrats*: entry for 22 March 1967 in Richard Crossman, Volume Two, p. 287.

p. 228 *Charter of rights*: Barbara Castle 'Why my reforms were right' in *The Sunday Times*, 13 January 1980.

p. 229 *Popular support*: Peter Jenkins, p. 44.

p. 229 *Basically academics*: Jack Jones *Union Man* p. 204.

p. 229 *Harold and Barbara*: Tony Benn *Office Without Power: Diaries 1968–72* p. 187.

p. 230 *Fraction of second*: Tony Benn, p. 293.

p. 230 *Public relations*: Kenneth O. Morgan *Labour People* p. 261.

CHAPTER TWELVE

Endings

p. 232 *NUT*: Bernard Donoughue *Prime Minister: The Conduct of Policy under Harold Wilson and James Callaghan* p. 110.

p. 232 *Sea-change*: Bernard Donoughue, p. 191.

p. 232 *Common sense*: Peter Kellner and Christopher Hitchens *Callaghan: The Road to Number Ten* p. 75.

p. 233 *Gaitskell on Callaghan*: Philip M. Williams (ed) *The Diary of Hugh Gaitskell 1945–1956* p. 540.

p. 233 *Zebras and cat's eyes*: James Callaghan *Time And Chance* p. 97.

p. 233 *Following unions*: Lord Wigg *George Wigg* p. 254.

p. 233 *Over 50 committees*: Robert Jenkins *Tony Benn. A Political Biography* p. 168.

p. 233 *Wilson missing NECs*: Joe Haines *The Politics of Power* p. 13.

p. 234 *NEC move left*: see Michael Hatfield *The House the Left Built*, passim.

p. 234 *Three groups radicalised*: Patrick Seyd *The Rise And Fall Of The Labour Left* pp. 47, 74, 139.

p. 234 *Stagecoach*: 1964 interview with Wilson quoted in Edward G. Janosik *Constituency Labour Parties in Britain* p. 193.

p. 236 *IRI's record*: Stuart Holland *The Socialist Challenge* p. 182.

p. 237 *Party in sight*: Michael Hatfield, p. 57.

p. 237 *Idiotic*: David Coates *Labour in Power? A Study of the Labour Government 1974–1979* p. 89.

p. 237 *No experience*: Denis Healey *The Time of My Life* p. 367.

p. 237 *No direct experience*: Bernard Donoughue, p. 54.

p. 237 *Balance sheet*: Joel Barnett *Inside the Treasury* p. 3.

p. 237 *Manufacturing decline*: Michael Barratt Brown 'The Growth and Distribution of Income and Wealth' in Ken Coates (ed) *What Went Wrong?* p. 52.

p. 238 *Majority of three*: David Coates, pp. 150–1.

p. 238 *Around this racetrack*: Bernard Donoughue, p. 11.

p. 239 *Walking wounded*: Philip Whitehead *The Writing On The Wall* p. 144.

p. 240 *Titanic*: Bernard Donoughue, p. 183.

p. 240 *Fourteen budgets*: David Coates, p. 12.

p. 240 *Moral for spending Ministers*: Joel Barnett, p. 94.

p. 241 *Father Christmas*: Martin Holmes *The Labour Governments, 1974–1979* p. 182.

p. 241 *Political constraints of full employment*: see Robert Skidelsky 'The Political Meaning of the Keynesian Revolution' in R. Skidelsky (ed) *The End Of The Keynesian Era* pp. 38–9.

p. 241 *Fossilised*: Martin Holmes, p. 58.

p. 241 *Treasury advice*: Joe Haines, p. 42.

p. 241 *Treasury misestimates*: Denis Healey, pp. 380–1.

p. 242 *Suddenness*: Harold Wilson *The Labour Governments 1964–1970* p. 460.

p. 242 *Restraint of schoolgirls*: James Callaghan, p. 428.

p. 243 *Gaitskell and Clause Four*: John Mortimer 'Probably the best Prime Minister we haven't got' in *The Sunday Times*, 13 July 1980.

p. 243 *Political bully*: Ian Mikardo *Back-bencher* p. 202.

p. 243 *Withdrew into citadel*: Stephen Fay and Hugo Young *The Day The Pound Nearly Died* p. 39; there is a very detailed account of the crisis in Tony Benn *Against the Tide: Diaries 1973– 76* pp. 681–90.

p. 244 *Three co-operatives*: Joel Barnett, p. 35.

p. 244 *£10/£800 million*: Robert Jenkins, p. 215.

p. 244 *Sponsored MPs*: Ken Coates 'What Went Wrong?' in Ken Coates, p. 22.

p. 245 *Jones and ACAS*: Jack Jones *Union Man* p. 245.

p. 245 *Anti-intellectualism*: Robert Taylor *The Fifth Estate* p. 91; insular outlook, p. 224.

p. 245 *Men running show*: Barbara Castle *The Castle Diaries 1974–76* p. 309.

p. 246 *Incomes policies*: Michael Stewart *Life and Labour* p. 195.

p. 247 *Low wage country*: Robert Taylor, p. 135.

p. 248 *Radical bookshops etc*: see Elizabeth-Anne Morgan *An Overview of the Radical Booktrade* (unpublished Sheffield University thesis, September 1981).

p. 248 *Coming decade*: Tariq Ali *The Coming British Revolution* p. 209; in a recent letter to me (dated 27 March 1991) Tariq Ali says that he did not write all of this book and not page 209. I suppose the reference should therefore read 'Tariq Ali' The Coming . . . etc.

p. 248 *Tuesday mornings*: Robert Taylor, p. 189.

p. 248 *Subordinate role*: Philip Whitehead, p. 310.

p. 248 *Women's movement*: see the excellent essay by Sheila Rowbotham 'The Women's Movement and organising for socialism' in the collection *Beyond the Fragments*.

p. 248 *Protest's limited life*: Beatrix Campbell *Wigan Pier Revisited* p. 201.

p. 249 *Clarity*: see the remarks of John Wood, deputy head of the IEA, in Michael Davie

'Men who told Thatcher there was an alternative' in the *Observer*, 24 March 1983. The intellectual origins of the New Right are discussed in Andrew Gamble *Britain In Decline* pp. 143–64.

p. 249 *Whitehall gentleman*: Ben Pimlott *Hugh Dalton* p. 398.

p. 249 *We Know Best*: Ferdinand Mount 'Socialism: the package that's past its sell-by date' in the *Daily Telegraph*, 13 March 1987.

p. 249 *Pigeon-keeping*: Roy Hattersley *Choose Freedom* p. 134.

p. 249 *Ideological stranglehold*: Colin Ward 'Self-help socialism' in *New Society*, 20 April 1978, p. 140.

p. 250 *Big Brother*: Robert Skidelsky 'Fantasy not history' in *The Sunday Times*, 11 January 1987.

p. 250 *No miracles*: Joel Barnett 'Realism and the socialist way to cut public spending' in the *Guardian*, 25 September 1979.

p. 250 *Consumers*: *Guardian* editorial 'The spirit of '45, the facts of '79', 8 May 1979.

p. 251 *Poverty figures*: Frank Field 'The Poor' in Ken Coates, p. 146.

p. 251 *5 per cent too low*: interview in *Denis Healey: The Man Who Did The Dirty Work*, BBC 2, 12 October 1989.

p. 252 *Meeting round clock*: Joel Barnett, p. 160.

p. 252 *Tanks into ICI*: Bernard Donoughue, p. 174.

p. 252 *Passage of time*: James Callaghan, p. 537.

p. 252 *Manifesto row*: see Geoff Bish 'Drafting the Manifesto' in Ken Coates, pp. 187–206.

p. 253 *Callaghan's campaign*: David Butler and Dennis Kavanagh *The British General Election of 1979* p. 325.

p. 254 *Paynter and Annan*: Will Paynter *My Generation* and Noel Annan *Our Age: Portrait Of A Generation*.

p. 254 *Error to neglect*: Noel Annan, p. 449.

CHAPTER THIRTEEN

The 1980s

p. 257 *Good on television*: Michael Cockerell *Live From Number 10* p. 287.

p. 257 *Distinctive*: John Biffen 'Ivory tower goes into orbit' in *The Spectator*, 17 December 1988.

p. 258 *Mentality*: George Orwell *The Lion and the Unicorn* p. 63.

p. 258 *Ship due North*: R. W. Johnson 'Watership going down' in *New Society*, 30 August 1979, p. 462; this essay is not reproduced in the author's collection *The Politics of Recession*.

p. 259 *Packaged together*: Graham Turner 'Why Britain's eggheads look down on Mrs Thatcher' in the *Sunday Telegraph*, 10 January 1988.

p. 259 *Squalid, ugly etc*: Hanif Kureishi 'England, bloody England' in the *Guardian*, 15 January 1988.

p. 259 *Extreme statement*: The *Independent*, 25 October 1988.

p. 260 *Czechoslovakia*: Timothy Garton Ash 'Czechoslovakia Under Ice' reprinted in his *The Uses of Adversity* pp. 55–63.

p. 260 *Bring university down*: Jack Jones *Union Man* p. 341.

p. 260 *First essential*: Richard Crossman 'The Lessons of 1945' in Perry Anderson and Robin Blackburn (eds) *Towards Socialism* p. 146.

p. 261 *Adolf Hitler*: see Tony Benn *Arguments for Socialism* p. 11 and also the cartoon reproduced in Tony Benn *Office Without Power: Diaries 1968–72* p. 457.

p. 261 *Stamps*: Robert Jenkins *Tony Benn. A Political Biography* p. 105.

p. 261 *Forty-four volumes*: Tony Benn *Office Without Power*, pp. 397–8.

p. 262 *Benn and Marx*: Tony Benn *Against the Tide: Diaries 1973–76* p. 12, p. 692.

p. 262 *Immatures*: quoted in Robert Harris *The Making of Neil Kinnock* p. 154.

p. 262 *Bought move*: Martin Holmes *The Labour Government, 1974–1979* p. 42.

p. 262 *Referendum campaign*: Tony Benn *Against the Tide*, p. 485.

p. 262 *Squash ball*: Bernard Donoughue *Prime Minister* p. 55.

p. 262 *Watch everybody*: Brian Connell 'A dedication to the idea of accountability' in *The Times*, 18 July 1977.

p. 263 *Frequently unrepresentative*: Beatrice Webb diary entry, 19 May 1930.

p. 263 *Crossman at NS*: Mervyn Jones *Chances. An Autobiography* p. 230.

p. 264 *Benn on tube*: Tony Benn *Conflicts of Interest: Diaries 1977–80* p. 548.

p. 264 *Cripps and Cabinet*: James Jupp *The Radical Left in Britain* p. 144.

p. 265 *Good Samaritan*: Ian Mikardo *Back-bencher* p. 220.

p. 265 *Political riff-raff*: Roy Hattersley *Choose Freedom* p. 4.

p. 265 *90,000 members*: James Hinton *Protests and Visions* pp. 182–3.

p. 266 *Absence of self-seeking*: James Callaghan *Time And Chance* p. 401.

p. 266 *Pax Britannica*: James Hinton, viii–ix.

p. 266 *EEC amazed*: Keith Richardson 'Foot shocks his comrades' in the *Sunday Times*, 14 February 1981.

p. 267 *Rag, tag*: the *Guardian*, 6 June 1983.

p. 268 *New brand*: Johnny Wright 'Advertising for a change' in *Marxism Today*, January 1985.

p. 268 *In the end*: Robert Fox 'Michael Foot's Nemesis' in *The Listener*, 16 June 1983.

p. 268 *Fighting spirit*: Michael Foot *Another Heart And Other Pulses* p. 91; saw little TV, p. 91.

p. 269 *Red Ken*: John Carvel *Citizen Ken* p. 18

p. 269 *1,000 organisations*: John Carvel, p. 208.

p. 270 *Bunch of amateurs*: Michael Barratt Brown 'Positive Neutralism Then and Now' in Oxford University Socialist Group *Out of Apathy* p. 84.

p. 271 *Pit closures*: Mark Adeney and John Lloyd *The Miners' Strike* p. 34.

p. 272 *Miners' QC*: Michael Crick *Scargill and the Miners* p. 68.

p. 272 *Might have won poll*: Michael Crick pp. 103, 108.

p. 273 *Mardy closures*: see the moving requiems in the *Guardian* and *The Times*, both 21 December 1990.

p. 274 *Forward March*: Martin Jacques and Francis Mulhern (eds) *The Forward March of Labour Halted?* pp. 1–19.

p. 275 *Strange indeed*: R. W. Johnson, p. 257.

p. 276 *Counter-hegemonic force*: Stuart Hall and Martin Jacques 'Introduction' to Hall and Jacques (eds) *New Times* p. 17.

p. 276 *Hate ghetto*: 'The couturier of designer Marxism' in the *Sunday Telegraph*, 25 November 1989.

p. 278 *Left-wing programme*: 'Who's the leftest of them all?' in the *Economist*, 11 June 1983, p. 61.

p. 278 *Campaign Group and polls*: James Naughtie in the *Guardian*, 23 January 1985.

p. 278 *Hair cut*: Michael Cockerell 'The Battle for No 10' on *Panorama*, BBC1, 15 June 1987.

p. 278 *1987 election spending*: Robin Oakley 'The Tories spent £3 million in four days to seal poll victory' in *The Times*, 26 October 1987.

p. 278 *Costs of campaigning*: for the American experience, Frank I. Luntz *Candidates, Consultants and Campaigns* pp. 25, 43, 222–4.

p. 279 *19 per cent in polls*: Colin Hughes and Patrick Wintour *Labour Rebuilt* p. 26.

p. 280 *Colour of books*: William E. Paterson 'The German Social Democratic Party' in William E. Paterson and Alastair H. Thomas (eds) *Social Democratic Parties in Western Europe* pp. 185, 186.

p. 280 *Requires switching*: Colin Hughes and Patrick Wintour, p. 5.

p. 280 *Exorcism*: Martin Jacques 'New start for Labour too' in *The Times*, 28 November 1990.

p. 280 *Basic stance*: Bryan Gould *A Future for Socialism* p. 112.

p. 281 *Don't actually believe*: Miriam Gross 'An Interview with Eric Hobsbawm' in *Time and Tide*, Autumn 1985, p. 55.

p. 281 *Terrible insularity*: Eric Hobsbawm *Politics for a Rational Left* p. 235.

p. 282 *Evil woman*: quoted in, for example, the London *Evening Standard*, 26 November 1990.

p. 282 *Conservatives and winners*: David Butler and Dennis Kavanagh *The British General Election of 1987* p. 277.

CHAPTER FOURTEEN

The 1990s and Beyond

p. 283 *Most people*: Paul Hirst *After Thatcher* (London: Collins, 1989) p. 180.

p. 284 *Dead generations*: Karl Marx *The Eighteenth Brumaire of Louis Bonaparte* (1852)

p. 285 *Soviet behest*: see, for example, recent revelations about Stalin's decisive influence on the CP programme drawn up in 1950 and 1951: George Matthews 'Stalin's British Road?' in *Changes*, issue 23, 14–27 September 1991.

p. 286 *Labour-intensive manufacturing*: Charles Handy *The Age of Unreason* (London: Business Books, 1989) pp. 39–43.

p. 286 *Henley Centre*: 'The coming of "telecommuters"' in *The Times*, 3 January 1991.

p. 287 *Seventy-odd years*: David Marquand *The Progressive Dilemma* (London: Heinemann, 1991) p. 1.

p. 287 *Kinnock and Clause Four*: David Wastell 'Kinnock drops "nonsense" of nationalisation', *Sunday Telegraph*, 1 September 1991.

p. 288 *£150 million*: *Report of the Commission on Citizenship* (London: HMSO, 1990) p. 31.

p. 288 *Management and change*: John Harvey-Jones *Making It Happen* (London: Collins, 1988) p. 122.

p. 288 *No transnational links*: 'Brother, we just missed the 1992 balloon' in the *Economist*, 23 June 1991.

p. 289 *German unions*: Andrei S. Markovits and Christopher H. Allen 'The Trade Unions' in G. Smith, W. E. Paterson and P. H. Merkl (eds) *Developments in West German Politics* (London: Macmillan, 1989) pp. 290, 295.

p. 289 *Blunkett and consumers*: Colin Hughes and Patrick Wintour *Labour Rebuilt* (London: Fourth Estate, 1990) p. 158.

p. 289 *Lucas Aerospace*: Ken Coates and Tony Topham *Trade Unions in Britain* (London: Faber, 1988 ed) pp. 280–2.

p. 290 *Anti-consumerism*: Beatrix Campbell *Wigan Pier Revisited* (London: Virago, 1984) p. 227.

p. 290 *Join us*: Bryan Gould *A Future for Socialism* (London: Jonathan Cape, 1989) p. 77.

p. 290 *Manny Shinwell*: quoted in Peter Jenkins 'Bevan's Fight With The BMA' in M. Sissons and P. French (eds) *The Age of Austerity* (London: Hodder and Stoughton, 1963) p. 248.

p. 291 *EC harmonisation*: Hamish McRae 'Can't tax, won't tax is the reality for Labour' in the *Independent*, 25 September 1991.

p. 292 *Tawney*: J. R. Williams, R. M. Titmuss and F. J. Fisher (eds) *R. H. Tawney, A Portrait by Several Hands* (London: Shenvall Press, n.d.) and Norman Dennis and A. H. Halsey *English Ethical Socialism* (Oxford: Clarendon Press, 1988) pp. 149–70.

p. 292 *God's children*: William Temple *Christianity and Social Order* (London: Penguin, 1942) pp. 14–15.

p. 292 *Variety of life*: Morris quoted in Linda Parry *William Morris Textiles* (London: Weidenfeld and Nicolson, 1983) p. 9.

p. 293 *Co-operative movement*: Karl Marx's inaugural address for the First International, 1864, in L. E. Mins (ed) *Founding of the First International* (Moscow: Co-operative Publishing Society, 1935) p. 36.

p. 293 *ESOPs:* Bryan Gould, p. 143ff; also see Roy Hattersley *Choose Freedom* (London: Michael Joseph, 1987) pp. 190–208 and Paddy Ashdown *Citizens' Britain* (London: Fourth Estate, 1989) pp. 129–30. There are now 50 ESOPs in Britain: Clive Woodcock 'Increasing number of firms learn the Esops lesson' in the *Guardian,* 2 August 1991.

p. 293 *Citizenship in war:* James D. Wilkinson *The Intellectual Resistance in Europe* (USA: Harvard University Press, 1981) *passim.*

p. 293 *Control of immigration:* Geoff Andrews 'Introduction' in G. Andrews (ed) *Citizenship* (London: Lawrence and Wishart, 1991) p. 13.

p. 293 *York charter:* Douglas Broom 'Major to study Labour model for Tory charter', *The Times,* 1 April 1991.

p. 294 *Rights and duties:* David Selbourne 'Who Would Be A Socialist Citizen?' in G. Andrews, pp. 96–7.

p. 294 *Citizenship not exciting:* Colin Hughes and Patrick Wintour, p. 174.

p. 294 *Lie upon heritage:* E. P. Thompson 'An Open Letter to Leszek Kolakowski' reprinted in *The Poverty of Theory* (London: Merlin Press, 1978) p. 116.

p. 294 *Westminster model:* David Marquand *The Unprincipled Society* (London: Jonathan Cape, 1988) p. 202.

p. 294 *Elaborate conspiracy:* Aneurin Bevan *In Place of Fear* (London: Quartet, 1978 ed) p. 26.

p. 295 *Cabinet meetings:* Richard Rose *Politics in England* (London: Faber, 1980 ed) p. 65. For analysis of the power of the Prime Minister, see Tony Benn *Arguments for Democracy* (London: Jonathan Cape, 1981) pp. 26–31.

p. 296 *Clever thing:* Brian Walden 'Labour must discard its old ideological baggage' in the *Sunday Times,* 19 November 1989.

p. 296 *The Treaty:* Tony Benn *Arguments for Socialism* (London: Jonathan Cape, 1980) p. 169.

p. 296 *Women:* Joni Lovenduski 'Feminism and Western European politics: an overview' in D. W. Urwin and W. E. Paterson (eds) *Politics in Western Europe today* (London: Longman, 1990) p. 149.

Index